THE COLLECTED LETTERS OF
KATHERINE MANSFIELD

VOLUME THREE

1919–1920

THE COLLECTED
LETTERS OF
KATHERINE
MANSFIELD

EDITED BY
VINCENT O'SULLIVAN
AND
MARGARET SCOTT

VOLUME THREE
1919–1920

CLARENDON PRESS · OXFORD

*...d digitally and produced in a standard specification
... ...r to ensure its continuing availability*

OXFORD
UNIVERSITY PRESS

Great Clarendon Street, Oxford OX2 6DP

Oxford University Press is a department of the University of Oxford.
It furthers the University's objective of excellence in research, scholarship,
and education by publishing worldwide in

Oxford New York

Auckland Cape Town Dar es Salaam Hong Kong Karachi
Kuala Lumpur Madrid Melbourne Mexico City Nairobi
New Delhi Shanghai Taipei Toronto
With offices in
Argentina Austria Brazil Chile Czech Republic France Greece
Guatemala Hungary Italy Japan South Korea Poland Portugal
Singapore Switzerland Thailand Turkey Ukraine Vietnam

Oxford is a registered trade mark of Oxford University Press
in the UK and in certain other countries

Published in the United States
by Oxford University Press Inc., New York

Letters © The Estate of Katherine Mansfield 1993
Extracts from letter of John Middleton Murry © The
Estate of John Middleton Murry 1993
Introduction and editorial matter © Oxford University Press 1993

The moral rights of the author have been asserted

Database right Oxford University Press (maker)

Reprinted 2007

ISBN 978-0-19-812615-7

Cover illustration: detail of a photograph of KM during her time at Menton, early 1920.
Alexander Turnbull Library.

CONTENTS

INTRODUCTION

In one of the last letters in the previous volume, written to her Russian friend Koteliansky a few days before she left England, Mansfield spoke of what it was that made 'these last days hideous'. It was not her illness, she said, but the lack of privacy, the desire of people to 'share' her. There was something 'indecent' in such proximity (5 September 1919, *Collected Letters*, II. 354). Within a fortnight she was writing again to Koteliansky, from the hotel in San Remo where she would stay for another week before renting the Casetta Deerholm in Ospedaletti. Travelling south had proved more troublesome than expected. The weather was uncomfortably hot. The insects plagued her – as they would until December – and she quickly and typically picked up the signs of human corruption. She accurately described what she was in for in one italicized adjective. 'I have found a small *solitary* little house away from everybody, hidden by olive trees, overlooking the sea' (19 September 1919).

Four of the five volumes of Mansfield's correspondence are progressively dominated by her bad, failing, and finally irreversible ill-health. In these present letters between September 1919 and the end of April 1920, she touched bottom in the despondency and antagonisms that were part of her disease. It is also the period during which she wrote most extensively to John Middleton Murry – one hundred and ten thousand words in the half year they were apart – and wrote least to anyone else. Although Ida Baker was with her during those six months and generous friends in Menton were caring for her for three of them, it was a period when 'solitary' best defines her own view of her life. Solitary, 'but really . . . mad', as she was to say once she had left Ospedaletti (21 January 1920). When fever and loneliness were less intense she acknowledged that all this, in one form or another, had happened before. There was an increasingly detached wariness about expecting too much to improve. 'Work' and 'home' continued as her talismans, her incentives towards how things ideally should be. Yet for all the grimness, distress, and marital misunderstanding that defines so many of the letters in this volume, Mansfield kept up as the correspondent she always had been – vivid, entertaining, switching from deft analyses of her feelings to exquisite, frequently witty cameos of what went on about her as she guided and harried Murry, excoriated Ida, thought obsessively of both writing and the idea of writing, and returned to why it was that she felt increasingly dissatisfied with her own assumptions and the mood of her contemporaries. Taken with those in the next two volumes, these letters reveal a movement towards something which is never so schematic as a 'philosophy' but is an intellectual stance, an emotional perspective, that would suffice in confronting the business of living when death was so often in mind.

One advantage Mansfield saw in this enforced separation from home was that she might press on with work. This meant, to begin with, the Chekhov 'translations' she shared with Koteliansky. Several selections from these had already been published in the *Athenaeum*, and a few more would appear over the next year. The intention to bring these together in a book would come to nothing, although Mansfield's enthusiasm for Chekhov, and for Russian writers generally, was unabated. Her English contemporaries seemed small fry beside them, and Chekhov himself remained her touchstone for excellence. He was also something of an exemplar in how to cope stylishly with her disease. But most of her energy during these months went into meeting the demands of her weekly column reviewing fiction in the *Athanaeum*. Considering the effort, even the distress, with which she wrote them, and the almost unrelenting mediocrity of the books she received, her reviews read as remarkably ebullient assessments. One of the lesser mysteries of her relationship with her editor-husband is why, in the light of his extravagant praise of her as a critic, he persisted in sending her such dull fiction, while he saved Chekhov for himself, and commissioned long and serious literary essays from a range of friends. Mansfield liked to joke that she was quite uneducated alongside highbrow Jack. Murry may have agreed with this rather more than he declared.

She wrote few stories during the span of this volume. Only 'The Man Without a Temperament' is important in her *œuvre*. Two others, 'This Flower' and 'The Wrong House', Murry placed in a posthumous volume, but otherwise there were simply fragments she either discarded or destroyed. Whatever her intentions before she left Hampstead, a tangle of emotional and medical factors worked against any kind of fiction that was not (like that group of abrasive poems she so casually posted to Murry early in December) directly related to how she mirrored herself at that moment, or to her dominating feelings of paralysis and suspicion. The last entry in her notebook jottings before she left England remarked on the pleasantness of planting 'cuttings of futurity', even if only one in ten managed to take (*Journal* 1954, 179). By December she copied a sentence from one of Chekhov's later letters. 'I am in the condition of a transplanted tree which is hesitating whether to take root or begin to wither.' She added, 'So am I exactly' (*Journal* 1954, 189). Her slide over these few months from muted optimism to as close as she came to disabling despair is minutely documented. It is the central movement of this volume.

Mansfield's customary first response to the Continent and to the South, to its warmth, colour, un-Englishness, *joie de vivre*, soured more rapidly than usual. The beauty of the coast she immediately responded to. But the British were not popular in Italy after the War, and the Italians made no secret of it. They were also openly fearful of those infected with tuberculosis, and regarded the presumably wealthy convalescents who sought their climate and services as fair monetary game. Nor was the weather what its promoters claimed. Mansfield quickly realized what it meant to exchange Hampstead for Ospedaletti, a home, husband, servants, the stimulation of friends, and the one doctor she ever totally trusted, for a room above an oppressive sea, her hands bandaged from bites, enough fear in the night for her to buy a revolver, doctors she lost faith in within days of consulting them, and, above all, the constant presence of a woman whose gauche attempts to help became a refined form of torture. Against the pressures that she felt conspiring against her, it was her commitment to Murry that offered the final defence. 'All the while, as you know, with my daily life but running deep and true and silent, is my life with you which is the *living* part of me. If I fly from one odd thing to another you must know the other is still there and depend on it. For it is my religion and defence and all that keeps life possible' (10 October 1919).

In ways she could not precisely define, there was a line that sometimes ran from that certainty she knew with Murry – and hoped for even at the worst of times – to what she wanted to strike in her writing, and experience as a mode of life. 'The sea is my favourite sea – bright bright blue but showing a glint of white as far as one can see – that lift of white seen far away – as far as the horizon moves me terribly. In fact it is *the very thing* I should like to express in writing – it has *the very quality*' (12 October 1919). One needn't labour the connection between that 'glint' and the 'glimpses' she once defined as her way of seeing the world. In writing or in life, it had much to do with the way experience was apprehended at its rare best, a quality (as it were) of elation through simply being open to things as they occurred. It threaded her letters, even the grimmest of them, with that sense of gathering in, with delight and determination and quickness, whatever confronted her. One might well be reminded, again, of Walter Pater's 'Conclusion' to *The Renaissance*. This was the text which more than any other shaped Mansfield's thinking as a schoolgirl and young woman, with its message that to a certain kind of mind alertness to drifting phenomena might indeed be as much as one could expect in a modern world. Or at least, so it might seem before other forces set in. But where could one go when the certainties of that vivid 'stream' might so quickly be replaced by the certainty of its opposite? When that flow of coherently satisfying moments was overtaken by 'this great cold indifferent world like a silent malignant river . . . I try to keep to one side, to slip down unnoticed among the trembling rainbow covered bubbles of foam & the faint reeds – I try to turn and turn in a tiny quiet pool but its no good – sooner or later one is pushed out into the middle of it all' (20 October 1919).

Mansfield wrote 'This Flower' early in 1920, but made no attempt to publish it. The story describes a woman, during a visit to a doctor, experiencing a moment of spontaneous elation.

> As she lay there, looking up at the ceiling, she had her moment – yes, she had her moment! And it was not connected with anything she had thought or felt before, not even with those words the doctor had scarcely ceased speaking. It was single, glowing, perfect; it was like – a pearl, too flawless to match with another . . . Could she describe what happened? Impossible. It was as though, even if she had not been conscious all the time that she was fighting against the stream of life – the stream of life indeed! – she had suddenly ceased to struggle. Oh, more than that! She had yielded, yielded absolutely, down to every minutest pulse and nerve, and she had fallen into the bright bosom of the stream and it had borne her . . . She was part of her room – part of the great bouquet of southern anemones, of the white net curtains that blew in stiff against the light breeze, of the mirrors, the white silky rugs; she was part of the high, shaking, quivering clamour, broken with little bells and crying voices that went streaming by outside – part of the leaves and light.

That condition of standing outside of things, and yet being more intensely in them, will be recognized by any reader of the fiction Virginia Woolf later came to write, or of similar, less extended occasions in Mansfield's stories and letters. Its role here, however, is to measure what the unnamed woman is deprived of by the man who arranges for her to be examined by this 'rather shady' doctor. The story is short and elusive. The doctor *may* be an abortionist, the man may have been as much concerned about pregnancy as about the woman's heart. Certainly his own relief, rather than her well-being, turns the ironical conclusion. And the man's name is Mr King. Murry's pseudonym for the poems he published in the *Athenaeum* was 'Henry King'. These oblique biographical filaments, and their casting of her husband's shadow, as it were, as a source of illness that poses as compassion, were more strikingly present in the longer story she wrote the next week.

On 10 January Mansfield heard from her sister that their father had remarried in Auckland the day he arrived back from Europe. During an 'Appalling night of misery deciding J. had no more need for our love', she 'thought out' a story called 'The Exile' (*Journal* 1954, 192). The next day she wrote out her depiction of an invalid wife in the South of France, a painstakingly patient husband, and the chill that springs between illness and duty. The story's initial title suggested that the husband as much as the wife was the victim of circumstance. When Mansfield renamed it 'The Man Without a Temperament' before posting it off to Murry, the emphasis was thrown back on the spouse whose husbandly attendance drained his own life to a husk. This drawing together of memories and present regret, the fact that Mansfield frequently set her father's warm behaviour as a husband against Murry's patent failings, the pervading distress of her recent letters and even more so of her notebook, variously contributed to the poignancy of her story, and the penetrating, punning bitterness of its final lines:

'I sometimes wonder – do you mind awfully being out here with me?'
He bends down. He kisses her. He tucks her in, he smoothes the pillow. 'Rot!' he whispers.

These stories written during those first weeks of the new year – 'The Wrong House', a shorter piece, is a sketch of undertakers coming to the wrong address – place Mansfield's obsessive concerns at a remove from herself. The January letters continued to draw her into a kind of sociability that diverted her from introspection; the notebook preserves cryptic details of 'the worst days of my whole life' (*Journal* 1954, 192) and what she fully recognized as the vileness of her temper. There is often a touch of the surreal as she attempts accurately to set down the fluctuations of her moods. She recorded as she sorted through old letters 'the *feeling* that comes – the anguish – the words that fly out into one's breast my *darling* my *wife*. Oh what anguish! Oh will it ever be the same? Lay awake at night listening to the voices. Two men seemed to sing – a tenor and a baritone: then the drowned began' (*Journal* 1954, 194).

When in late January she moved the short distance from Italy to France, from the isolated casetta to a bustling nursing home and the attentions of older women she admired, it was a move made, like several in recent years, and several more that lay ahead, in the expectation that her health must benefit, if for no other reason than that somewhere unsatisfactory was being left behind. Things had already been patched up with Ida Baker, those long days of silence or sheer rage replaced by a more enduring warmth that conceded just how essential her friend's devotion was. The weather would soon turn to spring. It was a matter of only ten weeks until she returned home to Portland Villas, and to the house in the country that Murry was looking for. She was pampered in Menton by her cousin Connie Beauchamp, and made important new friendships with Violet and Sydney Schiff. She quite knew and joked about the *snobisme* that came into this, for their wealth meant as much to her as their admiration.

And her cousin's Roman Catholicism struck her as attractively severe. She read *The Imitation of Christ*, and contemplated conversion at least until her quick eye for imperfection in others tempered her zeal. It was, as she said, the confusing of spiritual yearning with the erotic that she found distasteful, as well as the prudery of those kindly, well-bred women who, alas, had no conception of what it was to be an artist. 'I try to pretend she can see our point of view but then she says in Je ne parle pas 'how *could* you say her big belly. I feel Our Lady would have disliked it so much.' *Well* – what are you to say to that?' (4 April 1920)

Mansfield noted down soon after she moved into L'Hermitage that 'the people are newly risen.' She did not quite think that about herself. But in those easier, far more relaxed, less recriminatory letters from Menton there is the feeling that there could only be a return from the depths of the past few months. She was moving towards that notion of 'authenticity', the insistence that what one chooses to be is what one is, that was later to characterize the Existentialists. As Mansfield read Virginia Woolf's *Night and Day* the previous November, it was not – as Woolf herself believed – the novel's carefully traditional structure that disturbed her. It was something more essential than an aesthetic judgement, although the *Athenaeum* review did express a deep reserve about the novel's 'air of quiet perfection'. Mansfield's deeper objection was 'the absence of any scars' on that huge fictional craft, the refusal in Woolf to indicate that the novel 'must accept the fact of a new world' (The *Athenaeum*, 21 November 1919). She put it more frankly in writing to Murry. 'My private opinion is that it is a lie in the soul. The war never has been, that is what its message is.' It was the fact of the War, its immense carnage and its rupture of civilization, that Mansfield often referred to, as did many of her contemporaries, by way of explaining why 'I feel in the *profoundest* sense that nothing can ever be the same . . . We have to face our war' (10 November 1919).

Mansfield is speaking there as a woman aware of the fracture that set post-war Europe so vastly apart from the comforting certainties of pre-war England. More and more over the next two years it would seem a fine line indeed between how Mansfield read the aftermath of war historically, and as an allegory, a parallel for her physical condition, her own state of mind. 'I believe Bogey, our whole strength depends upon our facing things. I mean facing them without any reservations or restraints. . . . I feel almost I have been ill for so long for that reason: we *fear* for that reason' (10 November 1919).

That insistence on 'facing things', the inevitable fluctuations as she sought 'to *break the iron ring*' (4 December 1919) as she put it, without the assurances of any sustaining framework of belief, inevitably led her to where Existentialism would focus. There was that initial dread which she would later call 'the greatest failing of all', and the imperatives of 'the soul's desperate choice' (18 October 1920). There was the need to make sense of things, both immediately and ultimately, by attending to where one was, and why, and to what limited freedoms ensued. To acknowledge contingencies, then, yet to be neither intimidated nor confined by them, becomes Mansfield's dominating concern. The question that exercises her from now on, beyond even her love for Murry, her concerns as a writer, her diminishing dependence on people or circumstance, is how to arrive at a satisfying acceptance of oneself. As she wrote just after she had moved to Menton, as one phase was left behind, so she hoped, and another began, 'One must be . . . continually giving & receiving, and shedding & renewing, & examining & trying to place' (23 January 1920).

VINCENT O'SULLIVAN

TEXTUAL NOTE

The text attempts to reproduce what Mansfield wrote as accurately as possible. There has been occasional editorial intervention in providing full stops when this omission was clearly inadvertent; in regularizing single and double inverted commas when these were omitted or mismatched; and in silently emending the very few obvious slips of the pen. When a word or phrase finally resisted attempts to read it, the word 'illegible' appears in italics, within square brackets. When a phrase has been crossed out, the deleted words are enclosed in angle brackets. Any words supplied by way of clarification are in square brackets.

Mansfield's emphases have been rendered in the conventional manner, with words underlined once printed in italics, those underlined twice in small capitals, and further underlinings printed as in the manuscript. The sketches with which she occasionally adorned her letters have been reproduced as they occur in the manuscripts. When these were too small to reproduce, or the originals were not available, they have been briefly described.

When Mansfield did not herself date a letter or provide an address, the date supplied is enclosed in square brackets; where the date is uncertain or approximate it is preceded by a query or the conventional '*c.*' for *circa*. Complimentary closures have been standardized, with vertical rules indicating line breaks. Where Mansfield sometimes drew a line between paragraphs or sections of a letter a printed rule has been used.

Important literary figures and personal friends already identified and noted in volumes I and II have not again been annotated in this volume.

ACKNOWLEDGEMENTS

The editors are obliged to the various institutions and private owners listed under 'Manuscript Sources', who have allowed the use of original letters or transcriptions of letters in their possession.

All unpublished material by Katherine Mansfield and John Middleton Murry is copyright by the respective Estates of Katherine Mansfield and John Middleton Murry, and appears here by permission of the copyright owners. Thanks are due to the Murry family, especially Mr Colin Middleton Murry, for their kind support of this edition, and to Messrs Constable and Co. for allowing quotations from C.A. Hankin's selection, *The Letters of John Middleton Murry to Katherine Mansfield* (1983). Published material (such as the text of the *Journal of Katherine Mansfield*) has been corrected against the manuscripts.

As with any research on Katherine Mansfield, this edition is indebted to her biographer and editor, Professor Antony Alpers, and her bibliographer, Miss Brownlee Kirkpatrick. The work of both has been drawn on constantly. Two other Mansfield scholars, Gill Boddy and Dr Nelson Wattie, have variously provided invaluable help.

In this volume, as in Volumes I and II, the transcriptions of the letters were made by Margaret Scott. Vincent O'Sullivan is responsible for all annotations, dating, and other editorial aspects of the edition.

The reader is referred to Volume I for a Chronology of Mansfield's life (1888–1923).

Vincent O'Sullivan
Margaret Scott

Wellington
March 1992

LIST OF ABBREVIATIONS AND
MANUSCRIPT SOURCES

KM = Katherine Mansfield

The following abbreviations and short forms are used in the description and provenance given at the foot of each letter:

MS autograph original
TS typescript original

MANUSCRIPT SOURCES

Institutions

ATL Alexander Turnbull Library, Wellington
BL British Library
Newberry The Newberry Library, Chicago
Texas The Humanities Research Center, University of Texas at Austin

Private owners

Lawlor Pat Lawlor Estate
C. Murry Colin Middleton Murry
R. Murry Richard Murry Estate

SOURCES OF PREVIOUS PUBLICATION
and short forms used in the annotation

Adam 300 *Adam International Review*, No. 300 (1963–5)
Adam 370–5 *Adam International Review*, Nos. 370–375 (1972–3)
CLKM I *The Collected Letters of Katherine Mansfield*, ed. Vincent O'Sullivan and Margaret Scott, vol. I (Oxford, 1984)
CLKM II *The Collected Letters of Katherine Mansfield*, ed. Vincent O'Sullivan and Margaret Scott, vol. II (Oxford, 1987)
Dickinson John W. Dickinson, 'Katherine Mansfield and S. S. Koteliansky: Some Unpublished Letters', *Revue de littérature comparée*, no. 45 (1971), 79–99
Exhibition *Katherine Mansfield: An Exhibition*, Humanities Research Center, University of Texas (Austin, Texas, 1973)
Journal 1954 *Journal of Katherine Mansfield*, Definitive Edition, ed. John Middleton Murry (1954)
LJMM *Katherine Mansfield's Letters to John Middleton Murry, 1913–1922*, ed. John Middleton Murry (1951)
LKM *The Letters of Katherine Mansfield*, 2 vols., ed. John Middleton Murry (1928)
Meyers Jeffrey Meyers, *Katherine Mansfield, a Biography* (1978)
MLM Ida Baker, *Katherine Mansfield: The Memories of LM* (1971)

Murry   *The Letters of John Middleton Murry to Katherine Mansfield*, ed. C. A. Hankin
             (1983)
Poems   *Poems of Katherine Mansfield* ed. Vincent O'Sullivan (Oxford, 1988)
Stories   *The Stories of Katherine Mansfield*, Definitive Edition, ed. Antony Alpers
             (1984)

The place of publication is London unless otherwise noted.

I
ITALY – OSPEDALETTI: SEPTEMBER–DECEMBER 1919

By the end of summer 1919 KM was faced with what by now was a customary set of dilemmas. Her health compelled her to leave for the Mediterranean while her husband was obliged to make a living in England. The loneliness and the difficulty of living abroad would be mitigated by Ida Baker's companionship, yet to be at close quarters with her friend was an almost constant irritation. She determined to work hard at stories, but would find depression, illness, and the pressure of keeping up weekly reviews for the *Athanaeum* more draining than she anticipated.

A few months earlier, during the celebrations for the Peace Treaty at Versailles, KM had told Lady Ottoline Morrell, in a Swiftian echo, that 'Truly one must hate humankind in the mass – hate them as passionately as one loves the few.' During her time abroad there again would develop that pattern established during previous separations, the swing between her 'black mood' of despondency and the conviction that 'Life might be so wonderful' (*CLKM* II. 339). The hopes for recovery and stability that accompanied KM, her husband, and her closest friend as they left England on 11 September, and settled a few days later at Ospedaletti, veered sharply soon after Murry returned to London. By early December, there was the most bitter misunderstanding yet between herself and Murry.

To S. S. Koteliansky, [19 September 1919]

(The cheque came safely; thank you)   Poste Restante | San Remo |
Italy.

Koteliansky

This is the first day I am able to answer your letter. We were at the last moment forced to travel a day in advance. This I telegraphed you on the Tuesday but Lesley Moore forgot to send the wire, she says. I hate to think you came & there was nobody there – We had a dreadful journey and this place is terribly hot and swarming with insects and hotel profiteers. But I am better today and I have found a small *solitary* little house away from everybody, hidden by olive trees, overlooking the sea. In 8 days I shall be there. Please send me *as soon as possible* some more Tchekhov – as much as you can.[1] I will work fast here – and anything else – This address is quite safe, but for legal reasons I must add 'Murry' to Katherine Mansfield as I have to show my passport before I can get letters. I will write again when I am stronger. This is just to let you know I am thinking of you. Goodbye.

Katherine.

MS BL. *LKM* I. 242.

---

[1] S. S. Koteliansky sent his drafts of Russian translations to KM, who then shaped them into acceptable English. Thirteen selections from Chekhov's letters translated in this way were published in the *Athenaeum* between 4 Apr. and 31 Oct. 1919. The payment was shared between Koteliansky and KM.

To S. S. Koteliansky, 1 October [1919]

Casetta Deerholm | Ospedaletti | Portomaurizio.
October 1st

My dear Koteliansky

The box arrived today, with your letter and the manuscripts and the cheque – all safe. It was very nice, somehow, opening the box . . .

I, too, am sorry to have missed you, but we shall meet another day – a happier one. I shall start immediately on the manuscript, and if there is such a thing as a typewriter here they shall be typed. But my impermanent home is remote and the small town, Ospedaletti, has nothing but a laundry, a flower market and a wine shop. So I expect I shall have to send the MSS to England. You shall have your copy back as soon as I have done . . . Let the book be a 'token' of our friendship. This idea pleases me so – *very very* much.

I wish you could pick up a hundred pounds. It has just begun to rain – immense drops. If they were only gold I would send you an envelope full. You would not object to receiving an *act of God*, would you?

I have taken this little villa for the winter, perhaps for longer. It is nice, Koteliansky; you would like it. It is on a wild hill slope, covered with olive and fig trees and long grass and tall yellow flowers. Down below is the sea – the entire ocean – a huge expanse. It thunders all day against the rocks. At the back there are mountains. The villa is not very small. It has a big verandah on one side where one can work and an overgrown garden. No hideous riviera palms (like Italian profiteers); everything very simple and clean. Many lizards lie on the garden wall; in the evening the cicada shakes his tiny tambourine. I have often pictured you here. We walk up and down, smoking. If only the mosquitoes were not like roaring lions – but they are. On the 14th is my birthday. Please send me a letter for that day if you are in the mood. I am working. I wish your eyes were better; I wish you had good news. Goodnight.

M. is back in London.

Katherine

MS BL. *LKM* I. 243–4; Dickinson 89.

To J. M. Murry, [2 October 1919]

[Casetta Deerholm, Ospedaletti]
3.30 p.m.

Darling,

Your card has just come. Figurez-vous my happy surprise. I am disgusted that you had the extra bother[1] but *much* relieved to think you will be comfortable in the first-class express (or moderately so). Of course you couldnt have waited and then travelled in such a caterpillar. There is feltie[2] in the hall. Signs of you are everywhere. I jealously gathered your clothes & sent them to the donna bella this afternoon, making the list *myself*, so that no other hand should touch them. By this same post goes Swinnerton to the office,[3] written in spite of the flies. I hope it is alright. After you had gone I coo-eed when I saw you on a part of the road which was visible – then, when I saw you at the station, I ran up to the bonne's bedroom & remembering your old eyes, waved a *chemise*!! I felt sure you'd see.

No sign of Vince.[4] I sent L.M. to phone. He says the people are *here* working but deep in the mountain like gnomes & we may expect them to appear above ground tomorrow & the water the day *after*. No Mrs. Vince or Miss; they are frauds & Ive received their bill. They charged us 2.50 for those custards with our own eggs & milk. Oh a plague on human beings, only you & I are really the right kind. Here is a letter from Rendall.[5] Kots parcel came today with a cheque for £1. The parcel contains sheets & sheets of translation to be "ultimately published in book form in America".[6] What a bother!

L.M. refused lunch today but only tore a piece of bread, she said she was not hungry. I did not get angry and later discovered her *having her lunch*. Proved at last! She *is* a silly. Ill not mind her, though. The sea is white, with silver fishes of light in it. The waves say Boge – Boge as they come in. Yes, find the house.[7] Yes, the 28 weeks will pass. Then comes our month of May, and after that our home. Eggs are to be had in Ospedaletti, good ones & figs & mutton cutlets. I love you.

The good things that happen to you you may leave untold if you like but you are to tell me *all* the bad things that happen. Then I feel secure of your confidence and I don't worry, see?

I am going to start bang in on McKenzie & Gilly[8] – so that I shall be a bit ahead. So send along some more books soon please.

You will be in London when this reaches you and at home. Give it to Wing[9] to sit on for a moment. Oh, darling Heart – *how* I love you. All must go well. I want to know about the house & Violet[10] and if she really does all you require in the way you require. Its so hot – the flies are eating me up. Oh, Bogey, you come up the steps, carrying the pail – a geranium in your waistcoat pocket. You are more loved than anybody in the world by your

Wig

MS ATL. *LJMM*, 314–17.

[1] Murry sent a card from Ventimiglia, saying he had just read of a railway strike in England.
[2] A large grey felt hat owned jointly by KM and Murry.
[3] 'Portraits and Passions', her review of Frank Swinnerton's *September*, the *Athenaeum*, 10 Oct.
[4] Thomas Vince, the English manager of the Villa Flora, San Remo, where KM and Murry stayed when they first arrived, and the agent for the Casetta Deerholm.
[5] Vernon Rendall, a copy reader with the paper.
[6] This planned edition of Chekhov's letters was prevented by the publication of Constance Garnett's *Letters to His Family and Friends*, in Feb. 1920. In 1925 Koteliansky and Philip Tomlinson published *The Life and Letters of Anton Tchekhov*, which revised Koteliansky's and KM's earlier translations. Her help is acknowledged only with Chekhov's letter to his brother Alexander, Apr. 1883, first published in the *Adelphi*, June 1924. See letter to Murry, 5 Jan. 1920.
[7] KM continued, as ever, to hope for 'The Heron', their ideal cottage in the country.
[8] 'Humour and Heaviness', the *Athenaeum*, 17 Oct. 1919, was a review of Compton Mackenzie's *Poor Relations*, and Gilbert Cannan's *Time and Eternity*. For KM's earlier friendship with Cannan, see *CLKM* I. 119.
[9] One of their cats.
[10] The maid at Portland Villas.

To J. M. Murry, [4 October 1919]

[Casetta Deerholm, Ospedaletti]
By the time you get this it will be nearly the beginning of the 27th
week.

```
    X     X     X   X       X       X
  X X   X X   X X   X X   X X   X X   X X
  X X   X X   X X   X X   X X   X X
```

Darling Bogey,

No letter from you yesterday. So far I've just had the 2 cards from
Vintimille; I do hope for a line to catch on to from Paris, perhaps, this
evening. The evening post goes *out* here 5.45, comes *in* after six so I
cant tell you whether or no I shall hear. *No* Vince yesterday of course
and *no* workman at the water job today; it is gettng damned annoying.
No locksmiff either. I think there are disadvantages in the Granville[1]
type.

I am sitting outside in the bastick chair[2]: its a mild, cloudy day. This
morning was quite chilly – so was last night. Talk about the bounding
horizon . . . As I sit here I have to throw everything I write against it
& it seems to me the pink geranium beats me out of hand. It is a
lesson in humility to write *or* think with that sea and sky there.

Where are you **?**
How are you **!**

When I know those things and how you found everything I shall
feel really settled, but while you are en voyage Im restless. You
understand that? Augusta, the maid has disappeared. She must have
seen that furniture arriving.

L.M. has broke

(1) the big fruit dish
(2) our plate
(3) a saucer

all at one go from leaning on the sideboard. I shall buy crocks here but
put them in your suitcase against the Goldene Zeit.[3] And the worst of
it is I always feel she thinks it "so nice and homey" to occasionally
smash a thing or two. You must keep me from getting over stern, over
strict and over tidy. Its an obsession. I realised it this morning. Even
out here I had to rearrange the pick, the shovel & the rake before I
could do a thing. Even though they were behind me. I hope I wont say
to our darling little boy "As long as your mud-pies have *form*, darling,
you can make them. But there must be no slopping over the mould."
He will like you best. You know how, when we get hungry, we are at
last even unable to play demon[4] for wanting the hashhammer to

sound. That is precisely my state of mind *re* a letter from you to say you are at home. Once Ive got it, sat down to table with it, fed my soul on it, eaten every single scrap with all the appetite in the world I fire ahead with other things. But you do understand dont you darling, that especially as affaires are si graves I am very specially anxious.

We got superb filet today for 2.75 – a whack of meat with a bone attached & a kilo of peaches for 1.50. Your figs on the footstool are still there. Ill never eat them.

> My ros-ary – my ros-ary
> Each fig a pearl each pearl a prayer etc.[5]

Forgive a silly. But I have decided to steal two of these wooden stools when we go home – one at each end of my big box.

Be happy. Keep well. Tell me everything. Never spare me. Remember at odd moments how I love you and how happy we shall be. My very darling of darlings.

Wig.

MS ATL. *LKM* I. 244–5; *LJMM*, 316–17.

---

[1] Charles Granville, who as 'Stephen Swift', a fly-by-night publisher, cost them so dearly with the collapse of *Rhythm* in 1919. See *CLKM* I. 110.

[2] i.e. basket chair.

[3] That is, the 'Golden Time' when they would live together in their cottage.

[4] A card game, a variety of Patience.

[5]
> Each hour a pearl, each pearl a prayer,
> To still a heart in absence wrung;
> I tell each bead unto the end and there
> A cross is hung.

From Robert Cameron Rogers's words of the popular song 'The Rosary'.

To J. M. Murry, [5 October 1919]

[Casetta Deerholm, Ospedaletti]
Sunday.

My own Love

Still there is no news of you later than the 2 p.c.s posted at Vintimille. This means you cannot have had the time to send me a p.c. in Paris, and yet that seems to me *queer*. By the time you have this letter I shall have heard from you and my present anxiety will – please Heaven – be over. But since last evening when the last post brought nothing, my anxiety has run away with me & it will not stop until I see your darling handwriting again. It seems so horribly mysterious. Not a line from you. There was a storm all last night & today is strange and passionate. I can do nothing but *wait*. No further post today – none until tomorrow & its only midday here – Dont worry about this. You know how one feels. I live for letters when I am away from you – *for* them – *on* them – *with* them. Its as though you had gone to San Remo & train after train passes & I go out & lean over the fence with the cotton plant & wait to see my darling at the bottom of the hill & he isn't there. But don't remember this. Only remember how I shall rejoice and be made new again when your letter comes. Sunday today. Now there are only 27 Sundays. Oh, God, send May along quickly. I can wait *perfectly* if I have letters but I tremble when you are en voyage & silence falls. Its no good saying 'wire me' – I know you realise my anxiety & thats all – Ill write about other things after I have heard. All is well here outwardly. I keep my anxiety hidden – but there it is. No good pretending it isn't.

Your longing wife
Wig.

MS ATL. *LJMM*, 317–18.

To J. M. Murry, 6 October 1919

Casetta Deerholm, | Ospedaletti.
(Monday October 6, 1919)
Your postcard from Paris has just come. Why it has taken so long God only knows. I felt certain you'd have sent me one from there, yet yesterday I gave up all hope of getting one – indeed of hearing at all until you were back in London. I feel quite different with this postcard. When I die, just before the coffin is screwed up, pop a letter in. I shall jump up and out. . . .

L.M. has broken my thermometer. *Good.* I got another for 12 francs, which seems to play the same tune, though the notes are not so plain. 'I was pulling your cupboard away from the nets and it just rolled on to the floor'. I suppose in Rhodesia you just have notches on a bamboo or a tchetchetchetche branch.

I have been out since 9 o'clock. The sea is divine. It's very hot. All last night I chased the midges Buzzing in the nets afar Each one bearing, as it kindled, Message of the open war. (Macauley)[1] It's perfect except for the 'afar'. They are a scourge here, now; in hundreds. On dit that they will go when the fruit goes, and that flowers in the house are fatal for them. Well, what a silly country!

I started a big story yesterday.[2] I don't think it's very good but I am going straight on with it, whatever it is like, just for the practice and for getting into my stride. . . .

MS ATL. *LKM* I. 243; *LJMM*, 318.

To J. M. Murry, [6 October 1919]

[Casetta Deerholm, Ospedaletti]
Monday

Oh, Boge!

I have just had an interview with a bonne who does not speak 1 word of French – a pretty, nice, awfully nice girl with pearly teeth. What *she* said, what *I* said, I really don't know. *Me*: La lettiere nonne arrivato attendre duo giorni venuto Bordighera?

She: Si, si, cuisino.

Me: Oh, dear, what a bother!

She: Si, si, dimano-sabbato.

I finally gave her a letter in french for the woman at the dairy to translate – and off she went. When (to make it plain) I showed her the empty room with 2 coat-hooks & a sheepskin in it, she seemed to think it was superbly furnished. "Bono, bono, molto bono!" A sort of Maori haka! Wise old Feltie, listening in the hall, is still shaking with laughter at your Wiggy.

I think she is just the person – young, strong, pretty, with black, laughing eyes – a bit grubby, but only de la terre – a kind of Italian Marie[1] of a lower class. She gave a little half curtsey when we parted. What will come of it? She also wrote on a bit of paper da muni vineri si. Whether that means she is coming or that she is fond of wine I am still not certain . . .[2]

Its a lovely morning. I am working and very happy. Its hot – grilling. I think I shall have a pet lizard here. L.M. said a *sissida* (ciccada) was buzzing round her electric light all last night. What do you say to that?

Sitting here, I have had your most disturbing P.C.[3] If only you had some money. Isn't this just our luck. I shall be more than eager for the letter saying you are safe home. Oh, Bogey, you'll borrow from Valéry[4] I hope – you'll not go without. Wish I knew more.

I had also a letter from Sorapure[5] today which really boxed it. I mean, he said it was only my "indomitable will" (!) which kept me alive this last year, & he is sure I shall now get absolutely well and "grow into your dream of achievement". This, of course, makes me feel *cicatrisé* all over and also rouses my pride. I *will*.

He also says he has been at our house twice and got no reply. Kot said the same. When I read that I suddenly felt very suspicious of Violet and Gertie[6] and that they have played us false. It can't be true. Is it? I had a horrid moment when it seemed so.

We got excellent butter today from Ospedaletti and fresh haricots verts and figs and two perfect whacks of mutton (2.50). There is a vegetable and fruit stall there which seems to supply all needs. No sign of Vince, no Mrs. Vince, no cart "with the other things", no water. L.M. is going to phone as she posts this. I expect he is in prison. That's always my idea. I have been out all day and feel burnt. That table is excellent for writing. Oh, I do wish you were home and settled in. Then I shall be at rest about you. Take care of that precious self of yours. The sea dances, the olives dance with tiny flickering leaves . . .[7]

MS ATL. *LKM* I. 247–8; *LJMM*, 319–20.

[1] The maid at the Hôtel Beau Rivage, Bandol, where KM had stayed in late 1915.

[2] Murry enlightened her when he wrote on 13 Oct., 'The bonne sounds superb, particularly when I translate the hieroglyph you could not understand as *domane venere* – I will come tomorrow.' (ATL.)

[3] Murry's card, posted from Paris on 2 Oct., said that he might have to spend the night at Folkestone.

[4] Paul Valéry (1871–1945), poet and essayist. Although they did not become close friends until later, Valéry and Murry were acquainted through the French writer's contributions to the *Athenaeum*.

[5] Victor Sorapure, the consultant physician at Hampstead General Hospital. (See *CLKM* II. 292.)

[6] The housekeeper at Portland Villas.

[7] The ink at the end of the letter has faded irretrievably. The letters to Murry between 6 and 11 Oct. are now particularly difficult to read.

To J. M. Murry, [7 October 1919]

[Casetta Deerholm, Ospedaletti]
Tuesday

The pages are rather groggily numbered because I am outside and I havent any blotting paper. Kiss Wing for me on his head and on his nose.

My own,

A workman has come who says they will have finished their part of the job today and after that its only a matter of quelques jours before the water is turned on here. Wonderful people! Its another summer day. As the waves break they are full of gold, like the waves we saw at Bandol. This early morning (6.30) the sea was *pink*, pale pink – I never saw it so before – and it scarcely breathed . . . The washerwoman brought home your clothes last night (yes, the change of subject isnt a really absurd change. Id think the pink sea all the lovelier if it had a boat in it with your blue shirt for a sail.) I have just put the clothes away among mine – and the carnation sachets. There are tiny false links in your cuffs which impressed me greatly. Here they are waiting for you.

The insect plague is *simply awful*. No nets or veils will keep them out. I am bitten to death. The tiny, almost invisible ones, who are so deadly, the laundress tells me are called "păpĕtechīkŏs".

(Zuccinis are not cucumbers. They are a kind of elongated pale yellow marrows. L.M. bought one yesterday. I don't at all see why we should not grow them in Sussex.) I am longing to get out of the garden and make a small tour of Ospedaletti. Every day a new shop seems to arise; and the butcher is evidently a fascinating man. But I shall stick to the garden for the present and get my cough down. I feel wonderfully better, wonderfully stronger. I feel myself walking about like a normal person at times – quite lightly and quickly. Soon it will be always like that.

Shall I have a letter today, Boge? No, not till tomorrow, says my sensible head, but *Wig* says Perhaps. I hope I'll get more novels quickly, for the last 2 go today. They make very excellent *pasta* here – very fresh. I think it's much better for shopping than San Remo. It's not cheap to feed very well, and I think it will cost us 30/- a head per week for food. That is really dearer than London. Of course, the amount of butter, eggs and milk is not normal. If one was well, one could do it on 25/- each but not . . .

I keep the strictest accounts so that we shall know for another time. All the while I keep wondering how you are – and the house and WING and the office and the weather and Violet. Are you warm enough? Do you feel hard up? How is Richard?[1] Give the old boy my love; he is part of *our* family – not yours, not mine, but our special family tree.

John Murry – Katherine Murry

— Murry   — Murry   — Murry   — Murry   — Murry

(Oh, Wig, how stupid!) No, I'd like that. They would be so useful in the garden . . .

Corporal Love-in-the-Mist is coming out in that place in the garden.

You have all my heart and I am yours.

MS ATL. *LKM* I. 245–6; *LJMM*, 320–1.

---

[1] The name KM often used for Murry's younger brother, Arthur.

To J. M. Murry, [8 October, 1919]

[Casetta Deerholm, Ospedaletti]
Wednesday
A week today. 27 weeks to go.

My own,

Ida had to go to the Town late last night and she returned with your first letter from home. *This was breath of life to me*, to know that your journey was over. Was Pa's account of the revolution all my eye?[1] For how did you get to Hampstead? It's puzzling. I am very interested in Betts and his garden-Bett (joke!).[2] I believe every word. One of my specialities will be Italian tomatoes and Italian things like marrows. They'd sell in England, you bet. (Oh dear, *no* not again!) "My Lord she hath been eating honeycomb".

Precious little Wing! Keep him. I shall see him again, after all; and all the tears I shed for him here were in vain. Bless his nose! I see him grubby and a bit hungry. But I grudge his whole little derrière on your letter.[3] He must only write with the tip of his tail. You sounded tired, my darling. Was there food for you? Was the house in good order? Fancy Violet not having my letter. You mean tho' my *last* letter, not my Sydney one, don't you?

It is awfully hot here – as hot as when we came. The insects are *simply awful*. It's a good thing you left before they got really bad. My leg is so swollen I can only hop today. It is maddening because otherwise I feel so well and strong. curse these confounded countries!! We have double nets, powder, bathe in verbena, oatmeal, milk, salt water, fresh – but nothing cures them. I think they make the idea of a life in this country absolutely impossible. Enough of them.

I took the revolver into the garden today and practised with it; how to load and unload and fire.[4] It terrifies me, but I feel "like a new being" now that I really can handle it and understand it. I'll never give it back to Vince. They are fascinating things; one is childishly fascinated. I almost understand old Brontë père.[5] No more coffee to be had in San Remo. The government has taken it over as it has the rice. Dear knows when we shall get any more. It doesn't matter really.

Please send me some books to review. I have none for next week. Dearest of all, you tell me to write about myself. But then you must write about yourself. That is only fair. I want to know about YOU.

L.M. waits to take this to the post. I am going to look at my plants. I found some lovely roots in the lower garden which, like the wedding guests, are being put up higher.[6]

Look here! I am so much better that I feel like your old goblin girl –

in spite of the bites, and my old S. of F.[7] hunger is coming back again. So you must take care of yourself and be my goblin Boy.

Love, dearest Heart – all my Love forever.

Wig

MS ATL. *LKM* I. 246–7; *LJMM*, 321–2.

[1] Murry had called on Harold Beauchamp, who was staying at the Langham Hotel, Langham Place. KM's father would have held strongly conservative views on the current transport strike.

[2] A steward who put Murry up at his home in Folkestone, and offered him advice on gardening.

[3] Murry noted, *LJMM*, 322, 'Wingley had been lost before we left England. He was sitting on my note-paper when I wrote, so I wrote my letter round him.'

[4] The landlord had loaned KM a revolver for protection. Often she could not sleep because of nervousness.

[5] After the emergencies of a threatened Napoleonic invasion, and the Luddite riots of 1811–12, the Revd Patrick Brontë, father of Charlotte and Emily, primed his pistols daily and fired them each morning for fifty years.

[6] A memory of the parable in Luke 14: 8–10.

[7] South of France.

To J. M. Murry, [10 October 1919]

[Casetta Deerholm, Ospedaletti]

Friday

I wish Wing could write letters. I should set him papers of questions and give him prizes for full answers. The weather is marvellous, like *silk* – very hot and still. People are bathing below. It's so clear one can see their legs and arms, almost their toes. This house is rather like a fairy house. It is an adorable place to live in – and then the garden – and the view of Ospedaletti is exquisite. The view is always subtly changing. It's far more beautiful and remote than Pauline.[1] The fact, too, that one is forever conscious of this huge expanse of sea . . . God knows I don't want to live here, but for a place to get well in, it could not be more ideal.

L.M. is off to San Remo to see if she can find a *litre* of fine muslin. Just as I thought, she loves that jaunt in, and "you don't mind, Katy, now you have your revolver, do you?" No, I don't . . .

Later.

Darling of darlings,

There is *no* letter from you today. I expect with luck there will be *something*, at any rate, tomorrow. One came from Chaddie for my birthday containing her *wishes* and that's all. So you needn't bother to say what I would like. Ida has returned from San Remo and is making tea. The workmen have gone and *water flows*. A man climbed on to the roof and the deed was done. The sound of the plug is rare music. I have been walking up and down the garden, having a rest from work and thinking of you. My morning letter to you was scattered. Forgive it. All the while, as you know, with my daily life but running deep and true and silent, is my life with you which is the *living* part of me. If I fly from one odd thing to another you must know the other is still there and depend on it. For it is my religion and defence and all that keeps life possible. Love, dearest love, only you and I know what it means. The letters from other people who are in the other world and never have known ours jar me so – and at the same time they make me feel how wonderful we *are* and *have been* and shall be. You, my noble angelic Boy (I am sincere) – how could I love you enough. I could not – not if I had fifty pairs of lungs.

Wig

Still later. I have opened the letter to say:

Ida went to the Banque d'Italie today with another letter from me. They have been told nothing – so they must be given up. She then went to Benecke with £1 to cash for herself; they gave her 40 francs. She took my £5 to the Italian Bank (at the corner of the Via Colombia) who gave her 41 francs for each £1. Last week Benecke gave 39 to the £1 and this same bank 40. So what am I to do? I must have this decided pretty soon because my purse begins to show its lining. Advise me please, my little lawyer in chief. Isn't it a bother? I have decided what to send you by Vince. Some of those *chemises de Byron* OR polo shirts you liked so. The extra 5 lire will be the first egg in the nest for the Heron.

Darling,
Precious,
Boge

MS ATL. *LKM* I. 244; *LJMM*, 322–4.

[i] The Villa Pauline, Bandol, where KM and Murry stayed in early 1916.

To J. M. Murry, [11 October 1919]

[Casetta Deerholm, Ospedaletti]

No. 5 Tuesday letter and Wednesday morning letter both received and this is only *Saturday*.

My dearest,

Just a line more. Ive got three letters this afternoon; its a perfect *festa* today. Those before my Swinnerton review fetched up. Would to G. I had some books. But I'll write something for this week and post per usual on Tuesday.

(1) I long to know about the house[1] [2 words illegible.]

(2) I am very glad you saw Pa. I sent you his letter. Please note re Bank of Italy. What is this game? In future I shall do as you advise and get Kay to send my money per registered insured post. I wouldn't mind if he came for a fortnight.[2] I can always plead fatigue and do my work.

Don't go to Wood Hay[3] unless you can help. You'd be miserable. They are not *ours*.

I'd love to see Dent's old ladies[4] – love to any time. Please tell him. I am beginning to feel so dreadfully *affectionate*, just en l'air. Not for anyone I know particularly but just that I'd so like to be very nice to old ladies from Nice. [One short paragraph containing the word 'Sorapure' has become illegible due to faded ink.]

Tell Tommy [H. M. Tomlinson] we have small and big flies by day – that the mosquitoes are of various kinds – some really poisonous. They raise a great swelling, others big blisters. It's just as bad as his old place. Give him also my love.

This was to have been just a line. I had a sweet letter from Violet, telling me about the cats and you and asking whether you'd like anything special in *your* saucer.

> Dear Bogey,
> Dearest Bogey,
> Darling Precious Bogey,
> Yours for ever
> Wig

MS ATL. *LJMM*, 324–5.

[1] Murry wrote that Duncan Grant had told him of a house to let at Wilmington on the South Downs.

[2] Murry also told KM on 7 Oct., 'Last night I went by request off to the Langham to dine . . . I think yr. Father was very friendly (perhaps friendly wd. be more accurate) and, what is more important, he spoke of a plan of going to the South for a fortnight before he sailed.' (Murry, 180.)

[3] The house Harold Beauchamp bought at Lyndhurst, Southampton, where KM's sisters Chaddie and Jeanne lived rent-free.

[4] Edward Dent (1876–1957), who had written for the *Blue Review*, was now music critic for the *Athenaeum*.

To J. M. Murry, [11 October 1919]

[Casetta Deerholm, Ospedaletti]
Saturday.

Treasure brought to shore today: Monday nights letter. No. 3. No. 4. Lyttons letter.

My Precious Own

When I got up this morning I put on my hat first and as soon as the food had been arranged went out for a small walk. The day was so – what *can* one say – there isn't a word – perfect is not enough – that I had to go. First thing I saw was a large daisy at the bottom of our steps – in a pinafore – you know the kind – a Wingley flower. Then I walked along the Boulevard which smelled of pines, gumtrees, heliotrope, geraniums and a dash of the sea and really had a look at Ospedaletti. But Bogey! I had not the faintest *idea* of what it was like. Its just a fairy tale; thats all. And the country above and beyond it – these immense romantic glimpses! I sauntered along – gripping Mother's walking stick. My heart was bursting with happiness. The sun had his arm round my shoulder. The sea made a sound you would have liked: there was a breeze that filled the mouth with pleasure like wine does. Hardly anybody about. A small scene from an opera being enacted at the one cab stand between two lovely girls carrying baskets of fringed linen on their heads, a boy in a blue undervest eating a loaf of bread and the cabdriver in white. That was all. Then I keep coming to these glimpses of the old town, seen between the trees, and then to pine trees with rose red geraniums climbing up to their topmost branch. The only work being done was gardening – One heard people gardening & felt them gardening & that was all. By the time I got to the Poste I knew something very good was going to happen & three letters were handed across. You know that row of darling little oleanders [drawing] – little trees like that. I sat on a bench & read them – & then walked off clasping them very hard stopping occasionally and saying to a bush or a plant – *darling*! – very quietly.

Really when you come in May I dread to think of what we shall do. When its spring here, as well as everything else. You see we shall trundle off with our filet in the morning & then well come home – ravenous like I did & see this little house as I did perched on the hill half in sun half swept by the dancing shadow of the olive trees – – And there will be flowers everywhere – I didn't feel in the least tired. I stopped at the drug store & bought 4 bottils of Saint Galmier: it wasn't a luxury – I think one needs to drink here – especially while the skeeters are so skeeterish. Such a nice woman in there, extremely pretty & awfully nice jujubes on the counter. Blow! everything was awfully nice. Beams came from the toothbrushes. She says it is like this all winter except for an occasional day of wind or rain – just as hot, & people who come pour se reposer go away on wings. Cherry pie grows in trees in the Jardin Publique at Ospedaletti – Did you *see* that wonderful park-like place with all its flowers? Lawrence was working in the garden with a handkerchief round his neck.

Well Bogey – ı don't know – but really we seem to have found the most ideal place we could have found. I can *whistle* again. Look here – won't May be perfect. *Remember May* – Hug the thought of it – its going to be our new life.

(1) I am so glad about Violet.[1]

(2) As you face it the lefthand back leg is the one to prop with a match end & a french stamp folded small. Both front legs must be off the ground.[2]

(3) I think much the best plan is to come home early in the afternoon. I wish you would. Then you can change, & put on your slippers & have a good fire & tea & not feel you have to go out again . . . see?

(4) Everything is now done except the lock on the door. Vince came yesterday with still more linen. We shall lie in fair sheets in May. He will persist in wanting to bring *more* carpets – a set of *lovely* blue china ornaments, tapestry etc. "I feel I cant make it nice enough for Mrs Murry –" He is a good soul after all. Ive turned again.

(5) Augusta has disappeared. Half the town is looking out for another. There's no hurry: it keeps L.M. quiet but she is a most rotten cook – However she *learns*. Perhaps its because I am always hungry – even had to eat bread & butter in bed last night.

Please send the BOOKS & if you don't do something about poor little Wig's money soon she will not "have a bean left" – I'm still at the long story. It makes me *groan* but I must do it: its a form of practising to get back.

Must start a new page after all because I wondered if you would ever publish a column from a Note Book. It is going to be called *From the Casetta* and its a kind of daybook about things like flies or a certain light or a fragment of talk over a table or workmen going home in the evening . . . I want to write a whole book – ready in 6 months – of these . . . *observations*.[3] I quite understand if you don't want them, dearest.

Wasn't Lyttons[4] letter a nice one? Queer how some people seem to see things: I thought that a *bad* review.[5] Oh Bogey it is cruel to say how warm it is here – I never saw anything like the shadows in this house cast by the delicate trees outside. I have already noticed 5 different grasshoppers. They are great favourites of mine as insects: they are such *characters*. As for the cicada every night he is here. I cant tell you how good the stove is here – It is a gem now that it is accustomed to go. Yesterday when L.M. was out I made my tea with about 2 leaves and a twig & the whole kitchen felt so warm & lived in.

Forgive a drunken girl who loves you & you alone – I am so glad you are finishing Cinnamon & Angelica.[6] Please let me know if you have other plans.

A warm warm hug. A big kiss – *love* enough to last all the winter through.

Your own
Wig

Tell Wing how much I love you. See he dont catch cold after his bath. You ought to buy him a tiny jaeger wooly.

MS ATL. *LKM* I. 248–50; *LJMM*, 325–7.

[1] Murry had sent favourable reports of the maid.
[2] KM's shepherdess clock, which needed to be propped up in order to go.
[3] This was neither completed nor published, but the entries for this time in the *Journal* 1954 may comprise parts of it.
[4] KM had met the biographer and critic Lytton Strachey (1890–1932) towards the end of 1915. His attitude to her wavered between attraction and distaste.
[5] Murry wrote 8 Oct. praising her review of Frank Swinnerton's *September*, 'Portraits and Passions', in the *Athenaeum*, 10 Oct. 1919.
[6] Murry had resumed work on his verse play.

To J. M. Murry, [12 October 1919]

[Casetta Deerholm, Ospedaletti]
Sunday

My own Bogey

I am sitting in the Bastick chair[1] covered with the Jaegar rug as although the sun is hot the air is chilly (its about 4.45 p.m.). It has been a mavellous day here; Ive not moved except for meals. Ive been reading & writing & after lunch I fell asleep from the general *shipboard* atmosphere. Speaking of ships such a small jewel of a sailing ship passed the house today – riding close enough in to see the men on board. She had two small sails at the bows, one big one at the stern & a medium *very* movable one amidships. The sea is my favourite sea – bright bright blue but showing a glint of white as far as one can see – that lift of white seen far away – as far as the horizon moves me terribly. In fact it is *the very thing* I should like to express in writing – it has *the very quality* – Here comes another most interesting little steamboat – a very small trader, she looks, painted black & red with a most ridiculous amount of smoke coming out of the funnel. [drawing] No, I cant draw her. From where I sit I cannot see any ground below the balustrade – that is threaded through with sea. One would think it was a sheer drop from there into deep water. What a place – eh Bogey?

I had a nasty jar last night. As there was no water last week the laundry was put 'out' & it came home, exquisite, covered with white net with a rose on top, carried by the nicest old body on her head who seemed to take the greatest fancy to me as I did to her – *long* conversation – 'comme vous êtes bien ici' etc. etc. etc. etc., & under all this a bill for <u>37.85</u>. This of course after the old un had gone & the rose had been smelled admired & Wig had thought how *much* better, after all, they order these things in Italy. L.M. did not really "think it very heavy. I don't think you could have expected it to be less, Katie" – . This with her overall *4.50* & an immense white petticoat *3.85*. As to serviettes at 1 lira a piece "oh well, my dear thats not quite sixpence IF the exchange is still at 41 for a £1 – its about – let me see, *hardly* fivepence" and so on & so on and so on. How I should beat her if I were married to her – its an awful thought – She thinks Im made of money – thats the worst of it. On her last but one journey to San Remo she bought 1 hecto[2] of coffee for 4.50 from 'SUCH a funny little shop' & when I protested she "thought the parcel was small for the money but the beans felt very tightly packed." Could you believe it – However, let her go. And I shall never shoot her because the body would be so difficult to dispose of after. One couldn't make it into a neat parcel or put it under a hearthstone & she would *never* burn –

Every day I love this house more for some new grace – & every day I hold a minute review of the garden & there is always something fresh & wonderful. Then there is the wild hill never the same – *satisfying* ones deep love for what is living and ancient in literature. I look at the hill, dearest Bogey, & because I have not had a classical education it seems to me full of the spirit of those old boys – the wild fig & olive, the low growing berries and the tufts of sweet roots –

This is a place for lovers. (Hullo! there goes a swallow.) Yes, it is made for lovers. You know, don't you, how even now I am preparing it for you. I look at it & think I shall put net curtains here – & the baskets under the verandah shall be flower baskets and – It is enough to keep one busy until May – My very own. Another Sunday, thats two gone – now there are only 26.

Yours for ever & ever amen.

MS ATL. *LKM* I. 250–1; *LJMM*, 327–9.

---

[1] i.e. basket chair.
[2] Three-and-a-half ounces.

To J. M. Murry, [13 October 1919]

[Casetta Deerholm, Ospedaletti]
Monday

No letter.
Weekly Times.
A. for October 3 & the 10th.
Nation fetched up.
My Precious

The weather has completely changed, its chilly with a thick thick fog & heavy downpour of rain. The sky is grey – its like living inside a pearl today – very lovely for a change.

The October 10 number of the paper I have just gone through. Good Heavens! How good it is – What different eyes, different hair – to the little measles that came out all spotty while you were away. *This one simply thrills me.* Ill have to get a flagstaff in this garden and when Ive read my copies through, fly them – just out of pride – The leading article was excellent – it went so well.[1] I think one ought to begin by – not knocking the reader down exactly but by showing him who is 'master of the house' as Wilkies girl would say.[2] Scott-James too is admirably to the point and is a very good article to have.[3] Sheppard is one of your most valuable men, I think.[4] An excellent mellow quality in what he writes & altogether —— just what the A. can publish so well.

I wish the 1st letter from America had not been so particular. Its first chop to have secured it but we don't really care so passionately about Mr Kreymborg – do you think?[5] I do so love a general *survey* or at any rate an ordnance map – before I visit the various paths & farms. Now again this chap gives one an idea he could write very well –

Most excellent letter from Italy,[6] I thought, & awfully good dramatic criticism of Tolstoi – so *fresh.*[7] In fact the whole appearance, contents, everything has form & substance again. You are evidently a genius as an editor – nothing short of that – a perfect genius. I adore working for you but I do *wish* you'd send me some novels. I am sending an article tomorrow on some novels here, in the bookcase but it is a bit steep to be left without a single one – Yes the paper is a noble paper, my son: it most certainly is. I don't know what to do – I am so damned proud of you – you little marvel. I feel if only I had some books here I *would* write a review & thats what all your team feel, I believe. What about Ripmann.[8] Have you ever thought of him again as a possible contributor – an article on languages in the *production of books.* He is a very great nut on printing and so on.

L.M. has surpassed herself today – At 1.30 I staggered in to ask

where the lunch was & it was *not*. She had *no* kindling & the olive root
wont burn with just paper – After all these days when every afternoon
she is up in the hills roaming the pasture wild. *Then* there were no eggs
– then she boiled the coffee in the water she had prepared for
spaghetti, reeking with gros sel – I got a bit fierce but I apologised at
once and really I dont get upset by her at all now – I think she is *very
queer* though. You know that lovely room of hers with that view. I
asked her yesterday why she didn't make it nice – and she said she
hadn't unpacked "as you are sending me away in April and at any
rate my room is just a passage isn't it – to the lavatory" ——

Visitor last night. A *very* nice one. While I was waiting for the beans
I saw two honeyball eyes looking at me from the hall (the front door
was open). When they saw me they *flashed* away but I immediately
said as much Wing language as I knew & went quietly to the door
with my soup plate. A perfectly lovely tiny cat came in – *gold, white* &
black with a body rather like a rabbit. It simply bolted the stray pasta,
then I gave it some milk & it more than bolted that. Then it purred
more loudly than any cat Ive ever heard. Its purring machine must
have been wound up until that moment – It sat under a chair singing
like this for a little & then fled into the night again. In my mind I
called it 'Gênet'.[9]

I have just looked up – the fog has rolled away – the rain has
stopped – the air smells of the geraniums. Tomorrow the gardener
comes for the day – the ground will be just right for sowing. There are
carts going by yip-y-y-y-ip-yip say the drivers & the bells go tring-
tring-tring. The sea sounds as though it were somehow exquisitely
refreshed by that mist – all the grass blades are bowed down by a
diamond. Oh dear, *Im awfully happy*. It has been so lovely lying here in
the rain – I feel renewed too and bowed down with a diamond, too. I
love you. I love you. Shall I have a letter by the late post. Oh Bogey
look at the new leaves on the rosebush – bright red. Were they there
yesterday? There is one hidden frog here; he croaks every evening. He
shall be invited to the festa in May. Isn't this rotten paper – its oiled in
places and you cant write on both sides really.

After all a birthday present came from C. [Chaddie] & Jeanne
together. An ordinary small 1d matchbox, enamelled yellow and
painted (very badly) with an ugly little Chinaman – oriental
department 1/11¾ "To our darling Katie with our united love & best
wishes" – they couldn't have said more if it was a carpet. I shall keep
this matchbox for ever and remember the size of their hearts by it.

Goodbye most precious. Bites are still going strong – Does Tommy
know a fly – just like an ordinary housefly in the face that stings? *It is
here*.

And now I hug you tight & hold you a minute.

Wig

MS ATL. *LKM* I. 252; *LJMM*, 329–31.

[1] Murry's leading article for the *Athenaeum*, 10 Oct. 1919, 'Art and Industry'.
[2] A character in *The Night Watchman*, a sketch by the comedian Wilkie Bard (1870–1944), which KM also quoted from in writing to Murry, 14 June 1918, *CLKM* I. 239.
[3] R. A. Scott-James, 'Should Journalists be Educated?'.
[4] John Tressider Sheppard (1881–1968), then Lecturer in Classics at King's College, Cambridge, wrote 'Procopius and Others', a review of three volumes in the Loeb Classical Library.
[5] Conrad Aiken's 'Philosophy for the Flute' was a review of Alfred Kreymborg's *Plays for Poem-Mimes*.
[6] 'The Latest D'Annunzio', no. IV of 'Letters from Italy' by Guido de Ruggiero.
[7] 'Tolstoy at the St. James', signed P, was a review of *Reparation*, a translation of Tolstoy's *Living Corpses*. Murry identified the reviewer in his letter 11 Oct. as E. M. Forster.
[8] Walter Rippmann, KM's German teacher at Queen's College, with whom she had once been infatuated. See *CLKM* I. 11.
[9] 'Gênet Fleuri' was KM's favourite perfume.

To J. M. Murry, 13 and 14 October [1919]

[Casetta Deerholm, Ospedaletti]
October 13th.

My precious little husband (this title is reserved for State Occasions)

It is not only that the spoon is the most exquisite perfect little spoon, a spoon that faeries might go to battle for – a spoon that fascinates – that just to hold and turn & balance & feel is a joy – it is over and above these things a sign between us – a secret message from our real house. It is come from the tea table on the southern terrace, where we sit, idle, drinking tea & there it lies, winking bright in the late sun. And it shall be the spoon our own little boy shall eat his first strawberry and cream out of – standing by you, clutching your knees while you prepare the marvellous dish & make eyes at him. Ah the darling! Ah, *both my darlings*. All this & more the little spoon brings.

October 14th.

No 6 Wednesday
No 7 Birthday letter
Thursday, both here.

My Precious

You see that spoon came a day early even though it was registered, just to please us. It wont happen again. There are two Letters Extraordinary from you. Letters with icing, candles, marzipan, cupids & sugar Wingleys on them with angelica eyes. They *are* my birthday. Next one – where shall we be? We shall be in our own home eating off

Italian plates, drinking out of honey coloured fluted cups. But stop! You are nice enough. Don't be any sweeter, more adorable, more Bogey-like, more precious, more cherished than you are – or I shall fly off into a shower of stars.

I *note* the saucepans. It was high time we had them – I hope they were not 2 dear. Violet will give them a mothers care I expect & not leave them to cook themselves away. Fancy Sydney being there.[1] May fortune favour the arrangement. See that you both eat enough. Do get home to tea as often as you can.

Fancy 2nd the Moults[2] to dinner on Wednesday – That thrills me. I see you at the top serving or *not* serving or serving with your own spoon & then licking it afterwards & Wing under the table playing a tune on Sydney's shoe laces – Oh dear.

I send what I have penned. But I cannot make up every week. Where are the novels? How disgraceful it is. Conduct an enquiry. Have some menial burned.

You ask me how I am –

Oh, first, about my other birthday presents. Told you about the 1d matchbox[3] didn't I? That curve over the 1d is a *fling* of disdain. Thank Heaven Ive scratched a bit off the Chinaman's hat already. Then L.M. gave me a bottil of Genêt Fleuri. Wasn't it remarkable – the chemist had it *here*, same bottil and all. It must have cost an awful lot. Well, Ive given her her money for this month – & it is a heavenly scent. Thats all I got. Father sent me a communication not mentioning it – so all my fervour has gone to nothing so far. I thought my opinions on the Labour Crisis were good for a fiver – but *no*. He gave Marie £10 in hers. Isn't it *awful minge*. Never mind. We dont want them. They can go on eating their Wood Hay. *Very* Wood Hay –

It is a brilliant glancing day. You should have seen after the rain was over yesterday little old men appeared from nowhere in peaked hats crawling over the wild hill looking for snails. They carried coloured handkerchiefs which *frothed* – Flowers are coming up everywhere on the hill. I just went for a glance today – not more than five steps high and there were 8 kinds there.

Caterina came yesterday (the pretty one from the laundry). She brought me vivid pink carnations & two eggs in cotton wool for a present. But I felt she could afford to. All the same, she was fearfully nice, laughing, gay, beautiful, *healthy* creature. She says May here is magnifique beyond anything – the whole place is covered with flowers – and all the little kinds pour les distillations are out – tiny hyacinths – violets – small roses –

Well now Ill tell you about myself. I feel marvellously better. All that remains is my cough. It has bad moments still, but that terrible boiling sensation when I cant stop I have not had *once* since you left.

Nor have I *once* had a temperature. I get short of puff if I cough but my lungs don't hurt at all. The pain in my joints is – well its not outwardly better yet I feel it is. So it is evidently on the mend. Think of last October 14th. Sydney Beauchamp[4] came & at night I had fever in that North room & felt I was going to die.

Here's Ida for my letter. Shes off to San Remo for supplies – Tram waiting.

Yours for ever
Wig.

MS ATL. *LKM* I 253; *LJMM*, 331–3.

[1] KM's relative Sydney Waterlow (see *CLKM* I. 326 n. 2) was staying with Murry at 2 Portland Villas.
[2] Thomas Moult (b. 1895), minor poet, journalist, and sports writer, who occasionally contributed to the *Athenaeum*, and his wife Bessie.
[3] The cheap present from her sisters.
[4] Her cousin Sydney Beauchamp, an eminent physician. (See *CLKM* II. 281 n. 2.)

To J. M. Murry, [15 October 1919]

[Casetta Deerholm, Ospedaletti]

No 8 Saturday letter
Two books, Weekly Times & Nation all here.
Wednesday
My Blessed Bogey
I am in the middle of a review of Brett Young[1] which I will post tomorrow to the office unregistered. I had just got ready for post an article on a non-existent novel called A Fine Day by Emilia Lanteri, published by Paolo Littardi, Milan – but these books came & did the trick. Im *thankful* to have them. The Brett Young is interesting, too from the reviewing standpoint and the other has an interesting preface – so thats O.K. The Bianca d'Italia acknowledges me, so I can get money. Also good. I don't want *any* of your old money, not a crumb. Never dare to send it me –

I am very glad that K.M. is liked a bit.[2] She wishes she was more worthy. That's *sincere* from my soul. But whenever Im praised I always want to fall on my knees & ask God to make me a better girl – It just takes me that way.

I saw and shuddered at the Lit. Sup. campaign.[3] Very fierce. And how awful about Jack Squire[4] – you bet we won't be asked. But it means a pull doesn't it: we must beat them. Ill send you extras as soon as I can for my part. I wish we could do the drama together. I feel there we could collaborate & be perfect wonders – I long to see your notice. Fancy you & Arthur sitting there watching it, its so lovely where Portia & Jessica meet their men at the end[5] – I want an order form for your book; every copy tells[6] – So please ask Arthur to send me one immejite.

That Wing! What a fellow he is. I wish you could bring him in May but he would eat his way out of a suitcase just as you were in the Customs Office. How I would love to kiss him. Its only L.M. who had a bad influence on Athenaeum; he'll be alright now.

Yesterday ended in such a blazing glory of a sunset that I was quite frightened. It really was the most superb day and at night (all the windows open) the sea sounded like an immense orchestra; I could truly hear violins, especially, and great rushing passages for the woodwind. The skeeters drank my blood last night & Im awfully bitten today – but to death – both hands, one face and one leg.

You know I cant write letters here – only to you – other people are not when Im away. I am very glad you are going walking with Eliot; perhaps you'll tell me about it. And what kind of food do you have? And how are the household bills? And wont you & Sydney share in a dinner wine? The Australian Wine Companys address was on my table; its so good in winter to drink wine at least once a day & you need it. You have no vitality to spare, as you know & you bolster up the lack of it with your WILL which is a big strain on you. Health, darling as we BOTH know is really cheap at any price –

Food here is much better. I am dead nuts on *pasta*. We eat it once a day & for 2.50 to 3 lire we get quite good meat. Is that a great deal of money do you think? Z.B.[7] we get two veal cutlets for 3 lire; that seems to *me* reasonable. Last week my bills were huge but then net for a new mosquito net & £3 for L.M. and the laundry came in but even with all this I shall manage admirably on money *and* save. So that when you come there will be a lovely nest egg ready for spending – you & I together.

I wish I was more of a stoic about underlinen, perfumes, little boxes for a toilet table, delicate ribbons & silk stockings. But the older I grow the more exquisite I want to be – *fine* down to every minutest particular, as a writer, as a talker, in my home, in my life and all my ways – to carry it all through. Even now, sometimes when I write to you a word shakes into the letter that I dont mean to be there – an old windfall – you know from a tree in an orchard Ive long forsaken . . . Do you know what I mean? It is my illness which has made me so bad-tempered at times. Alas! one cant fight without getting battle stained – & alas! there have been so many occasions when Ive never had time to wash away the stains or renew myself – but have come to you – just as I was. You must forget these *melancholy melancholy things* my own precious darling. A year ago I thought I was going to die and

I think I *was*. And now I know we are going to live. Dont lets forget how Sorapure[8] has helped. I really think I should have just died in that room upstairs if he had not taken me by the hand, like you take a little girl who is frightened of a dog & led me up to my pain & showed it to me & proved that it wasn't going to eat me. Thats what he did.

I must go on with my review, my own. Im glad Sydney is there now; it "makes a difference" to hear another step on the stairs & to have someone at meals – How soon can you get any anthracite?

Bogey I am getting *absolutely well*; theres no doubt about it, no doubt at all. You see I live in the open air all day long & at night I practically sleep in it. I shall see Ansaldi[9] next week & tell you what he says. But dont even have the ghost of a worry about me. Dismiss me as a worry – Oh, dear, on the wild hill today I found thyme and rosemary – it reminded me of Bandol in the early morning. Very large astonished daisies are beginning to flower everywhere – even in the gravel. The cotton pods are huge. Exquisite pale yellow butterflies flutter by – the Marygolds unclosèd are –

Goodbye for now – I love you more than ever now I am 31.

Wig.

A huge fawn-coloured rat just ran over the verandah. Tell Wing.

Did you see the easy chair advertised in the Nation to be bought of Waring & Gillow[10] for £4.10.0.

It seems that prices are going down.

MS ATL. *LKM* I. 253–4; *LJMM*, 333–5.

[1] 'A Plea for Less Entertainment', a review of F. Brett Young's *The Young Physician*, the *Athenaeum*, 24 Oct. 1919.

[2] Murry had told her of hearing her reviews praised.

[3] Murry intended mounting a modest publicity campaign for his paper. In the following week the *Times Literary Supplement* was giving away 10,000 copies.

[4] J. C. Squire (1884–1958), poet and literary editor of the *New Statesman*, was about to launch a new monthly, the *London Mercury*. Several of the *Athenaeum*'s writers were invited to contribute, but not Murry nor KM.

[5] Murry reviewed the Court Theatre production of *The Merchant of Venice*, the *Athenaeum*, 17 Oct. 1919.

[6] *Poems: 1917–1918*, printed by Murry's brother Arthur on the hand press at Portland Villas.

[7] Zum Beispiel ('for example').

[8] See p. 11, n. 5, above.

[9] An Italian doctor she was now consulting.

[10] Waring and Gillow Ltd., Furnishers and Decorators, 164–180 Oxford Street.

To J. M. Murry, [16 October 1919]

[Casetta Deerholm, Ospedaletti]

No nuffin.

Thursday.

My own Precious

My review is just finished too, thank goodness. L.M. is off to post. There was no letter today – I have been so spoilt lately that I expect one every day & then the post punishes me – Its bitterly cold, pouring with rain, a hard heavy wind blowing and the sky like an iron shutter. 4.30 and the light is on – I went outside this morning but was blown in again and Ive been writing at the dining-room table. My little table is too small. I am so thankful after all that I brought really warm clothes. On a besoin, today – thick jaegers, jersey & cardigan & deux pantalons –

That cat I made such a fuss about got in the larder last night & stole our meat. It sprang in the window today again & looked like a devil when I shooed it away. I shall have *no* cats here – And *she* has broken our glass jug. Well, well. First thing I saw was the fragments outside the back door. It can't be helped. She said "it was very frail from the beginning". I suppose one would make the same excuse if one dropped & broke a baby! I hope my review is alright. I feel far away when I am writing: as though I am being confusing; you can't *hear me*. It makes me anxious.

Heavy thunder prowls round the sky. Now it is sunset & the shutter of the sky lifts to show one bright band of gold – I am just a little bit tired; it is the weather – the thunder & sudden intense *heavy* cold – like lead. Oh, what a good idea – Ill drink a glass of wine. Getrunken. Really England is never colder than this today. Now it is hailing, enormous hail. Id like to be in Sussex, Bogey, and very very *snug*. But don't think Im depressed, my own darling Boge; Im not – only <u>so</u> parky after such a long taste of heavenly fair climate. And very angry because in spite of the cold the mosquitoes & gnats persist; both my hands are bandaged today – Why don't they die? L.M. caught one today & put it out of window – instead of killing it. I expect theyve passed the word round that this house is an asile – for them.

Give me a very tight small hug & then hold me close till Im warm.

Until tomorrow my treasure.

Your Wig.

MS ATL. *LKM* I. 255; *LJMM*, 335–6.

To J. M. Murry, [17 October 1919]

[Casetta Deerholm, Ospedaletti]
Friday.

My own Precious

The Four pounds and letter 9 that is your Sunday letter both arrived last night & filled me [with] warmth and light again. I ate a large dinner, went to bed with a hot bottil & had coffee bread & honey there ad libitum. Today the sun is shining in the sky: it is real winter again and though the sun is warm the wind blows in it & through it & you have to wrap you very lively. I think winter has come for good. Ive a feeling it has, at least as much winter as we have here – and I am sure it will be cold whatever they have told us.

Last night's letter was just – just the letter I wanted. It told me everything – all about Violet & the house – I *lapped* it up. Zuccini is good to look at *&* good to eat. You remember it? What we called cowcumber and even saw the seeds. When its not cooked its about twice the size of a cowcumber & its pale yellow. We have got our sugar alright. I wish we could get rice but it does not exist. The other foodstuffs seem abundant though; the *butter* here is excellent. I find the Bank of Italy charges 1 lire in every pound – so I shall do as you suggest – get £25 a month from Kay.[1] It was like you to send that £5 – & what a picture of you running out of the office, trying to hide twenty books, all in a pile, like a conjurer's boy, tripping on the stair or bumping into Bernard Shaw[2] & then buying half a pair of blankets! Oh dear, how NICE you are, Bogey. My eyes have gone all bloodshot; I am resting them today; its trop de soleil – nothing. So I am looking at the flowers instead just for a change –

And I *love love love* you.

Your
Wig.

MS ATL. *LJMM*, 336–7.

[1] The plan was that at the beginning of each month KM would send a cheque payable to herself to the Bank of New Zealand in London, where Alexander Kay was manager, and have the money sent her in notes. She would then change these at the Banca Italiana di Sconto.
[2] George Bernard Shaw occupied the flat above the *Athenaeum* office at 10 Adelphi Terrace, WC2.

To J. M. Murry, [17 October 1919]

[Casetta Deerholm, Ospedaletti]

Dearest of All,

I had just given your letter to L.M. to post. I had put on my cape & after walking through the rooms & thinking how delicious apples & pot au feu smelt when they were cooking ensemble I went to the door to see the sunset. Up our steps came Caterina with a gardener in tow – Caterina has established herself a kind of guardian here – She it was who brought me the eggs in cotton wool & the pink flowers & who tells L.M. where to get things. Alors, she had found me this gardener; she talked as though she had just picked him up somewhere on the path. He was very nice – a big grey kind old dog in a cap. Caterina was very cold. She had her hands tucked in the cuffs of a small grey woollen jacket; her nose was pink – charmingly pink and her eyes sparkled. "Do you mind work on Sundays? He can come on Sundays." Not at all. And he will bring you plants – Would you like quelques geraniums? At that I held up my hands & I saw Caterina was having a joke, too – So I asked for violets & he said he would bring them, both savage & mild —— little blue growling darlings – & white meek as milk ones – She says they poussent *comme rien* here – All roses flower in le mois de noël. It is just time for jonquils narcissi tulips rather late, in fact. He will also bring roses – but when he asked me if I wouldnt like some little palms I said 'no' I loved plants with flowers – I saw by his shrug & his 'moue' that he rather despised me – "Ah – ces femmes avec ces fleurs!" was what I felt. Then he asked if I'd like a lily that grew about the size of the villa – *enormous*. By the time you came you would have had to hunt for me & the house among the lily leaves & the big white flowers – You would have said "there they are" – and then "no thats a snail" because on such pasture snails would grow huge too. This rather frightened me – I said if he had a smaller one – Id have it please but not "those of the Lar-gest size" – Then in the late pale light with Caterina & the gardener outlined against the olive, the deep blue sea & the red sky we had a little talk. The gardener meanwhile spat very splendidly over the olive boughs – He was greatly impressed by his performance.

(Enter L.M. Katie do you mind if I put the pot au feu through the sieve?

Me: terribly.

She: Oh, I am so sorry. I was only thinking how beautifully it would have gone through. It was just an idea. Do you mind? I won't interrupt again)

Now its dark. The big daisies in the vase on the table have shut their pretty eyes – The shadows are wonderfully quiet – The sea sounds as though it were sweeping up hollow caves. A dog is barking: a bell tinkles on the road – now it sounds far away. Through the window I see an olive tree growing in a room just like this one and a girl sits at a table under its branches writing to her love –

Ah, to love like this!

Wig.

MS ATL. *LKM* I. 256–7; *LJMM*, 337–8.

To J. M. Murry, [18 October 1919]

[Casetta Deerholm, Ospedaletti]

No 10 received. The new schema noted & approved.[1]

Saturday afternoon.

My Very Own Bogey

First I will answer your cherished letter which arrived by the noon post. Why I thought London was une ville morte was because Pa more or less conveyed: there are cannons in Langham Place; all the life of the place is at a standstill; starvation stares us in the faces in a few days![2]

I am delighted to hear of the books. I do not like Virginia's woman; she is as clever as you like but frightfully pretentious & precious and like a foreigner who knows her Paris – *from within*. But its an interesting book to review.[3] Please always tell me at once of the faults in my reviews. Haul me over the very hottest coals. It is only kind. I expect you to do this. I respect your opinion & I want it. If anything is alright – let it be – but otherwise – do please beat me . . . Elizabeth Stanley[4] is sending 2 poems on Monday; she wants to hold them over till then. One longs to write poems here. Dearest – that Samuel Butler! We knew it – didn't we. The ironing board & the sewing machine, they are in *all* his books – he gave them to himself as well – was an expert in the use of both really. What a surface he put on things – what little crisp frills how neatly turned – *how beautifully enfin he 'got up' other peoples' washing* – As to the sewing machine, the 2nd half of *The Way of All Flesh* is all machine sewn – I turn from him in disgust. I wish I could see the woman's letters; I'd *dearly* love to.[5]

This afternoon I have been to San Remo. A great Ausflug – the first since you went away. We took the tram & went 1st class – velvet seats – very fine – but iron seats in velvet gloves alas! as the journey progressed. It was a beautifully light gay afternoon – I don't feel in the least tired; I feel *rested*; in fact I went partly to rest my eyes. Oh, dear, if I could tell you all I saw – but the very very thrilling thing was that I went to our china shop & bought another plate (I am beginning our

collection with ½ dozen soup plates; they are a late *dowry*, darling)
and the woman said at the end of this month she will have cups &
saucers in this ware *all* sizes from large café au lait downwards – also
teapots & jugs. This is of international importance – isn't it Bogey. I
shivered with joy seeing the large fluted cups, the sun on the breakfast
table, honey in the comb to eat – Bogey one end me the other & three
each side with their cups tilted up to their noses. But seriously isnt it
Great News. Then I bought 2 lbs of honey, curry powder, tea,
medicine, toothpaste (german: but in an italian wrapper. Calve *said* it
was german) peaches, apples, brioches, letter paper – <u>&</u> heard from
the market woman she will have baskets of large freshly dried figs next
week – I hope in time to send them to you by Vince. This also thrilled
me greatly. The money flew out of my purse – but it was worth it.
Then we caught the tram home. L.M. carried the parcils – & soon the
kettle was boiling & we were having Tea. That is like the end of a
'composition' – *Describe an Outing*. The villa trembling in the late sun
& shadows was beautiful to return to – it *is* so beautiful: if only I did
not get so bitten. Worse than ever – both my arms & hands.

I heard from Chaddie today written on my birthday – *All* wishes – a
Panegyric on the matchbox she sent me – so *like* me – it would fit in so
beautifully with your belongings – so *eastern* we know how you
appreciate "things Chinese" – It really is *very funny*. The day Pa goes I
am going to send it back to them – say Ive had a little patchbox given
me which fits my bag better & I would so love to think of them using it
among the Indian rugs & brasses. Alas says she there were not so
many rugs as she had thought – not enough in fact. So *ours* have gone.
They are *made for a comedy*. I *must* write it here – This matchbox
business is the comble: it is almost perfect.

Take care of that cold. Please nurse it and tell little Wing to wrap
you in blankets & bring 2 saucers of mustard & water for your feet –
But I am really serious – you will – wont you darling – treat it as
though it were a roaring lion or the Dragon with Seven Bellies.

San Remo is all in readiness for its visitors. Every second shop a
cake shop: little cakes about the size of a cup for 3.50 – & *Victory* with
her car full of chocolates – you know the style – two sugar horses with
silver wings & little lovers holding – staggering under the bon-bons –
& then the stern majestic helmeted figure with her sword upraised in
a chariot of bouchées. How strange human nature is! An English
clergyman & his waife in front of the postcard shop. "My dear that
view I am share, was taken from our window!" "Oh do you think so,
Arthur?" "There is no question of doubt." "Well — perhaps so"
"Perhaps? What do you mean by perhaps. Why should I be so
positive if it were *not* so" "Yes, I see what you mean now." And they
walked away, poor silly creatures and he said *niente* niente to a boy

crying newspapers who was not for a moment crying them at him –
and remarked "these Italians are famous Beggahs!"

Do please send me Art & Letters. Does my story look bad?[6] I feel
rather anti-Johnny & Howard de Walden & it was not I it was *you*
who interested Bentinck in his work – I did nothing.[7]

I weighed myself today 7 st. 1 lb. 3 ounces just exactly the same.
But that is good I think. It takes I am sure a month to settle down to a
place before one begins to put on weight. I certainly have a *perpetual
appetite* & we feed very well. Dinner tonight is

Filet de boeuf aux oignons.

Pasta – sauce tomate.

Salade.

Haricots verts neufs sautés.

Gebäckte Apfeln.

My own darling Treasure. Think of those cups & saucers & the
plates & everything we shall have. There will be *no* holding us.

Goodbye. Heaven bless you.

Wig.

MS ATL. *LKM* I. 257–9; *LJMM*, 338–41.

[1] Murry wrote, 13 Oct., 'In future I wont number my letters except by the number of days to
May 1 1920. Thus the next will be 199 and so on.' (ATL.)

[2] Her father's reaction to the transport strike.

[3] Helen Hope Mirrlees, a Cambridge classics graduate, novelist, and friend of Virginia
Woolf, was, as Murry wrote, 13 Oct., 'very anxious to be reviewed by you. Serve her right, seems
the proper answer.' The book Murry sent was the recently published *Madeleine, One of
Love's Jansenists*, but KM did not review it.

[4] KM already had published several poems in the *Athenaeum* under her maternal
grandmother's name.

[5] Murry's 'The Life of Samuel Butler', a review of Henry Festing Jones's two-volume *Samuel
Butler, Author of Erewhon*, appeared in the *Athenaeum*, 24 Oct. 1919. He discussed Butler in his
letter to KM on 13 Oct., praised the letters of Eliza Savage, on whom Alethea Pontifex in *The
Way of All Flesh* was based, and repeated the story he had heard that Butler used to visit a
woman for sex, rewarding her with a sewing machine and an ironing board.

[6] 'Pictures' in *Art and Letters*, Autumn 1919.

[7] Murry had interested Lord Henry Bentinck, Lady Ottoline Morrell's half-brother, in the
painting of their close friend J. D. Fergusson. He in turn introduced Fergusson to Lord Howard
de Walden, who bought two paintings.

To J. M. Murry, [19 October 1919]

[Casetta Deerholm, Ospedaletti]
Sunday morning.

25 more Sundays.

Bogey darling

The Gardener is here; he arrived at Aurora's heels, thumping his
tail. I think he has done wonders but oh, I feel inclined to cry to the

garden like I do to you when youve been to the barber: why did you let him take off *so much*. When will it grow again! My cotton plant has lost its curls, a ruthless chopping of them; the roses that had all started what I thought were the most exquisite promising shoots are cut down to the bone & told to try again. I must plant sweetpeas immediately. And he is so *delighted* with his work; his good face beams; he shows me all the stones he has taken out (it sounds like an operation) and there on the path lie the pink geraniums – oh weh! oh weh! I feel theres an awful moral to be drawn out of all this & except ye can bear this to be done unto ye, ye shall not bring forth. At any rate some old gardener or other has been doing it to us for years: and God knows we've had our naked shivering moments – so now I shall *fill this* garden with flowers – I shall make it to blaze & shine & smell ravishing and look celestially beautiful by the time you come just to point the moral further.

The wind, with light, faint footfalls walks over the sea; the water rings against the shore, like a bell, striking softly.

No letters today, my darling. L.M. has just returned from the post. She went down to see if there were any by the 3 o clock but the post was shut. I knew it was – Sunday, but she made the effort. She has just broken my medicine glass. It grieves me. Ever since you 'noticed' it at the Flora Ive had a feeling of affection for it. But each fresh breakage confirms me in my determination *not* to have our new plates used until you arrive. Then they will all be on the table. The gardener has gone, there is a smell of bluegum, that means the tea kettle is on. After tea I am going for a walk up the *road* behind the hill. It's a most marvellous day – warm and yet *refreshing*.

Love, I have miscalculated the time. Its nearly 6 oclock. This letter must fly to the post.

Such a sunset – neapolitan ice on neapolitan ice.

My

own

darling

Bogey,

I

am

your

Wig.

MS ATL. *LKM* I. 267–8; *LJMM*, 341–2.

To J. M. Murry,[1] [20 October 1919]

[Casetta Deerholm, Ospedaletti]

198 received

(*no* 199). Books received: Benson & Weyman.[2] Oh Bogey why are people swindlers? My heart *bleeds* when they swindle me, doesn't yours? This gardener – he promised to come & put the garden in order for 10 francs & bring me some little plants, too. It was to be 10 francs a day *with* the plants & now his wife has come & explained the plants are *10 francs more*. And he only came for ½ a day yesterday but she says he spent the other half looking for the plants – so they between them charged me 30 francs. It isn't the money that matters – though I felt ashamed as I gave it to them & could not look at their eyes – it is that *they are dishonest*. That hurts so! Yes, put the wall round the house. Why will people do such things? Id rather they turned & beat me. The sun streams through the folded clouds on to the sea in long beams of light – such beams as you see in picture books when the Lord appears. It is a silent day except for the sound of this *false* pick as he digs up the little beds. L.M. is in San Remo. I have to hide from this old man now. I wish he'd go. His wife was all in grey, with big black hollow places where her teeth had been & she said *firmly* "c'est moi qui vient tous les soirs arroser votre jardin pour vous". When I said no – her "c'est bien" was like *steel spittle*. Well, Ive cried my cry to you. But my dear love – this vileness – this snail on the underside of the leaf – always there!

199 is lost – is roaring in the wilderness. Perhaps I shall still get it. Its awful to miss letters – This today – Mrs W. seems established[3] in the house. Oh I hope not. Its what I had feared. Can't you send her away. She mustn't be there long. No, thats childish. You know what is best from where you are & you will do it. But *another woman* – it *hurts*. Still, be sensible, Katherine. Don't mind. What does it matter – she goes & comes on the stairs. She waits in the hall & I expect she has a key – I *knew* it would happen, I *knew* it. She pulls the chairs forward. It makes me feel exactly as if I were dead. I see it all. She talks to Violet & would Violet mind doing this instead of that. Oh, curse my heart – curse it!! Why am I not a calm indifferent grown up woman . . . and this great cold indifferent world like a silent malignant river & these creatures rolling over one like great logs – crashing into one – I try to keep to one side, to slip down unnoticed among the trembling rainbow coloured bubbles of foam & the faint reeds – I try to turn & turn in a tiny quiet pool but its no good – sooner or later one is pushed out into the middle of it all. Oh, my enchanted boy I am really sadder than you, I believe. At any rate if they weighed us in the scales we'd both dip as deep –

Two books have come. Stanley Weyman & Stella Benson. Good. Ill do them. Stella Benson seems to me just to miss it; she reminds me of Colette in a way. But Ive only *dipped* into her book. A very attractive creature –

Father wrote to me: he is only coming as far as Nice or Cannes. Guaranteed no infection, I suppose. I shall go on writing away to him so as to be sure of my portion. L.M. is at San Remo buying butter – This week I hope to work more – My hands are still poisoned by the bites & my eyes are not Dorothy Wordsworth eyes.[4] Its a bore. Shall I send this letter? Or write another one – a gay one? No, youll understand. There is a little boat – far out – moving along, *inevitable*, it looks & *dead silent* – a little black spot like the spot on a lung –

Dont mind me: I am very foolish and ought to be punished. Even as I wrote that the little boat is far away & there have come out of the sea great gold streamers of light such as I never before saw.

Your own
Wig.

MS ATL. *LKM* I. 259–60; *LJMM*, 342–3.

[1] Although it is clear from the next letter that KM rewrote much of this in another version on the same day, both letters were posted to Murry.
[2] KM reviewed Stella Benson's *Living Alone* in the *Athenaeum*, 14 Nov. 1919, and Stanley Weyman's *The Great House*, 7 Nov. 1919.
[3] Sydney Waterlow had brought his wife Helen to stay at Portland Villas.
[4] From early childhood Dorothy Wordsworth possessed fine sight and powers of close observation. In 'To a Butterfly' William complimented her, 'She gave me eyes, she gave me ears.'

To J. M. Murry, [20 October 1919]

[Casetta Deerholm, Ospedaletti]

198 received
no 199.
Benson & Weyman received.
Monday.
My dear Heart,
199 is evidently roaring in the wilderness – strayed. I do hate missing letters. This – today tells me that Mrs W. is also established in the house. Its what I had feared. When I read your letter telling me I wrote you one on the spot which I don't send. No, its not fair to you to send it. *I simply must not mind*, thats all. You do whatever is best: I *knew* it would happen. Pincheys girl again,[1] on the stairs, in the hall, moving things & talking to Violet – Oh well, I must bear it. I wish I

were a calm indifferent grown up woman. *Why* do things hurt so? There's no answer.

The gardener has just gone. He swindled me. He promised to come for a day for 10 lire & for that to bring me some plants. His wife however came this afternoon parceque mon mari ne parle pas bien le français & explained it was 10 lire for the day & 10 for the plants (a basket of roots worth perhaps 50 centimes from his garden.) She was all in grey with a mouth of black teeth & she said firmly: c'est moi qui vient tous les soirs arroser votre petit jardin pour vous, M*adame*, & mon mari vient tous les dimanches – alors comme ça vous aurez avoir . . .' When I said *no* to both, she folded her dirty spotted hands & said *c'est bien*: it hissed out like steel spittle – I don't mind the money so much; I mind the shame & the longing to cry out that I felt when I knew they were swindling me – Oh, it is agony to meet corruption when one thinks all is fair – the big snail under the leaf – the spot in the childs lung – what a WICKED WICKED God! But it is more than useless to cry out. Hanging in our little cages on the awful wall over the gulf of eternity we must sing – sing[2] –

Father wrote to me: he has been ill. You wouldn't just look him up – would you? Or send a note? He is not coming further than Cannes or Nice – guaranteed infection proof – I shall go on writing to him however for *my reasons*.

I had an extraordinarily nice letter from the dear old Boy. Bless him – This week I hope to work more. My hands are still very poisoned, but my eyes are better.

L.M. to say she must go to post.

Goodbye, darling, *alls well*. Its grey here & raining, but *alls well*.

Heaven bless you for

Wig.

MS ATL. *LJMM*, 344–5.

---

[1] Murry noted, *LJMM*, 344, 'This refers to an episode in 1912 when Katherine was outraged by the familiar behaviour of the fiancée of an acquaintance.'

[2] An image taken up in her last completed story, 'The Canary', written in Sierre, Switzerland, in July 1922.

To J. M. Murry, [21 October 1919]

[Casetta Deerholm, Ospedaletti]

199 fetched up & 197 with cheque.   Tuesday.

My little Lion

I hope by now your cold is better: it sounded like one of your specialités de la maison and its not only unfortunate its horribly disgusting that you had so much extra work to do while it was ramping. If only you could find someone for the routine work: it is ridiculous that the editor should have to peel the potatoes as well as squeeze the white & pink icing over the puddings & be responsible for the savoury and the plat du jour (its just after lunch: this is *too digestive.*)

About that O.K. sauce. I was always reading that bit about it taking the place of fresh fruit & vegetables – W.L.G. should have it on a paper wrapper or done into latin for a motto perpetual for the House of George.[1]

Id like to have heard you & E. about minds.[2] I miss talk.

L.M. brightly & lightly: Wouldn't it be awful if one hadn't got hands and one lived in a place where there were a great many flies. Wouldn't it be simply dreadful – That is NO substitute.

Its a queer day here, all greys and purples and very chill. The sea seems to be growing bigger & bigger pushing further & further out. People shout as they pass, against the wind. Two exquisite birds have been walking in the garden. They had long narrow, pale yellow bodies, little jackets in black and gold, very long silver grey tails. Happy tiny creatures – quite unafraid, walking over the gravel and having a gay, gay little talk. I have a feeling, Bogey my darling, that my letter yesterday did not *ring* properly. Please blame the insects – My hands feel as though they were on fire – all swollen and inflamed – They will be better in a day or two. Its so strange the insects should persist for its really *very cold* at times – as cold as it was in Marseilles – Yet, in the evenings, even with the windows shut & powder burnt out they come. Bother them. I finished Stella Benson last night. I thought I might do her with Hope Mirrlees – two women, both protesting in the preface that their books are out of the ordinary – But no bridge could be thrown from one to the other. Miss Mirrlees lives in another world – & her world would *shudder* at Stella Benson. I don't. On the contrary – They are two interesting problems – *very* intriguing. I hope I manage to say what I want to say.

Oh how dull this letter is! And yours were so wonderful – They had their hands full of wonders – Oh my own Bogey, I love you beyond all the dreams of man. I want this letter to warm you – to creep into your heart & blow – very gently – until all is tiny flames. Let us think for one moment of our *own home*. Early autumn, say, evening, our first fire, we are curled up in armchairs before it: and all the world is shut away. It is no dream – it is all at the end of this voyage – isn't it. I couldnt *not* believe it. Now Im going in & Im going to ask L.M. to make me a tiny fire in *my* room. Mr Parky is certainly spending the day.[3] *But all is well, my darling heart* – perfectly. I expect Ive got a mild attack of poisoning from these bites, that's all. I wrote Ansaldi yesterday – just for him to report how much better I am. I hope your dinner with Pa is not too tiring: I cant think of those girls any more the Wood Hay pair – Please give Wing a four square kiss from me – & Athenaeum[4] a *plain* (non-currant) kiss. Arthur spoke of my four brothers, you, he & the cats: we sound like a fairy family, don't we.

Love love love
Wig.

MS ATL. *LKM* I. 260–1; *LJMM*, 345–6.

---

[1] The first friend they had in common, the novelist W. L. George (1882–1926). Murry wrote, 16 Oct., 'I saw in a 'bus today an advertisement for O.K. sauce which might come in useful to you when describing a novel of the W.L.G. kind. "O.K. Sauce consists of 'fruity' elements mixed with a choice selection of oriental spices, and a natural acidity derived from pure malt. The free use of this sauce compensates for the absence of fresh fruit & vegetables from the daily diet."' (ATL.)

[2] In the same letter, Murry said that he had dined that evening with T. S. Eliot and his wife Vivien. 'High falutin' talk with E. about minds, based upon my conviction that I haven't got & don't want one. Strange to say E. agreed.'

[3] That is, the day was parky, a colloquialism for bitterly cold.

[4] Their other cat.

To Richard Murry,[1] 21 October 1919

Casetta Deerholm | Ospedaletti | Porto Maurizio
21.x.1919.

My dear old Boy

I can't tell you how pleased I was to recognise your handwriting this morning. I have thought of you often, and was only saying to Jack the other day that I feel you are part of *our* family. By *our* family I meant the same band of brothers that you referred to: Jack, Arthur, Athenaeum, little Wingli and Wig – I think we're an awfully nice Family Tree – don't you – Jack & you and me underneath & Athenaeum & Wingli in the branches. I wish you would make a woodcut of the subject – with lovely wavy muscles on Athenaeum's back – Jack sitting under the tree, you, leaning over him with a page of print between you & me somewhere, small, admiring you all ——

Im awfully interested in all you tell me about your job. I agree with you that the production of a book should not assert itself but I think you're rather too hard on yourself when you say it shouldn't be noticeable. True, the writing is the important thing, but I think fine production, as it were, sets the seal upon its importance – & do you think its too far fetched to say its an act of faith on the part of the producer in that he considers it worthy of a "setting" and its also his expression of delight in honouring it. I suppose if a thing is really good and sound and honest there's no *need* to call attention to it – no *need* to praise it; but I like to think that people who are rich in life can afford to praise things – in fact, cant help praising them. I dont think any of *us* will stop at what is necessary. Take a domestick example. I suppose a baby is the important thing and its just as happy and content in a strong banana box. But I can't help feeling that if Jack & I saw one flying in the direction of the Heron, or on the Heron's back (he looks a safe old bird according to Fergusson) we would make that banana box as marvellous as a banana box could be. Of course the whole difficulty about noticeable production is that if the idea gets into the minds of wrong workmen, vain workmen, there's no stopping them – and you cant see the great man for the wreaths and banners, so to say. But you and Jack cant afford to worry about that – To be fantastical, I think a book should *look* like a herald – the author's herald – and as heralds *dont* carry trumpets it wouldn't be assertive but just very fine and on the proud side – (I just then had a vision of Wing as a herald, but he would, in defiance of all the laws have a most awful trumpet to blow in Athenaeum's ear –)

I note what you say about Ivor Brown,[2] sir, and will take down my harp when it arrives. You make Thavies Inn sound awfully attractive. That irregularity of old houses always fascinates me. I am glad to think you are there, and I'm very proud of you, too, as you jolly well know.

I expect Jack has told you about this little house – right in the sun's eye and the sea's eye – It is built on the slope of a wild hill covered with figs, olives, and tamarisk trees and a thick small shrubbery – and herbs like lavender and thyme and rosemary – There are very small paths winding up it in all directions: I long to follow them – I shall, by next spring. We three could spend a wonderful time in this house. Its a bit faëry – the light trembles on the wall from the water and dances in flecks from the olive trees until you wonder if youre living in a bubble. Down below – *sheer* down there is the sea with a fine flat rock for you to walk out on and dive off. Green sea with blue streaks in it and violet shadows – so clear that from here I can pretty nearly count the starfish star-gazing on the floor of it. (Thats nonsense – Its lunch time and Im getting what Jack calls "shiny in the head".)

I wish though that the things that bite were not so fierce. They are like the dragons my Papa used to draw – Dragons with Seven Bellies – i.e. never satisfied. They must have had pints of me and you can't think Id be anything but rather inferior government ale – can you – poor stuff compared to these rich fruity Italians.

I spend all day long in the open air, writing, reading, looking at things, eating and – writing again. I am determined to get well this time and take my part as one of the crew henceforward. Tell me how you think Jack is, old boy, will you? And snatch him away from work sometimes. Its so queer – *this* time I almost feel as if he was with me. That doesn't make me long for him less, though. However, the ship has weathered the worst of the storm and shes bound for home –

Dont ever feel you've *got* to write to me – but when you are inclined to – lets have a talk.

> Yours ever
> Katherine.

What about Gibbons?[3] Has he found a job?

MS R. Murry. *LKM* I. 262–4.

---

[1] Richard Murry (1903–82). Although Murry's younger brother was called Arthur by his family, KM expressed her dislike of the name, and he adopted Richard as his official name at her suggestion. She became very fond of him, regarding him as something of a mascot because he had suffered from tuberculosis and recovered. At that time he was developing his interest in book production, and was both designer and operator of the Heron Press. Recently he had begun working for the publisher R. Cobden-Sanderson, whose premises were at 17 Thavies Inn, Holborn.

[2] Ivor Brown's *Lighting-up Time* was published by Cobden-Sanderson the following year. KM did review it, but without enthusiasm, in the *Athenaeum*, 30 Apr. 1920.

[3] Arnold O. Gibbons, a school-friend of Richard Murry's. He sometimes visited Hampstead and KM read his attempts at writing stories.

To J. M. Murry, [22 October 1919]

[Casetta Deerholm, Ospedaletti]

Tuesday, no Wednesday.

My own dear Love

I owe you a small explanation. The truth is I haven't felt quite well these last 2 days (since Sunday) and I think thats why I have been such a dull mouse. See? Nothing on earth to worry about, Im sure. One cant have a disease & be O.K. all the time – can one. My heads been aching & my cough going & yesterday after Id written your letter I just went bang to bed with hot water bottles and had a good rest. I organised L.M. and made her give me good food – twice as much as she would have given me – whipped up egg-wegs & meal broth and hot milk and honey. There I lay, and rested. My temperature went up a bit, but it went down after a few hours & this morning it was normal. I also took *Guiacol*:[1] so you see how sensible I was. Couldn't have been more so. Having no doctor makes one awfully wise and careful. Thank God for Sorapure. I just follow his instructions and cure myself. Ida rang up Ansaldi last night but hes not back for 3 days. Not that I want or need him: I DONT. I think it was just a bit of a chill & praps because of my head-box a touch of sun.

Anyhow I EAT & I got up this morning & came straight outside & here I am resting in lovely weather, repairing – so don't you worry. Im a kind of doctor, you know.
Doctor Wig.
At the Sign of the Fig.
Now thats off my conscience. I won't write any more till I see if a letter comes from you. Galsworthy[2] came last night & another parcil I didn't open & cant get at just now because L.M.'s out & I am so enveloppé. Ill tell you plus tard.

Afternoon.

My dear Treasure – and Luck was with me. *196* arrived & the A. & the Nation & another whack of books. Now I have food for weeks & shall get ahead so that you have articles in hand. Now about your letter. Your letters are *changed* this time: they are almost too much for me: they make me feel breathless and as though I must face the sea and say: *How shall* I tell him how I love him? The little waves come in, fold upon fold – folding up my love for you. It seems to me Bogey when we have our new home – when we are *safe home at last* that we shall really turn into fairies & disappear from sight of man –

When you say "by the way, old girl" I just have to wave my hand at eternity and smile. Its as though youve known me & Ive known you ever since those queer trees grew that we looked at in the garden of Villa Flora.[3] Ill do that about Sons & Lovers & incidentally get a whack in a perlite one at the Bloomsberries.[4] I wont send you any more of that note paper: it *felt* like mottled soap, too. If you write that novel you've got to have a chapter called *The Birth of Wingli*, don't you think?[5] I have, as I always have, a sort of sweet scent in the air, a sort of floating mirage of your novel – But I feel one would be torn between tears & laughter all the while – everything would be in rainbows. Already long before your child is born I see the light above its head – a ring of light – so lovely. Would it have cats and flowers in it and would Bogey wander there wearing old Feltie & Wing wave at him from a high window? There would be pain in it, too, *agony*. Would there be a description of *the house* after they were in bed – the fire dying in their room – Athenaeum on the stairs – the moon coming through the window & shining on to the Shepherdess clock – on to her gay little dreaming figure sitting on the hill with her basket of fruit . . . And then his dark head on the pillow . . . Do not be cross with me. I am only dreaming to myself of what your book might be – I pray God I am not "heavy fingered", dearest Love . . . Dont call me a genius – *you* are. It makes me embarrassed when you say it of me.

This copy of the Athenaeum is really excellent – *full* of interest. Your Shaw is *most admirable* and your Merchant of Venice, putting Moscovitch in his place could not be better.[6] How very fortunate there should be *your* Shaw against Squires.[7] There's an orange and a lemon for the public to choose from – I bet they will come on to our side after that. All the paper I feel has been through your hands. Sullivan & Huxley are different creatures – so *tightened up.*[8] I haven't read it all yet because I have not had the time. *L'Hote* is a great acquisition – a most interesting chap – and so alive to himself as a painter & so free from c'est moi qui vous parle. Dent also I like very much this week.[9] I feel it is the Athenaeum way of writing about music – S. [Sullivan] might call it superficial but its not. I long to tuck into all these books & do my best with them. I shall, darling. Please if you get a letter that might interest me would you send it over? Like that American's par example,[10] and any letter which says you're a great man. I can stand any number of them.

Its a marvellous day – the flies appreciate it as much as I do – they are appalling. Ive just sent L.M. off for an extra supply of milk. I don't care what I spend *well I will be*: thats how I feel – and since Sorapure wrote me that letter which was really a kind of diploma (this is to certify that K.M. has passed the examination & is fully qualified to look after herself) I don't feel as though I *could* get really ill again. L.M. is stupidity personified but I am learning just to take it quietly & make her redo the thing thats wrong – and not do it myself.

I wish you were here, just for a little minute – with me. Im in my room, lying down, the door & window open – The wind, thinking the house is empty is taking a quiet *look through*, humming to herself. The shadow dances from the olive & theres no sound except the sea. Ah, my precious one – to have you here just for a moment, to hold you – *look* at you – have you call me 'Wormie'. But the boat has only 196 waves to ride over & then there's the dazzling shore! I dreamed last night I had come home (a fever dream, horrible) & it was still October, dark foggy, bitterly cold. And I was ill. I sent a note to Sorapure who came. I was still in my travelling clothes: a black velvet cap & my peach coloured shawl for a coat. He came & did not speak to me: you & he started talking about a new tobacco to be bought by the *sheet*: he had some to show you. Then you said 'well Id better go' & left us alone. And Sorapure wiped his glasses and said, very dryly: "Well Im afraid you've broken more than your journey." I said "Oh, but I am leaving for Italy again next week." He put his glasses on again. I said "Dr Sorapure I can see you'd rather not attend me any more." We shook hands & he walked out – and I saw the greenish fog in the window . . . and knew I was caught. To wake up and hear the sea and know I had not done the dreadful thing – that was joy. Boge, I feel much better now – more normal. If it were anybody but you I could not say this but really the gardener's wife had something to do with it. I felt her in my lung. Perhaps the truth was I was feeling weak

& she stabbed – What about the house Duncan [Grant] spoke of? Have you made any plans for weekends or has this extra work made you put all aside. Its a pity really you can't take the old boy into the office & train him; he would save you & know how to do it.

Goodbye for now. Tell Wing to send Gan'ma a message.

Your own Wig.

MS ATL. *LKM* I. 261–2; *LJMM*, 346–9.

[1] Guiacol, a liquid related to phenol, administered orally or by injection for lung abscesses and a variety of inflammations.

[2] John Galsworthy's *Saint's Progress*, which KM reviewed as 'A Standstill', the *Athenaeum*, 31 Oct. 1919.

[3] Where she and Murry had stayed in San Remo.

[4] Murry wrote her on 17 Oct., 'By the way, old girl, I would like to give D. H. Lawrence a leg-up. What do you say to writing on *Sons & Lovers* one week – either extra to or instead of your ordinary novels.' (Murry, 188.) KM did not, however, review the novel.

[5] In the same letter he said he would like to write a novel with 'among other things some real you and me love in it'.

[6] The *Athenaeum*, 17 Oct. 1919, carried Murry's 'The Vision of Mr. Bernard Shaw', a review of *Heartbreak House*, *Great Catherine*, and *Playlets of the War*. In addition, in 'Shylock and the Ghetto' he admired but also admonished the acting of M. Moscovitch, who 'interpreted his part as a genre picture from the Ghetto, even to the point of uttering a Yiddish imprecation in the trial scene'.

[7] In his weekly column in *Land and Water*, 9 Oct. 1919, J. C. Squire said of Shaw's new collection of plays that 'a worse volume has never appeared under the name of a man of reputation'.

[8] J. W. N. Sullivan wrote the unsigned 'Recent Advances in Medicine', and Aldous Huxley, under 'Literary Entertainments', reviewed Edmund Gosse's *Some Diversions of a Man of Letters*.

[9] In the Fine Arts section, André Lhote wrote on 'The Necessity of Theories'. In 'Landscape with Figures', Edward Dent contributed an essay on folk-song.

[10] Murry wrote, 15 Oct., 'I had a charming & enthusiastic letter from an American man & his wife the other day. . . . They are mad on the paper – the man called it "the last defence of civilization" or words to that effect.' (ATL.)

To J. M. Murry, [23 October 1919]

[Casetta Deerholm, Ospedaletti]
Thursday.

No letter yet.

My Bogey,

I wish you could see this glass of flowers on the dining room table – daisies & roses. Field daisies, but larger than English ones, and very wide with the fringed petals dipped in *bright* crimson and crimson roses from the wild garden at the side of the steps. I have just gathered the third rose and remarked hundreds of buds which will be blowing in a week or two. The sea is very pale today; small boats go sailing by. I don't suppose I ever see a little boat on this sea without thanking Heaven you are not in it – just as I never read the Shelley story[1]

without thinking: "there but for the —— of God goes Wig & Bogey."
I was out in the garden all the morning: now Ive come in to write.
Don't you find it very difficult to work without a large table & four
walls? I try everything – I work on a tray – on a chair – on a book – sit
up high – arrange the ink & papers on Table Mountain – on the
verandah, but *no* at the last I have to come in. In our Sussex home we
shall have a real table and a real chair & a real 'abri'. Except for my
head today, darling, Im well again. I again went to bed after tea
yesterday rubbed my lung with Capsoline,[2] ate a very nourishing
dinner & then had hot milk & egg later & really I am cured. Im very
glad to have had the experience: it makes me feel so secure. I should
have had a doctor in London pour sure, but here I did without one –
treated myself and cured myself. This makes me feel so safe in case we
should ever find ourselves on a desert island – just in case. If there are
cannibals there our lives will be spared because of Wig the Healer and
if there are none theyll be spared pour le même raison. But please
don't be cross. In view of the state of my *head* I am doing Galsworthy
this week: I know what I think about him: I mean he has been in my
mind for years and only wants dusting, bringing to the light & *proving*
by this new book.
(Oh why why did the Lord make the Fly
And when we die shall we find them spry
In Eternity?)
To be *spry* in Eternity seems to me particularly awful: eternally spry! I
don't want eternity at any rate so it don't signify. Now it will be ideal
for L.M. – time for everything, time to get to know everybody & to
wonder about "this & that and the other" to her hearts desire. She is,
indeed, made for eternity – one of Gods Own – as you might say – But
no – If the Lord will give me 30 years with my Bogey starting on May
1st 1920 he can do what he likes with whats left of my bones and
feathers after that . . .

I send you Violet's letter just so that you may realise who is in the
kitchen. What do you think of it? And what fortune to have found her.
And would she and Roger[3] come to the country with us? That is my
dream now, of course – a little cottage for them or at any rate their
own rooms in the house so that they may have babies of their own –
You might *sound* Violet on this (leaving the babies out) one day – will
you?

There are 25 more Wednesdays before we are together. Twenty-five
more copies of the paper. Do you feel – as I do this time – that its *not
much*. Its just two months to Christmas after that the New Year & in
February snowdrops – and they are the flowers of *our* spring. What are
you doing about the garden, darling? Anything? Have you replanted
the bulbs. I am sure youll want them next March. Please tell me if you

do. Then I *see* you but not as I did last year – from my window, thinking of all that was to come between, of the dark dark bridge to be crossed before the flowers would be discovered. But this time from the terrace by the cotton plant . . .

I have 6 packets of cigarettes – at 1 franc the packet – black soldiers cigarettes I should think made to be distributed to dying Zouaves in hospital and – held over. But they are a great deal better than nothing.

Bogey, is there *any* life of George Eliot so that I can write an article for November 22nd.[4] Less than a month to do it in – or if you could send me one or two of her novels – *Romola*, Adam Bede – whichever are best. I feel Id love to do something, but if there are other people on the spot more competent & with more material – *c'est entendu*. At any rate we mustnt pass her by. Oh, that *PAPER. It simply fascinates me.* If only I were by your side, sharing the work more, discussing it more, seeing the people more, helping more. Next year we shall make it very living: we'll have Eliot down & Sullivan and Sheppard and whoever is *there* – subjeck to your approval. Now I must finish my review. Goodbye my darling Heart. Keep happy, keep well, keep warm, *dont work too much.*

Your true love
Wig.

MS ATL. *LKM* I. 264–5; *LJMM*, 349–51.

[1] Shelley drowned in the Gulf of Spezzia in Aug. 1822.
[2] Capsoline, a proprietary ointment containing capsicum resin, applied as a counter-irritant for deep-seated inflammations.
[3] The housemaid of Portland Villas had recently married.
[4] The centenary of George Eliot's birth. The books were not sent to her.

To J. M. Murry, [24 October 1919]

[Casetta Deerholm, Ospedaletti]

195 Saturday,
   194 Sunday received.
   Friday le soir.
My own precious Bogey,

I cant understand why you have never received my letter about the spoon. I *cant* understand it; for I sent it I thought, on my birthday: it is a blow if its lost. When you talk about Wing I don't know what it is: something in all you tell me goes to my heart. I see him as he used to lie in a kitten coma while you kissed his nose – never shall we have such an adorable kitten again. When he slept on our bed too, &

wouldn't settle down, you remember – *would* dive off & swim about under the cupboard & up the screen pier. I do wish you'd take his pigglecher & send it me.

(OH the midges!!! There are 3) Your Sunday brought you & the house to me very very clearly. It was wonderful how you conveyed the quality of the day – the one thing happening after another thing – in a silence. But I wish you didn't always have a *duty* ahead – a horrid duty walking off that you have to follow – at such a round pace after – just when youve put one in its stable, so to say.

No, I don't think youre like a deep dark pool: I think youre like a deep silent sea – with wonderful ships in it, wonderful ships – but there again my own precious darling, you never have time, never, to sail where you will and how you will. I know what you mean about *people babbling.* Even though je ne suis pas une silencieuse, moi. But the *years* one has spent sitting with a strained smile trying to appear OF the party, IN the know . . . What foolishness – what waste of time.[1]

But on those rare occasions when you & I talk I do – I do feel the heavens opening and our thoughts like angels ascending and descending – Time, peace, freedom from anxiety – these things – must be ours. Time to be silent in and to talk in. But especially that last. The *strain* we have lived under. No-one will know. Isnt it queer, my little brother, what a cold indifferent world this is really. Think of the agony we've suffered. Who cares? Who dreams? If we were not 'set apart' for ever before this has been enough to do it. We could not, knowing what we know belong to others who know not. If I can only *convey* this difference this vision of the world as we see it: Tchekhov saw it, too, and so I think did Keats.

I am sending a parcel of books to Thorpes[2] tomorrow & here are the names writ on a page for you to put in your pocketbook. I have told him you will call for the money. That's best, don't you think? Anything else would be so confusing & you dont mind 'passing by' do you darling? But dont forget, mignonette, because it is real money & buys things.

Goodbye my love

Your
Wig.

(Wing, my duck-box, let me kiss you.)
Athy, a warm wave of the tail.

MS ATL. *LKM* I. 265–6; *LJMM*, 351–2.

[1] On 19 Oct. Murry had written, 'The older I get, the more I am amazed at the amount people talk and at the things they say. Compared to them I feel myself like a deep, dark pool, and I wonder whether there's anything at all going on inside it. I trust there is; but who can say? All that I can say is that, if there is, it is something utterly different not from what is going on

inside other people – I don't know anything about that – but from what they say & talk about. It all seems so incredibly childish – incredibly – never to touch even the fringe of important things. Babble, babble, babble.' (Murry, 190.)

  [2] Thomas Thorpe, bookdealer, 93 St Martin's Lane.

To J. M. Murry, [26 October 1919]

[Casetta Deerholm, Ospedaletti]
Sunday on the verandah

193 & Tuesday received.

My own Precious Heart,

I am thankful you got my letter about the spoon. Could you imagine for a *moment* that Id not have written? It was awful to have to wait so long though. I was simply *dying* for letters today, none yesterday or the day before: the posts are really very uncertain. These two make me feel Ive not been fulfilling my trust in my last letters: make me LONG to see you for a moment & tell you that *all is well* here. You simply must never worry about me. I am as safe as a rock. Just think of the seas that have washed over & all the same Im not only here – Im getting better all the time. I repose myself absolutely – and eat & sleep. The chill is tout à fait parti, and when I get some spegglechicks my eyes will be A I eyes. It IS cold but look at all the warm things I have. I simply rejoice in them & am sitting out now in the lamb – with jaegar underneath & on top snug as can be. Then when its cold my little room by virtue of its being against the kitching keeps a warm wall, and I dont stint firing a little bit – nor shall I. Nor do I deny myself anything but eat butter & honey, meat and eggs as if they were provided by ravens.[1] You believe all this – don't you? The insetti I must say are a real trial, worm. They make work really difficult. You cant get away from them. *They are a real pest.* But I suppose they will go. I confess they have awfully discouraged me at moments. These constant swellings & the heat of them, and the trying to write, waving off moustiques & moucherons. But you see what an external thing they are – aren't they? If theyd go Life would be 100 times easier.

Now I'll read over your letters & answer them. I am thankful you have sacked Gordon.[2] I agree *absolutely* with you about him & about a man like Orpen.[3] One must have an open mind. Its so difficult not to find a *sneerer*. Whats the good of sneering? Imagine what Strachey or V.W. would think of a man like Brett Young – but hes WORTH considering. One must keep a balance – i.e. one must be critical. Theres your mighty pull over your whole generation – and there's what's going to make the Athenaeum what it is in your imagination. Ill look up Wilenski[4] & tell you what I think tomorrow – and Ill carefully read his stuff next week – Ill tack the 6/- for Phillips[5] on to my cheque for you next month.

Your cold is *still* there? Boge, please do see Sorapure. Why don't you get injected against colds? It can be done! You cannot afford to have them for so long. This is IMPORTANT. Now your Monday letter. You are so overworked that I don't know what to say – A dramatic critic must be found – Does Strachey himself know no one?[6] In despair I even think of Aldington.[7] My darling, try and slow down just a bit. You cant keep up this pace. Youre running the whole show – and then dinner is brown stew and an apple. Really its not good enough. I *did* want to see my Pa – Now – well I dont mind if I do or if I don't. I was careful to extend a pressing invitation 'for the sake of the firm' and to give Wood Hay one in the eye. Im desperately anti-family now – Youre my family I am yours (you can have your own too, if you like, darling: but mine doesn't exist). We must form a brand new family with Mansfield and Middleton for family names. Im very glad you have heard from Gogarty.[8] Couldnt he put you on to an Irish correspondent? Or to say some chap who might write an interesting article or two. You must try & get some time off. I hope you do spend a bit of time in the garden: I know you cant plant bulbs with your pen. The lemon verbena ought to come in: its next to the scented geranium. But I expect both of the little dears are sitting in golden pots about the Throne of Grace ere now: frost kills them.

When you say forgive me for talking shop thats all nonsense, you know, precious. Bogey you cant say anything which doesn't affect me. But I am worried that you have to work so dreadfully hard.

Its Sunday. The sun hangs in the dappled sky like an uncertain silver star. The wind blows over the calm sea and then traces rivers, creeks, little lakes & bays in violet on the blue. On the horizon clouds like white crumbling mountains. Five men down below are fishing, hauling the net into an open boat. Oh, I long to be *well*, quite well and with the albatross off my neck and in Rhodesia.[9] These are convalescent longings. Where are you now? Take me in your arms darling Boy. This time we are not going to fail. All will be a success and in May all will be perfect.

Your own Wig.

MS ATL. *LJMM*, 352–4.

[1] When Elijah was in hiding, 'the ravens brought him bread and flesh in the morning and bread and flesh in the evening'. I Kgs. 17: 6.

[2] J. G. Gordon, etcher, painter, and graduate of the London School of Art, had been dismissed as one of the paper's art critics.

[3] William Orpen (1878–1931), an Irish painter more respected in 'fashionable' than in artistic circles. Murry wrote on 21 Oct., 'don't you agree with me that it's simply silly to dismiss a man like Orpen with a sneer', implying that such a view was held by Clive Bell and Roger Fry. (Murry, 194.)

⁴ Reginald Howard Wilenski, later an eminent and prolific art historian and critic, had done some recent reviewing, and was given Gordon's position.

⁵ A bookseller Murry had paid on KM's behalf.

⁶ James Strachey, Lytton's younger brother, who contributed drama reviews to the paper.

⁷ Richard Aldington (1892–1962), novelist, biographer, journalist, husband of fellow-Imagist Hilda Doolittle.

⁸ Oliver St John Gogarty (1878–1957), Irish poet, surgeon, wit, and later Senator.

⁹ Ida Baker was from Rhodesia.

To J. M. Murry, [27 October 1919]

[Casetta Deerholm, Ospedaletti]
Monday.

My darling,

I am sending 3 novels together this week so as to be ready for the new ones. As Madeleine & Virginia¹ are evidently on a like tack (from what V. told me of her book) Ill do them together. No letter came today, but the paper did. We had the devil of a great storm last night, lasting for hours, thunder, lightning, rain & I had appalling nightmares! I think it must be the noise of the sea which makes me dream so: it excites ones nerves at night & one longs for it to 'lie down' . . . Old age, I expect. After the thunder the day is very lovely cool but so *definite* and on a *big scale*. I began to write an article for the paper yesterday called Eternity;² I hope it will be finished today. If you dont care for it, please just keep it: it will go in some book sometime or other. Its so nice to walk in this little garden. After tea yesterday I went up and down, up and down, thinking out things. It was then I hit on the subject for the article. Ive been out of doors all day. I still am, in fact, under a sunshade on the verandy; I feel quite alright, Bogey, not a suspicion of anything is wrong with me but Im FLAT. Its the alabatross round my neck. Never mind she will be cut off in April & fly back to Rhodesia. But its weary living with her – and never seeing another person. I come up out of my pool & there she is on the side staring down into the water, glassy eyed to find me. Oh, I do *hate* her so. Theres nothing to be done, a maid would not help matters in the least. Of course nearly all the time I am working but to come out of work to a person, the person whom you really *hate* – this is very horrible. No-one can ever know what it is like, for the form it takes is so strange. Her passion for me feeds on my hate. I wont talk about it, Bogey. I have only mentioned it because it accounts for my *flatness*. Awful isnt it? However let us put a penny in the box – Let us have a tune. Let us nod and grin while the others get up and do our dancing for us as we sit over here in the corner – waiting waiting, for the bead curtain to jingle to be pushed aside for La Santé to come laughing

laughing in, running over to our corner, putting her arms round our neck & saying my friend – my darling friend. The garçon hovers by, biting his nails & shooting me a glance or two. Ive read *all* the illustrated papers – *all* the comics. Suddenly he swoops forward & piles two chairs on the table next to mine. Good heavens its nearly closing time! Why doesn't she come – why doesn't she! . . . I don't know why I am writing this – please forgive it, my angel. And forgive me for not being gay – forgive me for that. I always want to be like a little bell, ringing in our happiness when I write to you – but then at the same time I cant be insincere. Its such a predicament! And oh my Bogey, *dont worry about me.* Ill get out of this – See in your minds eye Wig under an umbrella much too large – thinking its still raining – & open the window & tell her how silly she looks and how that policeman with his scythe is laughing at her –

Your life is so dreadfully hard I feel – I ought to give you all thats fair – L.M. has gone off to 'look' at 'Bawdygerra' as she calls it & wont be back till evening, so Im quite alone. Now Ive come in to get out of the glare and am sitting in my room – Your spectacle case is on the mantelpiece. On the table with the russian bottle & Ottolines book & the green paper knife is your spoon. I don't use it. I cant have it washed and polished here. I only eat fairy soup out of it. There's a strong eager wind blowing – very cool – Ill write about the Athenaeum tomorrow, dearest for I am giving this letter to Caterina when she comes up for the laundry and here she is. Otherwise it will miss the post.

"Bonjour Madame."

"Bonjour Caterina. Que vous êtes jolie aujourd'hui."

"Ah, c'est mon nouveau golfe!"[3]

Goodbye my precious – I am for ever,

Your own
Wig.

MS ATL. *LKM* I. 273–4; *LJMM*, 367–8.

[1] The plan to review together Hope Mirrlees' *Madeleine* and Virginia Woolf's *Night and Day* was not pursued.

[2] This article seems later to have been lost in the confusion of a postal strike.

[3] A current fashion-word for a sleeveless pullover.

To J. M. Murry, [27 October 1919]

[Casetta Deerholm, Ospedaletti]
Monday.

Darling,

Here is your cheque for the rent and for Phillips. I made it up to £3.0.0. L.M. has just said *en passant*: 'And Katie I must order another load of wood today: theres only enough for another 3 days. It *does* seem to disappear so.' This is the kitchen fire *only – 80* francs a month! Its all gone. Remember when they put it in & Wig & Bogey said a good three months? What little optimists they are!

Wig.

She has JUST realised about the draught. 'I realise it now, Katie. I have always left it wide open & thats what makes the wood roar away so'—— 'Never mind, Katie, it will go better now.' Did – you –ever?

MS ATL. *LJMM*, 354–5.

To J. M. Murry, [27 and 28 October 1919]

[Casetta Deerholm, Ospedaletti]
Monday night.

My Precious Precious Darling,

This is most important Bogey, listen to me – listen faithfully – Dont think of anything but of what Im going to say. *Your Life Must Change.*

Bogey, this partner of the Firm cant stand your goings on; she cant stand them. Her heart stands still with horror; she feels as if she were crumbling away. Your Thursday letter came: too tired to do the garden you fell asleep – WORN OUT, and you woke up "I CREPT downstairs to a frugal meal because I have to be very careful what I eat."

BOGEY I CANT BEAR THIS. I feel as though the South of France swept over me: its raining, its very cold, with a high wind & sea again – I persuade myself things will get better – may be better now but PROMISE me to see Sorapure AT ONCE, for my sake. Think Love, these six months are the most important of our lives. Your letter pulled me up – I swore cross my heart straight dinkum never to give way to depression again. I WILL not and I [will] KONKER my albatross & work & live on letters and be gay as I can. This time we must succeed. But HELP me – by not overworking, by eating, by seeing doctors, by resting. No, Ill not listen to the weather. I shall just work. Let us be very strong itharm – two Indian braves making a path through the forest towards each other – 188 trees to chop – Oh, my precious husband – thou dearer than Life to me – feel my arms tightly round you, kissing those tired lips – Then Ill kiss your hands & the top of your head your eyelids and your cheeks. Then Ill kiss the stud showing above (or below) your tie. *Now* laugh. *Now* say I am silly.

Your very own for ever
adoring wife.[1]

[28 October 1919]

Next day.

A picture. Figurez-vous your Wig on the verandah in all the clothes she has topped with the wooly lamb and with her cherry sunshade up – under a green fly-net! It is so perishingly cold today. A wind like ICE – But for the first time I seem to have weapons to fight it with & I am as snug as can be. As I walked in the garden wearing the wooly lamb I leaned over the green gate which is my *confessional* & said to the daisy who remarked on it: oui c'est le jaquette militaire de mon mari, qu'il a porté pendant les trois hivers qu'il était au front. Le khaki était affreusement sale, alors je l'ai . . . etc . . . If the daisy had been Caterina the same histoire would have been recounted: I am *fascinated* by these ideas sometimes. I saw you in this british warm tucking your pocketbook away pulling on immense gloves & going off somewhere by motorcar . . .

Bogey at break of day I went through all the paper & had a good read of it. The printers seem to get a bit scrimpy at times & will cut the noses off the words: its very annoying. But – here goes. Your Butler I think is awfully good:[2] the beginning paragraphs are 1st chop writing. They are so free. But then I think you do show traces of fatigue: I am sorry you didn't say what his relations with Miss Savage were & how they failed. That 'quote' made me curious for more. However I know how you felt – youve ticked him off before – et voilà. Who wrote What is Bolshevism?[3] Its one of those reviews which begins with a bouquet & then gradually takes the flowers back again. And sentences like: it is of course impossible to estimate the number of people etc – are footle. Of course it is. L.M. might try. At the end the reviewer decides to give him back a stalk or two – but . . . Its a bad style of reviewing dont you think?

MS ATL. *LKM* I. 268–9; *LJMM*, 355–6.

[1] Another version of the letter to this point exists. It is almost identical in wording, with four hearts pierced by arrows at its head, and with the sentence after the signature Wig, 'Terrible storm raging here, bitter cold and rain & wind.'

[2] Murry's 'The Life of Samuel Butler', a review of Henry Festing Jones's two-volume *Samuel Butler, Author of Erewhon*, the *Athenaeum*, 24 Oct. 1919.

[3] The review of John Spargo's *Bolshevism* was by J. W. N. Sullivan.

To J. M. Murry, [28 October 1919]

[Casetta Deerholm, Ospedaletti]
Tuesday.

Bogey,

About the paper for the 24th. Can I go over it a bit with you – All I say I do say as you know dead sincerely & with all respeck to you who know the difficulties as I cannot & the ins & the outs. I wish the printers would not be so scrimpy, cutting the noses off the words – don't you – Bren, for instance, and *Lyn*.[1]

Santy is full of the eyebrow this week. But its good stuff to publish – awfully.[2] Your Butler whatever you may think is extremely good. The writing of the first column is 1st chop, it is so free. True, I don't feel you spread your wings as you might have but then youd said all you had to say before. I always want you to *go on* as children say – always want to say – take your time – please please don't pull me past the doors. YOU know whats inside & youre the only person who has the key – But thats this cursed Life which puts these horrible demands on you & makes it impossible. Who wrote What is Boleshevism? Its one of those reviews which begins with a bouquet & then goes on to take the flowers back again – At the very last he hands back a stalk or two – but its a bad *style* of reviewing, I think.

Our Welsh King *must* have been by a B.A. My aunts! "Henry VII turns out the more we study him to be" – I smell a B.A. there AND "traits which *smack* of the Celt." Take 3d off *her* cheque for that (its a lady?).[3]

I dont think Eliot has in the least justified your generosity in his review of Pound.[4] I quite understand that you *had* to give him the chance, but its lamentable all the same for there is no doubt Pound is a cheat and a charlatan. It makes Eliot look very silly too, to be carrying cannon balls for the prestidigitator. K.M. is tame I think and there is not enough shape in her review.[5] Shes not looking at it from above as well as all round it. 1/- off her cheque.

As to the Notes from Ireland – Oh! Oh! Oh! They begin like Fashion Notes *exactly* and what about "much may be said as to the value of *wide culture* but if the *reading of modern literature* etc." – Back to the Taypot Mrs H.T.S., je vous prie. Also "when the curtain falls & we come to earth again" – Oh![6]

Sullivan is alright dont you think but undistinguished.[7] I always feel hes on the point of choosing the Idylls of the King as his great poem – But its serious & interesting and the wires are quite well laid. Which is, I think, his part of the job in literature. Dent gets better and better. Really the Busoni is *famos*.[8] Its excellent. It is indeed like a fine piece of pianoforte playing by Busoni.

The Drama is of course nobodys child & it feels it. The Tempest is just like a review of the Tempest "we left with the firm intention" is rather an awkward ending isn't it.[9] I *did* smile to find our song in your review.[10] Oh Boge, *do* you think it necessary to put the names of actors in Brackets. Good God! its maddening. (Here I am, exaggerating again.) But Im sure its not a good plan – What can Mr Percy Parsons mean in the criticism? I don't think The Net ought to have *been* reviewed.[11] After all the Athenaeum goes to the theatre to say what the Athenaeum has to say – to look at it very very specially *from its own angle.* These critiques (the Tempest for instance) is so like any review of the Tempest. You'd never let a book reviewer say such things as: "she seemed to have but an imperfect control over her instrument of expression" for thats been cliché for years and years, & the *way* in which 'the Net' is seen – No, I think the Theatre wants a New Broom in it – not necessarily a Hard Broom – but a new one – who *speaks out* with wit and sympathy & gives the impression of a man of some learning who finds himself at the theatre for the first time – (I know what it means to find such a man, tho.)

If you knew how I have this paper at heart! Turn down anything of mine you dont care for – but I am whacking in this week. I am sending 3 novels under one cover & a review of Stella Benson for you to use when you want to & the little essay.[12] Its a wonderful paper – wonderful but too big to be carried by one pair of shoulders. I should be there to share the dogs work & make your personal life very easy & look after you – I shall be there after May. Can you stick it as long as that? In May I shall be well again and on the spot. Save yourself all you can till then but *keep it in mind, darling.* Wont Bertie write some articles? Or some fabulous tales – an account of his journey to China & his discussions with the philosophers he met there.[13] Am I mad?

Your

K.M.

MS ATL. *LJMM*, 356–8.

[1] For 'Brent' and 'Lynd'.

[2] George Santayana (see *CLKM* II. 304), wrote essays for six issues under 'Soliloquies in England'. His essay on 24 Oct. was 'Occam's Razor'.

[3] 'Our Welsh King', an unsigned review of *Henry VII* by Gladys Temperley, was by Archdeacon William Hutton, Reader in Indian History at Oxford.

[4] T. S. Eliot's 'The Method of Mr. Pound', a review of Ezra Pound's *Quia Pauper Amavi*.

[5] Her review of F. Brett Young's *The Young Physician*.

[6] 'Notes from Ireland', by Mrs H. T. Smith.

[7] J. W. N. Sullivan wrote on 'Science and Art'.

[8] 'Busoni and the Pianoforte', by Edward Dent.

[9] The review of the Royal Victoria Hall production was by Aldous Huxley.

[10] In reviewing William Mack's *Tiger Rose* at the Savoy Theatre, Murry quoted from the music-hall song:

It's only a knockabout shanty
And furnished as plain as can be;
'Twas built with an axe and a hammer,
A bagful of nails and a tree.
The walls are not hung with old masters
Or furnished with fine tapestree;
It's only a knockabout shanty,
But it's home, sweet home, to me.

[11] Murry also reviewed *The Net*, a play by Mark Ambient at the Scala Theatre.
[12] The essay on 'Eternity'.
[13] The pieces were not written, but KM at least anticipated Bertrand Russell's first visit to China in 1920.

To J. M. Murry, [28 October 1919]

[Casetta Deerholm, Ospedaletti]
Tuesday.

My Precious Own,

Forgive this bit of paper; its just a note Im writing you because your 190 letter has come & youve got my Monday letter and this one of yours is about the kettle holder I haven't got – you remember. Its a divine letter, a perfect kettle holder in itself. Thank you my darling of darlings. But I have determined after this – no looking back, no minding so dreadfully – the journey is too important. Ill not fail you again.

(a) Ill write to Sylvia Lynd.[1]

(b) And to Grant Richards[2]

Later on I feel that Arthur[3] ought to come in to the office don't you? I don't think Dickie C-S[4] will last very long – I shall be a week ahead with the novels this very week: I had decided already because of the uncertain posts. I *long* to do Waley.[5] There is a flower out in the garden which is the first sentence.

Half a stone is a terrible amount to gain in 2 years isn't it – my little optimist. But then Ill always be in fear that you're going to break – Ill try my best not to let you know & to look the other way when you hang over precipices and lean out of trains & dangle out of boats – but its a poor pretence – Im never certain of you unless Im hanging on to a handful of your jersey. Ansaldi is due back in three days. Ill see him then just to see how things are going. I feel they are going well – yes, well. My cough is less frequent; Im stronger. I eat *terribly*. My joints are still very painful, thats true, but Ive no temperature again. Theres my 'statement'.

Ive just looked out of the window. L.M. is at San Remo. There is going to be an *enormous* storm; terrible lead coloured clouds are pulling over; the sea is almost silent – just a deep beat & the wind has arrived to clear the court as it were for the Elements. The cold is immense here, Bogey, but I don't feel it at all as I did in the S. of France, thanks to all my warm woollies. But its absurd to say this coast is warm *all the time.* Perhaps next month will be finer. Now I must work again & pray the house isn't struck by lightning. Its the moment to shut all the windows – you know that moment. Well, Ive done it. Ive also been into the garden picked a rose and brought in a bundle of kindling from under the verandah table and I haven't coughed once or got out of breath. So I must be *furiously better* really. Goodby my precious.

Your
Wig.

MS ATL. *LKM* I. 269; *LJMM*, 358–9.

[1] Sylvia Lynd (1888–1952), a friend of KM's, who contributed poetry to the *Athenaeum*.

[2] Murry wrote on 23 Oct. that Grant Richards, novelist and publisher, had written to Sullivan 'complaining that he never had an answer to the letter he wrote you' (ATL).

[3] The publicity manager of the paper was proving incompetent, and Arthur (Richard) Murry had been helping to design advertisements.

[4] The publishing firm recently set up by Richard Cobden-Sanderson, for whom Richard now worked.

[5] Murry said he was sending her Arthur Waley's *More Translations from the Chinese*, but no review appeared.

To J. M. Murry, [29 October 1919]

[Casetta Deerholm, Ospedaletti]
Wednesday.

My own love,

No letter today so far. I may get one this evening. I have heard from Father at Menton. Poor darling! he was robbed at Boulogne of his wallet – all his money, addresses, papers, £50 in Bank Notes, a letter of credit for £500. This really wrings my heart. I cant help it. If he does mind so terribly about money it must have been so *ghastly* to be *alone* among foreigners having to keep up & be a man of the world and look out of the railway windows as tho' it hadn't happened – I really literally nearly fainted when this swept over me – and I 'saw' him with a very high colour 'putting on' a smile – I do hope to God people don't suffer quite as I think they do: its not to be borne if they do.

I am writing this in a hurry. I seem to have such acres to plough & the horse is going so slow. I wish I could change the horse, Boge. He just sits on his hind legs & scratches his ear & looks round at me when we're ½ way through a furrow. Its icy cold, thundering – blue grey with a flash of steel. I should think it was going to snow – I will write to you again later, my precious when this review is done, but I wanted to catch the post with this. Would you send me the Times review[1] of Virginia? Id *very* much like to see it or any other. I want to read the book but dare not so much as put my nose in till Ive cleared off this accumulation.

Take care of yourself, my *very own* Bogey. Love me: I love you.

Wig.

MS ATL. *LKM* I. 270; *LJMM*, 359–60.

[1] A very favourable review of *Night and Day* in the *Times Literary Supplement*, 30 Oct. 1919.

To J. M. Murry, [30 October 1919]

[Casetta Deerholm, Ospedaletti]
Thursday.

My darling.

I am sending a review today and I shall send another tomorrow. Things have not gone as fast as I wished (as usual) but from now onward they will improve. I expect you wonder why with such unlimited opportunity I do not just waltz through with things. Alas! Up till now it has been – not so much my health, indeed, except for that chill and mal à la tête not my health at all – but my 'domestic' arrangements. Now I have discovered how I can live with L.M. It is by not speaking more than is necessary for the service of the house. Two nights ago we had a 'crise' which made me realise it must be the very last, that if it occurred again Id have to ask her to go & to make other arrangements. This, of course, I dont at all want to do, so the other plan is adopted. I don't know what she thinks. I imagine she is furious but I don't care. Its *such a rest* – you cant imagine. No shouting, no quarrelling, no violence, just quiet: I am basking in it. I can keep it up, too, by an effort of Will; I am *sure* I can. Otherwise there would have been no work done – nothing done – nothing written – for our hate had got to such a pitch that I couldn't take a plate from her hand without shuddering. This *awful relationship* living on in its secret corrupt way beside my relationship with you is very extraordinary; no-one would believe it. I am two selves – one my true self – the other that she created in me to destroy my true self. Still Ill write no more about it & try & think about it less and less so that the fire gets more & more covered. But thats what makes my work so hard, what *paralyses my mind*. Its just like a terrible fog; Im lost in it and I go mad – just like L. [Lawrence] used to. Here I have thrown things at her –

yes, even that – called her a murderer, cursed her – Her three standing remarks "give me time", "Ill learn by degrees, Katie" and "you must just teach me, thats all" are to me too sinister. I haven't the time to give – However, its over. And I shall live in silence with her now and put it away. Better a thousand times be lonely than speak to her. But that is *the real reason* why I cannot work as I could – L.M. L.M. and L.M. So after this Ill do better – see?

No letters came today, none yesterday. I am longing for the post. There'll be two tomorrow I expect. Its fine today though still bitter cold: Ive been lying still in the sun all morning – haven't moved. The sea is wonderfully beautiful, so deep and dark – yet with the light on it, moving and glittering.

I heard from Chaddie & Jeanne, yesterday, both full of Wood Hay. 'How I wish I could send you a great hamper from the orchard of nuts and apples' . . . Its a safe wish at this distance. One page was devoted – this is *dead true* – to the matchbox. She knew it would appeal to me – so delighted it had fetched up safe. J & she both said '*K*' when they saw it, etc. It made me violently jealous that they should have a house and nuts & apples. I *yearn* to beat them – I feel I shall buy all the china I can get here to beat their china & oh if we had more money you could be looking out for oddmints too. We must have our house Bogey, next year. Is there any star on the horizon? Chaddie also sent me a photograph of myself at three months old. It was a *dreadful shock*. I had always imagined it – a sweet little laughing thing, rather french, with wistful eyes under a fringe, firmly gripping a spade, showing even then a longing to dig for treasure with her own hands – But this little solemn monster with a wisp of hair looked as though she were just about to fall backwards head over heels. On her feet she wears as far as I can make out a pair of ordinary workmen's boots which the photographer, from astonishment or malice, has photographed so close up that each tootsie is the size of her head. The only feature about her is her ears which are neatly buttonholed on to the sides of her head & not just safety-pinned on as most babies' are – Even the spade she clasps with the greatest reluctance . . .

Now I must work. The hot water runs at last, for the first time yesterday. Vince is not going to London until the end of *November.* I thought Id let you know. Oh, I do hope there is a letter tomorrow darling with news of you in it. I am anxious about this ghastly press of work. Otherwise all goes well here and under my new regime it can only go better. Goodbye my own precious Bogey. When you get this it will be November – 2 months to the New Year.

Your own Wig.

MS ATL. *LKM* I. 270–1; *LJMM*, 360–2.

To J. M. Murry, [31 October 1919]

[Casetta Deerholm, Ospedaletti]

189
188.
Friday.
My love and my dear

Two letters today: *the first since Monday*. Oh, how welcome they were! I had begun to think that L.M. made away with them. I often have a moment of doubt as to whether she's going to post what I give her or throw it into the sea . . . Your Saturday letter, darling telling me your cold still hangs round you was a sad one. I know how you felt – Yes, one *has* a lonely furrow and all I look forward to is *our home*. There is nothing else, you know, Bogey, absolutely nothing for me – I sent a review yesterday – Boge, before I forget will you change the last sentence of all – substitute another word for the word *great*, or . . . "farewell meeting between father and son it would be a great deal more."[1] I can't just remember how the thing went but I woke up in the night with the Lord crying 'Samuel'[2] to me & saying "cut that bit out about a great novel" — I am going to do my best to send another review off today. I am sending L.M. to San Remo pour faire les commissions on purpose. The sun came out this morning – took a cloud or two, did a little extremely high class modelling on the grand scale – "The Banquet" – "Greek Warriors Resting", "A Grecian Lady with a Bowl" and so on, all along the horizon for the benefit of a tiny little sailing ship and me – then it went in again & heaven knows how many doors are between us – It is bitterly cold and windy with great puffs of dust rising. I wonder if it will get warmer again? I don't see why it should & yet who would come for a saison d'Hiver to get a blue nose and fingers? A mystery to me.

Your portrait of you & Wing gardening is one of the wittiest most charming things *in the world*. Who are we? What are we doing in *this* world? We are the only original Babes in the Wood as has been played for the last —— years – Life is the old woman in the bonnet who gets our engagements for us, waits for us in the wings & rubs the black stuff round our eyes – and Wing must have a tiny veskit painted on him and be a robin with his *own private* leaf to lay upon us –

Oh my precious darling *how* I love you – Let this be our last separation. I cant help feeling – in view of this intense cold – why didn't I go to Ventnor or some such place. Why go so far? It couldn't be colder in the Isle of Wight – Well, it only determines me never to do it again – Peace still reigns between L.M. & me. She talks to the bread instead – its a perfect listener for it lets her fill herself with it to her content & is made to be devoured.

My lung isn't exactly painful but it creaks like a Sam Browne belt.[3] Ive no temperature. I go to bed every night after dinner & rest all day. Perhaps it is healing & thats what makes the noise – I am sending her to Ansaldi today to see if she can get news of him. Boge, could you find time to send me that Italian grammar soon? I wrote it on your little list, you remember. You know I cant bother about a *soul* in England but you. Theyre just *gone*. Yet I am very lonely. But only for *you*. I am so glad you were in the garden my darling.

Yours for ever

Wig.

MS ATL. *LKM* I. 271; *LJMM*, 362–3.

[1] Murry either emended or dropped the sentence she referred to, as it is not possible to identify the review KM speaks of.

[2] '. . . and Samuel was laid down to sleep [and] the Lord called Samuel: and he answered, Here am I.' 1 Sam. 3: 3–4.

[3] A leather belt for dress uniform, with a strap passing over the right shoulder, named after the British army officer Sir Samuel Hames Browne.

To J. M. Murry, [31 October 1919]

[Casetta Deerholm, Ospedaletti]

Bogey,

L.M. is just back from San Remo. The chemist can no longer make my cough mixture for lack of this ingredient. He has tried for it everywhere. This is important for my cough has got the upper hand still. Would you ask Doctor Sorapure to make me a new prescription or failing that would you have the medicine sent to me from a chemist. It is rather urgent. You might explain to the doctor if you see him that my cough is certainly no less troublesome than it was and at the slightest exertion I am very short of puff (such as dressing, doing my hair, etc.) so Id rather it were stronger than weaker – see? I am fighting all the time the most *overwhelming depression*: that I am sure is what keeps my cough going & keeps me feeling weak. I merely state this. I am determined to be 'gay' but I am *desperately* lonely & depressed – This is just medical truth.

Your own

Wig.

MS ATL. *LJMM*, 363.

To J. M. Murry, [1 November 1919]

[Casetta Deerholm, Ospedaletti]

A blank day
Saturday
My darling Bogey,

I had thought to have your Monday letter yesterday – but no: it wouldn't come. You must throw them more quickly down the letterboxes, darling, *hurl* them, send them *flying*: tell them that if they come quickly there is nothing – nothing she wont give them. They can take whatever they please, pull off her rings & put them on their thumbs, peacock in her flowery shawl, eat all the honey jar at once . . . Oh *no* they are not children. I won't have them children. Little children must never travel. How could I have written so! It breaks my heart only to think of them. No, they are just – birds to whom the journey is no labour – up they fly, out of sight with one beat of a delicate wing . . . But birds are so heartless, alas!

It is a fearful day; long cold rain, a homeless wind crying at the windows, the sea like ashes. I am sitting in my little room in a corner, wrapped up with a hot brick at my feet. I must work hard today – Thank God for definite work – work that must be done. Bogey darling, precious, do tell me when my reviews are not up to the mark – criticise them & *please* let me see the Lit. Sup. I really am a bit lost without it over here – If you cant send it to me then Ill write direct. Just let me know. Couldn't I have the office copy?

November 1st. Six months to May. After that don't leave me alone. I am not made to live alone, not with an enemy. Hating L.M. as I do I should have gone to a place like Mentone where I could sometimes go for a small walk without a climb and *lift the shutter* that I live behind. But work work work – simply to thy cross I cling[1] (why must it be a cross. Ah why! What a question to ask at 31!) ((But I *do* still ask it.)) Six months. Bogey. Let us look across them and sign to each other. Only six months to cross – a mountain a month – six mountains & then a soft still quiet valley where no wind blows – not even enough to fray the one o clock dandelions – And we are there and hidden – *Love* me. You MUST love me – as much as I love you. Send me a very brave piece of love to pin in my bosom.

Wig.

MS ATL. *LKM* I. 271–2; *LJMM*, 364.

---

[1] 'Nothing in my hand I bring, | Simply to thy Cross I cling', from the third stanza of A. M. Toplady's hymn 'Rock of Ages'.

To J. M. Murry, [1 and 2 November 1919]

[Casetta Deerholm, Ospedaletti]

Darling Heart,

Saturday.

No letter. Oh, what a disappointment. I have only heard once since Monday – True, I got 2 then but I did at least hope for your 'Monday' letter today.

I am sitting in the dining room, the front door is open, the cold salt air blows through. I am wrapped up in my purple dressing gown & jaegar rug with a hot bottle and a hot brick – On the round table is a dirty egg cup full of ink, my watch (an hour slow) and a wooden tray holding a manuscript called *eternity* which is all spattered over with drops of rain & looks as though some sad mortal had cried his pretty eyes out over it. There is also a pair of scissors – abhorréd shears[1] they look & two flies, walking up and down are discussing the ratification of the Peace Treaty & its meaning re our civil relations with Flyland – I am just sending L.M. in to San Remo to ask the Hochwohlgeboren Doktor Bobone[2] to come & see me. Curse Ansaldi! He'll never be back. I *must* know from somebody how I am getting on & what is the state of my left lung. i.e. I must be cheered up. Ten years passed this morning as I sat in my darkish little room. I am now 41 and can't afford to lose a moment. I must know. If my depression continues, my precious, I shall try & get out of here in January – because if it does go on we shouldn't have a May here, wed be flinging our daisy chains round the tops of cedar trees. But on the other hand if Bobone consoles me & so on, I may feel better. Its being alone with L.M. Things have gone too far, you know; we positively *loathe* each other – Its such a complex with me that only fear of the consequences stops me from shooting her – I see myself at the top of the stairs & she at the bottom & then to know she'd never never stare at me again —— *Later.* L.M. is back from San Remo. She has been to the post again. No letters. I feel simply paralysed with dismay. Think! Ive NO "negative tonic" here – theres my only link with Life with reality & in the whole week Ive heard ONCE. Pray darling tell me not to expect them or for Gods sake send them. Bobone comes tomorrow at 9.

Sunday in bed. This man has just been. I think he is a very good doctor indeed, highly scientific. VERY terrifying – He finds the apex of my right lung only affected – the left infiltrated to the third rib. He says "so long as you have not the fevers you do not die. It is the fevers that kills" – Well I have been very much without fever here so that is hopeful. I dont think he has at all a great opinion of me – Im to see him once a fortnight and as you get better once in three weeks. He is giving me a medicine for tuberculosis – not for my cough. He says this villa is very good for fine weather but for any other is no good. "You must stay in bed when de weather is not fine." Because of its bad heating and no stoves. At any rate he says if I cant get out I must stay in bed but I must, of course, get out as much as I can and eat everything. He is I think a german. He stayed about an hour – and most thoroughly examined me – His one constant remark is "it is *hopeful* you have no fever – When the patient has no fever the patient do not die." I think he came expecting to give me a death certificate! But when I tried to tell him of my appalling depression he (like everybody except Sorapure) made no reply – did not hear.

MS ATL. *LKM* I. 272–3; *LJMM*, 364–5.

---

[1] 'Comes the blind *Fury* with th' abhorrèd shears | And slits the thin-spun life.' John Milton, *Lycidas*, ll. 75–6.

[2] 'The honourable Dr Bobone.' As she often did, KM moved from doctor to doctor.

To J. M. Murry, [2 November 1919]

[Casetta Deerholm, Ospedaletti]

Sunday in bed

Darling of darlings,

I have heard from you twice this week – du reste – silence. If I do not get a letter today it will be *too* dreadful. My mind is paralysed with dismay and apprehension, and I am in bed with this terrible storm raging day & night outside – No-one to speak to – Like Robinson Crusoe – HE lived alone[1] – Worse – oh much, much worse –

I have just seen the Hochwohlgeborene Doktor Bobone. I did not want to wait any longer for Ansaldi. Yesterday was so terrible, Bogey, in my darkish room – like a cave – unable to write or think – no news – no letters – I sent her to San Remo: because I felt I must at least have some one in touch with me – He stayed about an hour and most thoroughly examined me. I think he is a very good doctor indeed – scientific – dry – *german*, and as frank with me as if Id been a student examining the case – with him. He says the fact I have so little fever is good – all on my side. "So long as you have not the fevers you do not die. It is de fevers which kills." I don't think he had at all a *great* opinion of me. On the other hand he said he thought I might go in to see him once a fortnight – go into San Remo! He says the apex of the right lung only is affected; the left is infiltrated to the third rib. He is giving me a medicine *for* tuberculosis. This I don't like. Sorapure said they were so often dangerous. This man said himself it is not one of the dangerous ones. "It do nothing or it do well." I suppose I must trust him, then. This villa he approves of for fine weather but when the weather is not fine he says I must stay in bed to be out of draughts & to be warm – Air, to lie out in the sun, food, and no worry, no fever, "and you will not die. It is the fever kills the patient." This was his one cry. But when I tried to tell him of my appalling *mental* state of depression he didn't even listen. No-one *listens* to a patient except Sorapure.[2]

Now listen. TRY to send me letters often or cards or papers from the office – anything. If I were there you'd spend 10 minutes with me. Give me those 10 minutes here. HELP ME HELP ME! If I veep I getta de fever and I am veeping strong!! I have no negative tonic. I am tired – I cant always write or work or read – Then I have nothing but darkness – I live on this desolate hillside with L.M. munching by me. *But I can fight through all this* if I am in touch with you. If you are ill *Arthur must let me know immediately* – Reality Bogey is ALWAYS less than my dreams and apprehensions. If you will bear that in mind you will make Life easier. SILENCE is the ULTIMATE BLACKNESS – I must stop crying & send this to post. Oh God – what an end of all my fine hopes – to be rewriting my S. of France letters because of these cursed posts. The weather is perfect hell, the sea roars: its never never quiet – it eats away the air. The room is half dark and Im alone all day all day all day every day every day – Mrs Jones[3] can do up a paper can't she? But you are so pitiful have pity on me & WRITE.[4]

Wig.

Nothing is hopeless. Nothing is lost. No new terror has been added no new fear really. But this loneliness is what opens the gates of my soul & lets the wild beasts stream howling through. I shall get over it. Let us keep firm – But write me AT LENGTH.

MS ATL. *LJMM*, 365–7.

---

[1] Murry noted, *LJMM*, 366, 'These are words from a music-hall song.'
[2] This repetition of much from the previous letter on the same day suggests that KM was in considerable confusion, as both letters were posted.
[3] Alice Jones was Murry's secretary at the *Athenaeum* office.
[4] Murry replied to this on 5 Nov., 'What can I do to help? I write & write; I try to keep in control of my work & behave like a sane being to the world. But when I feel that you feel that I have not written because you are not receiving my letters – I certainly become very nearly insane. Look here, you must keep things straight, & remember that a letter from me to you goes off every single day.' (Murry, 204.)

To J. M. Murry, [3 November 1919]

[Casetta Deerholm, Ospedaletti]
Monday.

186 Monday &
185 Tuesday received.

My darling Bogey,

I got your Monday & Tuesday letters yesterday and they reassured me that nothing was wrong. In fact everything seemed alright: Sydney there for tumpany & Eliot's poetry lecture[1] . . . It sounds Gaierty.[2] The storm at present is hanging over: it has withdrawn to await re-inforcements – a horrible lowering violet sky, a boiling sea like porridge – snow on the mountains. Fancy, with that – to get more air I had one side of the net up last night & I am bitten frightfully by mosquitoes. This is almost laughable . . . Everything about this Côte d'Azur is lies. Why does one believe it. One might as well believe that London is a rich magnificent city – or that the Midland Hotel Manchester is the most comfortable place in the world. Why believe *liars*: everybody lies. I don't know – but there you are. Dostoievsky at least understands through & through . . .

I feel a bit like the outside elements – at least I feel they've had their way with me for the moment & Im now high & dry – on a rocky ledge looking up at the sky and simply vaguely wondering. <u>Im not ill</u>. No temperature today. Ive taken it & written it down in my book. But I shall get up & go downstairs & lie in my little room – My joints wont stand any more bed. I hope to get work done today. I long to – ah! so much!!! If that were possible Id get back my *spirit*. When that goes (the power to work) then Im nothing. – Just a straw before the wind and I feel *one must hurry*. There are you & the paper, so important so enormously important – Your big number Nov 12th nearly there. Believe that I try ALL I can, every single bit I can. Nothing less than La Faiblesse (who is really the toughest old hag of them all) keeps me from the performance of my promises.

I had 2 letters from Father yesterday. He is ill too with the cold and of course terribly disappointed with the climate. Thinks it a 'perfect farce' . . . Cant keep warm even in bed with a hot water bottle and a Kaiapoi rug.[3] Very anxious to know if my villa is adequately heated. I only pray he doesn't come here while this cold spell is on: he'd be so cross & want to make other arrangements & I could NOT stand that.

Good God! Theres a little wavering gleam of sun on the wall – white, still: it makes everything look shabby & dirty. Its gone again.

Perhaps now I have encountered the whole troupe of fiends so early on I shall get better of them & be at peace. I suppose any one who has lived my life of the last two years is bound to have these moments.

That is what I hope. When I am with you I am furious because you will not see 'happiness' in the future.[4] Well, still if we're together in our own house, living our own life *I do see it* – Apart from that there is nothing: I mean there is just a living death or a dead one: it really dont signify (yes, it does.)

But to walk, kiss the earth, run, laugh, go in and out of houses & rooms, if I could do any of these things – "You are always an invalid – hein?" says Bobone, looking at me with absolutely inexpressive *red* eyes like an ox – no whites to them at all. "Vot is your age – dirty-five?"

"No," I said – "dirty-one."

"Zo."

Well, well, well. Why do I feel like this about Dostoievsky – *my* Dostoievsky – no-one elses – A being who loved in spite of everything – adored – LIFE even while he knew the dark dark places.

Arthur wrote me a little letter – so awfully nice. He is a very fine lad indeed. "Jack seems happy in his quiet way & very keen on his paper." He positively worships you. All his fineness is come from loving you. He is so young. You are in time to save him from so much that you suffered. There is no reason why he should not just go straight ahead & grow into a *real man*. He put at the end – 'oceans of love' – Wasn't that sweet? Fancy *oceans* of love – aren't they *boys* words – such a fling about them.

Tell Wing Ganma has been a very pore girl & would love to see him climb on to her bed now and would make him a whole cake for himself with Wing written on it in mouse tails of icing –

Well, my beloved Boy, goodbye for now. Perhaps this is partly due to the terrific shock of the cold and rain and dark – when one thought all was going to be so fair. It is well to look for reasons. I am always looking for reasons *why* my courage goes. But after all, here it is. I am not WELL. No good pretending I am. Im bound to get these fits of depression, I suppose. The only thing that helps is to feel you are there, to know about your life which is my *real* life – not my sick life, and to WORK. We must stick to our six months. Last night I felt in the middle of the night L.M. must not turn us away from our month here: one must conquer that & not let her win. I shall try. Remember always how long Ive been ill and don't think hardly of me. I have been ill for 200 years –

Love me. I am your true love

Wig.

MS ATL. *LKM* I. 274–5; *LJMM*, 369–71.

[1] On 25 Oct. T. S. Eliot had lectured on 'Modern Tendencies in Poetry' for the Arts League of Service.

² The erratic spelling KM several times adopted from the then rather modish *The Young Visiters*, by Daisy Ashford, which she reviewed in the *Athenaeum*, 23 May 1919.

³ A brand of woollen rug made at Kaiapoi, north of Christchurch, New Zealand.

⁴ Murry was clearly trying to see, if only to please KM. He wrote on 25 Oct., 'But, my darling heart, the good time, the secret happy time, is coming as sure as fate.' (ATL.)

To J. M. Murry, [3 November 1919]

[Casetta Deerholm, Ospedaletti]
Monday afternoon.

185 received.

Hardy Poem rec.

Darling Bogey,

I think your poem is extremely beautiful. So awfully like you too to have him *dead* first. But Hardy beautifully understood – you say.'

it has Please do send me the letter you speak of. It has not [fetched up] but then neither has Art & Letters or the Weekly Times or the American Letter or the Italian grammar or the Lit. Sup. They all lie at the bottom of Bogeys head somewhere —

Well if you've had terrible weather you have not had any worse than this place. Not a crumb worse. No-one could ever convince me of that – & England has comforts – carpet – fire – porridge – coal – and so on that these parts have not – I have heard from Thorpe; the books have arrived & he has credited me with 12/- which is quite good. Please get hold of it – will you – & do what you like with it. Its household money – isn't it. We decided that. Buy half a dozen serviettes or – something like that. I am longing to see the Paper. Did my Galsworthy get there?² Was it 'alright'?

I had a long characteristic most kindly letter from old Kay today. He said how Pa hated this coast & wished himself back in England. It was a really charming warm-hearted letter – I have sent Ida to San Remo today with a cheque to cash & the most extraordinary letter for the Bank Manager – all rubbish – I couldn't take the trouble to be perlite, curse him. So she's gone & Im alone for the afternoon, thank goodness.

My breathing is much better today so is my cough. Dont imagine I use up my new energy. Indeed I dont. On the 11th of last month I walked to Ospedaletti on the 18th I went to San Remo. But Ive done *nothing* since & am going to do nothing but lie about – & get up & go to bed – Dont imagine I exert myself physically & I eat quite double what I did. Im awfully hungry – always.

I have read your poem again. It is very noble and beautiful – and it is so finely *tempered* I mean like steel is tempered. You will always write elegies, it seems to me. Even your lullabies are to deaders, small & great, and Love is the darling small house on the mountain of loneliness. *The house on the way.* Isn't it so? The human soul is very mysterious – don't answer me. You *know*. Now I must work. Goodbye for now darling.

Ever your
Wig.

Later

L.M. has just returned with your Thursday letter with Hardys letter in it: I am more than glad you sent it me. It is a treasure. What a strange 'situation'. How strange to acknowledge a poem on ones own death! How great the character that can do so, how different to us impatient creatures *craving* for life's fitful fever.[3] Life Life! we cry – & Hardy writes so quietly as though he were already entering the quiet harbour – the sails furled – drifting in on a silent tide – You did very well to send them to him, unaltered. He is a man who I am sure would understand you very deeply. But after all, he is old, he has lived, he is a very old man – perhaps with age with long years desire dies –

I can imagine you writing this very letter to a jeune homme of the next generation, in all its particulars except your wife won't have a tomb – she'll have at most a butterfly fanning its wings on her grave & then off.

L.M. returned from the Bank. By cashing cheques there I drop a deal of money: I can't afford to do so again, but Kay had taken such pains to arrange the matter and as he said "tickle them up", that I felt I couldn't start another plan. Sentimentality you see which costs me 22 lire. It won't do. I always feel people's *feelings* are being hurt. I suppose they are not really & Im very silly to imagine they have such hurtable feelings. How dreadful Sullivan away & Aldous away[4] – you will have to begin slaving again. And then there will come my letters – Oh God – why do I write. Perhaps it would be better not to write letters – youd be alright, I'd pull through or not – just the same – I suppose. Anyway I am not ill and don't *cry* today which is a big relief!!

Goodbye precious.

MS ATL. *LJMM,* 371–2.

---

[1] Murry wrote on 29 Oct. that he had sent to Thomas Hardy a poem 'hot from the oven: considering I treated him as dead it was a bit thick. I send you what he sent me.' (ATL.) Murry's biographer F. A. Lea, *John Middleton Murry* (1959), 71, wrote how 'The *Athenaeum* sailed under the banner of Hardy. "Mr Hardy can speak for all that is noble in England as no poet since Wordsworth has been able," he [Murry] declared in one editorial; and scarcely a month went by without some similar salvo. . . . Not content with dedicating his *Poems, 1916–1920* "To Thomas Hardy . . . in Devotion and Gratitude", he out-Hardyed Hardy himself by despatching personally a poem on the old man's death. (The reply was perfect: "The verses are very striking I think, and they will keep. It will be for others to judge of their contents. I must limit myself

to admiring their form.")' For Hardy's reply, *The Collected Letters of Thomas Hardy*, ed. Richard Little Purdy and Michael Millgate, vol. 5 (1985), 336.

² KM's review of John Galsworthy's *Saint's Progress*, 'A Standstill', in the *Athenaeum*, 31 Oct. 1919.

³ 'After life's fitful fever he sleeps well', *Macbeth*, 3. ii. 23.

⁴ J. W. N. Sullivan was assistant editor of the *Athenaeum*, and Aldous Huxley second assistant editor.

To J. M. Murry, [4 November 1919]

[Casetta Deerholm, Ospedaletti]
Tuesday.

Chinese Poems and Monkhouse[1] received.

My darling Bogey,

The paper has just come & I am enjoying it tremendously: It seems to me to be an excellent number. The 'Preface' little essay is good.[2] I like RLS' remark don't you.[3] And Swinnerton is very sound.[4] That is a useful article from the *trade* point of view as well: good for the circulation – Who wrote Fatigue?[5] I love that kind of article – with a frog in it even though I pity the poor frog so I feel I *must* have him out of it. L'Hôte is really a splendid fellow[6] and I am ashamed that I did not realise how good Dent was until lately[7] – not only good – but such a personality comes through – something wonderfully unaffected, sincere, english and kind.

I wish J.S. would do the drama. Hes the man, don't you think? His Euripides is famos.[8] Its just right . . .

So we tickled Ambrose up.[9] Why not get Mrs Maufe[10] to write defending something or other or at any rate telling us how it should be done? I was very sorry to see that arch snorter, that ludicrous old sea lion Ezra blowing – Ill never forgive that creature a letter he wrote to Spender: it makes me utterly detest him – besides his letter with its 'tang, gusto' etc.[11] What rot muttered a stray lady in the crowd.

A funny foreign article in evening dress with kid gloves – a 'name day' bow on Couperus, but it has a deal of information.[12] I must go through all the paper again – at tea time. I am just reviewing Romer Wilson & Stella Benson together for this week. 'A Real Book and an Unreal One'[13] – the flowers go to young Stella – Romer Wilson is such a fraud – oh oh oh! She is one of the ladies of fashion who are teaching us how to put on our clothes. But she's tremendously absurd – Ive got her as she would say on a trident –

It was a fine morning, now it is very hazy – milk white. I feel *dead* emotionally & spiritually – just 'not at home' but mentally & physically I feel harder than I have since I got ill – You had better not pay much attention to me – perhaps part of my awful depression *is real maladie* – sickness – poison – a real symptom of tuberculosis. I don't know. When I say dead emotionally, my own darling, I mean to all people except you, to all external things. You, Wing, Arthur, our life is hidden away, deep – but all else – I dont care a straw for. Its good to be in this air because it makes one better physically – but I wouldn't care if the geraniums turned into cabbages – I don't want to look – no, *WORK*, thats all.

Ever your own girl

Wig.

MS ATL. *LJMM*, 373–4.

---

[1] Arthur Waley's *More Translations from the Chinese* and Allen Monkhouse's *True Love*.

[2] 'On Prefaces', by Bonamy Dobrée, was the leading article in the *Athenaeum*, 31 Oct. 1919.

[3] The article quoted Robert Louis Stevenson on prefaces: 'It is best in such circumstances, to represent a delicate shade of manner between humility and superiority, as if the book had been written by someone else, and you had merely run over it and inserted what was good.' From the Preface to *An Inland Voyage* (1878).

[4] On 'Author and Publisher'.

[5] 'Fatigue', under the 'Science' heading, was by Geoffrey Keynes.

[6] The second part of André Lhote's article, 'The Necessity of Theories'.

[7] In the music section, Edward Dent wrote on 'The Personality of a Teacher'.

[8] James Strachey on 'Euripides at the Old Vic', a review of Sybil Thorndike in Gilbert Murray's translation of the *Troades*.

[9] 'Art and Industry', the leading article in the issue of 10 Oct., discussed a hut converted into a working-class dwelling, on exhibition on Horse Guards Parade. Murry wrote that the hut was 'charmingly furnished', but at the cost of £350 was unrealistic. 'We do not suppose that the authorities who converted the hut, or the designers who designed the furniture, knew that they were making a bad joke. Doubtless, they were persuaded that they were helping to reconcile industry, art, and the working classes.' This provoked a letter from Ambrose Heal, of Heal and Son Ltd., who had made the furniture. He demanded, 'why drag in Art', wrongly taking the article as an attack on their products.

[10] Gladys Maufe, a neighbour and friend when KM lived at 141a Church Row, was an interior designer.

[11] Ezra Pound wrote a letter taking up 'The Method of Mr. Pound', T. S. Eliot's review of his *Quia Pauper Amavi*, in which he said that the reviewer 'seems to regard literature not as something in itself enjoyable, having tang, gusto, aroma; but rather as something which, possibly because of a non-conformist conscience, one *ought* to enjoy because it is literature (infamous doctrine)'. KM may also be referring to a letter she had seen from Pound to John Alfred Spender, political journalist and editor of the *Westminster Gazette*, and a friend of Murry's.

[12] 'Letters from Holland: III. Louis Couperos', by J. L. Walch, a piece on the Dutch novelist.

[13] The title of KM's review of Romer Wilson's *If All These Young Men* and Stella Benson's *Living Alone*, the *Athenaeum*, 14 Nov. 1919.

To J. M. Murry, [5 November 1919]

[Casetta Deerholm, Ospedaletti]
Wednesday.

183 with 10/- received & Pa's letter.

My own Precious Bogey,

This Friday 4 p.m. letter has a bit frightened me. You are for certain keeping something back. What is it? Is it that I am not sending enough work? Is that it? Are things not going well somewhere? Are you fatigued with writing letters? I have read & reread it; each time again I feel the *quelque chose*. Its true you drew a heart at the end but then I feel you did that to disguise the other – to fill up some vacuum which you were conscious of. Do I imagine this, or is it true. I wish you had not sent me the book money.[1] Keep it in future. I shall put this by & buy plates with it for our home. I shall do as you suggest henceforward with the books.

Be open with me, darling. What is it? You dont say to me "I am in the best form" – thats not us – its just your silly over courage – I am thankful you have Sydney there with you – tremendously thankful. He must take the edge off the empty house – & then there is our precious little grub, trailing ash over the carpet.

I finished my Benson & Wilson last night & am tackling Dosty[2] today. I cant go any faster just now. You must just give the overplus to others if I don't go fast enough. *I understand.* Its warmer today with a large wind blowing and working up for rain – all deep greys – The wind *tugs* at the trees – *tugs* at the waves. Its a vile wind. Yesterday the parson came to see me from San Remo and his wife – he a glazed old fish almost imbecile – she a grinning nightmare eating her veil as she talked – Rev. *Dudley Lampen*.[3] They said, with gay bridlings: "This is our *January* weather –" How very nice. I smiled away – L.M. was out. I think she thought me very fishy – To Hell with her –

I wish the sun would shine, I wish it would – hot bright sun day after day – Ive managed to get good porridge here which makes all the difference to breakfast and at last we can get *rice*. The foods alright, it couldn't be better really or more plentiful – unlimited excellent butter and so on –

Do you think, later on, you will be able to get away for weekends? Its no good now, because the weather is too bad & youre too tired. Youd get colds: you ought to *rest* at home, but you'll never do that. But later on – do you think? It would be wonderful to know of the house, even if we weren't there – Even Hampstead rests me to think of. It *is* my home, I *have* a home – I have every right to sit on the stairs & look at Wing come lopping up – I love 2 Portland Villas from here – Id kiss the gate & the door – often I go in and wander through & look

out of the windows – with love – with love – My room was so beautiful
– the long glass reflecting the books – the black monk[4] the exquisite
clock & the brass scuttle. These things I expect you take in your
stride. In my memory I caress them – they are beloved darlings. To
turn that unwilling key in the Black Monk – oh, what joy – to curl up
on the stickleback & to have Wing climb up the outer shell & then
walk over unimportant me – And my chest of drawers – the special
one – Dont let us ever give up our things – truly I *couldn't*. I dont like
foreign countries or foreign ways or foreign houses. It is only the sun
that tricks them out. When the sun goes it is as though the flesh were
gone – and there is nothing to tell over but ugly bones. Well, Bogey
my precious little husband Ill begin working – Thank God you found
our Wing again: he must never be really lost. And will you tell me
what the cream jug is like? Describe it when you have time.   This is
an ancient wind — In spirit I put my hands on you gently & kiss you
– but not interrupting – not interfering – *All is well here*. Don't worry.
We shall get through. We are winning, but the fight has been so long.

Ever your own
Wig.
Amen.

MS ATL. *LKM* I. 275–6; *LJMM*, 374–5.

[1] Murry sent 10*s*. from the books sold at Thorpes.
[2] 'Some Aspects of Dostoevsky', KM's review of *An Honest Thief: And Other Stories*, translated
by Constance Garnett, the *Athenaeum*, 28 Nov.
[3] The Revd Ernest Dudley Lampen, Anglican chaplain of St John the Baptist, San Remo, in
the Diocese of Gibraltar.
[4] Murry explained. *LJMM*, 375, 'The Black Monk, so-called from Tchehov's story, was a big
cupboard which I painted yellow and black for Katherine.'

To J. M. Murry, [6 November 1919]

[Casetta Deerholm, Ospedaletti]
Thursday.

My precious Bogey,
    It has just stopped raining and is steamy, misty and cool. Im out on
the verandah, the sea sounds heavy, so is the air – one feels
wonderfully *tired*. The Nation came yesterday but no letter. Father
wrote to me. He is motoring over here next Wednesday – it will be
alright, I suppose. It doesn't matter, anyway. Not having heard from
you I feel a bit dumb: I feel as though I were standing at a door
waiting for it to open – or sitting up against it, more like that, just
waiting. I wish I were a great deal more self supporting. Its a

thousand times harder for me to write reviews here where I have no one to talk things over with – Im 'out of it' and see so few papers & never hear *talk*. I have to get into full divers clothes & rake the floor of the unprofitable sea. All the same *it is my life: it saves me.*

The woodman & his mate came yesterday – I feel a bit sentimental about him because last time he was here you were here. He looked at the picture of Berne. "C'est à Londres – ca? Jolie ville – Londres est sur le lac de Londres, n'est-ce pas?" And finding it was also a mirror he twisted his mustaches in it. "How nice he is" I thought, etc. etc., until I had the bill. Same amount of wood – same size, 115 francs & it is to go up again this month. He declared also it is défendu to take the wood from the hillsides now – a new government order. Coal – does not exist for private houses only hotels. This is all rather a blow considering the climate but we shall have to manage. But now I think I must have the book money, darling, if you don't mind. Its 'odd money' isn't it and I had not reckoned on this expense. What do you think. Oh, as I write I *feel* the sun comes out in my heart at any rate – or in your heart and I am turned towards you – When I wrote that last 'darling' I suddenly changed all over, even physically as though you were here. I didn't feel blind and dumb and sealed up any more – but your true Wig – loving life. Its not six months now before we see each other – Ill be here in this Casetta & you will come here. Oh, God let us try & make this our last separation, at any rate it will be. Id never bear another. They are too terrible. Give Violet my love: I will write her on Sunday & Arthur too. But you have every single bit of me that is worth the giving – My own love.

MS ATL. *LKM* I. 276–7; *LJMM*, 375–6.

To J. M. Murry, [7 November 1919]

[Casetta Deerholm, Ospedaletti]
Friday.

My dearest Love,

I heard the front door bell – Its just after 8 a.m. and [I] knew it was a telegram. L.M. has gone off to wire you. I am frightfully worried that you should have felt compelled to send it. Ever since I had that crise of depression I have bitterly reproached myself for letting you know. Madness – madness! I shall never do so again if I am in my right mind. Let me try and be very plain with you. *All is alright* here. I thought in those first weeks it was going to be 'happy', & its not. But I have lost my capacity for happiness for the time. I am sure, even counting the climate, it is right to be here and to stick it out. I am lonely, very lonely. I somehow hadnt counted on that. Its like imprisonment. And I find it inconceivably difficult to work. Work is an immense effort of will such as I had never dreamed of. Now I know what *your* will is like. Nevertheless work is all I have. If I am not working I want to run up and down, just that – And I am fearful that my reviews are not what you want. It would greatly help if you would tell me. Would you? I am seem to be nothing but a great great drag on you – no comfort, no blessing – no help or rest. I just put out my hands & say 'please'. Its not really so. *Ill make it otherwise.* Tell me though if you feel a grudge against me or if you want to shut the door in my face – enfant trop gâté, am I? Do you think like that?

It won't go on – my mental state I mean. It will change. And physically I am really and truly much stronger. That's genuine. Id like to see Sorapure & find out from him whether it 'showed'. That would be immensely comforting and a great spur. No other doctor is of the slightest use; he knows nothing. I *ought* not to be so unhappy. After all I am able to – and there I want to make a line – able to – what? You see its like a kind of *blindness*. I only thought of Mentone because I thought there might be concerts there & music would help. I simply hate the sea. But *please* think and believe that physically I am better.

Then you have your paper and winter campaign. Oh to think I should bind you. It cannot be. Will you please, after this letter trust me not to do it again? And just plant your feet on a rock and say Tigs alright and so forget me – I mean forget me as a worry. Think of me as on a sea voyage or something like that – not much use (no use) to you while she's there but when she steps on dry land again all will be as it was before the blow fell. Nothing can take away from the fact that the blow did fall you know.[1] But I want to put myself away and think of you. For you are not to be worried. Do you FEEL that?

Forgive me. Can you forgive me? If someone was being attacked in a wood youd not be angry with them for interrupting would you? It was like that. Its sunny, today. No, only forgive me – forgive me.

Wig.

MS ATL. *LJMM*, 445–6.

[1] Murry had written on 3 Nov., in response to her recent depression, 'It's a fearful blow to me. It would have been that anyhow; but the consciousness that I can *do* nothing is too much.' (Murry, 201.)

To J. M. Murry, [7 November 1919]

[Casetta Deerholm, Ospedaletti]
Friday
181, 180.

My darling,

She came back with your Saturday night & Sunday letter (inclu. Butler.[1]) They heap coals of fire on my head. But I must tell you your Saturday letter when you spoke of us being lovers – was like a credo I believe to me. It seemed to bring the future near and warm and *human* for a minute. At sight of it – of so much life, the birds drew back – flew up and away. And then you seemed to tell me so much of what you were doing and it was home like. Our tiny Wing, clean in patches!

Early summer morning – think of it – a day before us – in the garden and the house. Peace – Holding each other, kissing each other until we are one world. It is all memories now – radiant, marvellous far away memories of happiness. Ah, how terrible life can be. I sometimes see an immense wall of black rock, shining, in a place – just after death perhaps – and *smiling*, the *adamant* of *desire*. Let us live on memories, then and when the time comes – let us live so fully that the memories are no nearer than far away mountains —

Arthur sent me another of his letters: you & he eating sausages & mash. *Hug* the old boy for me – tell him hes my brother. My 'Eternity' seemed perfect rubbish: Ill send it if you like. It seemed to go out as I wrote & I raked ashes. Ill send Butler back tomorrow. Ill send Dosty tomorrow. This isnt a letter: its just a word again with you, my precious lover.

Ive paid Porter.[2] Its alright. I wish youd go, though – Think of me as your own,

Mouse.

MS ATL. *LKM* I. 277; *LJMM*, 376–7.

---

[1] Murry sent her George Bernard Shaw's 'Samuel Butler: The New Life Reviewed', from the *Manchester Guardian*, 1 Nov. 1919.
[2] KM's dentist, William Porter, 11 Welbeck Street.

To J. M. Murry, [7 November 1919]

[Ospedaletti]

ALL GOES WELL DARLING ABSOLUTELY NOTHING TO WORRY ABOUT TIG.

Telegram ATL. Unpublished.

To J. M. Murry, [8 November 1919]

[Casetta Deerholm, Ospedaletti]
Saturday. 7 a.m.

Darling,

Ive been lying here while my dream ebbed away. I never have had such vivid dreams as I do here. Campbell[1] in this one came to warn me (we were at 'some strange hotel') 'Mansfield Id lock your door tonight. There are two Chinamen downstairs & theyre very *predatory.*' He repeated this word while he made some small tentative golf club swinging motions – immensely familiar. Campbell belongs to another life – doesn't he? But so does everybody – every single person – I feel they are all quite gone. Even Hampstead and the tapestry in the studio and the sommier. They are not in this world – not for me. What is in this world? – Nothing. Just a blank. Its fine this morning, sun and blue sea – and I dont even want to look out of winder. How long was Dostoievsky in prison. Four years, wasn't he? And he came out and did his finest work after.[2] If only one could rid oneself of this *feeling of finality* – if there were a *continuity.* Thats what is so intolerable. The feeling that one goes on – just as the sea does for hours & days after a storm presenting an appearance of agitation and activity but *its really all over.* Could it be possible that I am wrong? I think Id better not write stories but only my confessions here & keep them out of letters.

G.B.S. on Butler is very fine indeed. He has such a grip of his subject. I admire his tenacity as a reviewer and the way in which his mind follows Butler with a steady light – does not waver over him – find him lose him travel over him. At the same time its queer he should be (G.B.S.) so uninspired. There is not the faintest hint of inspiration in that man. This chills one. You know the feeling that a great writer gives you: "my spirit has been fed and refreshed – it has partaken of something new". One could not possibly feel that about Shaw. Its the clang of the gate that remains with you when all's over. What it amounts to is that Shaw is anything you like but hes not an artist. Do you get when you read his plays a sense of extraordinary *flatness* – They may be extremely amusing at moments but you are always laughing *at* and never *with.* Just the same in his prose – you may agree as much as you like but he is writing *at* not *with.* There is no getting over it: hes a kind of concierge in the house of literature – sits in a glass case – sees everything, knows everything, examines the letters, *cleans the stairs,* but has no part – no part in the life that is going on. But as I wrote that I thought: yes but who *is* living there – living there as we mean life – And Dostoievsky, Tchekov, and Tolstoi – I cant think of *anybody else.*

Oh God! what wouldn't I give for a TALK. Well it cant happen.

I did so love hearing about your walk last Sunday. To think of you in the open air & just walking & getting warm and refreshed – you darling darling Bogey – and then sitting at the yellow table in your velveteens. Dont move my shepherdess if you can help. I *see* her there so plainly: Id hate to think it was another dream. She wasn't there at all – only a little carriage clock. She is the gentle little spirit of the room to me. I always always until I die shall remember how we listened to the tiny bell striking – from a world of faëry. Please dont put her away, Bogey. Think what she has meant. Put the carriage clock on the writing table – cant you? But she is everything to the room – the poet to the landscape. Have you moved her? Tell me.

Goodbye for now my own darling. Keep happy and dont overwork. Keep warm. Is Violet alright and content? Your comfort depends so much on her. I feel inclined to end this letter with the Browning quotation that *cross my heart* I have sworn not to repeat.[3] I used to say it in fun: it was really I suppose a celestial warning. Its my whole life now & I used to just play with it & throw it away. Queer business.

Yours, yours for ever every bit of me with undying love

                                      Wig.

MS ATL. *LKM* I. 313–14; *LJMM*, 446–8.

[1] Their friend Gordon Campbell, later 2nd Baron Glenavy. (See *CLKM* I. 126.)

[2] Dostoevsky was arrested as a revolutionary in 1849. His death sentence was commuted to eight years in Siberia, four of them in a penal settlement in Omsk, and another four in a line-battalion at Semipalatinsk.

[3] Murry identified this reference, *LJMM*, 448, as the fourth and fifth stanzas in Browning's 'A Woman's Last Word', from *Men and Women* (1855):

> What so false as truth is,
>   False to thee?
> Where the serpent's tooth is
>   Shun the tree –
>
> Where the apple reddens
>   Never pry –
> Lest we lose our Edens,
>   Eve and I.

KM soon after took up the same form in her poem 'The Ring', with its concluding stanza:

> We will have no ring, no kiss
> To deceive.
> When you hear the serpent hiss
> Think of Eve.

(*Poems*, 80.)

To J. M. Murry, [8 November 1919]

[Ospedaletti]
Saturday. Post Office. I have just weighed myself and have gained Two Pounds.

Postcard ATL. Unpublished.

To J. M. Murry, [8 November 1919]

[Casetta Deerholm, Ospedaletti]
Saturday afternoon.

The Athenaeum for Ever!!!!!

My own Bogey,

I will give this letter to L.M. to post in San Remo. I went out today and weighed myself & found in a fortnight I had gained over 2 lbs. I weigh *46 kilos 70* and last time it was just on *45*. This is as you can see extraordinary. Now you will believe that I rest. I went then to the P.O. and found your Monday letter written after three awful ones of mine. What could I do? I could only send that p.c. *Now* I want to say – I would really count it almost as fearful if you gave up the A. and came out here as if all were lost.[1] It would in a way mean all were lost; it would mean scrapping our future. Never think of it; never do it. I can imagine nothing more horrible for us both than that. It would mean – looked at from whatever angle – that this thing had beaten us and it would mean – oh, it is not possible to contemplate such a thing. I had rather live here the 2 years than that. That is the solemn truth. You see I *am* getting better; my body is getting better. I have a theory that perhaps the creaking and pain I had were caused by the moist spot drying up in my bad lung. Its quite possible. Old Bobone of course would not know a thing like that. But then he, good as I think he is, does not believe tuberculosis is curable; its evidently a craze of his. I saw it & he said as much. "Quick or soon coma de fever" – But never come to me or give up a thing or send me money or bind yourself whatever I say *now or in the Future*. Please my own precious, NEVER do. We must see this through *successfully*, not otherwise. If you will just accept the fact that I am not gay – see? I will try not to talk of my loneliness & depression nor of L.M.

It is a bright sunny day today and I am not in the least tired after my walk – only hungry. As usual I thought I was going to have it all my own way – get well – be happy – the horror of my disease (it *is* a horror) over – peace with L.M., and ease to work in. What a fat head I am! Out of those – I'll get well – and thats all and enough. Let the others wait. *Work* of course – work is second breath. When you spoke [of] planting a tree of hope I felt oh – it was *you* to speak so. Plant it – plant it darling – I will not shake it. Let me sit under it & look up at it – spread it over me and meet me there often and let us hold each other close and look up into the boughs for buds and flowers. No, theres no God. That is queer. This morning I wanted to say 'God keep you' or Heaven guard us – Then I thought of *The Gods* but they are marble statues with broken noses. There is no God or Heaven or help of any kind but love. Perhaps Love can do everything. Lo! I have made of Love all my religion[2] – Who said that? Its simply marvellous.

L.M. is ready to go. I shall have the place to myself. Its nice. Then I turn into a real Mouse and make as tiny a noise as possible – so as not to disturb the life round me.

We shall not get another sou out of Father, darling, not on any account. I wish you would send him a farewell note to the Hotel Westminster – just for "the firm" – would you? It *does* please me enormously that he goes back to N.Z. enthusiastic about us, and he is. The worst of it is he keeps writing about us going there. "Pray God the day be not far off." It *is*, its very far. I want Sussex and you and Arthur & the cats but only <u>YOU</u>.

MS ATL. *LJMM*, 377–8.

[1] Writing on 3 Nov., Murry proposed that he throw in the *Athenaeum*, borrow £200 from KM's father, and come out to look after her himself, thus ridding her of Ida Baker. (Murry, 202.)

[2] KM is recalling 'Thou hast made love all thy religion', a line from Murry's poem 'Supplication'. It was published in *Poems: 1917–18* (The Heron Press, 1919).

To J. M. Murry, [9 November 1919]

[Casetta Deerholm, Ospedaletti]
Sunday

(b) The Lit Sup received.

(a) 178 received.

Bogey,

Your letter was terrible but I knew it would be because of my Hellish ones to you. It was the one in which you'd phoned Sorapure[1] – But by now you will know how things are and I swear I shall not fail again, however long I stay here. Trust me once again.

The papers have come; I have been reading them. The ad. of the London Mercury gave me a terrific knock of fright.[2] Then Ive read the Times, the *disgraceful* dishonesty of it, the repellant log rolling, the review of Dostoevsky & the one of Virginia![3] My God what has happened to this age. It cannot have been like this before. Look here! We must be bold & beat these people – We must be dead straight in our reviews. If they don't care for what we say – it doesn't matter but let us come bang out into the open while we have the chance & say it. I confess the world seems to me really *too* hideous – I felt after I had read the Times that it was all like Mrs Fisher's party (you remember, when we ran away.) and the *monstrous* idea of leaving you uninvited to contribute to the Mercury; my blood is up. Lets up and at em this winter. Send me as many books as you like. Ill do them. I have got my second wind from all this. Oh my darling soul – how could I have cried out so. Blow me & my depressions – What does my personal life matter – Let it go. Its hateful. But *we* matter: we have a chance to stand for something; lets stand for it. Of course I now see plainly we shall never be successful writers – impossible. But lets be honest on the paper and give it them strong. There must be young people who see through this crabbed malice. If it were not so tragic it would be – no it wouldn't. I am *all* for the paper now; I am with you every moment in all you do for it. I am your cabin boy –

Sweep me away Bogey – sweep me away – Lets work this winter & when we meet in the spring let us forget work. As regards the Times – there has been no war – all is as before – What a crew! I only wish I were with you. I could tell you what I feel. Besides we could work together. But we must do that from here – I have the Albatross against me the whole time which is maddening but I must beat her, too. Lets just win all the way round.

At the same time I hate and loathe it all: these sets and dishonesties – don't you? I mean it is the stern daughter of the Voice of God[4] that makes one fight, not a joyful impulse –

I wish Sorapure had not seen my private note.[5] That hurt a bit – you know I winced & hung my head & felt horribly ashamed – We must never speak of ourselves to *anybody*: they come crashing in like cows into a garden.

Love believe me: Ill not fail again. Fire away – old ship – sail out serenely into the deep waters – I shall never send another signal of distress – never – and may my precious little Boge sailor whistle to the morning star. Its bright sun today with a huge wind & sea like thunder.

The grammar came. Thank you darling – But the papers are a real godsend – Bogey, tell me you forgive me. I will never be ill again. Let us *fight* now & then lay down our arms & love.

Your own own
Wig the warrior.

MS ATL. *LKM* I. 277–8; *LJMM*, 379–80.

¹ Murry wrote, 4 Nov., that 'I took your note & the prescriptions across to Sorapure this morning.' (ATL.) When they spoke on the telephone Sorapure did not believe there was any cause for alarm over KM's condition.

² On 16 Oct. the *Times Literary Supplement* carried a full-page advertisement for the first number of the *London Mercury*, promising 'as its promoters believe, the most important and influential periodical of its kind in the English speaking world'. The same issue ran a much smaller advertisement for the *Athenaeum*, 'the most scholarly of the Critical Journals'.

³ Unsigned reviews of the Garnett translation of *The Honest Thief* in the *Literary Supplement* on 23 Oct., and of *Night and Day* on 30 Oct.

⁴ The opening phrase of Wordsworth's *Ode to Duty*.

⁵ Murry had sent on a letter from Sorapure which apparently made it clear that he had seen one of her letters to her husband.

To J. M. Murry, [10 November 1919]

[Casetta Deerholm, Ospedaletti]
Monday morning.

My own dear Love,

Here is another Monday. They do seem to come round so fast – like the horses we saw at the fair – no, the *roosters* – that was our one, wasn't it? Do you remember those little Princesses who went round for ever? They wore cotton frocks & tiny leather belts. Its a chill strange day. I breakfasted in Valhalla – cracks of lightning, thunder, tearing rain. Now Im on the verandy & the clouds are immensely near and distinct like mountains. Will you please say if my Dosty is alright? I sent it rather in fear and trembling, but I meant it. I am doing Virginia for this week's novel. I don't like it, Boge. My private opinion is that it is a lie in the soul. The war never has been, that is what its message is. I dont want G. forbid mobilisation and the violation of Belgium – but the novel cant just leave the war out. There *must* have been a change of heart. It is really fearful to me the 'settling down' of human beings. I feel in the *profoundest* sense that nothing can ever be the same that as artists we are traitors if we feel otherwise: we have to take it into account and find new expressions new moulds for our new thoughts & feelings. Is this exaggeration? What *has* been – stands – but Jane Austen could not write Northanger Abbey now – or if she did Id have none of her. There is a trifling scene in Virginias book where a charming young creature in a bright fantastic attitude plays the flute: it positively frightens me – to realise this *utter coldness* & indifference.¹ But I will be very careful and do my best to be dignified and sober. Inwardly I despise them all for a set of *cowards*. We have to face our war – they wont. I believe Bogey, our whole strength depends upon our facing things. I mean facing them without any reservations or restraints. I fail because I don't face things. I feel almost I have been ill so long for that reason: we *fear* for that reason: I mean fear can get through our defences for that reason. Weve got to stand by our opinions & risk falling by them. Oh, my own Bogey, you are the only one in the world for me. We are really absolutely alone: we're a *queer couple* you know, but we ought to be together – in every sense really. *We* just because we are 'like this' ought not to be parted. We shall not be after May. Ill come home then.

Do you want to know how I am? Yesterday upstairs in my room I suddenly wanted to give a small jump – I have not given a small jump for two years – you know the kind – a jump-for-joy – I was frightened. I went over to the window & held on to the sill to be safer – then I went into the middle of the room and *did* jump. And this seemed such a miracle I felt I must tell somebody – There was nobody to tell – so I went over to the mirror – and when I saw my excited face I had to laugh. It was a marvellous experience.

Blessed little Wing! Kiss his nose for me – & whistle in his ear & say your gan'ma loves you – She does – I wish he would have *one* kitten in May – Has he grown very big? And how is Athy? And how does the house look? Does it shine? And do you have nice food? Why cant we meet in dreams & answer all each others questions – Our nights are wasted. The sea is up to the brim of the world today –

Your own
Wig.
X   X   X
X   X   X

MS ATL. *LKM* I. 278–9; *LJMM*, 380–1.

[1] In 'A Ship Comes into the Harbour', her review of *Night and Day* in the *Athenaeum*, 21 Nov. 1919, KM remarked on a minor incident in Ch. XXII where William Rodney, picking out melodies from *The Magic Flute* on his piano, briefly recalls his future fiancée playing the flute: 'The little picture suggested very happily her melodious and whimsical temperament.'

To J. M. Murry, [10 and 11 November 1919]

[Casetta Deerholm, Ospedaletti]
Monday night late in bed.

My own Love,

Your Wednesday & Thursday letters have come & the note about the hydrobromic acid[1] & Sorapures note. About your letters I feel inclined to re-quote you – but only half the phrase: there's nothing to say.[2] I can only wait & wait till Wing brings you my postcard waving his tail & you know that all is well – I shall get the cough mixture made up as soon as the acid arrives: it will be a comfort. But what a Fate that my cough should have been in these last days so much better! It is almost cruel to say that because of the trouble you have had; the chemist is still unable to get *any* of the acid here or from any town in France or Italy – Darling, tell me what this has cost your pocket; I will send you a cheque. Tell me, please!

No – you will know by now I shall not go to Menton: or mix up with Connie & Jinnie[3] in any way – With all these my defences I can ignore L.M. I an not cruel. She goes to San Remo & spends her money on rank cake & is happy I know. She thinks it is all my illness, and bides her time. I am tired of cursing myself – tired of repenting. I can say no more & do no more. You will never have to forgive me again as long as you write. I WILL NEVER CRY OUT AGAIN. You make me feel like a vampire. I cant understand why you dont hate me. There was all your pressure of work & I chose the moment to *crash*. What a fool I was – how blind! It has been the lesson of my life. You are never to fear that again; *that* at least will not happen to us again. *Last moments* are always terrible moments. Those days here were the last moments of two terrible years: that is how they appear to me. All my . . . 'feelings' for the last 2 years went into them & I cried out & of course of course of course dragged you in – Yes, I feel as though I drowned you. You almost make me feel that it is unpardonable of me to feel better; that having made you suffer so I should have justified myself by getting worse and worse . . . Do you feel that? Its a bitter taste.

The A. is here & Art & Letters & the London Mercury – Let us talk about them a little. I am hugely relieved by seeing the lion after all the trumpets. J.C. Squire is quite a big enough flea in his ear to keep him from doing aught by scratching. What a piece of *grocery prose* is his editorial. Hes a rat. But the lack of style, poise, dignity – the boosting of his shop the crying down of the wares of the gentleman over the way – good God! His 'fungoid' writers & 'sterile' young men *and* so on[4] – I take a deep malicious delight that his vulgar literary Harrods[5] should be so bad. I had thought it would be a great deal better – Really his article on the 'Poet'[6] & Nichols mock opals[7] & the toothcomb run through Ruperts bright locks[8] *and* the reviews[9] – so undistinguished – I remembered Squire on Masefield in the old days – He was hatched out of the Everlasting Mercy, you know: wrote his first parody on it – & now he's back licking the hand he bit and cut his teeth on.[10]

But this makes me keener than ever on our paper (*our* in humility, love – its your hat – yes I know.) Bogey, Howe is not up to much is he. Can you get out of him? He cant write: hes *no* point of view. He hasnt a word to say about Fay Compton yet theres nothing but her[11] & look at his prose – 'need we say', 'needless to say', 'needless to specify' – He's absolutely colourless. The article on The Critic is excellent[12] but of course the paper has only one gem.[13] That is I think flawless. I feel I shall have to send you a telegram about it tomorrow. It thrilled me so. I had to run to the door & search the stars & the dark moving sea: I couldn't get calm after it – And all the while I felt how supremely good that Hardy should be so understood in his day – how supremely right that you should speak for this silent generation – We shall remember it with joy all our lives. Oh, I feel our responsibility is so tremendous: I wish now I could take back my review of Stella Benson & beat it into shape. I shall write far better from henceforward. And I am so strong now. I can tackle any amount of work.

You are at rest again, my beloved? I hardly dare to ask. I shall send little Wing as my messenger: "She says is it alright." And then he must come & tell me: "yes he says its alright but I don't know if he wants to see you." "Oh Wing, go back & see." He is gone. Ill have to wait.

Its midnight. The sea roars. I must lie down & go to sleep like a good girl. Today I have been gathering roses on the hill: the hedges are full of deep cream roses. But I cant tell you these things or anything until – Wing comes back.

Your love
Wig.

It is the papers that solve the L.M. problem. Thats why they matter so.

Tuesday. I wake up so happy my darling love. I just want to say this. If you can make somebody send me regularly the Lit. Sup., the Weekly Guardian, and of course OUR paper I can go on here *full of fire.* These papers have made me feel in touch with THE paper: I cannot exist without mental stimulants even though they are such that provoke my rage or contempt. They create a vacuum which is filled with ones own ideas. Is that foolish to you. But you see here: they are Society for me: my kittens, my acquaintances, all the talk I have, all the interruptions which send L.M. out of the room. Do you see what they mean? I will pay an extra 10/- a month for postage etc.

MS ATL. *LJMM*, 381–3.

[1] A diluted solution of hydrobromic acid was used as a cough suppressant.

[2] Murry wrote on 5 Nov., after receiving her letter of the previous Sunday, 'You have had no letters. I write every day, you know I do. I mustn't give way. I'll just say that I am in body perfectly well; but I don't know how long things will last if this strain goes on. Those silly lines I wrote when I was young keep singing in my head: There's nothing to say: my heart is dead. It isn't really; but there are moments when I feel it's on the point of giving out.' (Murry, 203–4.)

[3] KM's cousin Connie Beauchamp and her close friend and companion Jinnie Fullerton, who settled in Menton after retiring from their nursing-home in Hampstead.

[4] J. C. Squire's editorial in the first number of the *London Mercury*, Nov. 1919, was in part a tirade against new and recent movements in literature. He spoke of 'young writers who have strayed and lost themselves amongst experiments, many of them foredoomed to sterility', and observed how 'Year after year we have new fungoid growths of feeble pretentious imposters'.

[5] The large, reputable store in Knightsbridge.

[6] 'The Future Poet and Our Time.'

[7] A short story by Robert Nichols, 'The Smile of the Sphinx'.

[8] 'It's Not Going to Happen Again', a poem by Rupert Brooke.

[9] The magazine carried 43 pages of short reviews and notes.

[10] Although Squire does not mention John Masefield in his article, KM presumably regarded that poet as the kind of traditionalist urged on the reader. Masefield had published his long poem *The Everlasting Mercy* in 1911, and Squire in his *Collected Parodies* (1913) included 'If Wordsworth Had Written "The Everlasting Mercy"'.

[11] In the *Athenaeum*, 7 Nov. 1919, P. P. Howe reviewed *Summertime*, a play by Louis N. Parker at the Royalty Theatre, with Fay Compton as leading actress.

[12] Murry's unsigned leading article, 'The Social Duty of the Critic'.

[13] Murry's own 'The Poetry of Mr. Hardy', reviewing vol. i of *The Collected Poems of Thomas Hardy*.

To J. M. Murry, [11 November 1919]

[Casetta Deerholm, Ospedaletti]

Salzmann is quite a good chap but he needs watching[1] – A '*memory of pre-Pelman date*' is a bit thick in the A.[2] Aren't the Mercury reviews unthinkably bad! The vocabulary!! But we must get some poetry. Ou est Henri King?[3] E. Stanley is so slight & thin!![4]

I have this day despatched to the office (addressed to you) Richard Kurt 7/6

Splendid Fairing 6/-

Young Physician 6/-

If All these Young Men 7/-

Great House 7/-

Living Alone 6/-[5]

Three parcils. Two novels came today, no letter. I am doing Virginia for this week. Next week I shall do Hewlett,[6] Stackpoole[7] together & the week after Monkhouse[8] & Benjy.[9] That finishes all Ive got. I am on for *any* frisk you care to send me and have got (p.G.) my second wind.

Mistral blowing – v. cold, trees & sea like metal. But my room upstairs is as good as a verandy & warm & in the sun. Love to Violet & to Athy and to Wing (what is left over).

Wig.

Postcard. MS ATL. *LJMM*, 384.

[1] In the last number of the *Athenaeum*, 7 Nov. 1919, L. F. Salzman wrote 'Biblia-A-Biblia'.

[2] The well-known advertisements for the 'Pelman method' of improving memory.

[3] Henry King was the pseudonym Murry used for his poems in the *Athenaeum*.

[4] None of KM's poems, under the name of Elizabeth Stanley, had appeared since 'Secret Flowers' on 22 Aug.

[5] That week KM reviewed, under 'Three Approaches', Stephen Hudson's *Richard Kurt*, Constance Holme's *The Splendid Fairing*, and Stanley Weyman's *The Great House*. The other volumes are referred to in earlier notes.

[6] Maurice Hewlett's *The Outlaw* was discussed with Eden Phillpotts' *Evander* as 'The Plain and the Adorned' on 2 Jan. 1920.

[7] KM did not review H. de Vere Stacpoole's recent novel, *The Beach of Dreams*. An unsigned review had already appeared in the *Athenaeum*, 10 Oct. 1919.

[8] *True Love*, by Allen Monkhouse, and *Children of No Man's Land*, by G. B. Stern, were reviewed under 'Control and Enthusiasm' on 28 Nov. 1920.

[9] George Stevenson's *Benjy*, and Mrs Humphry Ward's *Cousin Philip*, were reviewed as 'A Post-War and a Victorian Novel' on 19 Dec. 1919.

To J. M. Murry, [11 November 1919]

[Casetta Deerholm, Ospedaletti]
Tuesday.

Good News!

175 received & Rutter[1] received.

[Drawing of a heart with an arrow through it]

My little mate,

(I shall answer your letter après.) I have just had the extraordinary comfort of seeing a really first chop doctor – the man Ansaldi. L.M. was at San Remo – it was getting dusky. There was a ring at the bell & I opened the door & nearly fell into the arms of a beaming glistening Jewish gentleman mit a vhite felt hat. I immediately decided he was a body snatcher & said, most rudely "Vous désirez?" At which he replied Ansaldi & abashed me very much. He came in – dark bright skin, gleaming eyes – a slight stoop and said "oh, vot a nice little house you have here!" The *spit* of the music halls. It made me feel terribly laughy. I don't know – L.M. away this solitary spot, this queer stranger with his stethoscope in a *purse* – it would be a purse – & me in less time than it takes Wing to pounce sitting draped in my flowery shawl with my discarded woollen coats strewing the floor like wictims. He examined me before he saw my chart. My bad lung he says is drying – there is only a small spot left at the apex (when I was in London there was the spot the size of a hand.) The other has also a small spot at the apex. I told him my history to date & he says that I have gained weight & can eat are excellent signs. There is no reason (bar accident) why I should not recover. "Never to be a lion or shoot the chamois or the hare (figurez-vous, my darling. Id rather feed them with rose-leaves) but to lead a normal life – not the life of an invalid. The chances are he says 99 to 100 that I can do this. He gave me no medicine, saw my prescriptions & said that was just what he would have prescribed. The fact of so little fever, my appetite weight & that I can sleep are all in my favour. He says it will take two years to cure me but I shall be a great deal better by April and able to live at home but *never* to be in London after September. He was urgent about no mental worry, *very* urgent but work all you like and be in the air & walk but never to tire yourself. Always stop everything before you are tired. Ill tell you the truth. He said I was not half warmly enough dressed. He was most emphatic on that – though I was wearing my jaegers & a jersey & cardigan – He says this climate is admirable & especially here because the air is *balsamic* & positively healing, but one must take absolutely no risk as regards a chill. Never to go out uncovered & really never to know what it is to feel cold. He says that wastes ones energy fighting the cold. This I am sure is sensible. But what was so good was his *confidence* in me. It made me feel so confident. He told me I had so much *life* even in my skin and my eyes and voice that it was abnormal for me to be ill and that was my great 'pull' over other consumptives. Hes coming again in a fortnight. But after closely examining my chart & reading *aloud* that writing we couldn't read he pronounced a definite improvement. Isnt that really superb. (Ill not always be such an egoist.) Of course he told me a chill or influenza might mean disaster, or mental worry – but I must try & avoid those things. And also he impressed on me that Ill never be a lion. That of course is bad; one wants to be a lion, but after these years to think I could lead a normal life is lion-like enough.

But here's a brilliant, clever, sympathetic doctor on the spot, see? When I go to San Remo I must please to call on him so that he may show me some little politenesses (as though he had a collection of them. I saw them, darling little tinies, sitting on his finger.) Then like the bee, the lizard, & the man in the poem 'he went away'. *I* went upstairs, put on an extra pair of stockings & a scarf & came down & had tea & ate four delicious fresh dried figs with it. Terribly good!

I wont spare money or fires. Ill be as good as gold & May will be *divine*. I shall spend the £2.10.0 on wood Bogey but now *keep* the book money. Keep little Wing & keep him warm.

Rutter is good. Ill do it. But Ive sent back Kurt so I must write & ask em for a copy.[2] Fancy calling my writing *critical essays*! I saw you wink at Wing & Wing, overcome, turning a catherine wheel (with a k).

Do you know what time I go to bed here: 7.00 or 6.45. There is not a chair or a sofa to sit on: I am driven there. But its a good idea. Everything seems to me good tonight except you. Youre BEST.

Answer me. Its so curious. I still feel positively shy of you. I cant ask you to kiss me even after I 'broke down' so.

Bogey, when you have the time & if it is *easy* can you send me a woollen scarf. Ill pay you by cheque (I *must* you *must* let me pay for things or I shall stamp and rage) but I mean one of those soft blanketty scarves that go round once & twice & cover ones mouth. Do you know the kind of thing I mean? Ask Arthur. I feel he might be very practical about clothes. But it must be *woolly* & long & warm. Ill pay up to £2.2.0 for it & you can choose the colour – a grey green I should think or purple – yes purple – or whatever you like. This is just when you have the time. I expect Jaegar[3] would have them. But I need it here. *Not* fearfully urgent – just when you have the leisure.

Now goodbye my One

Your One
Too
(a joke.)

MS ATL. *LKM* I. 279–81; *LJMM*, 384–6.

[1] Murry had sent on a letter from Frank Rutter (1876–1937), one of the editors of *Art and Letters*, a periodical which ran from 1917 to 1920. The Autumn 1919 issue had published her story 'The Pictures'.

[2] KM did not do the critical work Rutter apparently asked for. The reference to the novel *Richard Kurt*, by Stephen Hudson, which she reviewed in the *Athenaeum* on 7 Nov. 1919, may touch on the background to Virginia Woolf's enigmatic diary entry some months before on 14 June 1919, when she recorded, 'Katherine looks so ill & haggard', and observed, 'And then there's the question of Katherine's writing. Isn't she a little querulous & restless about that? Standing emphatically yet not quite firmly on her rights as an artist; as people do who must insist upon being one. In token of this she told me a long & to me rather distasteful story about her dealings with a man called Schiff, who wanted her to contribute to art & letters, & dared to offer her advice, upon which she got on her high horse, & wrote him such a letter that he replied humbly – in a style that I couldn't make anything of, & indeed the rights & wrongs of the whole business escaped me, though I protested, I'm ashamed to say, that I share Katherine's indignation. (*The Diary of Virginia Woolf*, ed. Ann Olivier Bell, vol. i (1977), 281.) Stephen Hudson was the pen-name of the wealthy art patron Sydney Schiff (see p. 268, n. 1), who provided the financial backing for *Art and Letters*. The KM letter Woolf refers to does not survive.

[3] Jaeger's, a shop in Regent Street selling its own brand of woollen clothes.

To J. M. Murry, [12 November 1919]

[Casetta Deerholm, Ospedaletti]
Wednesday.

My precious own,

I got a telegram from you today. It was an extra luxury, a *great* joy but it is not to happen again. A nice little boy literally *blew* in with it.

Strange strange day! My party has just gone. Connie, Jinnie (admirable person) and Papa. They arrived at about 10.30 (I expected them 2 hours later) but it didnt matter. The Casetta seemed to turn into a dolls house. Pa couldnt even find room for his glasses. The womens furs & coats & silk wraps & bags were scattered everywhere – Father suggested a run into San Remo which we took. I was I am just a little corrupted Bogey darling. That big soft purring motor, the rugs & cushions – the warmth the delicacy all the uglies so far away. We 'ran' long past San Remo. It was *thrilling* for me. I didn't dare to speak hardly because it was so wonderful & people laughing & silly Pa talking Maori down the whistle to the chauffeur. Very silly –

but very nice, somehow. It carried me away. Then we got up &
bought a cake & were as they say the cynosure of all eyes & it was
nice, too. I was glad the chemist saw me. (See what a snob you
married!) & then while Connie & Jinnie were at Morandis Pa & I
talked & the sun streamed into the car & he said we were like a couple
of hothouse plants ripening. They have just gone. Jinnie left me a pair
of *horn* spegglechiks of her grandfathers (the kind on a long black
ribbon, which suit me admirably.) She took photos of the Casetta, too,
& said 'theyll do to send your husband'. I don't know what happened.
They seemed to me so many. Father at the last, was wonderfully dear
to me. I mean – to be held & kissed & called my precious child was
almost too much. To feel someones arms round me & someone saying
"get better you little wonder. You're your mother over again." Its not
being called a wonder – its having *love* present close warm to be felt
and returned. And then both these women had been desperately
homesick for their dogs so they understood Wing. That was nice too.

Pa did not like this place, neither did they. They were horrified by
the cold. Pa said at Menton they have had *none* of this bitter wind –
that it has never been cold like today. He seemed to think I had made
a great mistake to be in such a thin house & so exposed. So, alas! did
they. They said Menton was warm, still, with really exquisite walks,
sheltered. I said Id consider going there in the spring. But I wont.
When the bad weather is over here will be warm too & I dont want a
town. I don't want to uproot. At the same time I was a bit sorry it was
so much warmer. I *fed* them & Pa left me five 3 Castles cigarettes!!! He
made the running, talking french – telling stories – producing
spectacles (he had *four* pairs of them – Connie had three & Jinnie had
three. At one moment they were all trying each others on – in this
little room – it was like a dream). [A drawing of six pairs of spectacles]
And here on the table are five daisies & an orchid that Pa picked for
me & tied with a bit of grass & handed me. If I had much to forgive
him I would forgive him much for this little bunch of flowers. What
have they to do with it all?

                                                            Wig.

MS ATL. *LKM* I. 281–3; *LJMM*, 386–7.

To J. M. Murry, [13 November 1919]

                              [Casetta Deerholm, Ospedaletti]
                                                      Thursday
My own Love,
    This is the third day without a letter. I believe the post office does it
on purpose. I have a box there which I bought for 14 lire where all my

letters and so on are kept so as to avoid any mistake, but they don't care.

I went to the post today, down the road past the railway station through a small 'place' & up some steps. Did you ever go that way? I did not cough once all the way to the station & then I came home past the shops & wasnt in the least tired. It is a brilliant day, bitter cold here but on the level – gorgeous. Theres no doubt about it Boge the Casetta is *not* a warm one. This morning, for instance, it was ICY here, really perishing cold, even in my room the wind was so sharp. I went out dressed in furs & a shawl & woolly coat & after ten minutes on the level was much too hot. There was no wind there either. But coming back as soon as I began to climb the steps the wind could be felt. The two front rooms are of course unlivable until after lunch but that shelter is as bad – even worse its a wind trap. I shall always when its fine enough to go out walk in the mornings now & then (as usual) write here in the dining room in the afternoon. But the difference of temperature between here & in the village! Did you ever explore the village, darling? It is so lovely – more beautiful than Bandol. All is seen against the huge background of the purple mountain. It was silent today except for an old woman crying fish & the boys flinging a ball among the trees of the place, but it feels gay – rather fantastic. The air smelled of pines and of deep yellow roses which grow everywhere like weeds: they even climb up the aloe trees.

I cant describe (yes I *could*) what real convalescence feels like. I decide to walk in the road & instead of stopping, putting my stick off the pavement, then one foot, then the other, I take a little spring with all three legs and have to hold myself back from crying to an indifferent native – *did* you see that superb feat? (That is not intended for a Pa joke.)

I am reviewing Virginia to send tomorrow; its devilish hard. Talk about intellectual snobbery – her book *reeks* of it (but I cant say so.) You would dislike it. Youd never read it. Its so long and so tāhsōme. By the way my dear I gave Connie the Oxford Book of English Verse to look at yesterday while she was testing somebody's specs, & she said a moment after: there are some quite pretty things here, dear. Who are they by? . . . What do you think of that? I *should* have replied Temple Thurston.[1] Instead I pretended not to hear.

Look here. I want you terribly today. I want to see you – hold you, touch you, play with you, talk to you, kiss you – call you. I want to open one of those huge great cotton pods with you & see whats inside. I want to discuss the novel with you & to tell you what a darling of darlings you are.

Wig.

MS ATL. *LKM* I. 283–4; *LJMM*, 388–9.

¹ Ernest Temple Thurston (b. 1879), prolific writer of fiction, plays, and inferior verse.

To J. M. Murry, [14 November 1919]

[Casetta Deerholm, Ospedaletti]
Friday

174, 173 received.

My Precious Own,

These are the first letters Ive had since last Monday & in them you say mine are not like stars appearing. What happens to our letters? If only one knew, theres some incredibly *silly* reason why they dont arrive, yet Pa said he got his regular & piping hot in three days. I loved your Sunday picture letter & saw it 'ever so' plain – you crosslegged, Arthur reading, & Wing discovering terra nuova in the chest of drawers.

I am glad you have seen Brett. I feel about Lawrence – that I dont in the least know whether I want to see him or not.¹ I do & then there sweeps over me an *inscrutable* knowledge of his feeling about *you* about you & me. He doesn't understand *us* or believe in *us* – & there you are. I cant do with people who don't. I am not one, individual, eternal, two in one, co-equal, co-eternal (or whatever it is). This, if people want me, they must realise. Thats one reason why I *hate* L.M. She's always always trying to make me 'one' again. But I must not speak of her. My life here with her must be between me and nothing.

Its a bitter cold day, pouring rain, wind, fog and air like acid. I am sitting in my room before the fire wrapped up snug with a hot bottil & Jaegar dressing gown over all. I am terrified of the cold & would go any lengths to avoid it. Ansaldis "chill in your case would be a fatal disaster" rings in my ears when the weather turns like this. At the same time God what courage we have to remain apart, knowing that. It amazes me. But we could do nothing else – nothing else at all. It would be very wonderful to be rid of these melancholy thoughts – for them to withdraw into the forest & not to come out again for – say 50 years. The fog and ceaseless drip of rain makes them very *impish*.

I wrote to Rutter saying 'yes' & to Grant R² the day before yesterday. Now Sylvia Lynd is on my conscience. Ill write her on Sunday.

How I hate furrin parts today! I feel numbed when the sun goes in. Thats a great mistake – to think it a good idea to live facing the sea. Ive discovered its a bad one. For this reason. When the sun is not out the sea is like a mirror without light. It simply *asks* for the sun far more than the land does. Theres nothing to say my heart is dead³ says the sea & goes on saying it in a loud keening voice. Another discovery is not to live alone & more or less tied to a house where the sea sounds so loud. If one broke up the noise with talk & kisses & walks it would be alright but it has a frightfully depressing exciting effect if one doesnt. Sometimes I lie awake literally all night – so excited that I play demon, *sing* & talk out loud to try & work it off. If there were a second person I don't think one would notice it. L.M. says she never does. These things one just has to find out.

I suppose Bogey darling there is not the vaguest hint of a house for us, is there? Do you feel its a great deal more difficult than you had imagined? I wish Fate would smile on our loves for once.

How awful about Marie Dahlerup[4] & yes, do please always open any letters for me – or anything that may come. I much prefer you to.

L.M. is taking the train in to San Remo to buy a few things for herself (???). No, I wont ask. But this letter shall be posted from there. Its almost too dull to send. Forgive me love; its the ugly weather and the COLD.

Its less than six months now before you come. And then we wont be separated again – no long separations – and we'll be *alone* and together. If Virginia should not come in time this week, youve got Dosty havent you? But I hope she will.

Goodbye my own precious darling. I am all yours & I love you for ever.

Wig.

Let me see Cinnamon when you can Bogey. How marvellous Hardys love poems must be – these last. But the earlier one you quoted, The Crucifix[5] – isnt it ——

MS ATL. *LKM* I. 284–5; *LJMM*, 389–90.

[1] Murry wrote on 9 Nov. that he had heard through Mark Gertler of Lawrence's plan to go to Italy. 'I am going to send him your address. He might quite well have the chance of coming to see you.' (Murry, 205.) KM had probably been told by Koteliansky of Lawrence's anger earlier in the year when Murry rejected his contributions to the *Athenaeum*. See *CLKM* II. 310 n. 2.

[2] Fellow of Trinity College, Oxford, the novelist Franklin Thomas Grant Richards (1872–1948) set up as a publisher in 1897. He had recently made approaches to KM for a collection of stories.

[3] KM is again taking up Murry's words to her on 5 Nov. 'Those silly lines I wrote when I was very young keep singing in my head: "there's nothing to say: my heart is dead".' (Murry, 203–4.)

[4] A Danish acquaintance of KM's and her sisters, who had written to say she intended coming to stay at Portland Villas.

[5] In 'The Poetry of Mr. Hardy', his review of *The Collected Poems of Thomas Hardy*, vol. i, in the *Athenaeum*, 7 Nov. 1919, Murry had quoted five stanzas from 'Near Lanivet, 1872', with its imagery of a woman's arms stretched along a signpost as though on a cross.

To Richard Murry, [14 November 1919]

S.S. Casetta (Homeward Bound) | Porto Maurizio |
Italia.
Friday night.

My dear old Boy, I am at present being stared at by (1) very old
wingèd beetle who is evidently looking in to see if this is his club or not
and whether there is an octogenarian or two to have a chat with. (2)
Three white moths with their little moths' noses pressed as flat as flat
can be. (3) An Unknown with six legs and the appearance of a
diminutive lobster. (4) One very large grey moth, apparently in a
shawl, who appears by her anxiety to be endeavouring to see if there
really *is* a large barrel of butter hidden behind the counter for regular
customers only or not. All these are on the outside of my windy pane
drawn to the light because I have not closed the shutters. It's a black
night, calm, with a great sweeping sound of sea.

Swear no oaths, young fellow, unswear them on the spot. I couldn't
risk your having the penalty exacted – I couldn't bear you to be in
New Guinea for six muns or weeks once I get home. This member of
the firm is far far too fond of you to have you away. It seems to me that
all of us have our work AND our play cut out for years. I see, attached
to the country house – The Heron of Herons – a large 'plain but
beautiful' barn – used for the printing BUT it has an outside staircase
(like you have leading to haylofts in the Best Barns) and this staircase
does lead to a kind of loft which has been turned into a bedroom and
den for Arthur M. It's about four o'clock on an autumn afternoon. I
run up the steps, knock at the door. Arthur opens it in his shirt sleeves
(I always see you in your shirt sleeves) and says 'come in. I've just put
the kettle on for tea.' I say: 'Oh Arthur this great parcel of books has
just been sent you by an Italian printer and when we have had tea
we'd better go over to the house FOR Thomas Hardy has driven over
and is having tea with Jack.' And so on while they live happier and
happier ever after . . .

Jack sent me a little pen picture of you and he at the top of the
house, with Wing exploring, the afternoon he read the play to you. He
hardly says a word about Cinnamon and Angelica – just wonders if it
is good and hopes it is. I think, soberly, it's a masterpiece. It belongs
to a different world to ours. There's a kind of stillness upon it –
something ageless, as though it had always been there waiting for Jack
to cause the light to fall upon it and so reveal it. Difficult to describe
quite what I mean. But it seems to me our brother grows more
wonderful every week. I do fight like billy-o but I can't help being
homesick for him all the same. Who could? You see we are not divided
up into compartments like other human beings seem to be. I haven't

got one nice little door called Jack which I can open when he's here and cheerfully shut when he's away, but printed in the largest lettering on all the doors and gates and outposts of my dwelling is 'This is the House that Jack Built' (decorations by Arthur Murry. Delapidations by Athenaeum and Wingli Murry.)

I wish you would come into this room now for a talk – sit before this wood fire with me and agree that one log has a head like a crocodile and one is like a poodle. The smell is good – of pines and bluegums – and I have one very large pine cone I would cheerfully sacrifice for a kind of illuminated address of welcome, my *dear dear* old Boy.

Here comes dinner. I must sit up and prepare to attack it. We have funny food here – macaroni in all the most fantastical shapes and devices – in letters and rats' tails and imitation lace and imitation penny stamps and triangles and shavings. It must be fun to run wild in the Macaroni Works. I wonder they don't have an Animal Series, camels, frogs and Nelephants in one's soup would be particularly nice.

I am afraid that this letter is not, on the whole, as serious as it ought to be. I trust, sir, by the time it reaches you its demeanour will be composed, reverent, grave, as befits one who is calling upon a young gentleman at a Publishing House in Thavies Inn.

Take care of yourself in these storms. Do not go up on deck without your big muffler; do *not attempt* to stow the top-gallant sail but *be certain* to let go the fore top-gallant halyards while a squall rages.

But here's to Fair Weather for us all. Yours with as much love as you wish,

Katherine.

MS R. Murry. *LKM* I. 266–7.

To J. M. Murry, [15 November 1919]

[Casetta Deerholm, Ospedaletti]
Saturday

Dearest Own,

I have just come downstairs & lighted my fire – do you smell the bluegum wood & the pommes de pin? Its a perishing coal black day – wet, dripping wet, foggy, folded – drear. The fire is too lovely: it looks like a stag's head – two horns of flame. I managed to get Virginia off yesterday but NOT without a struggle. I wanted to be sincere. I felt I had a duty to perform. Oh dear oh dear! Whats it all come to, I wonder?

This morning Jinnie Fullerton sent me a box of Khedive cigarettes.

That was very nice of her. I admire her terribly. Pa sent me a letter. I feel that between them they are going to *move* me from here. It is, I confess extremely cold and draughty but on the other hand – privacy privacy privacy. I *wont* go into hotels or pensionettes or rooms where I am not private. Thats the *essential*. They, that is Pa & his Co. seem to think of Ospedaletti as a kind of rock that rears its awful form.

Oh darling precious Jag Boge isnt it nice when I write so small? I am taking very tiny little stitches with my pen & making eyes of admiration at myself. Wish the Albatross would produce lunch. Its nearly *one* & lunch is at *12* & I am shaking like a leaf & trembling with want of it. Now a fly has walked bang into the fire – rushed in, committed suicide.

Lunch.

Lunch over. Pendant ce repas L.M. suggested I should take the train into San Remo & get another back in ten minutes – just to enjoy the sun. I wouldnt drive a *strong* pig to market today – its such a weedkiller, so this suggestion for me made me angry. She then said 'Of course it is damp, the damp went right *through* me but you do such funny things.' Now I *dont* do funny things, I havent for ages & I hate to be reminded. I came back & smoked a cigarette & got over it. On the cigarette paper it declares: Qu' aucun *moment* de leur fabrication, ni par quelque procédé que ce soit, aucune substance aromatisante, opiacée ou chimique, *en un mot*, qu'aucun *corps étranger* n'est introduit dans le tabac . . .

One feels there must be snippets of sheik brûlé in em after that.

Did I tell you – when I was in San Remo in that motor I went to a bread shop and there I saw a queer shaped loaf which looked nice for tea, a kind of tea bread. So I said Combien & he said I must pèse it Madame. Will you take it? So I said yes. And he pèsed it – and did it up in a paper with a pink ficelle and said cinq francs juste Madame, . . . Now what do you do then? I paid & took it and walked out – one living curse. But do the brave give it back? Which is the lesser humiliation? Have you ever decided that? I was awfully ashamed of myself. Then I realised that if it hadn't been for the motor I would not have paid – it was the price of corruption. All the same I read an article on small cars for tiny people (2 people, their luggage, a cat and its saucer & bastick) for 3d a mile – all round the world from door to door. Self starter, electrical installation and a bag for the money to roll into when you come to the place where money rolls. That sounded to me the spit of us. I thought Wing as cleaner would be so good – in overalls you know, wiping his little nose box with a morceau of cotton waste. The trouble with those cars is they ought to cost 3d to start with, it ought to be *all* 3d – 3d all the way through. "I'll have 3d worth of petrol please and a thrippeny horse to pull us out of this hole."

By the way Re Jeanne. She has been sending hampers of fruit even to *Kay*. Didn't you get one? Arent they prize mingies. I have been silly enough for today. I <u>wish</u> a letter would come. Id like some good news to put in this room – no to wear in my bosom. I am very well darling love, with an oldfashioned face coming back, very bright eyes and a pink colour like Bandol. I hardly know it when I powder its nose.

Addio my little mate,

Your Wig-wife.

MS ATL. *LKM* I. 285–7; *LJMM*, 390–2.

To J. M. Murry, [16 November 1919]

[Casetta Deerholm, Ospedaletti]
Sunday 8 a.m.

My own Bogey,

It was a fearful *blow* to get no letters yesterday again. I shall never understand it. When L.M. came back after the last chance I *hid* for a moment or two upstairs just to delay the 'no letters – nothing'. Perhaps my luck will turn today and the sea have a pearl.

Such a night! Immense wind and sea and cold. This is certainly no 'pensive citadel'.[1] This morning the storm still rages. Its a blow. I long to go out and have a walk but I darent face the wind.

What is this about the novel.[2] Tell me thou little eye among the blind[3] (its easy to see whom my bedfellow has been). But seriously Bogey, the more I read the more I feel all these novels will not do. After them Im a swollen sheep looking up who is not fed.[4] And yet I feel one can lay down no rules: Its not in the least a question of material or style or plot. I can only think in terms like 'a change of heart'. I cant imagine how after the war these men can pick up the old threads as tho' it never had been. Speaking to *you* Id say we have died and live again. How can that be the same life? It doesn't mean that Life is the less precious of that the 'common things of light and day'[5] are gone. They are not gone, they are intensified, they are illumined. Now we know ourselves for what we are. In a way its a tragic knowledge. Its as though, even while we live again we face death. But *through Life*: thats the point. We see death in life as we see death in a flower that is fresh unfolded. Our hymn is to the flower's beauty – we would make that beauty immortal because we *know*. Do you feel like this – or otherwise – or how?

But of course you dont imagine I mean by this knowledge 'let us eat and drink-ism'. No, I mean 'deserts of vast eternity'.[6] But the difference between you and me is (perhaps Im wrong) I couldn't tell anybody *bang out* about those deserts. They are my secret. I might write about a boy eating strawberries or a woman combing her hair on a windy morning & that is the only way I can ever mention them. But they *must* be there. Nothing less will do. They can advance & retreat, curtsey, caper to the most delicate airs they like but I am bored to Hell by it all. Virginia – par exemple.

Here is the sun. Ill get up. My knees are cold and my feet swim between the sheets like fishes.

Si tu savais com-me je t'ai . . . me.

Oh Bogey darling Heart, I shall never reconcile myself to absence from you – never. Its waste of life. But be happy, my precious.

                                                                        Wig.

MS ATL. *LKM* I. 287–8; *LJMM*, 392–3.

[1] 'And students in their pensive citadels', from William Wordsworth's sonnet 'Nuns fret not at their convent's narrow room'.

[2] In his letter of 13 Nov., Murry told her, 'You see, I reckon on you absolutely for the novels. Your novel page, I know, is one of the features most appreciated in the paper, and any interruption of it would do us great harm. . . . You are so *sure*, besides being so delicate. . . . What I feel, and what a great many other people feel, is that as long as your novel page is there, there can't be a really bad number of the *Athenaeum*.' (Murry, 210.)

[3] 'Thou best Philosopher, who yet dost keep | Thy heritage, thou Eye among the blind', Wordsworth, *Ode: Intimations of Immortality*, ll. 111–12.

[4] 'The hungry sheep look up and are not fed, | But swoln with wind', Milton, *Lycidas*, ll. 125–6.

[5] 'And fade into the light of common day', Wordsworth, *Ode: Intimations of Immortality*, l. 77.

[6]   But at my back I always hear
                Time's wingèd chariot hurrying near;
                And yonder all before us lie
                Deserts of vast eternity.

(Andrew Marvell, 'To His Coy Mistress'.)

To J. M. Murry, [16 November 1919]

                                        [Casetta Deerholm, Ospedaletti]

Cheque received.

Sunday night.

Yes my darling Love your mood travelled to me unbroken, perfect, exquisite. It filled my heart, filled it to the brim so that I felt a great stillness and could scarcely breathe for joy. Oh my own, I share, I share it all – your knowledge of how we have suffered, how we seem of all our generation to have been to the war, and your AND YET. I am looking at the letter as I write. Queer little fanciful things happen sometimes . . . Each time you write AND YET[1] these letters take a shape which is *like* you – they are a minute manifestation of you. The

A walks, the Y is a man waving his arms, the E is someone sitting down . . . Oh, all this is nonsense, but all this is true, too. I remember at the Villa Flora sewing a button on your pigglejams and the button became a little image of you – a *sign* – so that I fell in love with it and kissed it and said to it – now stay there for six months and I felt that it understood and felt very strong and determined every time you did it up. But your belongings are like that for me – they're sacred. When I see your hat it becomes the 'only hat in the world' for me. Do you know how I love you, you strange little husband? Do you know how I dream sometimes that your darling dark head is beside me on the pillows? How often Ive seen the dawn come into our top bedroom at Hampstead, waited until I could distinguish the figure of the man on the horse in the picture – how often I have just touched you, sleeping, with my hand – or watched that dark beloved boyish head turned away from me. Mysterious Love!

Beautifully you say our suffering might pass away as a dream.[2] When I am *really* with you it is gone. The day I watched you climb these steps you had been to the fountain, you wore Feltie & a sprig of geranium. I watched you coming up towards me, slowly, smiling and something within me cried: '*Here comes my world*'. We are like the twin doors of that *home* which is ours – I enter it through you & you through me.

This afternoon, sitting by the fire in my room I suffered from desire as I never have suffered before. Everything seemed to become suddenly almost unbearably vivid and alive and lovely. It was a hot summer day – early evening – and we were in a big room like a studio with a great low divan. The shutters were shut: we were terribly, terribly happy. We looked deep deep in each others eyes smiling at the happiness we gave, we were giving each other. You know that strange smile when the lips are so dark and the eyes gleam . . . I can't write about it even now.

Little Wing's telegram came this early afternoon. The postmistress must have known it was from him. She wrote Wing[3] just as he would have done. It was a VERY lovely surprise.

I return the American letters.[4] They are extremely gratifying. How nice the people sound. Of course you & I went to America & met them. '*Pleased* to meet you, *Mr* Murry.' She was charming. Now Ill go to sleep. Goodnight my precious.

MS ATL. *LJMM*, 393–4.

---

[1] Murry wrote on 11 Nov., 'I am convinced that you and I have suffered the war more than anyone, that we have really known, do really know, what sorrow and pain are . . . AND YET I have more happiness, I can touch moments of deeper and more certain happiness, than anyone

I've known.' (Murry, 207–8) Murry three times used the phrase in capital letters, to set their suffering against their more abiding contentment.

² Murry told her in the same letter of his 'feeling that we are children to whom nightmares of suffering happen, which still might pass away as a dream' (Murry, 208).

³ KM wrote the W with an elaborate flourish.

⁴ Letters from admiring readers of the *Athenaeum*.

To J. M. Murry, [17 November 1919]

[Casetta Deerholm, Ospedaletti]
Monday

Your Wednesday letter & the books received.

My Bogey,

After the poisonous day yesterday it was calm here this morning & I went to post. It was lovely in the village – warm as toast. I fanned my wings many times & at the post I found the letter about the table & the linen. I read it sitting under a tree that smelled of nutmegs – it was full of great bunches of flowers & the bees were busy in and out. Reminded me of old Dan Chaucer. I love to feel you are gathering the feathers for the *new* perfect nest & an oak table is a very big feather indeed. Oh, *what it means to get letters.* I wonder if you wrote me one on Monday? It never came. Here at this moment comes L.M. with your Thursday letter describing the dinner party & E.M.F. staying the night & the cutlets.[1] Violet is a treasure, Boge. It warms my heart chauffes it to hear they are keen on the paper. Oh, I am so *dissatisfied* with myself. You say lovely things to me & I feel Ill be better next time & then again I seem to *miss* it. You're right: Im not a real 'cricket' at all & only sing on our private hearth really. But I do my best & *thank Heaven if I please you.* But I feel such a fly beside you – and I feel I ought to explain myself more. My review of Virginia haunts me. I *must* improve. You know I just worship that old paper. There it is, your ship – I stare at it – examine it – wonder at it. Thank you for the cheque darling. Its a grateful sight. I am so glad you have gone to Porter. Hes good. He wrote me a nice little note here the other day hoping I was better. Hes a *sound dentist* too. The 4 books *all* look deeply interesting. Ill try & do them justice.

Its a TERRIBLY cold day – really shocking. I have a big fire & a rug & bottle and am wrapped up. The air is like ice, the sea like a sheet of lacquer. Truly this is a cold spot Boge. Yet I don't want to leave it. I *love* Ospedaletti. I dont want Menton & a *band.* Here one works, lives simply, is retired. If I got there people would call and so on and its no good: I am not that kind of person. But I do wish it were not so cold. Cold frightens me. It is ominous. I breathe it and deep down its as though a knife softly softly pressed in my bosom – and said 'dont be too sure'. That is the fearful part of having been near death. One knows how easy it is to die. The barriers that are up for everybody else are down for you & youve only to slip through.

But this is depressing. Dont mind it.

Love me. I love you. We'll *risk all all* – for our Love.

Yours,
Wig.

MS ATL. *LKM* I. 288–9; *LJMM*, 395.

¹ On 12 Nov. Murry and Sydney Waterlow had Bertrand Russell and E. M. Forster dine with them at Portland Villas.

To J. M. Murry, [18 November 1919]

[Casetta Deerholm, Ospedaletti]

168 received.

My precious,

First: I received your *Monday week* letter today (posted 10th arrived 18th) both the postmarks plain to see. Now how *can* that be? It had the cream jug & Hardy in it so thank goodness it wasn't lost. The cream jug is a pearl. Its two dear little feet look as though it was skating on cream or tobogganing on cream.¹ Heaven bless it and our Home!

Hardys letter was most revealing. Hes so frightfully *touching*. To say that poem really happened.² Oh God isn't that like *you*! You seem to me the next link in the chain after Hardy.

I received also your *Friday* letter & the paper & the Lit. Sup. & the Guardian. A great feast. Your Friday letter frightens me about my Virginia review. I missed it. Did I? Didnt walk round enough? I hope to God you *wont* pubish it if you feel that is true. Id rather write another gladly willingly than that. What a cursed little creature I am. Beat me.

The paper is simply *superb* this week. Its the best youve ever cooked. 'The tenderness & flavour, size and cheapness' – no that don't fit – but its a perfect corker. I had to send a telegramme to say so. Your review of Lewis is excellent – simply 1st chop.³ The Henry King poem one of the best of his poems & how apt it rang after Santy on Experience.⁴ Its an amazing good number altogether and is so well put together. That + the new advertisements makes one feel the child is "getting a big girl now Eliza."

Boge its a devilish day. 5.30 pm. Im just going to bed. Its too parky to be up. The robber with the knife is everywhere – hes not even afraid of the fire. No, darling this climate is a *fool* of a climate – because its dishonest. It smiles and it stabs. Never again. Father is ill in Menton – he has caught a chill. It goes through anybody. And you know how hard it is to work in extreme parkiness. And one plays the old game pulling down the wire screen, hearing a great roar, pulling it up, meeting a dead silence. But it can't be helped. I take as much care as a human being could – thats all one *can* do. But if one has to go abroad again it must be der Schweiz with *stoves and windlessness.*

I keep pondering over our new treasures, jug, linen and real serviettes. We shall sit at breakfast table, delicately poised on our chairs, like two butterflies hovering over a flower garden. Oh, that house. I want to feel the walls – to smell the fire to shut the door – to call you – "Boge come up here. There's a little room with a pear tree in flower at the window."

I cant write tonight dearest. My back aches. I must go and lie down in a garden of hot water bottles. Nothing serious, only the cold. And yet theres so much I long to say – I long to talk over. *Your* letters are so marvellous.

Peake is the Oxford Street end of Wardour Street, I *think* 141. He has a sign with his name on it from a first floor window – as you face the street its on your left, about six doors down. DO GO. I feel Id like you to sell all the office furniture bit by bit and put it into salt & pepper pots.

Your own adoring
Wig-wife.

MS ATL. *LJMM*, 396–7.

[1] Murry had sent a drawing of a cream-jug which he had bought for their proposed home.

[2] Murry wrote on 15 Nov. of receiving a letter from Thomas Hardy, written on 8 Nov., thanking him for his recent review article. 'I must say it gave me very deep joy to find that surprise letter from the old boy, saying that he had been impressed by what I thought the most valuable thing in it – the distinction between poetic apprehension & poetic method. That was the comble.' (ATL.) Hardy explained of 'Near Lanivet, 1872', which KM had admired in her letter to Murry on 14 Nov.: 'I forgot if I told you that the second poem you quote really happened, which now gives it a peculiar quality to myself – the white clothed form having long escaped all further possibility of crucifixion.' *The Letters of Thomas Hardy*, ed. Richard Little Purdy and Michael Millgate, vol. v (1985), 341.

[3] In the *Athenaeum* for 14 Nov. 1919, Murry wrote 'Our Art Executioner', a review of Wyndham Lewis's manifesto *The Caliph's Design: Architects! Where is your Vortex?*.

[4] Murry's poem 'Exploration', under his pseudonym of Henry King, and George Santayana's 'Soliloquys in England: Empiricism'.

To J. M. Murry, [19 November 1919]

[Casetta Deerholm, Ospedaletti]
Wednesday le midi

Dear Love,

A most beautiful man has just been here to put the lock on the door – really a superb creature. He could *not* put the lock on the door so he spent his time explaining (1) how easy it would be for a person to come in at night (2) how unpleasant (3) how much wiser to trouver quelqu'un to sleep here seulement pour la bien garder. Just give them a morceau de paille in the vestibule and the thing is done. Locking the horse in the stable *en pension,* so to say.

It has not been cold today – temperate air. The result is I am a different child. Ive been out for a walk and Im tingling with warmth & my bones don't ache so much & my lungs open and shut. The cold really *paralyses* me: I went to bed as I said last evening and felt in despair about it. First one couldnt work because of moustiques and moucherons, then because of L.M., then because of the cold – a sliding scale. But when the day is fair one forgets. I climbed about the hill at the back of the Casetta. After you get up a certain height theres a perfect little promenade – quite flat – only used by the sauterelles – full of gay small flowers and insects. Below are pines & the sun shining through them makes them smell sweetly. I was so happy there. I thought how much more my kind these little boulevardiers were – the butterflies the grasshoppers & the daisies than the crowd at Menton, par exemple. How much lovelier to look at are the wild thyme and the tiny honeysuckle than the shop fronts. I stayed up there (like M. Séguins goat I felt)[1] all the morning – & below ever so far as I came round a bend I saw the Casetta with its foreshortened geranium bushes – looking a jewel. Just as I left I said out loud "thank you very much its been lovely". But to whom? To the Lord who gave me consumption?

Just then lunch was ready, curried pasta, fresh bread, marmalade de pommes & dried figs and coffee. Ida is off to San Remo to buy oatmeal and 'have a *little* look at the shops' – so I shall write my review of Monkhouse & Stern & Stevenson.[2] The sun has gone – clouds have pulled over – soft grey ones with silver fringes – the wind is piping. Of course the locksmith man said they had never had such a year as this year – the flowers are nearly spoiled with the gêlée – and snow on all the mountains . . . Why do these things follow us. Wherever I go they never have known *such* a year. I take back my thank you.

Boge the Irish man is a deal better.[3] I smell he's a rank rebel and may use the A. for code messages to prisoners – but it doesn't matter.

He writes decently and hes a way with him. I dont think much of the Art man[4] – in fact I don't think anything of him – do you? He never gains ones attention. Dent is really top hole and old Sullivan was very readable this week.[5] An occasional *simple* article like that is very good for catching new readers I am sure. Clives curtsey & retreat is always worth reading.[6] It did show a tiny little soul this week – but he speaks well for himself. Voilà. Your Lewis was *as usual* masterly. It was *fair* in a way fairness isn't understood nowadays. It praised him, explained him, and *took him a bit further on his way*. Thats the difference between you and all other critics. I feel you do it even to Hardy. I have a suspicion that Eliot is finding himself as a poet in his analysis (not quite the word) of caricature. I feel he is seeing why he fails and how he can separate himself from Sweeney through Sweeney.[7] But this may be sadly farfetched. Santy is the sweet little cherub that sits up aloft far from our confusions and distractions. Im very glad you drew Heal.[8] But he ought to advertise with us. Thats why I think an article on the subject of the first article and the correspondence ought to appear. But who's to write it? And perhaps you think there has been enough. Did you ever approach Ripmann?[9] In view of the 'educational' public – modern languages, and so on. And have Forster and Lytton caved in?[10] This is a very tiresome letter. Ill stop it. Im always thinking of the paper & wondering about it. Wednesday is a kind of press day here: I think of you and wonder how all has gone. Goodbye my treasure. I must give this to L.M. to post in the town. I am so thankful about old Porter:[11] his attentions may make your *hair grow*.[12]

Always always and for ever your Wig-wife.

MS ATL. *LKM* I. 289–90; *LJMM*, 397–9.

---

[1] In 'La Chevre de M. Seguin', a tale from Alphonse Daudet's *Lettres de Mon Moulin* (1869), which KM had translated in the *New Age*, 6 Sept. 1917, the goat stays out late on the mountainside, with disastrous consequences. A wolf eats her at dawn.

[2] 'Control and Enthusiasm', KM's review of *True Love*, by Allan Monkhouse, and *Children of No Man's Land*, by G. B. Stern, appeared in the *Athenaeum*, 28 Nov. 1919; her review of George Stevenson's *Benjy* along with *Cousin Philip*, by Mrs Humphry Ward, in 'A Post-War and a Victorian Novel' on 19 Dec. 1919.

[3] E. A. Boyd, a new Dublin correspondent recommended by Beatrice Campbell, contributed 'Notes from Ireland', the *Athenaeum*, 14 Nov.

[4] R. W. Wilensky on 'Exhibitions of the Week'.

[5] Edward Dent wrote on 'Violincello Solo'; J. W. N. Sullivan on 'Science and Culture'.

[6] Clive Bell on 'Order and Authority', Part II, under 'Fine Arts'.

[7] T. S. Eliot's 'The Comedy of Humours' was a review of *Ben Jonson* by G. Gregory Smith, and Ben Jonson's *Every Man in His Humour*, edited by Percy Simpson. Eliot's *Poems*, including the Sweeney pieces, had been published by the Hogarth Press the previous May.

[8] There was another letter to the editor from Ambrose Heal, again taking up the leading article of 31 Oct. on 'Art and Industry'.

[9] See p. 23, n. 8.

[10] Both E. M. Forster and Lytton Strachey continued to write for the paper.

[11] Murry had visited KM's dentist, who 'talked about what you had told him of the *Athenaeum* with a great deal of intelligence' (Murry, 210).
[12] KM is twitting Murry on his receding hairline.

To J. M. Murry, [20 November 1919]

[Casetta Deerholm, Ospedaletti]
Thursday

Dearest of All,

Your Saturday letter has come when you are just off for the weekend & you tell me O. [Ottoline] has invited you there for Xmas. I strongly advise you to go. Its so comfortable and one always gets ideas for the house – from just being among those Spanish chests.

Its a very dull day here with wild ragged clouds and a cold halting miserable wind. My black fit is on me – not caused by the day altogether. Christ! to *hate* like I do. Its upon me today. You don't know what hatred is because I know you have never hated anyone – not as you have loved – equally. Thats what I do. My deadly deadly enemy has got me today and Im simply a blind force of hatred. Hate is the *other* passion. It has all the opposite effects of Love. It fills you with death and corruption. It makes you feel hideous degraded and old – it makes you long to DESTROY. Just as the other is light so this is darkness. I hate like that – a million times multiplied. Its like being under a curse. When L.M. goes I dont know what I shall do. I can only think of breathing – lying quite still and breathing. Her great fat arms, her tiny blind breasts, her baby mouth, the underlip always wet and a crumb or two or a chocolate stain at the corners – her eyes fixed on me – fixed – waiting for what I shall do that she may copy it. Think what you would feel if you had consumption and lived with a deadly enemy! Thats one thing I shall grudge Virginia all her days – that she & Leonard were together. We cant be: weve got to wait our six months but when they are up I WILL not have L.M. near – I shall rather commit suicide. That is dead earnest. In fact, I have made up my mind I shall commit suicide if I dont tear her up by the roots then. It would be kinder for us both – for you and for me of course I mean. We'd have no love otherwise – you'd only slowly grow to think I was first wicked and then mad. Youd be quite right. Im both with her – mad – really mad like Lawrence was only worse. I leaned over the gate today and dreamed she'd die of heart failure and I heard myself cry out 'oh what heaven what heaven.'

Should I *not* send this? I must. I want you to know so that when the time comes for her to go you will remember. The worst thing about hate is that it never spends itself – is never exhausted and in this case isn't even shared. So you come up against something which says hit me hit me hate me hate *feel strongly* about me – one way or the other – it doesn't matter which way as long as I make you feel. The man who murders from sheer hate is right to murder: he does it in self defence. Worst of all is that I cant write a book while I live with her. I tried now for two months. It wont go. Its no good.

Does this seem to you just absurd? Can you imagine in the least what it is like? I feel I must let you know even though you wave the knowledge aside & think it just 'Tigs tearing off at a tangent'. Its not. It is a curse like the curses in old tales.

Well thats enough 'in all conscience' as Mr Salteena would say.[1] I shall recover darling, as I did before. Ill get over the positive imperative overwhelming suffocating mood of it and pass into the other. But oh! 'let this cup pass from me'[2] in April. Its TOO MUCH.

Your (in a black cloud hidden away)
Wig-wife.

MS ATL. *LJMM*, 399–400.

---

[1] In Ch. 5 of Daisy Ashford's *The Young Visiters*, 'Mr. Salteena crossed his legs in a lordly way and flung a fur rug over his knees though he was hot enough in all conscience.'
[2] 'O my Father, if it be possible, let this cup pass from me: nevertheless not as I will, but as thou wilt.' Matt. 26: 39.

To J. M. Murry, [21 November 1919]

[Casetta Deerholm, Ospedaletti]

166 received.
Friday Morning 8.30 after déjeuner.
My own
It happened rather luckily yesterday that L.M. and I reached a crise at tea-time and after that the frightful urgency of our feelings died down a bit. So Ill not say more about it. It ruined yesterday and made me so tired that I felt I could have slept days and nights away.

Here is your letter from Oare, about the Waterlows House.[1] They are lucky – arent they. Shall we really have such a house? Its not too late? We don't just make up dreams – precious dreams – it's not "all over"? I get overwhelmed at times that it *is* all over, that we've seen each other for the last time (imagine it!) ((no, don't imagine it)) and that these letters will one day be published and people will read something in them – in their queer finality – that "ought to have told us". This feeling runs exactly parallel with the other – the feeling of hope. They are two roads, I cant *keep* to either. Now I find myself on one, now on the other. Even when you tell me about the table² I think how perfect but at the very same moment I think "will he sell it – of course not. He must have a table, after all." Its all part of what Ive said before – haven't I. I say it so many thousand times over in my mind that I forget whether Ive written it. Once the defenses are fallen between you and Death they are not built up again. It needs such a little push – hardly that – just a false step – just not looking – and you are over. Mother, of course, lived in this state for years. Ah, but she lived *surrounded*. She had her husband her children, her home, her friends – physical presences – darling treasures to be cherished – and Ive not one of these things. I have only my work. That might be enough for you in like case – for the fine intelligence capable of detachment – but God! God! Im *rooted* in Life. Even if I hate Life I cant deny it. I spring from it and feed on it. What an egoist the woman is!

And now Love, just supposing by a miracle the blissful thing should happen —— I dont remember where it was I stayed with the Waterlows. It was near Marlboro' and the country was beautiful. There were forest glades – a beautiful forest. They took me for a walk that was miles too long I remember that. I remember standing in a rank smelling field and seeing them far ahead and waving very gaily when they looked round —— But the country does not really matter a great deal does it? As long as it *is* country and one can grow things (oh *MAKE* it happen!) But the money question is pretty dreadful. As to furniture, that we can always accumulate Eric-or-little-by-little³ but I should think an anthracite range costs at least £30 or more and alterations – we know what they run in to. I think we might do it by not paying down. We overdo the paying down, I believe. Other people never have their money in bags – but first we ought to find the house – take it and then consider. That is my idea. The house (like the Jew) first. ((I never understood that text.⁴)) Oh God! when you say we'll have to get a builder in I suddenly dimly see – a hall, a staircase with shavings, a man with a rule and a flat pencil measuring for a cupboard. I hear a saw and the piece of sawn wood creaks and tumbles (such a *final* sound). I hear the squeequee of a plane, and the back door of the house is open and the smell of the uncared garden – so different to the smell of the cared one – floats through, and I put my hand on your sleeve and rest a little against you, and you say "do you agree" and I nod "yes" –

But these dreams are so dear that they feel unearthly – they are dreams of Heaven. How could they become reality? *This* is reality – bed, medecine bottle, medecine glass marked with tea and table spoons, guaiacol tablets, balimanate of zinc. Come – tell me – tell me *exactly* what I am to do to recover my faith. I was always the one who had a kind of overplus of it – you hated it in me – it seemed to deny you so many of your more subtle emotions. You made me feel it was so crude a thing – my belief that couldn't be shaken.

Take this all *coolly*; its all – what? Just add to my diseases a touch of melancholia, let us say. And remember how I adore you for as long as I live.

Wig.

MS ATL. *LKM* I. 290–2; *LJMM*, 400–2.

---

[1] Murry had spent the weekend with the Waterlows at Parsonage House, Oare, Pewsey, Wiltshire.

[2] A retired friend from Murry's time at the War Office had offered to make them a table.

[3] *Eric: Or Little by Little* (1858), a popular schoolboy novel by the Revd Frederick William Farrar.

[4] 'For I am not ashamed of the gospel of Christ: for it is the power of God unto salvation to every one that believeth; to the Jew first, and also to the Greek.' Rom. 1: 16.

To J. M. Murry, [22 November 1919]

[Casetta Deerholm, Ospedaletti]

165 received.

ACID from Roma received.[1]

Copy of Eve.[2]

Saturday morning.

My Precious Darling Bogey,

Per usual your adorable gay letter comes flying after my crows. I shall make L.M. wire you to ignore those two black things and forget them if you can. I can't help them my darling, yet I know I ought to. If the others make you so happy you *must* have the others.[3]

Find that house we must! I feel its absolutely necessary. Then to ask Violet if she and her husband would live with us. Is that a good plan? I feel Violet ought not to be allowed to escape and from what Chaddie says with all her competence & Belle's she can't get a soul. And I hope you do go to Bedford Square & see if there is anything for us there.[4] There might be a lovely mirror *or* a chest (it would be too dear) but there might be an exquisite 'bit' which would grace a whole room like our bergère does.

It is a brilliant bright day. The flowers against the sea flash and quiver with light. This house is full of roses, every jar, pot, spare glass has its share. Even the sauce boat has a little cargo with their heads over the sides and their leaves trailing in the mer imaginaire. I am going off to San Remo this afternoon if it stays fine, just to have a look at the gay world & to take the acid to the chemist. I ought to unwrap it & take just the bottle for I want the box. On the other hand Id like him to see the seals just for him to know what an important person I am —— You're shocked?

I sent off a review on Thursday night. Is it alright, Love? This copy of Eve is really too degraded. I wonder if Vogue is like it. Its written *by* imbeciles *for* degenerates. One gets so fastidious or I don't just know what it is – living alone on a wild hillside: at any rate what they call the 'semi-demi' shocks me no end. I suppose there are a great many women who care for this sort of thing or it wouldn't be produced. Its positively *foul* and *filthy*. I do shrink from this world and its ways – more and more. I am writing on Clemence Dane at present. She is another type of *falsity*.[5] But youll see what I think.

I had such a charming letter again from Arthur. He is a little trump to write to me like this. I want you to see this letter but I am nervous of sending it in case you leave it about & he finds it: he wouldn't understand. Shall I send it? And will you keep it in the file? Yes darling love I *do* wrap up no end. I am more frightened of catching cold than anybody. Its a terror to me in fact. And I can keep warm enough on the whole. The fireplace in this my small room is excellent; the others are no good – except the kitchen which is alright but wasteful since we have a fire there all day. Woollen goods dont exist in Italy. Even Ansaldi told me that. Father leaves Toulon today for Naples. Ive just written his farewell letter. Hes had an awful shaking since he was here – has been in bed nearly all the time with a severe chill & touch of congestion. We have had a rare tangi[6] over this climate.

Yes its a beautiful day today – an opal. I am so looking forward to San Remo – to lose myself for a bit and watch the people and perhaps the china will have come. I long to send you the superb fresh dried figs. L.M. is making enquiries about them today.

Darling I must give this to her for the noon post. Your marvellous letter is beside me. It *breathes* joy and life – you precious Boge. Take care of yourself. Try & keep the house warm. Have you enough coal? Does the house look shabby – or cared for?

With my meals I am drinking a Winters Tale. Its again one of my favourites. Its simply marvellous. Goodbye for now my precious. *The flag flies.*

Ever your true love,
Wig.

MS ATL. *LKM* I. 292–3; *LJMM*, 402–3.

---

[1] The hydrobromic acid, an ingredient for her medicine, was sent to her through the diplomatic bag to Rome – a privilege arranged by Sydney Waterlow.

² *Eve: The Lady's Pictorial*, a weekly which began publication in Sept., missed Oct., and began again in Nov. 1919.

³ Murry had written, 17 Nov., 'I think it is strictly impossible, as they say in the mathematical books, that I could ever have two letters that give me more joy than the two I had this morning, one giving an account of Ansaldi's visit, the other of yr. father's.' (Murry, 216.)

⁴ Lady Ottoline Morrell was arranging for the sale of furniture at 44 Bedford Square, before quitting the house.

⁵ KM reviewed Clemence Dane's *Legend* under 'Revival', the *Athenaeum*, 5 Dec. 1919.

⁶ Maori mourning ceremony.

To J. M. Murry, [23 November 1919]

[Ospedaletti]

IGNORE THURSDAY FRIDAY LETTERS FLAG FLIES FONDEST LOVE. TIG.

Telegram ATL. Unpublished.

To Athenaeum (J. M. Murry), [23 November 1919]

[Ospedaletti]

Dear Athy

Don't be frightened of what Ive marked with an X on the other side.¹

Your loving
Gran'ma.

Postcard ATL. Unpublished.

¹ A small recumbent dog in a photograph of Via Vittoria Emmanuele.

To Wingley [J. M. Murry], [23 November 1919]

[Ospedaletti]

With love and an X from his gran'ma (please show it to gran'pa.)

Postcard ATL. Unpublished.

To J. M. Murry, [23 November 1919]

[Casetta Deerholm, Ospedaletti]
Sunday

Cheque for Scarf enclosed.

My darling darling Bogey,

I have just read your letter about the scarf. I wish Id seen that girl asking you if terracotta suited me and you wondering if I was fair or dark or a hazelnut. Im sure I shall love it. Here is cheque for same . . . The ACID is here; a bottle has been made up & it has a most superb effect. Très potent – the best I have come across. You did not see the bottle it was sent in – did you – a round, glass stoppered, exquisite one which the chemist is not to be allowed to keep. I didn't go to San Remo yesterday after all. Got all ready & walked half way down the steps & the bells rang turn again Whittington:[1] I had no puff – my back ached. I felt it would only be going on my nerves. So I sent L.M. and lay down with the window open to rest a little. The bell rang. (The bell here when pressed, rings & goes on ringing till you open the door, unscrew the top & stop it. This is a common habit. I never think of a bell that stops by itself now. It makes all visitors sound extremely urgent.) *That* visitor was Catherina with her minute Gus Bofa[2] dog – *Flock.* She had just given him a bath & was attired for the occasion in a kind of white robe de chambre, très décolletée, with bare arms, her hair just pinned up, her feet thrust into wooden pattens. In her hand she had a large *brush.* Flock sitting in the garden, covered with what looked like prickles of black & white fur all on end shivered violently and kept his eyes *pinned* on the brush. He IS an adorable little animal – for sale for 150 lire!!! But hes worth it really, he's such a personality. Catherina had come to say three men were following her bearing in their arms a porcelain stove. When she & Madame Littardi had been discussing the *coldness* of the Casetta Madame Littardi had suddenly remembered she had this put away dans la cave and *they* decided it would chauffe toute la petite maison if it was installée, in the salle à manger. Would I like it? It was un peu cassée so Catherina had brought three admirers to mend it for me. Wasn't this very amiable. There must be a rat somewhere but I can neither see nor smell it up till now. Presently three good men and true hove in sight bearing a small *terracotta* crematorium. C. in her element, ordered them about, made them put it in the garden, sent them into the Casetta for a pail, a cloth, water for the cement, started them scrubbing, while she watched & Flock sat with an air of intense pleasure watching the sufferings of another while he still shivered & the blood showed red in the muscles of his delicate little hind legs. She came up today to have it put in the room. All my thanks were overborne with: je suis si contente, si contente d'avoir trouvé quelque chose. And when I said wouldn't she at least have a bouquet of des boutons de roses she replied seriously '*Demain*, avec grand plaisir: mais vous savez Madame, I cannot walk carrying a bouquet without my shoes on.'

After she had gone I lay down again & between my book I heard the workmen whistling & talking & then there was a new voice, a childs voice, very happy. It went on for about an hour. Vaguely curious, I got up to see who it was. C'était le petit de la poste qui porte les télégrammes, and he was beating up cement very firmly with a little flat trowel – in his *element*, a workman, in fact. When he saw me he paid no attention & I just chanced to ask if he had anything for me? 'Si, Madame' & off came his little cap with a telegram from Father inside it! I went in to sign the slip & he followed leaned against my table & suddenly picking up the pig, pointed to the old letters underneath & asked for the stamps for his collection then strolled over to the mantelpiece & looked at your photograph while I humbly tore them off for him.

I lay down again. The bell rang. A LADY, Miss Lionel Kaye-Shuttleworth, Villa Giovanni, San Remo, to call – a friend of Dents aunt in Nice. Elderly, typical, good family, dowdy gentlewoman with exquisite greenish ermine scarf, diamond ear rings & white suede gloves. The combination suggested *arum lilies* to me somehow. I liked her very much. She knows a great deal about Italy, she was *gay*, *sociable*, full of life and *pleasant talk*, and she was a 'perfect lady'. (I *do* like fine delicate manners.) I made her tea as Ida was out. But you know this form of social entertainment is quite new to me. It is like playing ladies. Are they playing too? They cant be serious, surely and yet . . . I see myself and hear myself and all the while am laughing inside. I managed to inform her: (1) we were not related to the John Murrays. We spell our name without the 'A' – yes from Scotland. The A was dropped generations ago. (Do you hear the 'A' dropping? Hullo! There's the A dropped. We cant put it back; its broken to bits.) My *private* idea is that the ships carpenter dropped it over the side – but never mind. Also – that Papa *motored* from Menton to see me: that my relatives there had managed to find *four* excellent maids & that my *cook* in London finds shopping so much easier that (this is the invariable final & always comes in as natural as you please) Elizabeth in her G. Garden is my cousin!!![3] It is Butlers Montreal brother in law.[4] She was rather horrified at the Casetta: the coldness and loneliness . . . the pity I was not at San Remo where 'we' could have looked after you if you had let us and at least introduced you to our friends. *What* do you do when it rains, especially as you are not strong etc. etc. etc. I am afraid I was a little brave-and-lonely at this: its so nice to be cared for . . . She is asking a few people to meet me at lunch on Wednesday and Im going. Do you wonder why? I will tell you. People steady and calm me – when I am not working, when Im in pain, and conscious every moment of my body and when my heart indulges in what Sorapure calls disorderly action & my joints ache Ive no one to turn to. I cant forget my body for a moment. I think of Death – the melancholy fit seizes me. Nature helps me when I am well but if the weather is cold and I am ill – Nature mocks & terrifies me. Then healthy people help *beyond words*. Ive noticed this many times. L.M. doesn't: she always makes me feel she is waiting for me to be worse but if I see people the strain of her, even, goes. I feel Ive cut away a few hundred octopus feelers, I feel refreshed. Do you understand? Does it sound to you unworthy? I swear when Catherina has come here sometimes – just to be with her – to feel her health & gaiety has been *bread* & *wine* to me. Bear with me. I had to explain. If I were well you see it would be utterly different & then the past is so *new*: its *not past* yet. Why Bogey, on Thursday when the wind blew & I was not well I suddenly *relived* the afternoon you and Arthur were in the kitchen and I came down and you 'teased' me. Dont move. Sit still. Dont poke the fire. Be quiet. Stop talking! And I felt distracted. I began to cry and cry. I saw Arthur laughing: I didn't know what to do. It was like great black birds, dashing at ones face. What *can* I do, I thought. If I go upstairs he'll say don't climb the stairs & now he says dont stay here. And I heard myself cry out 'youre *torturing* me' & the past and the present were one frightful horror. This is *sober truth*.

Its over now, done with. But I love you beyond words, your letters are *miracles* and after I have failed you I suffer, suffer. I want to keep you happy. But I cant lie and pretend. So if I do see a few people you will understand why and not think I am neglecting my work . . . This is so long. Forgive me. Put your arms round me. No-one in the world would understand but you. My fear of death – you do understand it? And the fact that you have thought of me *dead* & written as though I were & that L.M. is always preparing for that – you understand why, having been so near it myself, it made me terrified? As though I had nothing to help me fight it off except my own powers ——

I am looking at the little ring you gave me – the blue stone with the pearls round it. I love it so: I feel you made it out of a flower for me when we were children and it has turned into pearls . . . Glancing again at your letter I reread the part where you say you'd drive anywhere for a good table. Oh! how nice you are! *Too* nice. Terribly. I thought you meant *food* first . . . to 'keep a good table'. Then it dawned on me. It is the spit of you to say such a thing. But, my precious, be careful, if somebody asks you to 'take the chair' they wont mean what you mean. I now see you answering an invitation that you'll be very pleased indeed to take the chair on Friday 20th thanks awfully. How did they know we were short of chairs? And you will arrive at 8.30 as they suggest with a small hand barrow . . .

It has been the most perfect, exquisite morning. I went in to the village. There were no letters. The whole village is adorned with roses, trees of roses, fields, hedges, they tumble over the steps in a shower, children wear them, hideous middleclass women in chocolate brown costumes with black button boots & hard velvet toques pull & twist them from the stems. I walk about wishing I knew the name of that white beauty with petals stained as though with wine and long slender buds – those pink ones round and curled – those red ones with *silver shadows*. Ospedaletti *is* an enchanting little village, and the village people seem very nice. The visitors are simply APPALLING. All the men are forked radishes, but their strut, twirl, stare, ogle, grin, is so bewildering. And the women are all either chocolate brown or a colour I always think of as Belgian grey – a second class on the boat grey. They have cold, selfish faces, hard eyes, bad manners, mean attitudes and ways. Serpents come out of their eyes at sight of me – I don't know why – & they draw the radishes attention to me & then (*really*) burst out into a loud affected laughing. I, of course, don't notice, but I feel myself getting very *english*, but in truth ones heart is wrung. How *can* they be like that with all these roses, with the air humming with bees, with the great white bunches of sweet flowers on the promenade. How *can* they. Divine weather – a crocus coloured sea – the sun embracing ones body – holding one like a lover . . . You know people are *impossible* to understand. I think I only understand you of all the world. We MUST have children – we MUST. I want our child – born of love – to see the beauty of the world – to warm his little hands at the sun & cool his little toes in the sea. I want Dickie to show things to. Think of it! Think of *me* dressing him to go for a walk with *you*. Bogey we must hurry – our house – our child – our work. Goodbye for now my own little mate,

Your Wig-wife.

MS ATL. *LKM* I. 293–8; *LJMM*, 403–8.

---

[1] According to popular legend, Richard Whittington (d.1423), who four times held the office of Lord Mayor of London, was leaving London as an impoverished young man when he heard Bow bells ringing out, 'Turn again, Whittington, | Lord Mayor of London!'

[2] The pseudonym of Parisian comic artist Gustave Blanchot (d. 1968), who published during the War a satirical weekly, *La Baionette*. In June 1918 KM worked on a review which was never published of his *Chez les Taubibs Croquis d'Hôpital*, an account of his experiences in a French field hospital.

[3] KM's cousin, Mary Annette Beauchamp (see *CLKM* I. 8 n. 1), who as the wife of Count

Henning von Arnim published the enormously popular *Elizabeth and her German Garden* in 1898. After many years, she and KM had met again in June 1919.

⁴ In 'A Psalm of Montreal', first published in *The Note-Books of Samuel Butler*, ed. Henry Festing Jones (1918), there are several stanzas describing a museum custodian who boasts of his brother-in-law's connections.

To J. M. Murry, [24 November 1919]

[Casetta Deerholm, Ospedaletti]
Monday

Master of the Cats![1] Hail.

My precious darling Bogey,

Ive gone and gained another 2 lbs. I weighed myself and couldn't believe it & made the man weigh me as though I were beurre frais at least & still there it was – another kilo – thats a bit more than 2 lbs. Pretty good for a young 'un, don't you think? Please whisper the news in Wing's ear – I now weigh 7 stone 4 and when I left home I weighed 6. 13. Having found out this fact I phantasmagorically (see Miss R. Wilson)[2] danced off to the post & found hymn number 163 – the one hundred & sixty third hymn (why do they always say that) waiting for me. I read it in the public eye but when I found you had not given me the chuck absolute for my Virginia review I lost my head & kissed it – looked up and saw an old female leaning on a broom watching me & smiling very broadly. This was awkward because I blushed and had to climb up a flight of steps so as not to pass her. Her broom by the way was made of those great reddish stems that grow in the centre of palms with tiny dates on them – a very nice broom indeed.

Dont ever flatter me. Beat me *always* before you would beat anyone else. But God! to think that review was alright. Ive been on the point of wiring my regret that I had failed you. Thats enough to make a person gain 20 more —— I burn for the next number. Hinds letter was *exceedingly* gratifying.[3] How you have wiped the floor with those old Oxford people. They must feel pretty silly. Really letters like this ought to go to the managers. Won't you send this one & the other American one? They *ought* to see how it is admired.

I am so glad that the precious cats have won Sydney. I sent them each a card yesterday. I SEE little Wing rabbiting on the stairs. They are blessed creatures and must have perhaps a whole tiny cottage of their own in Sussex. I see Wing leaning out of the window pouring a jug of water onto Athy in the garden below. Athy will get very 'pa' in his old age – don't you think?

The Ottoline furniture makes my mouth water. A *chest* a *cupboard* a *couch* a delicious cabinet. I should like to have a cabinet – tall, you know the legs. Oh dear! why arent we rich – we want £800 a year *without* working, please and just a few lump sums – thats all. Its not much to ask. If I ever went to Mentone I might meet an old dying American there who for sufferings-nobly-borne might well leave me twice the sum. But I dont want to go to Mentone, Boge. Terracotta, the new stove, has been installed today. Its a regular German stove with a flat top. It looks awful there. But that round thing is where the red shows & below is a sort of baby oving. I should think it would box it – the cold I mean. You see I cant afford to go to Mentone and live there: it would cost quite double this place, I am sure. No, if I see tumpany here and go into San Remo & see people I think I can manage – & this place must be terribly healthy for me to have gained 4 lbs, stopped all my fever and planted in me a roaring appetite. And then —— MAY!! I feel so well today that only to write that makes me almost unbearably excited. I have to do the books for A. & L. [*Art and Letters*] this week – its a dreadful sweat having to *re*-read two & the Mask which I imagine I am supposed to admire I dislike intensely.[4] It is a very vulgar ill-bred book with 2 climaxes where the little Jew is forced to expose himself. Drey[5] would think it a masterpiece; thats the exact measure of it but I cant quite say that tho' Id like to.

I had 8 pages from Father at Toulon written just before he left. You know how in the old days you used to *wring* my heart in letters – *all* the ghastly things that happened just to you. Father does it. If he manages to secure one egg on a journey its a bad egg – he loses things, people cheat him – he goes to an hotel where they wont give him a fire – he "feeling very shaky". He peels the bad egg, letting the shells fall into the crown of his hat so as not to make a litter & the 'juice' spurts out all over the lining that he showed me with such pride the other day when he was here. And so on. Of course he *has money* but it makes no difference to him. He falls into absolute *pits* of depression and loneliness and 'wanting Mother'. Talking about Mother he told me such a typical little story about her in this letter. It was when they first took the Grange.[6] He was at a board meeting & was called away "in the thick of it" to the telephone. A voice said "its Mrs Beauchamp of The Grange speaking". He couldn't make out what was happening & thought she had wanted to ring up the *office* to give a "wholesale order". But when she heard his voice Father said 'all she said was "Hal dear, Im at home. I love this house. I simply love it. Thats all." and rang off.' Cant you hear that – I can.

I shall love to see Hardys poems. It will be interesting to read De la Mare on him, too.[7] Its a soft grey day with puffs of warm wind blowing. L.M. has gone to San Remo. Shes already borrowed 40 lire of her next month's £5. What *can* she spend it on? I suppose she sends it away or something & she buys the most awful smelling cakes but you cant spend £5 a month on cakes. Its all I can do *not* to ask. (Miss Kaye-Shuttleworth had 40 lbs of sugar sent her this summer to make peach jam with! I *dont* believe it.)

Clemence Dane will be sent tomorrow to be another odd review to have by you. The Times notice of it was really too funny.[8] Ive made a discovery. Its a very old book, touched up. Shes left some bits untouched which give away the show. But I think I made it pretty clear that she wrote it about 20 years ago.

Goodbye darling Bogey. Forgive the soap paper. Ill get some decent stuff tomorrow. Always yours

Your own
Wig.

MS ATL. *LKM* I. 298–300; *LJMM*, 408–10.

[1] A variant on Tybalt's nickname, 'Prince of Cats', in *Romeo and Juliet*, II. iv. 19.

[2] In Ch. XI of *All These Young Men*, which KM had recently reviewed, Romer Wilson wrote how her heroine 'phantasmagorically . . . enacted the utmost brutalities of war, then phantasmagorically she went through the pantomime of conversion to human sanity'.

[3] Murry had sent on another admiring letter, this time from Lewis Hind.

[4] *The Mask*, by John Cournos, which KM was reading for the 3,000-word commissioned article for *Art and Letters* that continued to hang over her head. Murry would report on 5 Jan. 1920 that its editor, Frank Rutter, told him he had received a telegram from her saying the piece had been posted, but that it failed to arrive. (Murry, 245.)

[5] The journalist O. Raymond Drey, married to her close friend, the painter Anne Estelle Drey.

[6] The mock-English mansion in Wadestown, Wellington, which Harold Beauchamp bought in 1917.

[7] Walter de la Mare wrote 'Mr Hardy's Lyrics', the leading article in the *Times Literary Supplement*, 27 Nov. 1919.

[8] The *Times Literary Supplement*, 13 Nov. 1919, carried an appreciative unsigned review of Clemence Dane's *Legend*, which KM designated a 'quaint old-fashioned little story' in the *Athenaeum*, 5 Dec. 1919.

To J. M. Murry, [25 November 1919]

[Casetta Deerholm, Ospedaletti]

162 received.

New Version

Boge (appassionato)	We want a house!
Wig (con brio)	Garden and cows!
Ath (sforzando)	Not forget-TING
Wing (con amore)	For Athy and Wing

All fortissimo diminishing to a pianissimo MOUSEHOLE FOR
MOUSE!

The paper has come. May I talk it over a little. And please
remember I am nobbut a cabin boy and you are the skipper. I dont
think S.W. brought it off with George Eliot.[1] He never gets under way.
The cartwheels want oiling. I think, too, he is ungenerous. She was a
deal more than that. Her English, warm, ruddy quality is hardly
mentioned. She *was* big, even though she was 'heavy' too. But think of
some of her pictures of country life – the breadth – the sense of sun
lying on warm barns – great warm kitchens at twilight when the men
came home from the fields – the feeling of *beasts* horses and cows – the
peculiar passion she has for horses (when Maggie Tullivers lover
walks with her up & down the lane & asks her to marry, he leads his
great red horse and the beast is foaming – it has been hard ridden and
there are dark streaks of sweat on its flanks – the *beast is the man* one
feels SHE feels in some queer inarticulate way)[2] — Oh, I think he
ought really to have been more generous. And why drag Hardy in?
Just because he (S.W.) was living with you and is I am sure like
certain females powerfully influenced by the climate of the moment.
Perhaps thats unjust. But I feel I must stand up for my SEX.

V.W. does it very well. Aint she a snob? But she does it very well in
her intellectual snobbish way. A Wyndham & a Tennant *no*
aristocrat[3] . . . I think D.L.M.'s review is excellent, don't you? Its so
informed, out-of-the-way and direct – and Saintsbury I like *awfully*.[4] I
wish we could lay down a little piece of excellent vintage. But ours will
be dandelion, elderberry, cowslip, and blackberry. (*Oh Bogey* won't it
be heaven).

I say who did Fisher?[5] Do you altogether approve? I read bits of the
book in the Times – hes a presumptuous self-conscious high-
stomached old roarer. No doubt the Admiralty was at fault – no doubt
everybody was a fool – but Fisher could have put nought right & as to
saying he was a great man — or are our sea legs being pulled?? I was a
bit sorry to read that.

I like the way Tommy keeps hitching up his trousers as he writes
and just not yarning. Hes always full of life, somehow. *Lewis* is
extremely interesting I think. He hurls lumps of sentences at you but
that doesnt matter. I think you ought to give him a chance. Youre *very*
clever to have seen him. R.H.W. is immeasurably more interesting
this week.[6] I don't know enough about Matisse to know if hes right –
but he sounds very right. Its got ideas – that article – hasn't it? Of
course Dent is as good as ever. And his remarks *re* the Boutique
Fantasque are I am sure *absolutely sound*.[7] Thats what I like about the
A. – the way it *steadies* opinion. You do it supremely. We tag along

after putting our two feets down on the bit you tell us to and trying to stand very firm.

Howe, Bogey – frankly disgusts me. Oh, I wish that first paragraph had *not* appeared in your paper. "Gave herself" in commas – oh the unspeakable journalist![8] Shoo him off. He simply revolts me. Apart from his vulgarity hes got nothing but a very old newspaper in his head.

The Duchess of Malfi is a useful little article very à propos.

I suppose you had to publish 'Thomas of Duddington' to fill space.[9] Its a pity you cant get better letters. I don't think one ought to publish irritation splenetic outbursts do you?

Now Duhamel is of course another eye opener.[10] The idea that they should surrender something of their personality . . . that started a terrific excitement bubbling in me. Its true of all artists, isn't it? It gives me another *critical point of view* about an artist, and quite a new one . . I mean, to find out what the man is subduing, to mark that side of him being gradually absorbed (even as it were without his knowing it) into the side of him he has chosen to explore, strengthening it, reinforcing it even while *he thinks* it is subdued away. Oh thats frightfully vague.

The letter from Italy was *peculiarly* interesting to me about the poet who had consumption & his "fits of blackest depression".[11] Its a very good letter, tho. I wish that old Valéry would write again. I think its time Lytton sent an article – don't you? Are you going to publish anything special at Xmas? A Christmas 'ode' by you? I *wish* I *wish* you would write a Christmas poem.

It is raining, a heavy misty rain – most beautiful. I went out to post in it and after so long it was thrilling to hear the fine rain sting the stretched silk of my umbrella, the sudden heavy drops down on it from the gum trees. All the coast is soft, soft colour, the roses hang heavy – the spiders webs are hung with family jewels. Aged men in pale blue trousers are sweeping up the dead leaves & there is a succession of bonfires – puffs of white fine smoke with the old figures moving in it, sweeping & bending. The sea is still very full – faint to see with dreamy lines upon it, and my two little royal birds are back in [the] garden.

Goodbye my darling. Tomorrow I send some *menus*.

Your Wig.

MS ATL. *LKM* I. 300–2; *LJMM*, 410–13.

---

[1] Sydney Waterlow's 'George Eliot, 1819–1880', the leading article in the *Athenaeum*, 21 Nov.

[2] 'In the Lane', Ch. XI of *The Mill on the Floss* (1860).

[3] In 'Maturity and Immaturity' Virginia Woolf reviewed *Edward Wyndham Tennant* by Pamela Glenconner, and *Joyce Kilmer*, edited with a Memoir by Robert Cortes Holliday. The opening

sentence of her review was, 'On his mother's side a Wyndham, but on his father's a Tennant, there is no reason, either in eulogy or in excuse, to call Wyndham Tennant an aristocrat.'

[4] 'Venice Decayed', a review by D. L. Murray of Ralph Nevill's *Echoes Old and New*; 'The Bounties of Bacchus', George Saintsbury's review of *Wine and Spirits: The Connoisseur's Text Book* by André L. Simon.

[5] 'A Great Man', an unsigned review of *Memories*, by Admiral of the Fleet, Lord Fisher, was by J. W. N. Sullivan.

[6] H. M. Tomlinson, under 'The Senior Service', reviewed *Merchantmen-at-Arms* by David Bone; Wyndham Lewis wrote on 'Prevalent Design 1. Nature and the Monster of Design'; R. H. Wilensky, in 'Exhibitions of the Week', discussed 'Méryon and Matisse'.

[7] Edward Dent's 'A Parade of Silliness', his review of Diaghilev's production at the Empire Theatre of *Parade*, with music by Erik Satie, and the Russian Ballet's production at the Alhambra of *La Boutique fantasque* by A. G. Rossini.

[8] P. P. Howe reviewed Arnold Bennett's *Sacred and Profane Love* at the Aldwych Theatre. The review began, 'Carlotta Peel, twenty eight, novelist, the author of eight progressively successful works of fiction, "gave herself" one evening, an equal number of years before Mr. Arnold Bennett's curtain in strict dramatic theory ought to rise, to Emilio Diaz, world-famous pianist.'

[9] 'The Date of "The Duchess of Malfi"' by W. J. Lawrence; a letter from Robert W. Napier, author of *John Thomson of Duddington*, disputing a review of his book by 'W. G. C.' (W. G. Constable) in the issue of 24 Oct.

[10] In 'Realism or Idealism', Murry reviewed George Duhamel's *Entretiens dans le tumulte* and *Lapointe et Ropiteau*.

[11] In 'Letters from Italy', VI, Guido de Ruggiero wrote on the poet Guido Gozzano (1883–1916).

To J. M. Murry, [26 November 1919]

[Casetta Deerholm, Ospedaletti]
Wednesday

Photograph enclosed: dont let it drop out.

My darling,

Its press day for you. How is the paper going? Whats the day like. I am thinking of you. I have got our house on the brain as well as the heart. I feel such a frenzy of impatience but that must not be. We must be wise children and hard to please – for this time it really is more important than ever before. This time we decide to live in the land with our flocks and our herds our manservant & our maidservant & our two sacred cats. All the same I keep seeing *chimneys* in the landscape of my mind, so to say – chimneys that are going to be ours. Think of the first time we visit it together, sitting on a step with our hats on our knees smoking a cigarette (man with a vehicle waiting for us somewhere round a corner) looking over the garden, feeling the house behind us, saying – we must have peonies under these windows. And then we get into the station cab & the man drives away and we hold each others hands and think how familiar this road will become . . .

Its a wild glittering day. I cant go to those people for lunch. The wind is like a great bird tumbling over the sea with bright flashing wings. I am upstairs in my bedroom sitting in the sun. The windows are open. It is very pleasant. One could make a charming room of this.

At three oclock I woke up into the middle of a terrific thunderstorm. The thunder seemed to set ones bones vibrating. One heard the sea – not breaking regularly – but *struggling* and only now and again with a great harsh sigh the waves spent themselves. It is strange to lie alone in such a storm. I kept feeling I must write this, I must write this but it must be a man who feels it rather an elderly man away from home and something must happen to him – something, you know which could not happen to such a man and then the morning must follow – still, clear, 'poised' like it is after such a storm and he . . .

At 7 oclock the front door bell ring. A telegram from Father at Naples (I had 2 from Toulon). This was to say goodbye finally. You know I have a feeling that he may buy us a farm in the North of Auckland. Wouldn't it be *too awful*. I shall have, every letter I write to accentuate the importance of your being in England for (at least) five years with the Athenaeum. He sketched the kind of place that would suit us in his last letter & it was so vivid that I hear him asking Mr Bob Fenwick[1] to keep his 'eye skinned for him' & let him know by wire if such a little farm comes onto the market. Wouldn't it be tragic! L.M. has gone to the post with my telegram of regrets. I should like a letter, a paper, and the scarf. But Ill leave this open in case the letter comes.

Later. Darling. A letter came from Jinnie enclosing this photo for you. It looks like Wing's house doesn't it? Nothing else came. Its afternoon. Ive just had *another* caller. A woman who lives here in Ospedaletti with her Italian maid her english maid her mother and I should think a few Spanish menservants. She asked me to tea on *Monday*. Her villa has a flat roof. She was smothered in fur, violent perfume, & I thought she was Mary Cannan.[2] The spit of Mary. Mary's eyes, teeth, extravagance *chicken 18 lire, butter 20 lire*!! Did you ever! You must go to Algiers next year. Algiers is *perfect*. She is I should think very rich & what they call 'fast' – plays golf, bridge, *our car*. No 'swank'. On the contrary. *Naive*, like Mary was. Speaks no Italian & I should think no French. She has a house in the South of England. I had no time in this *race* (so familiar!) to ask where but it was that which interested me. But I must have cards. Here are 5 people I ought to leave cards on – what an absurd predicament. Oh how nice our name is! My husband bulks very large in these conversations. What a dark romantic brilliant creature he is and as he never need see the people he is quite safe. Ive just seen her address. Her name is Mrs Frederick Temple, The Pond House, Chobham, Surrey, so its *not* the South of England.

Boge here are a few recipes. You see I don't know what the meat ration is or whats in season or anything, but they are sound – and I thought Violet might not know them. Are they at all what you want? My God! the wind. Its blowing great huge guns.

I send Jinnie's letter just to give you an idea of her. She is a nice woman – streets above these *callers*. This woman has left rather a faded taste of white suede gloves in my mouth after all. She is unhappy, dissatisfied, like Mary was. I dont know – ones work sets one *finally apart* from the idle world, doesn't it? You must like the little photograph *very* much please & look long at it. It fascinates me. Show it to Arthur will you? I wish you were here. Goodbye my precious. This is a dull letter: I am waiting for one from you. You know that state? I want one *terribly*. I love you love you love you.

Wig.

MS ATL. *LKM* I. 302–3; *LJMM*, 413–15.

---

¹ A Wellington business friend of Harold Beauchamp's.
² Mary Cannan (1867–1950), formerly the actress Mary Ancell, had been married to the author and playwright Sir James Barrie before marrying in 1910 the novelist Gilbert Cannan. The Cannans for a time were close friends of the Murrys before the First World War. (See *CLKM* I. 119 n. 1; 146 n. 1.)

To J. M. Murry, [26 and 27 November 1919]

[Casetta Deerholm, Ospedaletti]
Wednesday night. My precious little Paper Boy,

I dont want the Times as well as the Guardian. I didn't know the Guardian was going to be a regular: its of course 100 times more interesting than t'other.¹ (You see I am answering your Saturday morning letter.) About the 10 stories.² They wont all bear reprinting, Boge. I cant afford to publish my early Works yet. If you don't mind Id rather let them lie & deliver you the new goods in May. In any case I don't want the Woolfs to have any of my new work. We really *are* opposed. I know just how angry Virginia *et cie* are with me.³ They ought not to be for indeed I tried my best to be friendly & erred on the side of kindness. If you read that book you would realise what I feel . . . its aristocratic (?) ignoring of all that is outside its own little circle & its wonder, surprise, incredulity that *other people* have heard of William Shakespeare. Though what in Gods name THEY find in Shakespeare I don't know! Virginia's cry that she is the flower, the fair flower of the age – that Shakespeare & his peers died that she might be saved that she is the result of God knows *how* many hours in a library – is becoming a mania with her. Intellectual snobbery. She reminds me of Beatrice Hastings who had the same *mania*. B. saying that her work is the talk of *all Paris* my dear & Virginia imagining that England rings with Night & Day. Its boundless vanity & conceit – dreadful in woman or man.

The wind has been joined by the robber cold. Both are in brightest spirits. There is a perfect uproar going on outside. It makes my room feel like a lighthouse. I seem to see you in another lighthouse. I see my beloved seated at a table, reading or writing or playing with his little cat. All the rest of the world is in chaos – but there he is. It makes every gesture, every movement of yours – *beautiful*, charged with a kind of solemn quiet. Goodnight my love.

Thursday.

Hail, rain, wind, dark. The terracotta in full blast, smelling dreadful as the plaster bakes dry. No, the point about this climate is its extreme variability of temperature. It is never a whole day the same. Thats what puts such a terrific strain on one, I think, and thats what makes it truly preposterous for people who are not as well covered & as solid as L.M. They may win through – but why have to fight so hard? Why have to use up ones energies in keeping warm? Its so wasteful. The sea sounds like a big old rake. I was awake more than half the night. At one o'clock I called L.M. & she went down & made some tea. Bogey in my *home* I shall always have the things for tea in my room, so that in the middle of the night I can brew a cup. Mr Salteena's thrill for tea in bed I feel for tea in the middle of the night.[4] Ten years ago I used to have tea and brown bread & butter every morning at half past two. I don't know why it should be such a gay little feast then. I long for somebody to *laugh* with – I think of such funny little jokes – minute little jokes. Wing would perhaps be the perfect companion of such revels: he *shall* be. I see him stuffing his paw into his mouth or the end of his tail so as not to laugh out loud & wake you.

Oh Boge I hope I get a letter today or something. It is the *vilest* old day. However Ive *got* to stick it. Theres nothing else to do. God! how lonely I am! You know I sometimes feel a violent hate of Sullivan Eliot Tomlinson – all of them because they have never suffered what I have had to suffer & especially not THIS. Its just one of the many poisons I suppose. But to have been *alone* here – that – even you will NEVER know. Here's L.M. for the letter.

Goodbye Bogey

Wig.

MS ATL. *LKM* I. 303–4; *LJMM*, 415–16.

---

[1] Murry was sending her the *Weekly Times* as well as the *Guardian Weekly*.

[2] Murry asked on 22 Nov., 'am I to do anything with the ten stories in your cupboard. Shall I send them to Grant Richards? Or give them to Cobden-Sanderson, who, I'm sure, would be glad

to have them? Or give them to Virginia? Or do nothing? You see I was dining with Virginia last night, and she asked me point-blank about them.' (Murry, 221.)

³ Because of KM's recent review of *Night and Day*. The same letter from Murry went on, 'Of course, Virginia asked me, as I knew she would, to explain your review. I did my best. . . . I imagine that Virginia was more than a little gêné by it. I explained that what you meant was that she made an abstraction from life, which instead of being potentially complete (forgive the big words) left one important element completely out of account, or rather withered it. I don't suppose that was very comforting. She then said that she thought your novel reviews showed that you were not interested in novels.' (Murry, 221.)

Virginia Woolf recorded on 28 Nov.: 'K.M. wrote a review which irritated me – I thought I saw spite in it. A decorous elderly dullard she describes me; Jane Austen up to date.' *The Diary of Virginia Woolf*, vol. i: 1915–1919 (1917), 314.

⁴ In Ch. 4 of *The Young Visiters*, by Daisy Ashford, 'I say said Mr. Salteena excitedly I have had some tea in bed.'

To J. M. Murry, [28 November 1919]

[Casetta Deerholm, Ospedaletti]
Friday

My precious,

Forgive a note today instead of a letter. I must finish that review for A. & L. [*Art and Letters*] and its the devil. The cold is back; it is paralysing, and Im stiff as ever (!) & there were no letters yesterday or today. (The Observer came today for which Im very grateful.) But Ill come out of my hole when this review is over & Ive had a letter. The brick is the icy weather. Ones whole energy is taken up fighting it: theres *none* left over for work. But I must work – so there you are. L.M. will post this in San Remo: she is going in for my cough mixture. If only this climate were not so *intensely variable*: its never two days alike, it beats England. Now with a groan & a flick of a disconsolate paw Ill run away again. Ill come back & nibble a letter & then talk. But you know, old boy Im so *stale*. Oh for a 'weekend' or even a ciné or a theatre or the sound of music.

Your deadly dull
Mouse.

Dont be cross with me. Even L.M. thinks its colder than Hampstead.

MS ATL. *LJMM*, 416.

To J. M. Murry, [29 November 1919]

[Casetta Deerholm, Ospedaletti]
Saturday

My Beautiful Bogey,

Your Sunday letter is here – about Vanessa and Virginia. Yes I agree about Virginia.¹ I have only met the sister once. Id like to know her tho' I confess as a painter I think shes *awfully bad*. But she sounds very attractive. How I envy you seeing people – & yet of course it means nothing to you. I mean you are not like me, *dependent* upon contact with people. I am, yes, I am. By people I mean – not being alone. Id live all the rest of my life without seeing another human being if I had you.

We had a severe earthquake last night at 11 o clock. The little Casetta gave a *creak* and silently shook. And today it is dead calm, airless, real earthquake weather. Wasn't that nice about this weeks review which I did early [so] as to have the rest of the week for Rutter. I don't know – it beats me how she can do these things. She said last night it was because her brain had gone rotten but thats nonsense. Well I feel this last affair is not to be talked of. Ill have to take my work to post myself in future, that's all.

Vince comes this afternoon on his way to England: he brings you figs – *figs only*. Boge, youd better I suppose give him lunch & a cigar but be a bit on your dignity – will you. Tell you why. Hes a shady bird. I know his history. He came out here as footman to that old lady Miss Lockhart & betrayed her trust in every way & seduced the german maid (she made him marry her) and misbehaved with a child and when the old woman was ill told none of her friends shut her away even from the servants by saying she was infectious & then she left a will signing away her possessions to him. Its a good story & a true one but I think theres no doubt hes a pretty inferior devil. I feel he may ask you for some money. If he does make him sign a receipt to the effect that its part rent. You see you are such a *child* in bad people's hands. You are fairly safe with the lambs but you must not ever play with the lions unless Im by.

I couldn't get to sleep last night. When I shut my eyes *gardens* drifted by – the most incredible sort of tropical gardens with glimpses of palaces through the rich green. Trees Ive never seen or imagined – trees like feathers and silver trees and others quite white with huge transparent leaves passed and passed. My heart just fluttered: I scarcely had to breathe at all. It was like a vision brought about by drugs. I couldn't stop it & yet it frightened me but it was too beautiful to stop. One is almost in a state of coma – very strange. Ive often got *near* this condition before but never like last night. Perhaps if one gives way to it & gives way to it one may even be able to get there. Oh, I don't know but it *was* a vision not a memory. I am going to San Remo today to try & get some tea plates for you. Those two items *don't* hang together.

Filippi sent his bill for that chit yesterday – *40 lire*. I consider that an absurd swin. But I must pay it. Dont you think its too much?

No sign of the scarf yet nor of the acid that was posted here. Did I tell you Id paid 8 francs for a box for my letters so as to have them secure. Now L.M. tells me its *8 francs par mois*!!! I thought it was for the season for after all they won't deliver here – they refuse. Another robbery, alors, & I dare not quarrel with the gens de la poste. On the contrary L.M. takes the little box faced girl bouquets of roses from Madame. If shed like me to burn candles Im only too willing. But Bogey they do make one pay. This is a horrid letter. Ill be a nicer girl when I come back from San Remo. Goodbye for now my darling.

Wig

MS ATL. *LKM* I. 304–5; *LJMM*, 417–18.

---

[1] Murry had tea with Vanessa Bell on Saturday, 22 Nov., and the next day wrote, 'I think that Virginia & Vanessa, however much we disagree with them – and, as I said, I think we are profoundly at cross purposes with Virginia, at least – are the two women with whom you & I have most in common (except, perhaps, Brett).' (Murry, 223.)

To J. M. Murry, [30 November 1919]

[Casetta Deerholm, Ospedaletti]
Sunday Morning 8 a.m.

My Precious Bogey,

Its a real Sunday, calm, quiet with the sea practising over a voluntary while the verger tiptoes laying out the hymn & prayer books in the strangers pews. Theres a lovely piece of bright sun in my room but bother – it is moving towards great banks of unruffled cloud. Your letter with the house & the horse has come, darling. Yes I am a ⌇⌇⌇⌇ but I do my best all the same.[1] Im *prisoned*. Ill never be right until L.M. and I part company. About the parcels. The acid sent to Rome arrived: the other has not, neither has the scarf. But I believe the parcel post takes a month occasionally or even five weeks so they may turn up . . . I hope you do have a whack at the Georgians.[2] Is Nichols one?[3] There was a most disgraceful article by him in the Observer.[4]

I went to San Remo yesterday afternoon. It was *very* exciting. The shops are all prepared for the Great Fleece. A great many antique shops are open. I suppose they are all frauds. At any rate the prices would be appalling but by jove! they have got some lovely things! There was a chair yesterday that cant be a fraud covered in the most exquisite needlework in old ivory brocade. Figs and their leaves, pomegranates, apricots, pears, a spotted snake or two all in most gay delicate colours and then there was another great piece of embroidery, all flowers with a little running border of wild strawberry fruits, leaves, & blossoms. The shops are rather darkish. One looks in and one sees a flash of silver, a mass of copper, dark polished furniture, lace, a glass case or two of miniatures & jewels, & the old spider with a silk handkerchief over her head sitting quiet, on the watch. Id be the first fly to go in if my purse were full. I had to order some cards yesterday but they cant cut me a plaque here: the wretched things have to be printed. Boge *would* you send me out some decent ones? I must have them as soon as I can. No address – so Id better not have many.

I went to the market. It was gay there. You remember where they used to sell fried cakes? Yesterday there was a stall covered with them & to one side on a charcoal stove women were cooking pancakes. A queer feeling markets give me. I feel that – once every hundred years or so I walk about among the stalls, price the fruit, note that the new raisins have come, smell the fried cakes, and see the womans gesture as she rattles for change in the money bag at her side . . .

Waiting for the train Vince came up. Well! Hell commit murder one of these days. If ever man looked like a murderer. Hes a fascinating character – a *real* villain. Not a fool – not merely vague (*far* from it). Hell end by having a small hotel at a place like Boulogne or Calais or Dieppe and hell meet the trains wearing a straw hat and sandshoes.

Its autumn here now: the vines are red and yellow: the dark women carry pale chrysanthemums & oranges and lemons are ripe. I came home, lit my fire, began to take my shoes off & fell asleep. When I woke up it was dark – the fire just burning – not a sound. I didn't know how long Id been asleep. Everything was still. I sat there for about ½ an hour then I heard steps outside & L.M. came in back from the village. It was nearly seven oclock! I ate dinner came up got into bed & fell asleep again & woke at 11, bitten to death by three *huge* mosquitoes in the net. Murdered them. Went to sleep again & slept till seven! What a pa woman! Oh, Boge, find the house! I am *longing* for it. Christmas is near. *Shall* we next year really keep Christmas? *Shall* we have a tree & put it in a room with the door locked – only you and I allowed to go in & decorate it – & then have a small party on Christmas Eve?? We shall go out all wrapped up to the noses, with a pruning hook to cut holly & well burn a Christmas log. PERHAPS! You know its madness to love & live apart. Thats what we do. Last time I came back to France do you remember how we *swore* never again. Then I went to Looe – and after that we *swore*: never again. Then I came here. Shall we go on doing this? It isn't a married life at all – not what I mean by a married life. How I envy Virginia; no wonder she can write. There is always in her writing a calm freedom of expression as though she were at peace – her roof over her – her

own possessions round her – and her man somewhere within call.
Boge what have I done that I should have *all* the handicaps – plus a
disease and an enemy. And *why* should we believe this wont happen
again? Weve said as sincerely as we can ever possibly say: "it *will* not.
This is the *last* time. Well *never* let each other go again. We *could* not."
But the time comes, and theres nothing else to be done and – before
you say Jack Knife we're apart again, going through it all again.
Shall I be in Malaga next winter or Algiers? Odious, odious thought.
But really Id better get used to it. We are the sport of circumstance.
Its obviously impossible for us to do anything – but how tired the dice
get of being rattled & thrown!

Your
Wiggie.

I long to see Cinnamon & Angelica. I expect it will come today.

MS ATL. *LKM* I. 305–7; *LJMM*, 418–20.

[1] Murry's letter of 25 Nov. included a drawing of a house, a horse, and a rough graph
demonstrating with a rising jagged line how KM's emotions were 'always tumbling down. . . .
But you never tumble down as much as you've been going up.' (Murry, 226.)
[2] Murry felt extremely antagonistic to the anthology *Georgian Poetry, 1918–1919*, edited by
E. M. (Edward Marsh), which he told KM was 'spreading a miasma of sickening falsity . . .
sham naive, sham everything'.
[3] There were five poems in the anthology by Robert Nichols (1893–1944), who had published
three collections of verse, and also wrote short stories.
[4] In the *Observer*, 23 Nov. 1919, under 'A Serious Satirist', Robert Nichols favourably
reviewed D. S. MacColl's *Bull, and Other War Satires*. He prefaced his praise with a dismissive
survey of Pound, Eliot, Strachey, and Huxley, and the 'undoubted tendency among our younger
folk to make fun of the world when they can make nothing else of it'.

To J. M. Murry, [30 November 1919]

[Casetta Deerholm, Ospedaletti]

Weather report: Dead calm, warm – some sun, earthquakey.
I had a proof of E. Stanley. Did you like her verse?[1]
Sunday evening.
My precious,
What a fate you should have published the Dosty the very week my
review wont arrive. The Lord is *not* on my side. But to the extent of
having let me have two of your letters today it is. One mentions the
house.[2] Is there really a chance for it? What is the rent? What is it like
– old – young? Garden – fruit? Trees? I expect I would get very
friendly with the Waterlows if I lived near them. Well, thats that.
Your Wednesday letter about the paper gives me such a glimpse of

you – rescuing it. It is though an awful drag on you, isn't it? Aren't there many moments when you long to be free? What do you feel about running this paper. Do you feel the game is worth the candle? I often wonder. On the other hand how are we going to make money? We cant live on ha'pennies: I mean we don't want to. You don't want to – do you? I dont. The days of washing saucepans are over. Of course Id do it *like a shot* if need be – and be *perfectly happy* but I think its a waste of energy and time when we are together. No two lovers could possibly talk while they were cleaning the knives. No wonder you 'upped' with the bath brick! Oh I *do* love you Bogey. If we took it you wouldnt come here for May – would you? Id come back & wed spend the holiday looking at the outside. But your later letter says you're going to De la Mare on Sunday so praps the house is 'off'. No you *mustnt* go such long journeys: you're as bad as I am with your thank you very much instead of 'no'. When – if – we are together for good Ill always answer your invitations & you mine: then we'll be safe.

Old Rutter forwarded this letter today, together with a note from him asking where to send my cheque & would I send another story because people liked the last so.[3] Very rash. Yes, the *Fake*-ists quite overcome me.[4] That Observer had p.e. a review of Legend. If you read Legend!!! Humbug – deplorable humbug – rant – rubbish – tinpot provincial hysterics. But they couldn't have said more if Clemence Dane had written The Tempest. It makes me feel quite queer sometimes when I read that Saint's Progress is one of the great masterpieces of all time & yet I never feel for an instant Im not right. There cant be any doubt about such rot as Legend and the Times RAVED. Perhaps when 1200000 people a year buy Georgian Poetry we shall be burned together.

At that moment Vince and his babies came over & I gave him the figs for you, packed with my own lily-white hands, wrapped in a linen napkin which is ours. They are the figs *of* Ospedaletti – dried here – in this very place & sold by the panier. Chew them well, child, and dont swallow too soon. He promised me wardrobes & plants and /// (rockets) But do you think he is safe enough to convey a parcel for me? The thing is this. My cardigan that you gave me October 1918 is worn very thin. *No, no, no.* I don't want another. I *cant* just now. Ive heaps of things I can manage with really & truly. I stayed in bed all the morning & *slept*. Queer how I suffer from insomnia and then just make it all up by perpetual sleep. Last week I couldn't sleep. After my jaunt yesterday I have slept practically ever since. Oh, I *do* wish we were a bit rich – don't you? Money is a bore. I must get more wood tomorrow & pay old L.M. *She* is coming into some more money £300– £500. Its *hers*. And that other legacy was over £100. "But thats all settled & out of my hands" she said "I've spent that!" I feel a deep rage that it trickles away so – that the £5 a month I give her flows away & is not. Still, however I hate her I owe her the money for all shes done. Her sisters letter today I managed to see. She had been three days in Cape Town where their brother is but, 'of course', did not let him know.[5] I wanted to find out first for Mr Swain how he has been behaving & I have found out now – it was *just as well*. Theres the Chaddie attitude. Ida I know agrees. Gerald was very spoilt by the ladies on the boat . . . My Vord!

Theres tea. I must go and drink & eat it. Wasn't the sketch of the cats good?[6] Wing is the spit of Wing. It was nice of the old boy to send it me so carefully, little trump that he is. Give him a squeeze from his sissy.

Its getting dusky. The house is full of small shadows. I hear the kettle having its lid taken off & then its filled & now its on the fire again – all this very distinct. Its sunset. The windows are shut the sea is pale. Oh, my dearest darling, my wonder, how dare I lean on you as I do. Do you feel Im a weight? I want to lean so light so light & then suddenly I get heavy and ask to be carried. You ought not to have chosen me to travel with. Ah, I don't agree with that. We made the right choice, the miraculously right *choice* at any rate. *We've* done all we could. Its only the —— Boss Omnipotent whos been so horrid.

Yours for ever and ever as long as I live and after that all the flowers will come up small & starry with love.

Wig.

The A. not here yet nor scarf nor acid.

MS ATL. *LKM* I. 308; *LJMM*, 420–2.

---

[1] Two of KM's poems, under the name Elizabeth Stanley, appeared in the *Athenaeum* early the next year: 'Old Fashioned Widow's Song', 9 Jan., and 'Sunset', 23 Jan. 1920.

[2] Murry told her of a house to let close to the Waterlows, near Pewsey, Wiltshire.

[3] 'The Pictures', in the Autumn issue of *Art and Letters*.

[4] Murry wrote, 25 Nov., 'Oh, the *fake* of this *Georgian Poetry*! It really is a terrible condition of affairs that these people – Eddie M. & J. C. Squire – should have got such a stranglehold of English poetry.' (Murry, 227.)

[5] Ida Baker's sister May, and her younger brother Waldo, both of whom lived in Rhodesia.

[6] Richard Murry had sent KM a drawing of the cats at Portland Villas.

To J. M. Murry, [1 December 1919]

[Casetta Deerholm, Ospedaletti]

Darling,

Im rather dished today. Ive got fever and that makes me frightfully depressed. Ansaldi came yesterday. Dont *count* on him. Hes a charlatan. He owned yesterday that the reports he gave me were because "I saw dis lady vants vot you call sheering up. Like de Irishman[1] I told you you could trot and I hope you may be able to walk." You observe the polite smile with which I listened. The whole interview seems to have been more or less of a fake. He said yesterday for instance *emp*hatically that I could not winter in England next year or the year after: that I must have sun and warmth. In fact he behaved precisely like all other doctors in the world but Sorapure do behave. Sorapure is the only man one can trust at all. This one wasn't like Drey in the face for nothing. He *did* give me a good beating. And when I told him of my melancholia he said it was part toxin poisoning and part because you are alone wiz nobody near you to love and sherish you. I tell my patients dat is better dan medicine, Mrs Murry & so on & so on & so on & so on. And then he went away & I sat in my dressing gown & watched it grow dusk & then dark here – and REALISED how I had been taken in again.

Doesn't matter. What must be, must be. I am writing to Jinnie F. today to ask her if I may come to Menton for a few days. But whats the good? I couldn't go today: my temperature's 102. So one goes round & round & round like the squirrel in the cage. Its a cold grey day. L.M. is at San Remo getting money for me. When I 'get better' again though Ill go to Menton for a few days. I think I *must*. I am *too* lonely. You my own precious dont grieve for me. Its just my melancholia. Tigs black birds. Kiss Wing & know I love you.

Wig.

MS ATL. *LKM* I. 308–9; *LJMM*, 422–3.

[1] Christopher Costello, the doctor who treated her at Looe in 1918.

To J. M. Murry, [3 December 1919]

[Casetta Deerholm, Ospedaletti]
Wednesday

My own,

Your wire came this early morning. How it *could* have arrived so soon I cannot understand but there it was – *thank God*. I am sending 2 reviews this week so that you have one in reserve again. Im doing Couperus & Kuprin together as 2 foreign novels.[1] I thought that the best idea. Here is also your darling Friday letter about the new linen for the house & Wing saucepan rolling. It all sounds so wonderful. I am better today – my temperature is lower & though I feel a bit like a fly who is *just* out of the milk jug – ça va. Must have caught a chill I suppose. I don't know how. Its a very ugly day. I am lying in my little room warmly wrapped up with a hot water bottle & fire. L.M. has gone to San Remo. She dropped 32 lire on a cheque yesterday & as it was a 'mistake' I have had to ask her to go back with it today & see if she can get the extra. I suppose not.

Last night under the inspiration of a fever attack I wrote these verses. Keep them for me – will you?[2] I feel a longing to write poetry. Don't forget you were going to send me Hardy: I feel passionately eager to read his poems. Did he mention the De la Mare review in the Times. Bogey it was superficial, 'silly' and the snail on the nasturtium leaf again. That don't fit Hardy. Talking of snails, the Nation & Guardian came today. Did you see the one in the eye Wayfarer[3] gave me? He HAD his quarrel I own but he was unfair all the same.

Vinces old gardener is outside, bless him – sowing sweet peas. Hes a dear old root of a man. He peers at me through the window & when I open it to speak makes the gesture of pulling his coat round him so that Ill keep covered up & mutters 'd'vent d'vent' as though it were spelled *devant*. Its alright, precious. I shall be better still tomorrow. Its always a comfort not to feel worse. But don't rush a house. Who knows that Im not turned out of England by the Lord: that Im not a wandering tribe, complete with lamentations. It looks jolly like it to me. But even if I am *you* must have a house in the country – so go on collecting. Goodbye for now my precious. I LOVE you LOVE you LOVE.

Your own Wig-wife.

MS ATL. *LKM* I. 309–10; *LJMM*, 423–4.

---

[1] The reviews appeared separately: 'A Foreign Novel', discussing Louis Couperus' *Old People and the Things that Pass* in the *Athenaeum* on 12 Dec. 1919, and 'Alexander Kuprin', a review of *The Garnet Bracelet*, 26 Dec. 1919.

[2] The verses were enclosed with one of her letters next day.

[3] In her review of Virginia Woolf, the *Atheneaum*, 21 Nov., KM remarked, 'It is impossible to refrain from comparing "Night and Day" with the novels of Miss Austen. There are moments, indeed, when one is almost tempted to cry it Miss Austen up-to-date.' In the *Nation's* weekly column 'A London Diary', signed 'A Wayfarer', 29 Nov. 1919, this comparison was taken up and curtly dismissed.

To J. M. Murry, [4 December 1919]

[Casetta Deerholm, Ospedaletti]
Thursday

My darling Bogey,

I am sending my review of Couperus and Kuprin today. Don't the names go well together! I feel a bit better today. My temperature rose again pretty high last night tho' I went to bed at five. I expect its that which knocks me out so absolutely *morally*. Its pretty frightful – the loneliness the noise of ones heart pounding away – and the feeling that this is ALL there is. I can't master it. I must just go on with it & take what comes. There is nothing else for it. I reviewed the whole situation last night. The old gardener came again yesterday to sow sweet peas. We parleyed through the window, he roaring and I nodding. He wants to dig up the lower terrace & plant zucca, concombres, haricots, tomates, pommes de terres, kakis. And then he performed a pantomime of the servant maid emptying jugs of water into these delicacies and they growing round and fat – all by next spring.

Ive never seen or heard from les dames de San Remo since I did not attend Miss Shuttleworths lunch. That was the end of that. But it was an appalling day – impossible. Everybody seems to agree that the appalling cold this year has been quite exceptional – and that the worst is over. It has not been so cold these last few days. I begin to think that even *with* it this climate is vastly better than England. The sun does shine, the air is pure. If one were not alone here and conscious of every tiny smallest change in the elements and in ones sick body even the cold would not matter so much. And there IS sun. Ospedaletti itself is quite the most beautiful little place Ive ever seen – far lovelier than Bandol – and behind it that valley must be really exquisite. The cemetery bulks in my vision but then Im an abnormal creature. If it didn't and if people had to come abroad I should say come here. Its so small, theres no fashion, no parasitic life, the people are self-contained and pleasant – you and I in the old days would have been ideally happy here.

You know I am going to Menton I hope for a few days when I am better – to *break the iron ring*. I want to have a talk to Jinnie F. too. If I can be sure of getting better – absolutely sure – would you mind very much if I adopted a child? Its evidently on the cards I may have to spend a good deal of my life – alone – and I cant stick it. I think, Im sure in fact, I could manage as regards money and I want to adopt a baby boy of about *one* if I can get him. I cannot do it if you dislike the idea because of course he would be always with us when we were together just like our own child – and you might hate that. On the other hand when I am alone hed keep me from utter loneliness and from writing these agonising letters!! I thought Id ask Brett to be his guardian supposing anything were to happen to me. I think she would like it and that would free you from any possible responsibility should you not want to have him & of course you couldn't if I wasn't there. If I must spend next winter abroad I cant spend it alone – and a nurse for him kills two birds with one stone!

But at any rate, my dear darling, I can't face life alone not even for six months at a time. The prospect is unbearable. It can't be done. Neither can you and I be together. Theres the paper. You CANT give it up. We must have the money. You cant earn money away from England and even if you could you mustn't leave England. That is obvious. Your place is *there*. It would spell failure for you to live abroad with me – I absolutely fully realise that. I can imagine what hours we should spend when I realised and you realised the sacrifice. And then theres the house in England which I could come to in the summer & perhaps after a year or two live in always . . . But Ill never be sure that a moment of uprooting will not recur and this is what I cannot contemplate. I think quite seriously I shall go out of my mind if I have to suffer a great deal more. There's where the child comes in: Id love him and he'd love me. We'd look after each other. But when you reply to this consider that he'd be always with me. Id have to bring a nurse back to England. (She wouldn't cost any more than L.M. however.) But I want you to think of it and write to me as soon as you can for if I go to Menton Ill talk it over with Jinnie.

L.M.s off to the village. I must give her this letter. Goodbye for now darling Bogey. I hope O's sale was a success (for us I mean).

Ever your own
Wig-wife.

MS ATL. *LJMM*, 424–5.

To J. M. Murry, [4 December 1919]

[Casetta Deerholm, Ospedaletti]
5 p.m. Thursday.

My darling,

Your Saturday letter telling me of your cold and your Sunday letter are come. I do hope the journey to Penge[1] didn't make the cold worse; it seemed a bit like madness to go and risk waiting at the railway stations – but – what could you do? Wing ought to be trained to balance the paperweight on his nose, like Dora's Gyp did the pencil[2] – you remember? I have been wondering whether you marked the new linen and how: it *is* so important to have it plainly marked & to see it comes back from the wash. I expect Violet is careful, though. Would you put an *ad* of my story in the T.L.S.[3] Ill pay. I feel we must sell it now its been such a labour & thats the only way it will sell. But it ought to be in before Xmas.

Dont overwork, Boge. I wish I could see your Georgian Poetry review:[4] I tremble a little for you when you go 'eyes out' for or against a thing. I always feel you dont quite get the measure of your opponent – you expose yourself in your enthusiasm and he takes a mean underhand advantage. But perhaps that is nonsense. Its sunset, with a wide, wide pale yellow sky and a blue sea gilded over. I feel horribly weak after this fever attack but calmer – just now – thank the Lord. My heart is so hateful. If you had such a heart. It *bangs throbs beats* out 'tramp tramp tramp the boys are marching'[5] double quick time with very fine double rolls for the kettle drum. How it keeps it up I dont know. I always feel its going to give out. I think every day I shall die of heart failure. I expect its an inherited feeling from Mother. Oh – *envied* Mother – lucky lucky Mother – so surrounded – so held – so secure. Cant I hear her "child you mustnt be left here ONE INSTANT" and then shed make miracles happen and by tomorrow shed have wrapped me up and defied everybody.

But we are firmly held in the web of circumstance. Weve got to risk it – to see it through. If you were to leave there our future is wrecked. If I came there Id die. No, once Im better I go to Menton and Ill return here later in the spring when Im stronger with a maid so as to be ready for you in May.

L.M. is out to tea with some people in Ospedaletti – gone off with a big bunch of roses for them. The wind sighs in the house and the fire goes chik-chik – very small. My fever makes everything 100 times more vivid – like a nightmare is vivid. But it will be over in a day or two, I expect. A bad business! Brett sent me some photographs.[6] Will you thank her for me. I can't lash myself into any kind of a friendly cackle. I thought the photographs very weak, thats all, but she sent me a nice letter.

Can you get Lawrences address for me?[7] I should like to have it.

Goodbye darling.

I am ever your own

Wig-wife.

I am sure Menton will do wonders for my old depression – Ive great hopes of it. Bogey forgive me. All you tell me about the house I cant help feeling is all part of the hideous vile joke thats being played on us for les autres to read about in days to come. I *cant* see it except like this. I sometimes even get to the pitch of believing that subconsciously you are aware of this, too, and with colossal artistry are piling on delicate agony after delicate agony – so that *when* the joke is explained all will be quite perfect even to a silver teapot for her.

P.S. Darling please keep all these verses for me in the file – will you? Ill polish them up one day have them published. But Ive no copies –

so don't leave 'em about – will you. Just thrust them into the old file or
into my cupboard.

Wig.

MS ATL. *LKM* I. 310; *LJMM*, 426–8.

The New Husband.

Some one came to me and said
Forget, forget that you've been wed
Who's your man to leave you be
Ill and cold in a far country
Whos the husband – who's the stone
Could leave a child like you alone.

You're like a leaf caught in the wind
You're like a lamb thats left behind.
When all the flock has pattered away
Youre like a pitiful little stray
Kitten that Id put in my vest
Youre like a bird that's fallen from nest

We've none of us too long to live
Then take me for your man and give
Me all the Keys to all your fears
And let me kiss away these tears
Creep close to me. I mean no harm
My darling. Let me make you warm

I had received that very day
A letter from the Other to say
That in six months – he hoped – no longer
I would be so much better and stronger
That he would close his books and come
With radiant looks to bear me home.

Ha! Ha! Six months, six weeks, six hours
Among these glittering palms and flowers
With Melancholy at my side
For my old nurse and for my guide
Despair – and for my footman Pain –
Ill never see my home again

Said my new husband: Little dear
Its time we were away from here
In the road below there waits my carriage
Ready to drive us to our marriage
Within my home the feast is spread
And the maids are baking the bridal bread.

I thought with grief upon that other
But then why should he aught discover
Save that I pined away and died?
So I became the stranger's bride
And every moment however fast
It flies – we live as 'twere our last!

— * —

Elizabeth Stanley.

LJMM, 427–8.

He wrote

Darling Heart if you would make me
Happy, you have found the way.
Write me letters. How they shake me
Thrill me all the common day

With our love. I hear your laughter
Little laughs! I see your look
'They Lived Happy Ever After'
As you close the faery book.

Work's been nothing but a pleasure
Every silly little word
Dancing to some elfin measure
Piped by a small chuckling bird.

All this love – as though I've tasted
Wine too rare for human food –
I have dreamed away and wasted
Just because the news was good.

Where's the pain of ⟨making⟩ counting money
When my little queen is there
In the parlour eating honey
Beautiful beyond compare!

How I love you! You are better.
Does it matter – being apart?
Oh, the love that's in this letter
Feel it, beating like a heart.

Beating out – 'I do adore you'
Now and to Eternity
See me as I stand before you
Happy as you'd have me be.

Dont be sad and dont be lonely
Drive away those awful fears
When they come remember only
How Ive suffered these two years.

Darling heart if you must sorrow
Think: "My pain must be his pain."
Think: "He will be sad tomorrow"
And then – make me smile again.

— * —

Elizabeth Stanley

Journal 1954, 181–2.

Et Après

When her last breath was taken
And the old miser death had shaken
The last, last glim from her eyes
He retired
And to the world's surprise
Wrote these inspired, passion-fired
Poems of Sacrifice!
The world said:
If she had not been dead
(And burièd)
He'd never have written these.
She was hard to please.

They're better apart
Now the stone
Has rolled away from his heart
Now he's come into his own
Alone.

— * —

Elizabeth Stanley

Journal 1954, 182–3.

[1] Where Murry had visited Walter de la Mare.
[2] KM is remembering the episode in Charles Dickens's *David Copperfield*, Ch. XLI, in which the dog stands on a cookery book while it holds a pencil-case in its mouth.
[3] *Je ne parle pas français*, recently set by hand and printed by Richard Murry, was then being collated and sewn.
[4] 'The Condition of English Poetry', Murry's devastating review of *Georgian Poetry, 1918–1919*, and the periodical *Wheels*, Fourth Cycle, the *Athenaeum*, 5 Dec. 1919.
[5] The first line of the chorus from 'Tramp! Tramp! Tramp!', the well-known song of the Northern armies in the American Civil War, the words and music by G. F. Root.
[6] Brett had sent photographs of her recent paintings.
[7] D. H. Lawrence was then in Florence, later in the month moving on to Rome, Picinisco, and then Capri.

To J. M. Murry, [5 December 1919]

[Casetta Deerholm, Ospedaletti]
Friday in bed.

My dearest Bogey,
    I was thinking over Cinnamon and Angelica in bed last night and you know I think you ought to find something else for that bit where Cinnamon comments on his nose and Mace says tis the Cinnamon nose and tells him his grandfather was called Old Long Beak. For this reason. There have been so *many* royal noses so many Long Beak grandfathers that the idea is too familiar to the ear.[1] I am a perfect fiend about this play aren't I and Im afraid I come as Miss Dane would put it "savaging your Holy of Holies".[2] But you know how it is meant. Its what I want you to do with my stories. I feel you ought to have done it more to 'je ne parle pas' – don't, because youre exquisitely tender spare *me*. Id rather not be *sporn*.
    Your play suggests so much – thats the trouble and I cant be quite sure that what you have imaginatively apprehended yourself has *got into it enough*. You know how, beyond a certain point, if one is deeply in love with a piece of work its almost impossible to say what is there and whats not there. I think too, it might be more faëry, by that I mean

have more *songs*. I think when Angelica is found with Carraway and Marjoram she ought to sing. There ought to be indeed to my thinking a song for the three of them – Angelica's song with a line for Carraway here and a line for Marjoram there[3] . . . Perhaps this is because I do *shy* a little at blank verse. It makes the *quality* you want to get very difficult. On the other hand at Cinnamon's death – at Mace's account of it except for that (forgive my horrible cruelty) "*war Mace war*" you bend it wonderfully to your will. By mentioning that *war Mace war* I know that is precisely what you meant to convey – yet it seems to me *curse* the word reminiscent. I hear so many lovers saying with just that real feeling '*war Mace war*' but I dont, on the other hand, hear them saying "My darling" nor read how they drooped and died.[4]

At that moment I tried to *think* out what I wanted to see and instead – bending my mind to your play I saw you instead – in all your innocence and beauty. I saw that you which is the *real rare secret* you. Oh if only I could lift this dark disease from me. It did lift for the instant but then I realised how dark it is – and how it has poisoned me. It does not stop at your lungs; then it attacks your brain and then your heart. And I also feel I must make very very plain that I never want you here. Dont think that for one instant. I DONT. You must stay where you are. I must get through this and find my way out or not alone. I feel that to the bottom of my soul. The time is past when we might have been together in such a case. Now it would only spell tragedy for us both. You feel that, too, dont you? Of course that being the case it is not fair that I should tell you what I suffer. But the feeling is stronger than I. I cant know you and not tell. I dont write to another creature simply because I couldnt not tell them. Its all there is of me TO tell. Hideous, hideous predicament. I hope to hear from Menton today or tomorrow and as soon as I am well Ill go there for a bit. Ive still got fever but it is going. My temperature was only 100 last night. Ill get L.M. to buy a bottle of cognac today for a stimulant.

Well heres December. Does Arthur remember the paper flowers he made last December and how we decorated the hall and stairs. *Darling Memory.* I was very happy. If Im alive next year Bogey where shall I be? *Malaga* I think; it sounds so peculiarly odious full of the most beautiful *flowers* and *shops* and an english boarding house kept by a Mrs Cooper. But she wont take anybody who is ill or who wont dress in *low* evening dress for dinner. Thats one strange door mercifully shut then. Goodbye darling. Its a pity this all happened. Alas! Alas!

Your own Wig-wife.

MS ATL., *LJMM*, 429–30.

[1] The printing of Murry's verse play was more advanced than KM realized, so Murry could not take her advice.

[2] In Clemence Dane's *Legend*, p. 126, there occurs the sentence 'Love-sick – sick of love – savage with love – savaging her holy of holies.'

[3] At the beginning of Act III.

[4] At the end of Act IV, Colonel Mace reports to Angelica:

> Madame, he muttered something
> I could not hear, and then he smiled at me
> Into my eyes and whispered: 'War, Mace, war.'
> And then he tried to rise up from the ground
> And said in pain: 'My darling,' and his lip
> Drooped, and then I know he drooped and died.

To J. M. Murry, [5 December 1919]

[Casetta Deerholm, Ospedaletti]

My darling Bogey,

Your after the sale letter has arrived & I think you did very well. What you say about *clocks* is quite true, no room is complete without one – and the writing table sounds exquisite.[1] Will you put it in the hall for the present in place of that ugly? Or is it not the right shape or size? What a lot of new things there are even since my time! Now about your talk at De la Mares on poetry. No, youre NOT too serious.[2] I think you are a trifle over anxious to assure people how serious you are. You antagonize them sometimes or set them doubting because of your emphasis upon your sincerity. In reviewing again you cry sometimes in your sincerity: these are the things which have been done which have happened to *me* to us. I think as a critic that *me* or *us* is superfluous. If they must be there then you must write a poem or a story. People are not *simple* enough. Life is not simple enough to bear it otherwise. It fills me with a queer kind of shame. One hears oneself whispering in ones soul to you: "cover yourself – cover yourself quickly. Dont let them see." That they think you are asking for alms for pity doesn't matter. That of course is just their corruption – their falsity. Nevertheless though they are wrong I do not think you are right. If you speak for your generation *speak* but dont say I speak for my generation – for the force is then gone from your cry. When you know you are a voice crying in the wilderness *cry* but dont say "I am a voice crying in the wilderness."[3] To my thinking (and I am as you know so infinitely incomparably nearer the public than you) the force of either the blow you strike or the praise you want to sing is *broken* by this – what is it. Is it the most infernal modesty? Innocence? Do you see how all this which is non-critical in you proves & proves & proves & proves you *poet*. Heavens child! Youre quite capable of kicking off with

My lips have sipped oblivion, I have known
The Golden Hours chime through the charmed day[4]

while reading Mr ——'s essay on ——. No, that is extreme but theres
a big *pearl* of truth in it. The trouble ∴ is that when a book really
engages your passions you are dangerous. You can be trusted with
other books but if a book stirs you to real anger then theres the fear
that youll be all poet and miss it – and at the same time – what I call
expose yourself.

You have of course worked about a million times too hard and too
long. That *long breath* you never have time for. Youre not crippled,
your wings aren't injured (*real* wings now) but they are bound to you –
bound tight – and until youve had time to really really spread them –
to sail down a tideless breeze youll never really be the writer you
ought to be. Whenever a little spell has come – the smallest – you have
made these extraordinary beginnings of real flight – I mean *short perfect*
flights as in some of your poems – but you must know your *freedom* to
be the poet you are. If its not absurd to say so you are capable of
infinite expansion (see the Globe-Wernicke)[5] and ripe for it. In fact I
see you as a man *starved*. If we could – ah if theyll let us pull off the
house idea you're saved as well as I – you're saved as a poet. (Reading
Hardy made me realise this.) You oughtn't to *give out* except whats
just over-plus – you ought to *absorb* and receive.

I expect this is both dull and impertinent.
Later.

Oh! your new book has just come. It looks SUPERB.[6] I want to burn
all Ive written here. Ill read it tonight. It looks terrific. And when I
looked at the title page (and decided no, hes forgotten), & saw that *to
my wife* I had a moment Bogey of such ANCIENT BLISS you cannot
conceive. Now Ill go on with this. Really *C.S.* [Cobden-Sanderson]
has done you very proud – I mean its so distinguished looking – don't
you think? No, that *To my wife, To my wife* is written on every wave of
the sea at the moment. I see Michael Sadleir[7] lapping up that. Its to
me just as though Id been going home from school and the
Monaghans[8] had called after me and you – about the size of a
sixpence – had defended me and praps helped to pick up my pencils &
put them back in the pencil box. (Id have given you the red one.) I
had by the same post an awfully nice sympathetic letter from Grant
Richards asking me for a book. He can have "White Roses"[9] when
ready. I feel better today: the brandy was a great point. "Very old
pale cognac" – one can't help pitying it. Yet that it should have such
fire!! My temperature was only just on 100 last night. Now Ive got to
climb back again – curse it.

Bogey about that scarf – would you gather the insurance? I think its

gone for good alright and we cant just drop the £2.2.0. And if you get
it might I have it in notes to buy summat woolly here if I can? The
post is obviously quite untrustworthy.

The sea comes rolling in – rolling in. Theres not a sound but my
pen. L.M. is out somewhere in the village. Catherina came to see me
yesterday guarding against the infection de la fièvre with a shawl –
but an *immense* shawl! which she kept held up to her lips till I made her
smile & then forgot all about. I was asking her if she is going to help
with the tea room that Madame Littardi is opening. "Ah non
Madame, ce n'est pas mon métier, vous savez" and here she blushed
lightly & put her hands in her pockets. "Je suit *née* pour le repassage
e-t puis – c'est ma passion!"

Theres the secret of her charm. Heres L.M. back. Its ¼ to six. Post
time très juste.

Goodbye my darling own.

Your
Wig-wife.

MS ATL. *LKM* I. 311; *LJMM*, 430–3.

[1] Murry had attended Lady Ottoline's auction at Bedford Square, where he bought a writing-table for KM, and a Dresden clock.
[2] In the same letter, 1 Dec. 1919, Murry told of his visit to De la Mare, his condemnation of *Georgian Poetry*, and his fear that his seriousness might be taken as 'animus' (Murry, 230–1.)
[3] 'The voice of one crying in the wilderness.' Matt. 3: 3.
[4] These lines remain untraced.
[5] Globe-Wernicke Company, Cincinnati, manufacturers of filing cabinets, card-index systems and an 'elastic book case'.
[6] *The Evolution of an Intellectual*, published by Cobden-Sanderson.
[7] Michael Sadleir (1889–1957) had been a friend of Murry's since they were undergraduates together at Oxford. He had helped Murry establish *Rhythm*, and was now a publishing editor with Constable, where he was to become a director the next year.
[8] A family who lived in Karori at the same time as the Beauchamps, and attended the same primary school. KM had shared a desk with Lena Monaghan.
[9] Perhaps a title KM had in mind for a collection. No story with this name survives.

To J. M. Murry, [5 December 1919]

[Casetta Deerholm, Ospedaletti]
Friday.

Dear Editor,

I feel that this book demanded a review of its own. I shall send
(cross my heart straight Dinkum) Kuprin, and Hewlett & Philpotts &
Stackpool on Sunday.

K.M.

Sent this day Friday: Night & Day
                     True Love
                     Children of No Man's Land
                     Legend
                     Old People[1]
                     I certify this girl has had a temperature
                     this week & hasn't been able to do more.
                                           Doctor Wing.
                                           Priez pour Elle.

MS ATL. *LJMM*, 433.

---

[1] All books she had recently reviewed, and was sending back to England to be sold.

To J. M. Murry, [7 December 1919]

[Casetta Deerholm, Ospedaletti]
Sunday

Darling Own,

I wonder what you are doing with your Sunday? And if its fine or dreadful. Its very fine here – a little windy thats all. My day has been like my last few days. I rise at *12* lunch – lie on the sofa till *6*, and then say "are the hot water bottles upstairs", and go to bed. Its a small beat but there is a large Policeman on it who frightens me a bit. My fever returned last night: I dont know why. It decided me to take a step. Your "clock" complex is surpassed by my doctor complex – but my collection, unlike yours never is reliable, never tells the truth or sustains or strikes the real hour – except the beautiful clock Sorapure. But Im going to call in another: I dont want to see Ansaldi again. What IS the good. Who wants "sheering" up only? And besides he repels me. But yesterday that Miss Shuttleworth came here and though she was *far* too kind & concerned to be genuine she did implore me to see Foster the englishman.[1] In fact she asked if she could go back and phone him and I said yes. Perhaps its just as well. He comes tomorrow. But I must get Arthur to print off a decent little pamphlet entitled The Physical History of K.M., 1917–19? It is so wearisome, so – I dont know like ashes to hear myself recite my ONE recitation – a bird with one song. How the Fowler Trapped Me. Perhaps that's what all birds in cages sing. Next time you pass one listen and hear it: "I was flying through a wood – a *green* wood and spring wood —— it was early early morning" ——

This afternoon Ive been reading your book but I cant write about it till its finished. Thank goodness youre not going to De la Mare's tonight – all that journey —— you must not do it again.[2]

The fire is alright but its become a burning bridge with no heart – just an arc de triomphe. I cant get up and put it together I am so wound round in my jaegar rug. There WAS a purchase, Boge, my own. Oh, I DO love you. Its dusk here. My pen seems to make such a loud noise – the wind swings in the shadowy air – the sea cries. I love you and love you. Dont forget how I love you. Remember pour toujours. How long since weve said that. I expect this week Ill get well again. I know why I have the fever today its my left lung – but not intolerable by any means. Goodbye for now darling darling Heart.

Your
Wigwife.

MS ATL. *LKM* I. 311–12; *LJMM*, 433–4.

---

[1] Michael Foster, an English doctor who practised in San Remo.
[2] The visit the week before had meant a journey of one-and-a-quarter hours each way.

To J. M. Murry, [8 December 1919]

[Casetta Deerholm, Ospedaletti]
Monday morning.

My darling,

Its warm & still. Ive all the windows open – practically the *wall* open in my bedroom and Im looking out on to the hillside. There's just a gentle, gentle stirring of the trees – lovely to watch. Lets talk about your book.[1] I read it through last night. The quality that is ever present and that makes the greatest impression on the reader is your *honesty*. Your almost desperate struggle in a world of falsity to get at the truth. That is *very noble*, and the *imperative impulse* which urges you to speak for the sake of truth – whatever the cost, not, indeed, counting the cost – is again a noble noble impulse. Nevertheless it seems to me that the false world has wounded you – has changed your 'word' from what it should be to what it is. You ought not to have to say these things. It is wrong that they should have been forced from you. You see I dont believe that the war has done these things to you: I don't believe you are maimed for life that you *go on* certainly, but that you never can recover. (Your generation I mean that you speak for.) I think these are the conclusions arrived at by thinking: granted such a war, granted such a *reception* of such a war, granted such falsity, indifference, squalor and callousness – their effect upon an intellect would be so and so . . . But this intellectual reasoning is never *the whole truth*. Its not *the artist's truth* – not *creative*. If man were an intellect it would do – but man ISN'T. Now I must be fair; I must be fair. Who am I to be certain that I understand. There's always Karori to shout after me.[2] *Shout* it. Ive re-read The Question & the Republic of the Spirit. The Question is very brilliant. Oh, dear, but its an *étude* – isn't it? Tour de force sur les écharpes? Isn't it? The other is the best essay in the book I think but it might have been written by a famous MONK. As I read, I felt yes, yes, yes but now let me turn and kiss somebody and let there be music . . .

Now I do not want you to think its the female in me who wants to kiss somebody after these essays. It is not because I am incapable of detachment that they seem to me *unwarm* (in the sense that fertility is warm. I keep seeing a golden hen on her eggs.) For you are not detached. If you were detached you would not have been influenced in the same way by the spirit of the times. Yet it is not the *complete you* who is influenced: it is the intellectual you. The *complete you* rebels against the intellectual you at times and wrestles and overthrows it. Which wins out after the book is finished in the mind of the reader?

19. We are maimed & broken for ever. Let us not deceive ourselves.

86. Tchekhov's sense of the *hopeless indescribable* beauty of the *infinitely weary* pattern . . .

97. And even that to such contemplation our own *utter* discomfiture is beautiful . . .

110. Yet we feel that the effort to respond to the Sursum Corda will be as long and may be more terrible still.

110. A part, how great we do not know of our soul is become *for ever* numbed & insentient. But with what remains we feel and we feel no joy.

117. And while we reach back *timidly* into the past to discover the sequence of our wounds . . .

131. We are afraid to speak of it because we know in our hearts that the breath of the very word will find us *naked* and *shivering* . . .

156. The possibility which we had desired stood before us in the *frozen intolerable* rigidity of a law. Against it we might dash our minds but they would break.

166. The impulse is almost overwhelming to withdraw into ourselves and discover in the *endurance* of our souls . . .

216. In a life in which the gold has dimmed to grey.

218. A menacing instinct warns us that we are somehow maimed.

I have just copied those few things because though I know it is not all "like that" they are there – and they are important. They DO give the tone. You know Bogey they seem to me deathly. They frighten me. I dont believe them – but thats beside the question. What I feel is that they cannot be the VITAL you? Were the world not what it is that you would not be alive today. Whatever the world were the you of certain of your poems, of parts of Cinnamon & Angelica will always be there. It seems to me that the intellect only ceases to be a devil when the soul is *supreme* and *free*. I know that you have been naked & shivering, timid & frozen. Oh that you should have known Love as deep as ours and still feel *like that. Love that is of the soul.*

I cant write any more today. These are just 'notes'. Please forgive them. They have been interrupted by two Wednesday letters. I hope your cold is better, my darling. *Dont* send me a cardigan if you've not sent it. Because neither of us have the money at present. But if you have SEND ME THE BILL & POSTAGE. I shall carefully count my pages in future. I am sincerely deeply sorry to have given you the extra work.[3] I know how annoying it must be.

I had such a nice letter from Kot. Wing has charmed even him. "Small and slender and quick witted" he calls him. What a little briseur de coeurs he is!

L.M. is taking this to San Remo. Foster hasn't been yet. Its a perfect summer day. I feel a good bit stronger – I dont *fret* darling. Fretting always seems to me tearing at the frayed edge of a feeling. I tear the whole feeling into great black bits. Dont know what thats called. Im going to *flood* you with work this week & then have a holiday at Xmas.

No, Boge, dont sent the A. & L. [*Art and Letters*] Sun and Moon – if you don't mind.[4]

(1) Theyd not publish it.

(2) I feel far away from it.

I think your Xmas present for me of that writing table is just perfect. I could not have one I like more.

Ever your own true love,
Wig.

MS ATL. *LJMM*, 434–7.

---

[1] Murry's *The Evolution of an Intellectual* was a collection of essays and articles published through the previous three years. KM's many numbered references in the letter are to pages in the volume.

[2] She had lived in Karori, then a small settlement west of Wellington, from 1893 to 1898.

[3] Murry told her, 3 Dec., that her review of Clemence Dane was 'a bit long. . . . Yours is certainly the hardest copy to cut of any we have.' (Murry, 233–4.)

[4] 'Sun and Moon' was published in the *Athenaeum*, 1 Oct. 1920.

To J. M. Murry, [8 December 1919]

[Casetta Deerholm, Ospedaletti]
Monday night. In bed.

My dear Love,

All is explained. Foster has been. I have a SLIGHT attack of bronchial pneumonia. Ive often had them before you know when I was at my Doctor Sorapure's college. As far as anyone can tell at present it is not any fresh outbreak in the left lung – I mean any new tubercular trouble, but a local attack as any non-tubercular patient might get. This will keep me in bed of course and it accounts for my fever and for the unpleasant symptoms in my heart. I mean there is considerable nervous exhaustion which strains the heart (but no disease in it – 'no reason why it shouldn't last you out'.) He has given me a preparation to help my congestion and he advises me to take brandy at least twice a day – or two full glasses of marsala (oh, the relief it is to *know*: to know I was not just giving way!) My situation in this villa with L.M. to look after he said was quite satisfactory. He does *not* regard it as very exposed. He says those winds have been everywhere. No villa in San Remo would take me, nor any hotel. "They've all got the wind up about you since you tried for the Excelsior." That accounts for the fact that there were no villas for us! Its either this or a nursing home and there is no present necessity for the latter and "I certainly *dont* recommend it if you can be comfortable here." This is also the reason why I can't get a maid. He says they won't come because they *know* about me . . . Very nice! But 'can't be helped'. He examined me thoroughly. His verdict was "there is serious disease in your left lung of long standing. The right is at present quiescent. You stand a reasonable chance." He was quite frank and rather on the brutal side, which is pleasant and refreshing. He said, in reply to my question that if I managed to "pull round the corner this winter" I could return to England and live there – though for two years my life would be an invalid's life and I could only do it "provided you lived in great comfort." I said "please don't for one moment be over optimistic. Im just as prepared for a verdict against me as a verdict for." And he said "Quite so, Mrs Murry. Your first job is to get over this pneumonia and then I can examine that lung better but from a first inspection that is my opinion." He is going to notify me & I must sign that my sputum is disinfected and that my knife, spoon & fork are kept apart. How utterly repellant! But the Italians according to him have a perfect horror of this disease. He has told me my regime and you can judge the attack is not serious for he is not coming to see me again for a week unless I phone. Ill just keep here very still. Its a good room to be in bed with. When L.M. is out she locks the doors & I have the loaded revolver so no one can come in and steal your Wig. No thief in his senses would, Bogey my precious. Well, I think thats all my darling. He seems quite a good serviceable dining room clock – with an emphatic tick & a well-defined face. Ill keep him on the mantelpiece for the time being, at any rate, thankfully. He asks if old Vernon Rendall[1] was still in the office. Does Francis still edit Notes & Queries?[2] I dont know how he knew this. I forgot to ask. Sydney Beauchamp[3] made no *end* of a difference. They were at Cambridge together!! Bogey, it is a funny world. Well Ill take every care as you know & in a week Ill be better I expect. Tell Wing & hear him when he tells you I am alright. I *do* feel greatly better to know why I was feeling worse. Forgive me. I am for ever & ever your own little true love.

Wig.

MS ATL. *LJMM*, 437–8.

---

[1] A copy reader with the *Athenaeum*.
[2] J. Edward Francis was the Proprietor of *Notes and Queries*, the journal of scholarly enquiry, who at the end of the 12th Series, Volume V (December 1919) warned readers that he could not continue as Editor without salary, and that 'other arrangements for "N. & Q." will probably have to be made'. Early in 1920 the journal was taken over by *The Times* and its continuity assured.
[3] KM's cousin. See p. 25, n. 4.

To J. M. Murry, [9 December 1919]

[Casetta Deerholm, Ospedaletti]

Dearest,

Your wire saying will come for week Xmas has just arrived.[1] I beg you not to. I beg you to reply by wire that you will not do this. Please please forgive me and remember it was only my pneumonia which made me so miserable. Now I am in bed, and quiet and Ill get over it & be stronger. I know I have *driven* you to this by my letters. I don't want it at all. The idea is perfectly dreadful. We shouldn't be happy <u>and</u> you shouldnt get back. I caution you most seriously on that point. You'd never get your passport from Genoa in time. You'd spend the whole week getting ready to go. Yes, I know its my fault. I have left you no other loophole, but forgive me & DONT DO THIS THING. Its not only a question of the money. Its a question of the paper. The paper wont stand it – and more important still the journey is *preposterous* for so few days. You'd not get a week here. The doctor told me only yesterday that people cant GET here without a wait of DAYS in Paris. Xmas will be twice as bad. *Bogey dont do this thing.* Youve given me such a proper fright that I set my teeth again and will somehow or other get through. For Gods sake wire me that youll have a peaceful Xmas at Garsington. While Im ill its no good. I cant bear it. No, save the money for later in the year. Ive driven you to this. I don't want it. It horrifies me. DON'T COME: DON'T COME. Stay there. Ill be calm. I wont be such a vampire again. And consider carefully that quite apart from 'us' there is the fact that one's passport now takes from a fortnight to three weeks to recover from Genoa & that youd be detained in Paris. It would be a perfect disaster. I *feel* it. Dont do it.

In May I shall be better. All will be different. L.M. will be 'going' – not staying with me and you gone again. I really dont think I *could* stand that. Above all theres no need. The idea is like you. Thank you from my heart but please dont ever do it.

Wig.

MS ATL. *LJMM*, 438–9.

[1] When Murry received KM's letter of 4 Dec., with the enclosed verses, he was shocked and confused. His first reaction was to wire his determination to come out to her at Christmas.

'The effect of these verses upon me was shattering. At that time I did not fully understand how uncontrollable is the mood of despair which engulfs the tubercular patient, or how Katherine was from time to time possessed by it as by a totally alien power . . . they struck me as a terrible accusation of myself – the harder to bear because it was unfair: for it was not of my own free choice that I stayed in England at my job. My livelihood and Katherine's depended on it, at that time.' (*LJMM*, 428–9.)

To J. M. Murry, [9 December 1919]

[Ospedaletti]

IMPLORE YOU NOT TO WRITTEN DISMISS IDEA IMMEDIATELY GREATEST POSSIBLE MISTAKE BETTER TODAY TIG.

Telegram ATL. Murry, 244.

To J. M. Murry, [9 December 1919]

[Casetta Deerholm, Ospedaletti]
Tuesday night.

(Will you change the last sentence of my Kuprin to: "And what more has anybody said . . ."[1])

My precious,

After sending you the wire I want to send another to say that I do feel stronger. I have spent the day you see dead still and the pain is *much much* less – then to my joy the paper came.

Your Georgian Review is FIRST CHOP. Wing must decorate you with the O.M.T.: Order of the Mouse Trap. You couldnt have done it better, Boge. There's not a chink in your armour either. You have really wiped the floor with them: and I cheered you – to the echo (you know in my thumb). I had no idea you were going to bathe it in a kind of twinkling delicate light. I thought you were going to cry *woe*. You have cried *woe* but oh with what arrows to spear those sparrows to their very marrows!

I feel as though wed been through a naval engagement & now drew away – & heaved up & left them – tuned our fiddles, brought out the dishes of gold & the fishes heads of pure jade with lamps for eyes – Bogey, twas a famous victory! Swinnerton is very good & l'Hote excellent. So is Dent.[2] I must though say the Christmas Supplement is bad Boge to my thinking. What do you think. Its simply *rotten* for trade. You cant make an ad out of a single review and then they are so SLOPPY. Turner makes me burn in not mentioning a single book. But the women are simply squashed flies though I say it as shouldnt. After all in a supplement youre out to *sell* – I don't mean vulgarly – but youre out to – lets say make a point . . . And apart from that Rebecca West 2½ columns on a 1/9 book that she dismisses – whew! I shuddered at the look of the publisher turning it over . . . Sylvia Lynd on Crusoe[3] is not only so wrong in idea that the spirit faints – she writes as though she were baking a cake. Next year well do a *korker*.[4] Well have an article on what children like and *should have* & lists of books & poetry books & reprints. The copy all in advance – a dummy ready to be taken round for the ads.

Later. L.M. has just brought the post. Your Friday & Thursday letter & her income one. My own precious darling angelic little mate youre working to your eyes – youve a cold in your nose – Ive come down on you like a ton of bricks and away you smile. I must pray again. I must pray louder & longer and harder to my *cruel* God to make me not to fail. Oh, *you* MUST not come. It would be too awful!! Tell me the price of the cardigan. I shall love it. But now I *dont* want a scarf. Ça suffit. Look at the Lacket[5] when you have time. Yes I can easily do the work this week & send it off *easily* in time. Youll have Mrs H.W. & Bengy tomorrow by the noon post.[6] Ive only a page more. Hewlett & Philpotts ought to be for Xmas.

Take care of that cold please for our sakes. Why dont you have a few innoculations against cold? And are your teeth perfect? Talk to me *only* about yourself – not a word about me. Dont worry about me. Im here in bed – not moving, wrapped up warm, eating, all the windows open – my temperature descending by "slow degrees, by more and more". Another load of wood came today. The wood cupboard is full. Its filet for dinner. Oh *cruel* God help me not to sink into the pit again

– help me to give him all the love I feel. For tonight I am just love of
you – no more to me – and tonight I do believe. Bless me my brother.

Your Wig.

MS ATL. *LJMM*, 439–40.

Sir,

Re abatement and the questions in that clause

claimant does not remember

when it was

or

where it was

or

to what office her claim was sent

I advised her to leave all unanswered.

Was that right?

(Bet I don't get a sniff of that £7. She's *furious* with me!)[7]

Text *LJMM*, 441.

---

[1] This slight change was not made to the end of her review of Alexander Kuprin's collection
of short stories *The Garnet Bracelet*, published in the *Athenaeum*, 26 Dec. 1919. The review
concludes with a quotation she endorsed from the end of 'An Evening Guest', a story she
otherwise disliked: 'when we are almost inclined to call it childish, he cries "Every time that I
think of the vastness, complexity, darkness and elemental accidentality of this general
intertwining of lives, my own life appears to me like a tiny speck of dust tossed in the fury of a
tempest." What more is to be said?'

[2] Frank Swinnerton wrote 'Coteries', the leading article for the *Athenaeum*, 5 Dec. 1919; André
Lhote discussed 'The Salon d'Automne', Part II; under 'A Stormy Petrel', Edward Dent
reviewed *Impressions that Remained, Memoirs*, by Ethel Smyth.

[3] That week the paper carried a Christmas Book Supplement, in which W. J. Turner wrote
on 'Children's Songs', Rebecca West discussed Hawthorne's *Tanglewood Tales*, and Sylvia Lynd
considered *Robinson Crusoe*.

[4] A New Zealand colloquialism for fine, splendid.

[5] The house in Wiltshire which Murry had heard of through the Waterlows.

[6] Under 'A Post-War and a Victorian Novel', the *Athenaeum*, 19 Dec. 1919, KM reviewed
Cousin Philip, by Mrs Humphry Ward, and *Benjy*, by George Stevenson.

[7] A note relating to an income tax claim of Ida Baker's.

To J. M. Murry, [10 December 1919]

[Casetta Deerholm, Ospedaletti]

I entreat you not to come in the name of our love.

My dearest,

Another wire has come this morning and I have just prepared the
answer. You must please please obey me and believe me and not
come. The idea is more terrible than I can say. You *must* stay there till

May. We break our resolve, ruin our future by such a thing. Stay away. Dont come. What in Gods name would be the good? *What for?* To see each other? Why? We might even break with each other if we were to do such a thing. Youd 'forgive' me but youd owe me a grudge always & rightly. It would be a sign that we had failed – ganz definitif.

Waste of energy – waste of life – waste of money – a mad impulse grâce à moi yielded to – our *new* selves betrayed – the paper cant stand it either. Its rocky still as we know, & YOU WOULDN'T GET BACK.

MS ATL. *LJMM*, 443–4.

To J. M. Murry, [10 December 1919]

[[Ospedaletti]

URGE YOU MOST EARNESTLY NOT TO COME UTTERLY UNNECESSARY ENTREAT YOU TO WAIT UNTIL MAY LETTER SENT EXPLAINING TIG.

Telegram ATL. Murry, 244.

To J. M. Murry, [11 December 1919]

[Casetta Deerholm, Ospedaletti]
Thursday

My own love,
All day long Ive lain waiting for the bell that should mean your answer to my telegram saying you are not coming. Sometimes, for days, this bell isn't rung: today there has been an old woman and a child with grapes & a maid to enquire after Madame and a beggar. Each time the bell has rung my heart has felt *suffocated – fainting* and the moment when L.M. went and did not come to me has been an age – an age. I *must* have stopped you! I think of you leaving home – the cold – the dark – your cold – all this vile terrible journey before you – your fatigue. I think of your making arrangements to leave the paper – working, overworking at top top speed. I see you sitting in one of these *loathsome* trains, my tired boy and pale, trying to sleep, wrapped in your overcoat – the draughts, the rattle and your uneasiness – your *state of soul*. Oh, can Love keep this horror from you? Ill wire again tomorrow if I do not hear. Be calm, be calm, wait for his answer. It *must* come. I see you with your passport bending over a table, explaining that your wife is ill. I imagine you held up here, unable to get back. If I can only save you from this by those messages. Tonight I

would promise to stay here a year I think rather than you should come.

My love goes out to you – running out to you down a dark path saying keep away, keep away, Bogey! Can you hear? Will you realise my relief when I know Ive been in time? I feel it will make me well again. God forgive me for what I have done. Those words Chummie spoke as he died.[1] Ever since Ive had your telegram they seem *mine*. Can you forgive me? I lie here wondering. Oh my love, oh my love – stay in England!

Your own true love,
Wig.

MS ATL. *LJMM*, 444–5.

---

[1] Leslie Beauchamp's reported last words, as he died on 4 Oct. 1915 after a hand-grenade accident, were, 'God forgive me for all that I have done', and 'Lift up my head, Katie, I can't breathe.'

To J. M. Murry, [12 December 1919]

[Ospedaletti]

TELEGRAM RECEIVED IMPLORE YOU FINALLY ABANDON PLAN DON'T COME TILL MAY ALL GOING ON SPLENDIDLY HERE DON'T SPOIL OUR FUTURE WIRE TIG.

Telegram ATL. Murry, 244.

To J. M. Murry, [12 December 1919]

[Casetta Deerholm, Ospedaletti]
Friday

Jack your wire has come saying you are determined to spend Christmas here. I have wired finally begging you not to.
There is no need.
Our compact is broken.
Its one of our old *mad* flings.
We havent the money.
Youll not get back under 3 weeks at earliest.
We shant enjoy it. Im not well enough to have fun with you – L.M. is here. You know how before you left last time we were all at near breaking point. Id a million times rather you saw the Lacket & wrote to me.

Even if you have your tickets and visas I would not come if I were you. I can easily give you £5 to help with the expenses you have had. All goes well here – there is nothing to worry about in the very slightest. If you come I feel we have failed. I can now say no more but trust you to believe.

Your Wig.

MS ATL. *LJMM*, 445.

To J. M. Murry, [12 December 1919]

[Casetta Deerholm, Ospedaletti]
In the night.

I am awake and I have reread your letter.[1] It is stranger than ever. It is half an account of what I have done to you and the other half is all money. And you say I dont appreciate the seriousness of these your views about money. You do me great wrong. But I must not be kept in the dark. Have your creditors come down on you? But if they have – it is since Ottoline's sale? For were the burden of your debts so imperative & terrible you could not have spent any money there. What are these terrible debts? I must be told them. You cannot hint at them and then say I lack sympathy. You are not a pauper. You have £800 a year and you only contribute to my keep – not more than £50 a year at most now. You write as though there were me to be provided for – yourself, and all to be done on something like £300. I know you have paid my doctors bills and that my illness has cost you a great deal. IT WILL COST YOU NO MORE. I cannot take any more money from you ever and as soon as I am well I shall work to make a good deal more so that you have to pay less. But your letter frightens me for you – I think you have allowed this idea of money to take too great a hold on your brain. Either we must do nothing but pay off your debts or you must not care so greatly. Its madness to write like this to your wife & then to buy furniture. Its unworthy of our love surely to taunt me with my lack of understanding. How *could* I understand? I had no idea you still felt these crying claims: I thought all was going fairly smoothly. You must stick to the paper. I have never had another thought. Your being here is impossible from every point of view. I do not want to at all. I thought I had made that plain and about the paper – many many times. You say money is "fundamental to any decision you make". Yes of course it is. But I do not need to be told, and truly you should know that. I feel ashamed when I read that.

What I do beg you to do is to stay there, to live quietly and get the paper really going. *Live quietly.* I suppose you laugh. I have made that so impossible in the past. Youll have no cause to blame me in the future for it. I leaned on you – and *broke you.* The truth is that until I was ill you were never called upon to "play the man" to this extent – and its <u>not</u> your role. When you said you ought to be kept you spoke the truth. I feel it. Ever since my illness this crisis I suppose has been impending when suddenly in an agony I should turn all woman and lean on you. Now it has happened. The crisis is over. You must feel that. It won't return. Its over for good.

And I dont ask you to "cut off with nothing" or to sacrifice *anything.* All I do ask of each of us is to keep very steady and calm now and by May we shall have recovered. But please be calm. You are not asked to do anything quickly – theres *no* decision for you to make.

However ill I am you are more ill. However weak I am you are weaker – less able to bear things. Have I really put on the last straw? You imply in this letter I have. You make me out so cruel that —— I feel you cant love me in the least – a vampire – I am not. That is all.

I am not so hurried now – I want to talk more with you. God knows if I have managed to stop you. I can do no more.

Granted (and I grant absolutely) that I have sent you this 'snake' (though now Im not talking of the verses but of my depression in general), granted that – are you fair in punishing me so horribly? I know when I write happy letters they make you happy. You ask me to write more and you say if you want to keep me happy thats the way to do it. Listen. When I was in Hampstead with you were you always able to put all else aside and make me happy? Did you never come to me depressed, fearful, uneasy, fatigued and say "you cant expect me to dance – or act up to what you want"? Did I ask you to make such an effort that your whole nature should change and you should be *really* happy, *believing* in happiness. You have even denied you *wanted* happiness – on the Heath by a broken tree. I did not think I had to make the effort. I thought you alone – you, the secret, secret you would understand. The effort to keep perpetually radiant was too great. But you asked it of me. I did not *only* write to make you and keep you happy. That was important but not of first importance. Of first importance was my desire to be truthful before you. Love, I thought, could stand *even that.* Love could penetrate the isolation surrounding another and lovers did not suffer alone. Not that I required of you that you should suffer with me. Never. Never. From the bottom of my heart I can say that. But I took you at your word: it seemed to me almost my duty to tell you all in the greatest possible honesty – anything less would not be *our love.*

When you wrote thats the stuff to keep me happy I was full of despair. I knew that I could not go on giving it you. It was not as though you were ill and turned to me, strong and well, as a flower

would turn to the sun, crying: "I am in the shadow, shine on me."
Alas, I was no sun. I was in the shadow – and when at times I came
into a bright beam & sent it to you it was only *at times.*

I keep thinking of Wing as I write this and of our love. Will it all
come back or have I the snake laid everything waste. Peace! Peace! It
could not be helped. If I have done this it was a snake in my bosom –
yea in my bosom and not I. I will not receive your dreadful
accusations into my soul for they would kill me.

But here is your letter and you tell me I have driven you nearly
insane – ruined you – it seems – quenched your hopes even of getting
your money affairs straight. You tell me again that you are a
bankrupt. It cant be helped. No protestations now. Remember how
weve loved – remember it all all and let us not talk of *money*. It is not
necessary to tell me to hint that THEY will come after you & perhaps
put you in jail for debt if you run away. I dont ask these things. I
never asked them. I believed that the human being did not suffer
alone. I showed you my sufferings. I have learned the truth. Do not let
us talk of it again. Let us just go on. Let us bury the past and go on
and *recover*. We shall. Our only chance now is not to lose Hope but to
go on and not give each other up.

Your devoted – yours eternally

Your

Wife.

MS ATL. *LJMM*, 441–3.

[1] Murry wrote on 8 Dec. that he had received her letter with the poem 'The New Husband'.
'I don't think that at any time I've had a bigger blow than that letter & these verses. Even now
they hardly seem like a letter & verses – more like a snake with a terrible sting.' The letter also
said, 'At present I'm trying to clear up the remains of last year's debts. Until they are cleared I
shall stick to the A. That's callous, I suppose. But I can't help it. You know my position as a
bankrupt. I dare not leave our debts unpaid – I'm not supposed to have any. Once we're straight
– and if things were to do moderately well I shall be straight by April (as I hoped to be by
December) – I'll do anything. But I *know* that to cut off with little money coming in & heavy
debts would mean inevitable disaster.'

Murry went on to say, 'I'm not made of steel, myself. And it's becoming a great effort to do
what I have to do sanely – do you think I can do anything with this ringing in my ears.

> Who's your man to leave you be
> Ill & cold in a far country?
> Who's the husband, who's the stone
> Could leave a child like you alone?

There's nothing to say to that. All that I implore you is to say what you want. That will help.'
(Murry, 240.)

KM wrote on the back of the envelope that brought Murry's letter: 'This letter killed the
Mouse, made the Worm creep underground and banished the Dream Child for ever. Before I
had received it I had learned to live *for* Love and *by* Love. I had given myself up – and a kind of
third creature US was what I lived by. After I had read it, quite apart from me, my own self
returned *and* all my horror of death vanished. From this date I simply *dont care* about death! No

question of heroics – or life not being worth living or anything like it. I simply feel alone again. Voilà.'

She also underlined words in Murry's letters, such as his use of the first person singular, which she felt betrayed his egotism and his misunderstanding. (Murry, 239–41.)

To J. M. Murry, [13 December 1919]

[Ospedaletti]

TUESDAY LETTER RECEIVED[1] OVERJOYED IF EASY BUT PERFECTLY UNDERSTAND IF DON'T COME WIRE TIG.

Telegram ATL. Murry, 244.

---

[1] Murry's letter on 9 Dec. told KM to 'Forget all about that horrible letter I wrote to you yesterday'. He already had arranged his French and Italian visas, and intended leaving in a few days' time. ('But why in God's name, I ask myself now, did we not originally arrange to have Xmas together?') (Murry, 242.)

[*Murry joined KM at Ospedaletti on 16 December. On 15 December she wrote the following entry in one of her notebooks, analysing and attempting to come to terms with her state of mind.*]

When I had gone to bed I realised what it was that had caused me to 'give way'. It was the effort of being up with a heart that wouldn't work. Not my lungs at all. My despair simply disappeared – yes, *simply*. The weather was lovely. Every morning the sun came in and drew those squares of golden light on the wall, I looked round my bed on to a sky like silk. The day opened slowly, slowly like a flower, and it held the sun long, long before it slowly, slowly folded. Then my homesickness went. I not only didn't want to be in England, I began to love Italy, and the thought of it – the sun – even when it was too hot – always the sun – and a kind of *wholeness* which was good to bask in.

After a few days J.'s letters in response to *my* depressed letters began to arrive. There were a series of them. As I grew depressed, *he* grew depressed, but not *for* me. He began to write (1) about the suffering I caused him: *his* suffering, *his* nerves, *he* wasn't made of whipcord or steel, the fruit was bitter for *him*. (2) a constant cry about money. He had none; he saw no chance of getting any – 'heavy debts' – 'as you know I am a bankrupt'. 'I know it sounds callous.' 'I can't face it.' These letters, especially the letters about money, cut like a knife through something that had grown up between us. They changed the situation for me, at least, for ever. We had been for two years drifting into a relationship, different to anything I had ever known. We'd been *children* to each other, openly confessed children, telling each other everything, each *depending* equally upon the other. Before that I had been the man and he had been the woman and he had been called upon to make no real efforts. He'd never really 'supported' me. When we first met, in fact, it was I who kept him, and afterwards we'd always acted (more or less) like men-friends. Then this illness – getting worse and worse, and turning me into a woman and asking him to put himself away and to *bear* things for me. He stood it marvellously. It helped very much because it was a 'romantic' disease (his love of a 'romantic appearance' is *immensely* real) and also being 'children' together gave us a practically unlimited chance to play at life, not to live. It was child love. Yes, I think the most marvellous, the most radiant love that this world knows: terribly rare. We've had it. But we were not *pure*. If we had been, he'd have faced coming away with me. And that he would not do. He'd not have said he was too tired to earn enough to keep us here. He always refused to face what it meant – living alone together for two years on not much money. He *said* and three quarters of him believed: I couldn't stand the strain of it with you ill. But it was a lie and a confession that all was not well between us. And I always knew it. Nevertheless, I played up, and truly even in October I *clung* to him still – still the child – seeing as our salvation a house in the country, in England, *not later than next May* and then never to be apart again. The letters – ended all of it. *Was* it the letters? I must not forget something else.

All these two years I have been obsessed by the fear of death. This grew and grew and grew *gigantic*, and this it was that made me cling so, I think. Ten days ago it went, I care no more. It leaves me perfectly cold. Well it was that *and* the letters perhaps. Gone is my childish love – gone is my desire to live in England. I don't particularly want to live with him. I'd like to if it could be managed – but *no sacrifices, please*. As to leaning – as to being a 'little lovely darling' – it's not conceivable. I want to *work* – here – get a good maid in place of L.M. and that's all. Quite all? Yes, all. I am become – Mother. I don't care a *rap* for 'people'. I shall always love Jack and be his wife but I couldn't get back to that anguish – joy – sweet madness of the other years. Such love has gone for me. And life either stays or goes.

I must put down here a dream. The first night I was in bed here, i.e. after my first day in bed, I went to sleep. And suddenly I felt my whole body *breaking up*. It broke up with a violent shock – an earthquake – and it broke like glass. A long terribe shiver, you understand – and the spinal cord and the bones and every bit and particle quaking. It sounded in my ears – a low, confused din, and there was a sense of flashing greenish brilliance, like broken glass.

When I woke I thought there had been a violent earthquake. But all was still. It slowly dawned upon me – the conviction that in that dream I died [written later in the margin, 'important. For the confessions']. I shall go on living now – it may be for months, or for weeks or days or hours. Time is not. In that dream I died. The *spirit* that is the enemy of death and quakes so and is so tenacious was shaken out of me. I am (December 15, 1919) a dead woman, and *I don't care*. It might comfort others to know that one gives up caring; but they'd not believe any more than I did until it happened. And, oh, how strong was its hold upon me! How I *adored* life and *dreaded* death!

I'd like to write my books and spend some happy time with Jack (not very much faith in that) and see Lawrence in a sunny place and pick violets – all kinds of flowers. Oh, I'd like to do heaps of things, really. But I don't mind if I do not do them.

That quiet simplicity – that deep simple love *is* not. It only existed until we put it to the test. Then when I cried out, Jack beat me – because it hurt him to hear me – I stopped his play I made the house all wrong. . . . How clear it all is. Immediately I, as a tragic figure, outfaced or threatened to outface him (yes, that's exactly the truth) the truth was revealed. He was the one who really wanted *all* the tragedy. It must have been a fearful blow to share at all . . . I am glad its over. I wouldn't call it back.

Honesty (why?) is the only thing one seems to prize beyond life, love, death, everything. It alone remaineth. O those that come after me, will you believe it? At the end *truth* is the one thing *worth having*: its more thrilling than love, more joyful and more passionate. It simply can*not* fail. All else fails. I, at any rate, give the remainder of my life to it and it alone.   (15.XII.1919)

I'd like to write a *long, long* story on this and call it 'Last Words to Life.' One *ought* to write it. And another on the subject of HATE.

Journal 1954, 183–5.

To S. S. Koteliansky, [13 December 1919]

[Casetta Deerholm, Ospedaletti]
Saturday night.

Koteliansky

Your letter has made me very happy. Thank you for it. You know, it is still here, in my room, sounding like music that has been played. "Be well". And I am ashamed that I broke down in my last letter.[1]

That night I went to bed with pneumonia. That was why I was so depressed. Of course I am still in bed but it does not matter. *All is well.*

We are quite alone here tonight. It is so far away and still. Everything is full of silent life – complete with its shadow. From the sea there comes a soft *ruffled* sound and its beat is regular and soft like the beat of mowers cutting through a deep meadow. Yes, one day when we have the money we shall meet somewhere and talk quietly for as long as we wish. It will happen, I think. Your loneliness is precious to you, I know. Does it disturb it to know you are dear to me. Do not let it. It is such a quiet feeling. It is like the light coming in to a room – moonlight – where you are sitting.

I shall try and get well here. If I *do* die perhaps there will be a small private heaven for consumptives only. In that case I shall see Tchekov. He will be walking down his garden paths with fruit trees on either side and tulips in flower in the garden beds. His dog will be sitting on the path, panting and slightly smiling as dogs do who have been running about a great deal.

Only to think of this makes my heart feel as though it were *dissolving* – a strange feeling. But the Knipper[2] . . . You know Koteliansky, I cannot like her. There is a kind of false brightness about her. Perhaps I am very wrong.

Lawrence wrote from Florence.[3] Frieda had arrived – *thinner* – but very well. This thinness will not last. He said Florence was lovely and full of "extremely nice people". He is able to bear people so easily. Often I long to be more *in life* – to know people – even now the desire comes. But immediately the opportunity comes I think of nothing but how to escape. And people have come to see me here. *What* are they? They are not human beings; they are never children – they are *absolutely unreal* – mechanisms.

And those people in England – when one goes away the memory of them is like the memory of clothes hanging in a cupboard. And yet the beauty of life – Koteliansky – the haunting beauty of "the question".[4] Sometimes when I am awake here, very early in the morning, I hear, far down on the road below, the market carts going by. And at the sound I live through this getting up before dawn, the blue light in the window – the cold solemn look of the people – the woman opening the door and going for sticks, the smell of smoke – the feather of smoke rising from their chimney. I hear the man as he slaps the little horse and leads it into the clattering yard. And the fowls are still asleep – big balls of feather. But the early morning air and hush . . . And after the man and wife have driven away some little children scurry out of bed across the floor and find a piece of bread and get back into the warm bed and divide it. But this is all *the surface.* Hundreds of things happen down to minute, minute details. But it is all so full of beauty – and you know the voices of people before sunrise – how different they are? I lie here, thinking of these things and hearing those little carts . . . It is too much. One must weep.

Forgive a long letter. I shall send you the letters.[5]

I do not know if Murry is coming. I have sent him several wires asking him not to come. It is not at all a good idea.

Goodnight. When you think of me call me by my other name –[6]

MS BL. *LKM* I. 315–16.

---

[1] A letter which has not survived.

[2] Olga Knipper, who played leading roles in several of Chekhov's plays, and married him in 1901.

[3] Lawrence's letter does not survive.

[4] In a letter to A. G. Souverin, 27 Oct. 1888, translated by Koteliansky and KM in 'Letters of Anton Tchehov, II', in the *Athenaeum*, 6 June 1919, Chekhov wrote: 'You are right in asking from an artist a conscious attitude to his activity, but you are mixing up two things: the solving of the question and the correct putting of the question. It is the latter only which is obligatory upon the artist.'

[5] The translation of the Chekhov letters she and Kot were working on.

[6] Koteliansky frequently called KM both Katerina and Kissienka.

II

ITALY – OSPEDALETTI:
DECEMBER 1919–JANUARY
1920

The tangle of confusion between KM and Murry was resolved only by his leaving J. W. N. Sullivan and Aldous Huxley in charge of the *Athenaeum*, and joining his wife in Italy on 16 December. By the time he returned to England in early January they were convinced their love was as firm as ever; within a few weeks a postal strike, renewed loneliness, a constant brooding on their relationship, and a fresh crop of misunderstandings as their barrage of letters crossed, brought KM back to that earlier combination of tenderness and recrimination, and the conviction that 'J. and I are no longer as we were'. (*Journal* 1954, 192.)

∽

To Jinnie Fullerton,[1] December 16, 1919

[Casetta Deerholm, Ospedaletti]
Tuesday

The doctor came yesterday and put his British foot down on all the lovely plans. I am not to get up yet and when I do only to lie on a couch or on the verandah for a few hours a day at present. My heart which evidently feels its turn has come for a little attention has been playing me tricks and I'll have to give way to the jealous creature for the present. So bang goes the lovely Christmas! We're more than sorry and it was lovely to have been asked to the party and I hate to be such an unsatisfactory creature. Will you and Cousin Connie forgive me? But what can one do when ones heart gives the most marvellous imitations of the big drum in a brass band – first, heard very far away in the distance, then coming nearer and nearer, then thumping so loud that you think it must break the windows and then wonderful faint, far away 'distant' effects – and all for an audience of *one*! But it's not really 'serious' – only a temporary thing. I'll have to learn to play the fife to keep it company –

A comfortable old Scottish party from San Remo came to call the other day and seeing the chaste nudity of the Casetta she has since sent us a great roll of carpets and rugs that she had in store so we are a great deal snugger and warmer here. The doctor is definitely opposed to me moving at present. Ida takes little jaunts into San Remo and she has made several friends and I've plenty of work to keep me going. So that's my programme for the present, quite a satisfactory one except that it prevents me from spreading my wings.

Text *LKM* I. 316–17.

[1] Jinnie Fullerton (b. 1856) the close friend and living companion of cousin Connie Beauchamp in Menton. They had retired there after running the private nursing home in John Street, London, where KM had undergone a minor operation in 1905, and another in Hampstead. (See *CLKM* I. 16–17.)

To Richard Murry, [20 December 1919]

[Casetta Deerholm, Ospedaletti]
The woodcut of Wing is a *masterpiece*. I love to have it. And I owe you thanks for a letter and a drawing. Forgive me. Ive been ill with an attack of pneumonia and I couldn't run after my pen which would run away. It doesnt mean I haven't thought of you as you know. Jacks book looks awfully well,[1] and isn't the Wordsworth lovely[2] – it looks so tall and slender . . . We have been talking about the Heron this afternoon and the Family Tree. You can imagine what its like – having Jack here. He will carry the Third Brother's Xmas present back with him – its safer than posting it. First, a Happy Christmas, then may our wishes come true this Year for us all. We shall be thinking & talking of you.

K.

Postcard. MS R. Murry. *Adam* 370–4, 25.

[1] *The Evolution of an Intellectual.*
[2] An anthology of Wordsworth recently published by Cobden-Sanderson, set in the new Monotype Caslon type.

To Dorothy Brett, December 20, 1919

[Casetta Deerholm, Ospedaletti]
I've been ill with pneumonia, and too wretched to write. Forgive me. I have thought of you so often. And I want to thank you for the photographs, to talk about them. I will, at length, now I am 'better.' Now M. has brought over his exquisite little coals of fire for Xmas from you – So lovely. Such gay greetings. Thank you ever so much for

them. This is an exquisite little place – and the weather – like June. The whole village is under roses as other villages are under snow. I hope you have a happy Christmas and Joy in the New Year, real, real Joy.

Text *LKM* I. 317.

To J. M. Murry, [3 January 1920¹]

[Casetta Deerholm, Ospedaletti]
Saturday.

Darling of darlings,

My review went off – thank god; I do hope it is alright. Now I shall start another so that you have cash in hand. Youre still on your way. I keep thinking of you, my love, and hoping you are warm. It is a comfort to know youve a good bed to get home to *and* your Wingy Wingchik. That was my most pet name for him when we were quite alone in my room & he was watching the tail of a mouse (a very old feather tail) emerge from under my blotting paper & then *mysteriously* disappear again. I stayed in bed yesterday. It was cold & I was tired. Today I'm very rested & its as warm – tiède – a lovely day with silver leaf on the sea. I am going to walk in the garden and consider the peas how they grow.² Please mark in your diary *May 4th* which is the anniversary of our wedding & *Friday Avrilo 30th* which is the day I leave here. These and our birthdays I have enclosed in heavy squares. Really its marvellous how near the spring feels. If only The Lacket is notre affaire. Remember, my precious, that if its dark they may allow us to cut down a tree or 'throw in' a window. Bear these facts in mind. I feel the forest would be so perfect – so near. You could go riding in it before breakfast & I could go looking for wild strawberries in it before tea.

It has been lovely having you – lovely. I feel as though we are (you are – too?) mysteriously renewed. I feel that the spring is going to be so wonderful – that even our meeting in Paris will be wonderful. Do be sure to keep your diary. I am keeping mine.

And I shall by some means or other buy more of the lovely china. We must have it. We shall never get anything as good in England. I am going to ask Caterina to give me the address of the factory in Firenze where her aunt Madame Littardi orders it and then I shall write direct if naught else availeth.³ L.M. went to San Remo yesterday. Yes, I can get an english cheque cashed in french money – but she surely made some absurd mistake for she said the man would give me *123 francs for 100 lire*! Very nice for me! (L.M. got her £5 out of me this month. Would I mind starting it next month as she'd practically *spent* it this and had so much to pay off . . . What a mystery! The wood has come however. It cost 109 francs & looks good – though much smaller than last time.)

Oh I long to know of your homecoming and how you found everything. Will you tell me, please? I had a letter from Clara[4] today addressed to *Gentma Signora*. If the news is very good please address me like that and I shall know. A letter from Chaddie too – 'Do ask Jack to let us know . . .' Peace! Peace! You are far too busy to go to Woodhay before I return. We shall go down together – and have a look at the carpets & refresh ourselves with the knowledge of how much better we order these things – but not before.

After you had gone the house was so quiet – so quiet. The patience cards are put away. No more demon is played. The sea sprang up in the night & roared. I wondered where you were – and how you were – and felt again my old anxiety about you 'en voyage'. *Take care of yourself.* Remember my love for you is deep and abiding and I live by it.

Goodbye my own Bogey.

Your devoted
Wig.

MS ATL. Unpublished.

[1] Murry was obliged to leave again for London and his editorial duties on 2 Jan. On 3 Jan. KM recorded in her notebook, 'Storm of wind and rain. I had nightmare about Jack. He and I "separated".' And the next day, 'Cold, wet, windy, terrible weather. Fought it all day. Horribly depressed. . . . Immediately the sun goes in I am overcome – again the black fit takes me. I *hate* the *sea*. There is naught to do but WORK. But how can I work when this awful weakness makes even the pen like a walking-stick.' (*Journal* 1954, 191.)

[2] Cf. Matthew 6: 28 (Authorized Version): 'Consider the lilies of the field, how they grow'.

[3] 'Say not the struggle naught availeth,' the opening line of A. H. Clough's poem of that title.

[4] Probably Clara Palmer (see *CLKM* II. 298), an old Wellington friend who now lived in Rome.

To J. M. Murry, [5 January 1920]

[Casetta Deerholm, Ospedaletti]

Monday.

My own darling Bogey

Since I have put such a stopper upon my pen I feel as though dear knows when I *shall* write – if to write is to be merry. Yesterday I realised to the full the strangeness of a day when I didn't write to you. You know its for *years* that we have written to each other every day & I thought we *always* would – for toujours. But I see & still hold to the foolishness of it for people like us – I who can't *hold back* and you who can't bear . . . But should (God forbid) the situation be reversed & you away from me & unhappy you will write to me? I am of that nature that I can bear anything better than silence.

Ever since you left you have carried the sun in your pocket. Its bitter cold, raining fast – *sleeting* and an east wind. Dickinson[1] says he has never known the glass so low. The cold is intense – one's fingers ache. You could not believe this was the same place – and the sky seems to have great ink stains upon it. I am working – all day – all the evening – too. Your telegrams my thoughtful love were a great pleasure. But you were a *day late* weren't you? In arriving? I hope you are well at home now & with your Wing & your friends.

The post office has struck – no-one knows for how long. It just announces a strike. The country is in a queer state. Dickinson yesterday on his way here met the men from the railway below who shouted youd better pack up your traps & go. We dont want any more of you English here. We're going to clear you out. But 10–1 that is an exaggeration. He is an alarmist of the very first water & sat here yesterday suggesting that even at 3 oclock in the afternoon no-one would hear my screams if I were attacked – and that a revolver for a person like me was ridiculous. *They'd* knock it away in no time. I have come to the conclusion that hes not only a *real insane lunatic* but a *homicidal maniac*. I thought the first time he was here he was a trifle insane but then you liked him so & I felt you would laugh at me for always 'suspecting' people & for my 'horrible mind'. But I know Im right. His glance – without any barriers – cruel – cruel like a man raving with delight at sight of a torture, his *flat sounding* voice – somehow so repressed & held back – his physical great stiffness & the shape of his flat head – real criminal shape. See him in profile – his eyes glittering: hes a *terrible* object. He is attracted to me because he realises my sensitiveness. Im weak for him to terrify. It relieves him to sit in that small room & suggest that navvies will break in & "slit your throat" while Miss Baker is in San Remo. Well – well ——

The new maid is here. If to be a maid is to drop the stove rings on to the tiled floor shes an excellent one – and very cheap at 5 francs a day. Dearest I cut out this ad just because I wanted to tell you I really didn't recognise the paper without the imprint:[2] it loses *tremendously* I think.

I send a long Tchekov letter.[3] If you don't care to use it will you please have it typed for me (at my charge) & send the typed copy to Kot for our book? I hope to send off another review tomorrow.

Take care of your precious self. I long for news of you my dearest own. If only this black weather would lift. The wind *howls*. Please give Sydney my love but my Wing chick *kiss* for me. All goes well here. I

hope to hear from you tomorrow. I *work* & *work* and *work* & stay in bed
until the sun returns. Heaven bless you my precious.

Your Wig.

MS ATL. *LKM* II. 2–3; *LJMM*, 449–450.

[1] An English acquaintance who occasionally visited KM in Ospedaletti.
[2] Murry had dropped the head of Athena, set in a medallion, which the paper had carried
until that issue.
[3] Chekhov's letter to his brother Alexander, Apr. 1883, published by Murry in the *Adelphi*,
June 1924.

To J. M. Murry, [7 January 1920]

[Casetta Deerholm, Ospedaletti]

Wednesday.
Dearest Bogey
    The post office and the water spouts are open again. Heres the
Athen. the Lit. Sup. Mercury. 2 novels & letters which are not from
you & ∴ don't count as letters & here is the bedroom flooded, water
spurting through the window frame, great watery maps on the walls,
the continent of Australia (very true) on the ceiling. This plus a wild
gale & a boiling leaden sea. And the *cold*. Is it within the bond to tell
you that I had rather a bad heart attack yesterday morning at 8 a.m.
& languished all day unable even to read. But today I feel better and
Ive written to Sorapure. Hes my one remaining confidante . . . *zut –
alors*! I hate talking of this to you.

Bogey, I am really thankful you are at the helm again. Pages 12–13
– the bit o' poetry about the boarding house[1] and Poetry for Babes[2]
beginning with a capital I'VE (pretty, that!) and in my review *swish*
for *swim*[3] (malice?) made me shudder this week. Don't I pray you
leave the paper again. Sullivan appears to compose his pages after a
9d mixed hors d'oeuvres[4] . . . The review of your poetry in the Times
was very intriguing. What I felt was they had to judge you by extraordinary standards & they felt it. This pleased me. The quotations,
too. My word – what a jewel the second was![5] It gave me a deep thrill
of joy. I think the reviewer was really very complimentary (properly
so of course) to you. I really feel that tho' he didn't understand you *he*
felt it was because you were beyond him. I note Grant Richards
picked out the Firbank.[6] At the risk of your shouting me down – *please*
dont praise Firbank. Hes of the family of Aleister Crowley[7] – an 'otter'[8]
bird – a sniggering, long nailed, pretentious & very dirty fellow. As to

honesty – the fellow would swoon at sight of such a turnip. Huxley is very silly and young sometimes – & watery headed.[9]

I wish you were not so innocent in these matters. Please forgive my 'impudence'. Ive no earthly right to say these things – but dear me – I cant suppress myself *entirely*. If I agree to suppress the personal me t'other must come out.

I send you today to the office the first instalment of some autobiographical notes on Tchekhov.[10] Do you care for them? There are more to follow & they are *very* interesting. If you dont would you have them typed (at *my* charge) & sent to Kot. I send also 2 parcels of novels. If you will send me the money they fetch it will help me to pay Arina. I hope to send off a review by todays afternoon post & another before the end of the week.

The London Mercury is between [*sic*] contempt but it is evidently as fat as can be – bursting with fatness – curse it. Squire's *Moon* is the flattest orb that ever sailed the hevings.[11] This doesnt mean I dont enjoy seeing it (the paper I mean).

Oh the acid has come today – [12] – sent 5.11.1919 as the parcel states. This is a record I should think even for this horrible country. I shall get up again as soon as I behold bright Phoebus in his strength[13] . . . All's well, my darling. *Write to me as often as you can & love me.* For I love you. I am afraid to tell you how much I love you. Write to me even if its only a note you jot down and post. Well, heres Black January. I hope it is better with you. Goodbye my precious Love.

Ever your own
Wig.[14]

MS ATL. *LJMM*, 450–2.

[1] The pages of the *Athenaeum*, 2 Jan. 1920, that KM apparently found so dull, carried an awkwardly expressed review by F. W. Stokoe of Arthur Waley's *Japanese Poetry: The Uta*, and Ivor Brown's discussion of the Report of the Adult Education Committee, Ministry of Reconstruction, on 'The Extension of Educational Facilities'. There was also a poem by Jean Guthrie-Smith, 'The Sick Lodger', on the death of 'A piece of human furniture | Within a boarding house'.

[2] R. Robert Ellis, under 'Poetry for Babes', reviewed *Nursery Lays of Nursery Days*, by M. and C. T. Nightingale, and *The Fairy Queen*, by Rose Fyleman.

[3] A sentence in KM's review of Eden Phillpotts's *Evander* concluded, 'in the moonlight the naiads, tired of the water springs, come down to the lake to swish and sing'.

[4] As assistant editor, J. W. N. Sullivan arranged the paper's layout during Murry's absence.

[5] The unsigned review of Murry's *Poems: 1917–1918* in the *Times Literary Supplement* quoted the sestet of 'To the Poets of Old', and 18 lines from 'The Forgotten Past'.

[6] Grant Richards's regular half-column advertisements in the *Times Literary Supplement* took the form of notes by the publisher on his recent books. On 2 Jan. he noted of Ronald Firbank's *Valmouth* 'a gift for style, a capacity to write dialogue, an appreciation of the beautiful and the absurd'. The same phrases were repeated in a brief note in the *Athenaeum*, on 2 Jan., presumably placed by Huxley during Murry's absence.

[7] During the time of her association with A. R. Orage's *New Age* (see *CLKM* I. 97), KM had briefly met Aleister Crowley (1875–1947), writer, poet, and ostentatious Satanist.

[8] Gwen Otter, who claimed to be a direct descendant of the Red Indian princess Pocahontas, was for decades 'a leading Chelsea hostess – almost an institution, in the worlds of music, art, literature and the theatre – and entertained both the obscure and the famous with equal lavishness' (Douglas Goldring, *South Lodge* (1943), 44). In a letter to Anne Drey in 1921, however, KM wrote of Gwen Otter: 'Poor dear, it will never be over for me. I have a warm corner in my heart for that woman always. There's something very fine in her yet she's *missed* life.' (*Adam* 300 (1963–5), 93.)

[9] Aldous Huxley knew Firbank slightly, and admired his fiction.

[10] 'Anton Tchehov: Biographical Note', a straightforward unsigned account of Chekhov's life by KM and Koteliansky, appeared in the *Athenaeum* in two parts: 23 Jan. and 6 Feb. 1920.

[11] The Jan. 1920 issue of the *London Mercury* ran to 120 pages, and included J. C. Squire's expansive 'Moon', a poem of thirty-two stanzas each of ten lines.

[12] The hydrobromic acid prescribed for her by Dr Sorapure.

[13] '. . . behold bright Phoebus in his strength.' *The Winter's Tale*, IV. iv. 124.

[14] KM's notebook entry for 7 Jan. read: 'On the verandah. I don't want a God to praise or to entreat but to *share* my vision with. This afternoon looking at the primula after the rain. I want no one to "dance & wave their arms" I only want to *feel* they see too. But Jack won't. Sitting out there in the sun – where is my *mate. He* wants neither external life *nor* depression?!!! (*Journal* 1954, 192.)

To J. M. Murry, [9 January 1920]

[Casetta Deerholm, Ospedaletti]

My precious Darling

I have just received your Monday letter explaining about Wing. I had been so uneasy about him: now its alright. I DO love you – this adorable generous letter calling all things OURS. You are a wonderful lover. I shall be terribly proud of you. I feel your book is going to have a great success. Did you see Goldy's letter in the Nation.[1] It pleased me *terribly*. Print his poems – ask him to dinner – do anything: he admires my Bogey.

Now my precious please forgive what I have to say. And do not think you came here all for nothing or anything dreadful like that. Its just my peculiar fate at present which wont leave me. I must tell you but there is no action for you to take – nothing for you to worry about in the very slightest. I don't ask your help or anything & God forbid I should make your work harder. Just go on as you are and I shall manage what I have to manage.

Bogey I must leave here. The doctor has been today. He says I must go – there are no two opinions. I have been ill this week with my heart – and very nauseated by food & unable to sleep or rest with these fearful fits of crying. I have fought & fought against it but it is all no go. Today he came & I told him. He says I am suffering from acute nervous exhaustion and cant afford to stand any more. My *lung* is very improved but my heart is not and this causes the depression just as the depression he thinks has caused the heart. Ive had too much to fight – so he says. I asked if it was within my power to conquer this and he [said] "no – absolutely impossible". In fact he was kind & did not seem to think me a coward – so *you* must not. I have known these last few days that I was at the end of my tether – but we won't discuss them. Well, I have written all about it to Jinnie at Menton. The doctor thinks this much the best plan. If she cant find me a place there I shall go [to] the nursing home at San Remo & send Lesley to Menton to look round. She (L.M.) does understand at last & has been *kind*.[2]

It is not feasible to be here. She was away one day this week. I was alone. It was evening. I had a heart attack in my room & you see there was no-one to call. I had to wait till it was over & then get upstairs for the brandy – and I fainted. Well, this you see isn't good enough. Yet he says when I do get away I shall get better quickly – just as I did when you were here. When you were here my cough nearly stopped I was always hungry I slept all night. Now don't think that means I regret you are not here now. It does not. All it means is that I must not be alone. I will wire you when I do go. It will be by motor of course. But DONT worry dearest love. All is well.

This has of course thrown my work out utterly. But Ive sent the one review this evening & another shall go with this letter tomorrow.

Your letters are meat and drink. I think everybody but you is not to be trusted with the paper. S. & A. would have it ruined in a week. The Shestov![3] *Did you ever!* But you are just a little marvel. Oh, our Wing too late for your train. Did you kiss him *enough* to make up? Kiss him again for me.

Your true love
Wig.

The carol was lovely.[4] I am so glad about the Hardy.[5] Arthur sent me a really wonderful letter – dont be cross with the dear old boy. Give him a hug from me & tell him Ill write as soon as I *possibly can*. But my pen is very lourde at the moment. My love to Sydney & to Violet. *Did Gertie get my present?* Please ask Violet. Don't forget about chestnuts boiled put through the sieve & then made the consistency of mashed potatoes.

MS ATL. *LJMM*, 452–3.

[1] A letter to the editor of the *Nation*, 2 Jan. 1920, from the poet Louis Golding took up Murry's article 'The War Pictures at the Royal Academy' in the *Nation*, 20 Dec. 1919, noting his 'weariness' as 'disillusion', but judging him 'one of the few intellectual leaders of the younger generation in whom we can trust; his power of sheer thinking is matched by a fierce, proud honesty which is sometimes almost lurid in its intensity.'

[2] KM's notebook entry for 8 Jan. read: 'BLACK . . . A day spent in Hell. Unable to do anything. Took brandy. Determined not to weep – wept. Sense of isolation frightful. I shall die if I don't escape.' And the next day: 'BLACK. Another of them . . . I somehow or other wrote a column . . . In the evening L.M. and I were more nearly friendly than we have been for years. I couldn't rest or sleep. The roaring of the sea was insufferable.' (*Journal* 1954, 192.)

³ 'Leo Shestov, Chapters from a book', with the by-line 'Authorized Translation from the Russian by S. Koteliansky', was a series of rather ponderous *aperçus* on writing and moral questions by the Russian philosopher (1866–1938), accepted for publication during Murry's absence. Koteliansky's translation of *The Apotheosis of Groundlessness: An Essay in Undogmatic Thought* (1905) appeared in 1920 as *All Things Are Possible*, with a foreword by D.H. Lawrence.
⁴ Thomas Hardy had sent Murry a Christmas card with an accompanying poem.
⁵ Murry wrote on 5 Jan. that he had bought two unnamed volumes of Hardy, even though they could not afford them.

To J. M. Murry, [12 January 1920]

[Casetta Deerholm, Ospedaletti]

Monday.

My dearest Bogey

I received your wire yesterday Sunday and am sending by the first post registered this day (Monday) a story called *The Man Without a Temperament.*[1] The MSS. I send is positively my only copy. I cannot possibly repeat it. May I beg you to see that it is not lost? I have asked Rutter to send either (1) the story to you if he doesnt want to use it or (2) the proofs to you in case he does. But if he does send it to you I would most earnestly intreat you to have it copied for me (at my expense) as it is one of the stories that I am giving to Grant Richards and as I have not so much as a shaving or a paring of it wherewith I could reconstruct its like. I hope I do not exaggerate. If I do – forgive me. You know a parent's feelings – they are terrible at this moment. I feel my darling goes among lions. And I think there is not a word I would change or that can be changed so would you examine the proofs with the MSS? —

That my novel review did not arrive on the Tuesday proves that Friday posting is not early enough. Youll have no more of that worry I promise you.

I have just sealed up my story. I am sorry to say Im nervous about its safety. If you could wire me the word *arrived* when you know it has arrived you would give me very great relief.

Goodbye darling for now.

Wig.

Take care of it for me, PLEASE PLEASE.

MS ATL. *LJMM*, 453–4.

¹ 'The Man Without a Temperament', conceived under a different title, was written with extraordinary speed. On 10 Jan., after recording that she had heard that day of her father's remarriage in Wellington to his dead wife's best friend, KM wrote in her notebook: 'Thought

out *The Exile*. Appalling night of misery deciding J. had no more need of our love.' The entry for the next day reads: 'Worked from 9.30 a.m. to a quarter after midnight only stopping to eat. Finished the story. Lay awake then till 5.30 too excited to sleep. In the sea drowned souls sang all night. I thought of everything in my life and it all came back so vividly – all is connected with this feeling that J. and I are no longer as we were. I love him but he rejects my *living* love. This is anguish. These are the worst days of my whole life.' (*Journal* 1954, 192.)

This drawing together of memories and present regret, the fact that KM frequently set her father's warm behaviour as a husband against Murry's failures, the recollection a little earlier of the child lost eleven years before, and the general context of recent letters, disturbing verses, and her notebook entries since Murry's return to England, contribute an added poignancy to her new story of invalid wife and long-suffering spouse, as well as a penetrating bitterness to its concluding lines:

'I sometimes wonder – do you mind awfully being out here with me?'
He bends down. He kisses her. He tucks her in, he smoothes the pillow.
'Rot!' he whispers.

To Richard Murry, [c.12 January 1920]

Casetta Deereholm | Ospedaletti | Porto Maurizio

My dear old Boy,

I owe you letters, thanks – Im in your debt all round and you must be thinking I am an ungrateful creature – to say the very least of it. But I feel as though Ive been on a voyage lately – on the high seas – out of sight of land, and though some albatross post has brought *your* news under its wing Ive never been able to detain the bird long enough to send an answer back. Forgive me.

The little book is a rare find.[1] Ive not only read every word and stared the pictures (especially the crocodile and the little lamb who doth skip and play always merry always gay) out of countenance I've begun a queer story on the strength of it about a child who learnt reading from this little primer. Merciful Heavens! Think of all the little heads bowed over these tiny pages all the little hands tracing the letters, and think of the rooms in which they sat, and the leaping light they read by, half candlelight half fire, and how terribly frightened they must have been as they read about this Awful God waiting to pop them into Eternal Flames – to consume them utterly and wither them like grass . . . Did you read the poems? And did your eye fasten upon Mr John Rogers,[2] the first martyr in Queen Marys Reign, laughing, really rather callously as he burned away in sight of his wife and Nine Small Children? They certainly were peculiarly hideous children and his wife looks as though she had wasted his substance upon buying hats but all the same its a bit steep to show your feelings as he is doing.

I am awfully interested to know about your drawing. It will be very exciting. I think it is a perfectly first-chop idea – and I feel there is something in you that printing doesn't give expression to and that only drawing could satisfy. I feel you're one of those rare people who will find the '*word*' for a thing by a *line* – by a *curve* – do you know what I mean? Now, of course with my usual patience I want to see your sketch books, and . . . Text by John Middleton Murry . . . Illustrations by Arthur Murry. Etc. Etc. Etc. It is a fine little tree to have planted to mark the New Year by.

I am working very hard just now. I cant walk about or go out. Nearly all my days are spent in bed or if not in bed on a little sofa that always feels like lying in a railway carriage – a horrid little sofa. I have seen hardly any people at all since Ive been here – *nobody* to talk to. The one great talker is the sea. It never is quiet; one feels sometimes as if one were a shell filled with a hollow sound. God forbid that another should ever live the life I have known here and yet there are *moments* you know, old Boy, when after a dark day there comes a sunset – such a glowing gorgeous marvellous sky that one forgets all in the beauty of it – these are the moments when I am *really writing*. Whatever happens I have had these blissful, perfect moments and they are worth living for. I thought, when I left England, I could not love writing more than I did, but now I feel Ive never known what it is to be a writer until I came here.

Jack's book seems to be creating a stir. I feel Jack is on the eve of very great success. He's never looked for success – but then he never does look for anything – it just comes to him. I'm afraid he didn't have much of a time over here – the journey is so tiring and then he had neuralgia.

Goodbye, my dear old boy. And to show you forgive me – write again soon – will you? I love hearing from you.

Yours ever
Katherine

MS R. Murry. *LKM* II. 1–2.

[1] On 3 Jan. Richard had sent KM an old catechism for children, 'a little book that you might well like with fancy wordcuts' (ATL).

[2] John Rogers (1500–55), commonly identified with the 'Matthew' of 'Matthew's Bible', a translation of 1537, was burned at Smithfield.

To Marie Dahlerup,[1] *12 January [1920]*

Casetta Deereholm | Ospedaletti | Porto Maurizio
January 12th

My dearest Marie,

I have just received your letter and I hasten to answer it. Thank you a thousand times for accepting my offer so charmingly and so generously, but I am more than sorry to say that since I last wrote to you (since *yesterday* in fact) there is a great change in my plans and I shall no longer need a companion secretary in May. What has happened is this. Perhaps you know that for nearly two years now my old school-fellow Ida Baker has been living with me and looking after me. She was leaving me in May to join her sister in South Africa, but yesterday a letter came from the sister asking her not to go, putting her off indefinitely, in fact. This of course means that she must stay with me and go on doing what she has so nobly done for me these past two years. I could not send her away. It was only because I was losing her that I ventured to write to you – because I thought there was no possibility of keeping Ida in our household.

I simply hate to have to tell you all this when you have so exquisitely accepted, but, my dear, I can do nothing else. I can only hope that you will be our guest some time in the country and that we may be able to help you perhaps with some literary work. I am bound to Ida by not only ties of affection; she has seen me through some very bad times. It is only fair that now I am better she should share in the good.

Your letter is of course quite confidential, dearest Marie. Thank you for telling me so much. And now let me say once more how deeply I regret having to write this – how sorry I am that I could not let you know sooner. I can only trust that you will understand the position.

With very much love, my dear girl

Yours
Kathleen.

Unpublished, MS ATL.

[1] A shadowy Danish acquaintance almost certainly from her schooldays, considering the name KM signs off with. There had been a plan for her to go to the Riviera as a companion to replace Ida Baker. Murry apparently did not forward the letter.

To J. M. Murry, [13 January 1920]

[Casetta Deerholm, Ospedaletti]
Tuesday Night.

My dearest Bogey

Thank you for your letter today and for letting me see the two poems; I think they are exquisite and could not be improved on.[1] I return you them.

I return also Nevinson's letter.[2] It is an outrage; it made me feel quite sick and faint – the spirit of it seemed to get into the room . . . and to go on and go on. It is a really revolting letter.

I am enclosing a letter to Marie Dahlerup which I want you please to read before you send it to her. I am very much afraid that the contents will surprise and anger you. Will you please try to be patient with me while I explain. Bogey I am so sorry – when I have anything to explain to you now I have a kind of premonitory shiver – I see you turn away so quick and sharp . . . but you *really must* please be patient with me now.

I do not want Marie any more. Ever since you left here this time – since this last 'illness' of mine – (what the doctor calls acute nervous exhaustion acting on the heart) my feelings towards Lesley are absolutely changed. It is not only that the hatred is gone – Something positive is there which is very like love for her. She has convinced me at last, against all my opposition that she is trying to do all in her power for me – and that she is devoted to the one idea which is (please forgive my egoism) to see me well again. This time she has fed me, helped me, got up in the middle of the night to make me hot milk and rub my feet, brought me flowers, *served* me as one could not be served if one were not loved. All silently and gently too, even after all my bitter ravings at her and railing against her. She has simply shown me that she *understands* and I feel that she does.

Am I right in feeling you never would have disliked her had it not been for me? How could you have! I look back and think how she tried to run the house for us. She failed – but HOW she tried! I think of her unceasing devotion to us – her patience with me – her trying to help you and to efface herself when we were together. Who else would have done it? Nobody on earth. I know she loves US as no one ever will. She thinks (STILL thinks) it would be the ideal life to be near us and to serve us. In Hampstead she was in a false position. She cannot be a servant – a nurse – a companion – all these things. But to overlook – to help – to keep an eye on OUR possessions (precious to her because she knows what we feel about them) there is no one like her. My hate is quite lifted – quite gone; it is like a curse removed. Lesley has been through the storm with us. I want her now to share in the calm – to act Marie's part for us in our country house. Do you agree? I feel I cannot do without her now. Here is someone *tried trusted* – who understands who is really bound to me now because of what she has done here for me. I think I would have died without Lesley these last terrible times. You know she has such an affection for you, too, deep and true: "Jack is JACK". I know she is not perfect. I know she sometimes will annoy us. God – who wont? And who will leave us so utterly free and yet be *there* in *charge* when we want her. I confess that now I do lean on her. She looks after me; she has become (or I see her now in her true colours) the person who looks after all I cannot attend to. It was only when I refused to acknowledge this – to acknowledge her importance to me that I hated her. Now that I do I can be sincere and trust her and of course she, feeling the difference, is a different person. Her self respect has all come back. She thinks *for* me and seems to know my ways as nobody who had not been with me for years ever could.

This great change will I am sure astonish and I am afraid anger you. I think my hatred must have been connected with my illness in some way. I cannot explain it – only tell you and though I am afraid I must trust that you will believe me. Will you please tell me what you think? You must realise that now that we are at peace I am never exasperated and she does not annoy me. I only feel 'free' for work and everything.

My dearest, I am still waiting to hear from Menton. It is still early to expect an answer. Foster comes again tomorrow. I got up for an hour or two today but now I am in bed again. Did I tell you we have had an alarm here at night. Some men very late, ringing and ringing the bell until finally Lesley shot out of the window. It was so queer – like a siege – very dreadful, really. Lesley did not take off her clothes all night.

Thank you for sending me the Tchekhov.[3] I will do my very best. It is awfully good of you to let me do it. Tell me about *yourself* – will you? My darling, remember how I love you – If you knew what your letters mean to me!

Be happy. Fare well. I am your devoted

Wig.

MS ATL. *LJMM*, 454–6.

[1] On 8 Jan. Murry sent her the two poems for the Epilogue and Prologue of *Cinnamon and Angelica*.

[2] On 6 Jan. Murry referred to 'young Nevinson', whose letter 'almost makes me repent of having been so kind to him'. (ATL). C. R. W. Nevinson (1889–1946), painter, war artist, the son of H. W. Nevinson (1856–1941) the *Guardian*'s eminent war correspondent, and jilted by Dora Carrington for Mark Gertler. His autobiography, *Paint and Prejudice*, was published in 1937.

[3] Murry told KM on 7 Jan., 'I've sent the last volume of Tchehov to you today – do two first-chop columns on it.' However no review of Chekhov by KM appeared in the *Athenaeum*. (ATL.)

To Jinnie Fullerton,[1] 14 January 1920

[Casetta Deerholm, Ospedaletti]
Wednesday

Your letter has made me spring so high that 30 francs a day is mountain peaks below! I do not know how I am to thank Cousin Connie and you for this letter. Will you please believe that large warm beams of gratitude are coming out of this letter and that the inkpot is flashing and stars are dropping off the pen.

But *seriously* – thank you from my heart! The Hermitage[2] sounds the very place for me, and Ida is quite content to go to the Pension Anglaise. I know I shall be able to earn the extra money to keep us both quite easily in such surroundings. Besides, I shall get well at such a rate that they will turn me out for a fraud by the time April is over.

Could they take us soon? Ida is going in to San Remo to-day to see about our passports and so on and I wondered whether, if we can get a car, they would be ready for us to-day week (next Wednesday). Or is that too soon? We shall prepare ourselves for Wednesday, and then if we must wait a few days it will not matter. I should like if possible to take the rooms for a month to begin with, tho' I am sure I shall stay longer.

I keep re-reading your letter as I write. My dear, what trouble you have taken – and how soon you have answered. I had marked Friday in my diary as the day I could 'perhaps' hear.

I told the doctor man that I wanted very much to leave here and he said that I must – there were no two opinions. My lungs are much better and my heart is only temporary caused, he says, by the fever and 'acute nervous strain.' But that will vanish away as soon as the solitary confinement is over.

TS ATL. *LKM* II. 3–4.

---

[1] Unsigned and incomplete, this letter is clearly a draft.
[2] The private nursing home in Menton where KM would move the following week.

To J. M. Murry, [14 January 1920]

[Casetta Deerholm, Ospedaletti]

My dearest

Just hasty note enclosing the letter I have received from Jinnie. I have replied saying I will take the room at 30 francs a day & Ida is going to the pension at 15. It seems to me to be really ideal. I have asked whether it will be possible to go next Wednesday. Of course I must take a car. It costs £6 but I must do it: there is no other way. And once I get there to such a place I shall be able to do a great deal more work and earn the extra money. I can't really imagine a kinder letter than this and she must have acted *immediately* on receipt of mine and she's been ill herself and isn't at all fit to do these things. Such behaviour on the part of human beings surprises me *too* much. I cannot reconcile it with what I know of Life; it is "too good to be true". I will send you a wire immediately I know the date of our leaving & I will make the most careful and complete arrangements possible as regards the forwardings of my letters and parcels. *Will you see I have more novels sent?* Mary Hamilton's[1] for instance? You see I can work quite differently there and shall be so refreshed. *And please darling you will still send me papers and so on – won't you?* I shall want them just the same. After I send the wire to you will you address my letters, books & papers to the new address on the card.

You see this is all arranged and managed and perfectly simple. I know I am doing the only thing – and I am *sure* I can make the extra money necessary.

I only hope my darling that you approve and do not still think it queer of me to find this solitary confinement insupportable. But the past is past; I look forward to the future – with oh – such joy!

Goodbye my precious.

Be Happy.

Your own devoted
Wig.

Do you think you could just wire me if this plan satisfies you?

MS ATL. *LJMM*, 456–7.

---

[1] KM had met the political journalist and scholar Mary Hamilton in late 1918 (see *CLKM* II. 280 n. 7). KM reviewed her novel *Full Circle* in the *Athenaeum*, 6 Feb. 1920.

To J. M. Murry, 17 January [1920]

[Casetta Deerholm, Ospedaletti]
Saturday January 17th.

My own Love

We ask again and again at the P.O. but the strike continues and there is no news; no letters or wires are sent or received. We are quite shut off. My reviews are I suppose at Vintimille. I shall have nothing in this week. I sent the Chinese Poetry[1] on Wednesday and on Thursday Limpidus & Coggin,[2] but they'll not arrive. This is really very strange & terrible. On Wednesday I go to Mentone to *L'Hermitage Menton*.[3] We cannot get there before, neither can we communicate with Menton now.

I came downstairs today – it is a dark, very silent day. I began to prepare to go away – to sort & tie up your letters and to burn all others. As I went through them words, phrases, half sentences, started up – "my darling" – & "tell me about yourself" or "I hold you in my

arms". Oh – what anguish! What anguish! Will you ever write so
again? Love Love Love overcomes me. I knelt by the fire – trying to
bear it. Yet, whatever happens, if you no longer keep me in that
wonderful place in your heart where I lay so long – whatever happens,
my own Bogey – For this wonderful love you gave me may you be
blessed for ever more.

Here is the flower you painted inside the cigar box – yellow & red.
It is *us*: it smiles at me. It belongs to *those two*.

You were not made of steel. Oh, my Love, was I so heavy? If only
you could ever know what I have suffered here in this *desolation*. But
you will not listen: you will not hear – I ought to have kept quiet in my
box. I am in anguish today – I keep on thinking & thinking – trying to
remember the time in the garden trying to *forget* how you turned on me
& upbraided me & said 'God only knows what you *do* think'. *Christ* to
have heard that & then to be alone. But on Wednesday all will be
changed. This is goodbye from the Casetta. I cant see for tears.[4]
I love you for ever.

MS ATL. Unpublished.

---

[1] KM's review of Arthur Waley's *More Translations from the Chinese*, which on 28 Oct. 1919 she
had said 'I long to do', was not used.

[2] KM's review of *Sir Limpidus*, by Marmaduke Pickthall, was run under 'Amusement' in the
Athenaeum, 30 Jan. 1920, and that of Ernest Oldmeadow's *Coggin* under 'Portrait of a Child', in
the same issue.

[3] Murry wrote on Monday, 19 Jan. that when he arrived at work that morning he found her
telegram, which does not survive, informing him that she would leave for Menton on 21 Jan.,
and telling him, 'Postal strike still on.' Murry had not heard from her for almost a week.

[4] Tear stains in fact smudge this page of the manuscript. KM wrote in her notebook on
17 Jan.: 'Postal strike, no letters, no wires. Tearing up and sorting the old letters. The *feeling* that
comes – the anguish – the words that fly out into one's breast my *darling* my *wife* Oh what
anguish! Oh will it ever be the same. Lay awake at night listening to the voices. Two men
seemed to sing – a tenor and a baritone: then the drowned began.' And the next day: 'I am
haunted by thoughts of Jack perpetually.' (*Journal* 1954, 194.)

To Ottoline Morrell, [20 January 1920]

Ospedaletti | Porto Maurizio

My dearest Ottoline

I am leaving here tomorrow for Menton and that 'frees' me to write
to you. I have been on the verge or the brink of writing so often – and
your perfectly angelic letters have been a vile reproach to me – but I
could not break through. This experience has been such Hell that really
if I took up my pen to describe it the ink would be ashes. I have been
nearly out of my mind with misery and I don't feel (one always says
this but surely its true this time) that Life can ever be the same again.

Its as though one had had smallpox; one could never look in the glass and see the same face.

But – to explain? There was no villa or any place to be had in San Remo (a *horrid* town) so I came to this small cottage on the side of a wild hill just beyond Ospedaletti. It stares, glares, gapes at the sea. It is high up & the noise of the waves beating on rocks & rushing up caverns is never still. At night sitting up one *vibrates* with the noise, literally. It is a pretty little house – pretty like a doll's house with a garden & terrace. I could get no maid because of my DISEASE so L.M. & I were alone here. For months I have been unable to walk – or to move at all except from my bed to a sofa or just to crawl down to a tiny room for the afternoon. Literally *not a soul* to talk to – L.M. very often out for hours until it is dark – the day fading, fading out here – and the dark hanging over the sea. My heart has been affected by – they say – the fever. It isn't that. Its by misery. Really, I have simply wept for days. This appalling isolation – deathly stillness – great wind and sea – and this feeling that I had consumption and was tainted – dying here. If I moved – even to the doorstep – my heart beat so hard that I had to lean against the door – and then no sleep – nothing but going over and over ones whole past life – as one will do when one is dead, I suppose. I tried to explain this to M. But – he did not understand at all. Not in the very slightest.

Ottoline, I *adore Life*. What do all the fools matter and all the stupidity. They do matter but somehow for me they cannot touch the body of Life. Life is marvellous. I want to be deeply rooted in it – to live – to expand – to breathe in it – to rejoice – to share it. To give and to be asked for Love. I know you understand this for you are thrillingly alive – but few people do. Do you realise what it was like to find oneself here – in bed day after day – going grey with misery – utterly alone and ill? Dearest – I don't want pity. But its been *beyond terrible*. L.M. fat and rosy, runs to the village, runs to San Remo, comes back with her 'the woman at the laiterie told me –' and then I hear her upstairs – singing to herself.

Well, its over. I go to Menton tomorrow and I shall stay there for some months. *L'Hermitage, Menton* is the address.

In *strictest deepest* confidence the really horrible thing about all this has been that it has left me quite alone. I thought, until now even, that 'one' understood – that superficially perhaps I was alone but that really it wasn't so. And I find out I was wrong. For nearly six years I have felt *loved* (you know that feeling?). Now it is gone. It was all just a dream. But one must get over that and gather up Life for oneself and get in touch with Life again. One must not mourn or cry out if the sorrow is great – one can't afford to —— Mysterious Life! . . .

I would give anything for a long long talk with you, uninterrupted and very intimate. Other people are such shadows —— The day you wore your blue dress & stood outside the gate in the sun with all those delicate willows moving behind you —— Do you remember – you said the day was so lovely – and there was deep delight in your eyes – darkening them. I never forget that. IT IS YOU.

I have worked here. Some days from nine in the morning until twelve at night – only stopping to eat – just writing on and on. Rutter has one of the stories.[1] They're queer. I shall write again dearest dearest friend. This is just 'to let YOU know.'

Yours for ever
Katherine.

MS Texas. Cited *Exhibition*, 44; Meyers, 194.

---

[1] 'The Man Without a Temperament' would appear in *Art and Letters* in the Spring issue, 1920. The only other stories that survived from her time at Ospedaletti were 'Late Spring', later renamed 'This Flower', and 'A Strange Mistake', published by Murry as 'The Wrong House' when both were included in the posthumous *Something Childish But Very Natural* (1924).

III

FRANCE – MENTON:
JANUARY–APRIL 1920

By the time she left Ospedaletti on 21 January, KM hoped that to move from the anti-British sentiment then prevailing in Italy, to terminate the loneliness of living only with Ida Baker, and to be near her elderly and warmly protective cousin in Menton, would bring about that change in health she persisted in believing accompanied a change of abode. After three weeks in a private nursing home she moved in with her cousin at the Villa Flora. Living comfortably with women she admired, her dallying with Roman Catholicism, a new tolerance towards Ida Baker, Murry's buying the house in the country they had spoken about for years, a burgeoning friendship with the Schiffs, and plans for a new collection of stories, in their various ways brought a fresh buoyancy to her last months in France.

∽

To J. M. Murry, [21 January 1920]

[*drawing of a heart with an arrow through it, and three stars with the words* Boge Wig house *written inside them*]

L'Hermitage | Menton.

My own precious Husband

I have escaped. Do you know what that means? There has been a postal strike in Italy – no letters, no wires. *Nothing* comes through or goes out – a strike of the railways – and now from today a strike of automobiles. We just got through by taking a round about route & escaping the police.

ALL ALL my thoughts, hopes, longings were for an answer to my telegram, here. I managed to get a telegram telephoned to you at Menton – at what pains I cant describe – and I knew there was time for an answer. I simply TORE the telegram from these people & read *story arrived safely* not even a signature. Was that from you? Could it have been. I have sent Ida out with another – thats all I can do. For about a moment I nearly broke down but I must steel myself & wait wait wait again.

Bogey I have got away from that hell of isolation – from the awful ringing at night – from the loneliness & fright. To tell you the truth I think I have been *mad*, but really, medically mad. A great awful cloud has been on me & now if I hear from you & all is well it will lift & you will see your own Wig under it – the *old true loving* Wig – your OWN wife who adores you. Its nearly killed me. Yes. When Jinnie took me in her arms today & she cried as well as I I felt as though Id been through some awful deathly strain – and just survived – been rescued from drowning or something like that. You cant understand love – its not possible you should know what that isolation was when you left again and I again was ill –

Forgive me forgive me completely for ever will you. I ought never to have done it. Of course it was all an awful mistake but now at last it is over – & wont happen again. If I dont get well here Ill never get well. Here – after the journey – was this room waiting for me – exquisite – large with four windows overlooking great gardens & mountains – wonderful flowers – tea with *toast* & honey & butter, a charming maid – and these two dear sweet women to welcome me with papers books etc. This is really a superb place in every way. Two doctors live here. They are coming to examine me tomorrow. They 'called' after tea & just chatted & ordered my extra milk and dinner in my room & so on – awfully nice men. The cleanliness is almost supernatural. One feels like a butterfly – one only wants to fan ones wings on the couch the chairs. I have a big writing table with a cut glass inkstand – a waste paper basket – a great bowl of violets & *your* own anemones & wallflowers on it. The directress is a very nice french woman only too anxious to look after me & see that there is no change in anything. She will give me a litre of milk & butter as much as I want. There is also a sort of Swiss nurse in white who has just been in & says she answers the bell at night. She is so good to look at that I shall *have* to ring.

Boge Boge Boge. Ive got away from under that ghastly cloud. All is absolutely changed. Im here with people with care. I feel a different creature *really* – different eyes, different hair. The garden is gorgeous: there is a big shelter, chaufféd. What do you think of that.

Precious I have to catch the post – & heres my dinner in my room – all lovely. This is just on the spot to let you know I AM here and all goes marvellously well. Only YOU YOU YOU now thats all I want. A new-old Wig will come back in May. Ill write tomorrow & every day.

Your own wife.

MS ATL. *LKM* II. 4–5; *LJMM*, 457–8.

To J. M. Murry, [22 January 1920]

L'Hermitage [Menton]
Thursday 8.30 A.M.

My precious own dear

At the risk of not having a letter from you I shall still write another. For I am not so pressé this morning and I have so much to tell you . . . I have had such a gorgeous night in this huge room with stars coming through the west & south windows & little airs. At eight arrived the breakfast. Bogey I really hope this place is showing off a little & this present behaviour is abnormal. If it isnt pray see that our new house has folding doors – wide staircases . . . nothing else will contain me. Oh, blankets & sheets of such rare quality: blankets that feel like lambs – sheets glacés. Electric lamp by the bed under a small gold shade. Great pot of hot water muffled in a real soft thick bath towel. All these things are acting with such effect upon the infant mind of your girl & a west view of mountains covered with little pines & a south view of distant sea and olive groves (as seen from 2 marbil balconies) that she feels almost intoxicated.

Getting away yesterday was really pretty awful. Ma'am Littardi arrived asking 50 lire for the *hire* of the stove. The youth who has been sleeping arrived asking for 5 lire a night (8 nights). The laundry arrived with a bill for 57 lire. Vince arrived & carried down the boxes and behaved like such a superior courier that I felt we might employ him later. The taxi fare was £6 & he demanded 25 *francs* for having seen us through the police at Vintimille. I dont care – Im still alive and Im away. But the comble was that the day before yesterday when I was gone upstairs to fetch the revolver two beggars came & rang. The door was open – so I came down quick as I could. But theyd gone & were at the foot of the steps – an old man & an old woman *with a bundle*. I saw them get into a small mule cart & drive away. At 11 p.m. that night I asked Ida to fetch my overcoat as I wanted to sew on a button. It was gone with the green scarf – the woolly. Both must have been pinched by the woman. What do you think of that?

Italy – my Italy.[1]

Hold hard to your chair. This room I am in is forty francs a day twing-twang. But the post only takes 3 days to England & now Ill be able to work more. Im sending Tchekhov tomorrow. Forgot to say before the motor came Vince arrived to tell you there was a revolution in France & no motors allowed over the frontier. As we came into Menton we ran into a procession of hundreds of young men with banners who waved and called & thrust the banners into the air. *We want wages dont tip us.* It was the waiters strike. A train – a blessed train that goes to Paris connects with a boat lands me in my darlings country has given a faint far away rather exotic horns of elfland hoot. Oh my precious Bogey do write to me. You do really care about external life to the extent of hearing about it? Oh – you're my *all*. The trees outside whisper and the sun seems to be flying. I suppose this *is* nonsense but I breathe quite differently. Once I hear from you – once you take me in your arms – Im not thinking of that queer small unsigned telegram – I *cant*. YOURS

Your very own
Wig.

MS ATL. *LKM* I. 5–6; *LJMM*, 458.

<hr>

¹ 'Italy, my Italy!', from Robert Browning's 'De Gustibus', l. 39, *Men and Women* (1855).

To J. M. Murry, [22 January 1920]

[L'Hermitage, Menton]

My love

I have just received the 2nd wire. No news or reviews. Now you will understand why. This wire sounds even though of course it assures me the worst has happened & nothing has got through it sounds as though you arent angry.¹ *Boge*. That word is my talisman. Now Ill feed on this telegram burrow like a bee in sweet clover into the word *Boge* and wait again. Surely Waterlow told you about the grève des postiers? In time? And you had my telephoned wire saying *postal strike continues* so that you were not surprised to receive no reviews? This wire was brought by a nice boy whom I gave 5 francs to yesterday to make certain hed act as faithful messenger between us. He wore a little red jacket and a black & white linen apron. He has black hair & very large eyes like bulls eyes – the lollies I mean. *Ma-dame un-e te-le-grrāmmme!* BOGE theres your name. I shall sow it first in snowdrops then in crocuses then in tulips & then vergissmeinnichts in the garden I make for Dicky before Dicky is born.² (I wish you could see my writing table all in perfect order with the books the pig the flowers a box of Abdullah cigarettes (Jinnie) and a large calendar with yesterday's date marked in red ink. Jinnie again. These two items were brought round by her maid last night. "Miss Fullerton said please 'm it was to make it a red letter day". What a woman! Their villa is only 5 minutes away – we stopped on our way here & the cook & housemaid both ran out with "bonjour bonjour les dames vous attendent a l'Hermitage." As though I was an old friend. The villa looked superb with a grove of oranges. "Now Katherine my dear – the garden is yours – & you must take tea with us every day & when you come here to work *growl* when you see us and we'll disappear".

Well now thats enough about me. I only tell you because I want you to forget the creature who lived at the Casetta. It was all wrong – terribly wickedly wrong to have been there. You'll never know, & I felt your strangeness *your refusal to enter into it* – that was what overpowered me. That I shall *never* understand. Even when we sat there at evening & I said can you imagine what this is like when one is alone & ill & L.M. away? *Still* you would not see. But let us put all that away. Let us forget it. Bury it in cursed Italy. Let us look forward – and build and build.

I love you. You know I love you with my whole being.

Wig.

Result of the doctors examination.

I must add this page – just to tell you what these men have said. I am in a state of healing now. If I take les plus grands soins for 3 months I shall be énormement mieux. Im to stay in bed till 11 every morning then to get up & go into the garden, stay there till lunch. Spend the afternoon in a chaise longue – have goûter at four with toast & butter & honey and dine downstairs. Every morning the Swiss masseuse is to give me a friction all over to aid my awful circulation. They want my poumons X rayed to see just how they are so I must have that done. The Big Man said I am très fragile mais vous n'avez pas simplement bonne chance – vous avez toutes les chances. They would not have me here if I were not going to get well. *Car c'est une maison de convalescence.* Look here. This room I am in is only for a few days because the one I was to have at 30 isn't ready. This one is 50. The exchange is between 35 and 40. But no. Im mad. 30 IS my limit. At any rate my own husband HERE HERE HERE IS YOUR OWN WIG. When the Italian letters do reach you kill them. They are not me. I used to feel like Virginia but she had Leonard. I had *no-one*.

Heres your Monday letter come by the 2nd courier the one about Wells.[3] On what a treasure (*you* not H.G.). Oh Boge my precious own – I don't know what to say to it. Its a wonderful letter. Its the 1st for a fortnight. I dont know what will be safe in Italy as regards cheques or anything. Nothing is delivered. I have left 30 lire with the post for forwarding any parcels. Now I must write old Kay & tell him I mean to overdraw. I see the Wells family very squashy – wait till we have *our* house and *our* boys and our ball game.

Heaven bless our loves

Wig.

MS ATL. Unpublished.

¹ Murry wrote on 21 Jan. saying there were neither letters nor reviews from her for a week, but he had received a telegram telling him the postal strike was still on.

² The name KM assumes for their imaginary child.

³ Murry had spent the weekend of 17–18 Jan. at the home of the novelist H. G. Wells (1866–1946), Easton Glebe, Dunmow. For Murry's acerbic description of his host, who 'struck me as degenerated, shallow, vain and a ludicrous snob', see Murry, 253–4.

To J. M. Murry, [23 January 1920]

[L'Hermitage, Menton]
Friday.

Dearest

I thought when I had sent my letter yesterday that you don't really know where we stand. The last letter I had from you was on a Wednesday and you contemplated spending the following weekend with the Waterlows to see *the Lacket*.¹ Did you go? What happened? I know nothing after that until I received your letter about Wells yesterday. And what was the last you received from me I wonder? It is all terribly confusing. Have you got my cards of this place? Do you know how we stand? Oh, a hundred curses on the italian post. It is too distracting. . . .

Reviews of course – Chinese Poetry, Sir Limpidus, Coggin all have been sent & four parcels of books. Two I imagine arrived before the strike. If they did will you please let me have the money? I need every single penny I can get. You see in addition to my room I have *wine* & *medicine* & laundry & odd expenses and L.M. to not only keep but to give pocket money to and provide for. I don't care two figs. I feel perfectly reckless. Until Kay says the Bank will summons me Ill just *go on*. Its worth it. One day here makes me feel better – and only to have escaped that TRAP is such a triumph.

Connie came yesterday to see me carrying a baby Pekinese. Have you ever seen a really *baby* one about the size of a fur glove – covered with pale gold down with paws like minute seal flappers – very large impudent eyes & ears like fried potatoes? Good God! What creatures they are. This one is a perfect complement to Wing. We <u>must</u> have one. They are not in the least pampered or fussy or spoilt. They are like fairy animals. This one sat on my lap, cleaned both my hands really very carefully, polished the nails then bit off carefully each finger & thumb & then exhausted & blown with 8 fingers & two thumbs inside him gave a great sigh & crossed his front paws & listened to the conversation. He lives on beef steaks and loaf sugar. His partner in life when he is at home is a pale blue satin bedroom slipper. Please let us have one at the Heron.

I had a long talk with Connie yesterday. She and Jinnie are really – no joking – superb women. Its a queer queer relationship. C. obviously adores J. and refers everything to her but she is not in the least a parasite or overshadowed. She is a complete creature who yet *leans* on J. as a woman may do on a man. One feels her happiness to an extraordinary degree. That is what is so restful about both these women. They are deeply *secure* – and they are well *bred* – they are *english ladies* – which means a great deal.

I went downstairs yesterday for lunch & dinner. Dear love I am here on false pretences. I am the only healthy creature here. When I entered the salle a manger I felt that all the heads were raised all the noses sniffed a frampold[2] rampant lion entering. Its not that these people are *ill*. They look exactly as though they were risen from the dead – stepped out of coffins & eating again pour la première fois. Their hair is thin & weak and poor – the eyes are cold & startled – their hands are still waxen – & THIN! They are walking sticks. All the little arts & allurements they have shed & not yet picked up again. They are still sexless & blow their noses in a *neuter* fashion – neither male nor female blows. At the tables there are the signs & tokens of their illnesses – bottles, boxes. *One* woman gave me a nasty knock. She had a réchaud beside [her] – a lamp & stand & she reheated everything even the plates. There but for the grace of God went Wig. The waitresses of course thrive in this atmosphere. They are two pretty full-bosomed girls – with spider web stockings, shoes laced up their legs – little delicate wispy aprons – powdered necks – red lips – scent – & they move like ballet dancers – sliding & gliding in the fullness of their youth and strength over the polished floors. All this amuses me very much.

Later. The masseuse has just been and ironed me from top to toe. I am all tingling as though I had been a 10 mile walk. ♫ See how VERY silly I am getting. You just wait until we meet again and you find a bran new girl.

But never never shall I cut myself off from Life again. I haven't any illusions darling; I know all about it and am not really a baby saying 'agoo-a-gah!' but in spite of everything I know *il y a quelque chose* . . . that I feed on, exult in, and adore. One must be, if one is a Wig, continually giving & receiving, and shedding & renewing, & examining & trying to place. According to you I suppose my thinking is an infant affair with bead frames and coloured blocks – Well its not important. What is important is that I adore you & I shall go up in flame if I do not show you these cornflowers & jonquils.

The day is cloudy – but it doesn't matter. Landscape is lovely in this light – its not like the sea. The mimosa great puffs of mimosa & great trees of red roses & oranges bright and flashing. Some boys are being drilled outside. The sergeant major keeps on saying '*T'ois cinquante, n'est-ce pas,*' & there is a most forlorn bugle.

Here is a story my little femme de chambre told me. Please read it. Do you know Madam que les fleurs sont trop fortes to be left dans la chambre pendant la nuit & surtout les joncs. If I put them sur le balcon – n'est-ce pas & bring them in early in the morning. Vous savez quand me petite mère etait tres jeune elle etait la maitresse d'une petite école pour les tous petits enfants, et sur son jour de fête les bébés elle a apporté un bouquet énorme grand comme un chou – rond comme ça Madame de ces joncs. Elle les a mis dans sa chambre à coucher. C'était un Vendredi. Le soir elle est endormie, et, puis, tout le samedi, le dimanche – jusqu'a le lundi matin elle dort pro*fond*ement. Quand les petites eleves ont arrivés le lundi la porte etait fermée. Ils ont frappés – pas de reponse. Enfin mon père qui n'etait pas mon père à ce temps-la, alors est venu du village et il a forcé la porte et voila ma mère qui n'etait pas ma mère ni même marié a ce temps-la – toujours dans un sommeil *profond*, et l'air etait chargée de la parfum de ces joncs – qu'elle a mis sur une petite table pres du lit —

Don't you like that story? Do you see the infants looking in with their fingers in their mouths & the young man finding her blanc comme une bougie & the room & the flowers. Its a bit sentimental, praps, but I love it. I see such funny little worms with sachets and socks & large tam o'shanters.

Post has been. Your Tuesday letter is arrived & here is only Friday. Isn't it a COMFORT to be out of that awful silence? But here you talk of farmhouses. Does that mean the Lacket is off? Oh, shall I ever catch up?

Why did not Sydney tell you – or why didn't you enquire at the post office about Italy? Sydney MUST have known at the F.O. Yesterday tho' I saw a copy of the D. T. [*Daily Telegraph*] which said the strike was over on the 20th. What a lie! It is really only beginning – San Remo you know was guarded by the military. I feel this place is so near – so *easy* to get at. Its like being out in the garden with you in the house. It really is. But its so beautiful, darling, what I see of it at least – *superb*. The one brick is the expense. I wrote to Rutter yesterday. If *he* pays me it will make a difference. Did you see the story? Did you like it? What did you think? I must get up – & open the windows.

Goodbye my precious. Give my love to the pussies & to Violet & keep it all down to the last crumb for yourself. Did Arthur get a long letter from me? And a lovely inkpot posted in a diplomatic cardboard box? I shall be so thankful when you have heard from me. Perhaps you'll get a letter tomorrow or praps you'll be in Sussex . . . Goodbye my own. Do write as long a letter as you can and tell me a̲l̲l̲.

Your own wife
Wig.

MS ATL. *LKM* II. 6–9; *LJMM*, 459–62.

¹ A house at Lockeridge, near Marlborough, Wiltshire, which Murry was thinking of leasing, but was disappointed in when he saw it.
² *OED*, sense 2, 'Of a horse: fiery, mettlesome, spirited.'

To Richard Murry, [c.25 January 1920]

(That catechism in the primer was "for infants of 2½ years"!!! Just think of them standing up & saying: my original sin was the sin of Adam.) ((Dont send me any more books or drawings my young Millionaire)).

Hermitage | Menton.

My dear Petit-Frère,
Here is a letter with an Ominous drawing of yourself in Aids to Eyesight. I hope you won't have to wear them. You have as you doubtless know, beautiful eyes, very rare, expressive, original and seldom-seen eyes, the kind of eyes you might imagine a person having if he'd been born at sea while his wise parents cruised about among the pacific islands and had spent the first days of his natural little life wondering what all that blue was. However if you *do* have to have em glassed & framed – so do I. Mine – or rather one of mine is not at all the orb it used to be. Im going to wear horn specs those of the largest kind for working in. What a trio we shall present at the Heron. Pray make a drawing of us – surprised at our labours & suddenly all at various windows looking out to see who that is coming up the flagged walk – three faces at three windows – six prodigious eyes! Whoever it was faints among the pink peonies . . .

Yesterday – no the day before I received a copy of Je Ne Parle Pas. I want to thank you for having printed it so beautifully.¹ It makes me very happy to see your name on the back page. *My* share doesn't satisfy me at all – but *yours* fills me with pride. I hope a little handful of people buys it – for the sake of covering the expense. The page you send me of Cinnamon & Angelica looks very well. Are you going to make a *map* for the frontispiece with the arms of C. & A. very fairly drawn? Or a tiny tiny Durer like drawing of Apricia[2] – with a great flowery branch in the foreground. You know the kind of thing I mean? It is somehow *most right* that you should draw. When I come back you'll show me your sketches? Another quite small insignificant little half-hour job for *you* is a stone carving for the garden of the Heron – something that will abide for ever with somewhere about it our names in beautiful lettering saying we lived and worked here.

I am out of Italy as you see and in France. I shall stay here until the end of April if I can manage it. That italian villa got pretty dreadful and yet now the time there is over I wouldn't have it otherwise. I found out more about 'writing'. "Here" is a room with the window opening on to a balcony & below the balcony there is a small tree full of tangerines and beyond the tree a palm and beyond the palm a long garden with a great tangled – it looks like – a wood at the bottom of it. *Palms* Arthur are superb things.[3] Their colour is amazing. Sometimes they are bronze – sometimes gold and green – warm deep tiger-gold – & last night, under the moon in a little window they were bright silver. And plus that the creatures are full of drawing. How marvellous life is – if only one gives oneself up to it! It seems to me that the *secret* of life is to *accept* life. Question it as much as you like after but first accept it. People today stand on the outskirts of the city wondering if they are for or against Life – is Life worth living – dare they risk it – what is Life – do they hate or love it – but these cursed questions keep them on the outskirts of the city for ever. Its only by risking losing yourself – giving yourself up to Life – that you can ever find out the answer. Dont think Im sentimental. You know and I know how much evil there is but all the same LETS LIVE to the very uttermost – lets live all our lives. People today are simply cursed by what I call the *personal* . . . What is happening to ME. Look at ME. This is what has been done to ME. Its just as though you tried to run and all the while an enormous black serpent fastened on to you. You are the only young artist I know. I long for you to be rich, really rich. Am I a dull little dog? Forgive me, my dear old boy. I am working awfully hard & that always makes me realise again what a terrific thing it is – our job.

Three tons of the best, bright burning love

Katherine.

MS R. Murry. *LKM* II. 10–12.

---

[1] Richard Murry had set, printed, and bound the Heron Press edition of her story, which was officially published from Portland Villas on 15 Feb. 1920.

[2] She might easily enough visualize a Dürer-like depiction of Act III of *Cinnamon and Angelica*,

set in 'A remote hollow of the hill Apricia', with the characters grouped outside the mouth of a cave, while 'on the north side . . . the hill slopes steeply away'.

³ As she would note on 3 Feb., 'The beauty of palm trees. To fall in love with a tree.' (*Journal* 1954, 197.)

To J. M. Murry, [26 January 1920]

[L'Hermitage, Menton]
Monday.

Darling Heart
Letters are beginning to roll up from Italy. I am now up to Date to the 18th only there is not a *word* about The Lacket. Did you see it? Or did you just give it up? The cheques have arrived: they are *more* than grateful. As you can perhaps imagine I am terribly hard up & need every single sou. I meant to send Tchekov on Friday night but in the afternoon I was *stricken* with – a nervous headache – absolutely dished with it all that Friday. Saturday couldn't *move*. Sunday the same. I think it was the reaction after the strain. Also I havent slept since I left that cursed place. The brilliant doctors here prescribed me a forte dose of veronal (qui est si bon!) I refused to take it. They are mad. But today I can lift my head & walk. Feel a bit faible but that is all. I feel certain that the earliest of my reviews must have reached you for this week – the others will roll along & Ill send this week Tchekov. But that finishes my books. Don't novels ever turn up? Susie?¹ Or Mary Hamilton? Or anybody? I cant *make* them up. When you said we must have novels in the paper – was that really quite reasonable? Who in Godalmightys name doesn't agree? Could I stop the strike?

Oh you do make me want to *stamp* so hard sometimes. Wing ought to beat you with his tail. The weather here is simply gorgeous today – the room flooded with sun. L.M. is going to try & get a job here – to help with the keep. You see she costs at least 20 FRANCS a day – & then they order me wine & frictions & gouter which I *must* have. Oh – that reminds me – the Lit. Sup. has come. What a very nice advertisement.² But look here have you time to send a book of mine to *Grant Richards*.³ DO darling! Can you find time? Look here – you old boy I must have it sent. A book of short stories. Ill send a list of 'em & if you approve do for Gods sake let him have it at once. I don't know what terms he will make but let me see a copy of your letter to him. I'd sell outright for £20 of course but I want money *now*. Later on I can make it. But can you do this?

I've just written four pages and torn them up. A wave of bitterness came over me. I *must* never let it be known.

C. and J. are coming today with their precious dog. I regret to say I burn to let them know you are an Old Boiled Egg,[4] and have already told Pa same – and intend writing Chaddie and sending V. a card. What a woman – aren't I? I must stop writing. For some horrible reason a Casetta mood is on me. It will pass in two T's. Tell me if you see that story, will you?

Always your own
Wig

For Grant Richards.

> Je ne Parle pas Français
> Bliss
> Psychology
> A Man of No Temperament
> Sun and Moon
> 'Pictures'
> Mr. Reginald Peacock's Day
> The Black Cap

I can't remember the others. There were 10 at any rate, and now my new story will be 11. I'd like them called *Short Stories*. Will you discuss this with me?

MS ATL. *LJMM*, 462–3.

[1] *Susie, Yesterday, Today, and Forever*, by the Hon. Mrs Dowdall, which KM did not receive.

[2] A small advertisement at the foot of p. 49 in the *Times Literary Supplement*, 23 Jan. 1920, announcing *Je ne parle pas français* as 'the Second Book of the Heron Press'.

[3] The intention to publish a new collection of stories with Grant Richards was soon complicated by an approach from Michael Sadleir for Constable.

[4] Murry's own description on 17 Jan. 1920 when he told her of his receiving the OBE.

To Alice Jones,[1] [late January 1920]

L'Hermitage | Menton.

Dear Mrs Jones

Would you kindly send me a copy of the paper that had my review of *Agate*[2] in it – Mr Murry will know the one I mean. I have never received it. It is you who send me the papers – isn't it? If you knew how I look forward to them!

I hope your little boy is well again. I was so sorry to hear he had been ill. It ought to be spring weather all the year round for little people under ten – and never any winter.

Yours sincerely,
Katherine Middleton Murry.

MS Texas. Unpublished.

¹ Alice Jones was Murry's secretary at the *Athenaeum* office.
² KM's review of James E. Agate's *Responsibility*, the *Athenaeum*, 16 Jan. 1920.

To Sylvia Lynd,¹ 31 January 1920

Hermitage | Menton
31.1.1920.

My dear woman

I can't tell you how pleased I was to get your letter – how sorry to know that you've been so ill. You're better now? Its a cursed thing to have – I had an attack once ten years ago above a grocers shop in Rottingdean – no more than ten years ago or less – the year our great Edward the Peace Maker died.² He died when I was in the very thick of it. But its an absolute mistake that you should be ill – you're not at all the person to be ill. I always see you in my minds eye – sitting up and laughing – but sitting *up* in a way that few people have any idea of – delightfully.

Look here – Im coming back to England in May for a few months at least. Let us meet. Let us arrange it now. Will you come & spend the whole day? That is not half long enough but my plans are so vague. I don't know where we shall be living. John seems to be either camping in a wastepaper basket at Adelphi Terrace³ or walking the country looking for a real country house, far from station church & post office. But I don't want to miss you – so spare a day for me. Ill look for [the] review of Night & Day. I did it badly – very badly. The trouble with the book is its over-ripe. Its hung in the warm library too long; its gone soft. But thats the trouble with that whole set of people & with all their ideas, I think. One gets rather *savage* living in a little isolated villa on a wild hillside & thinking about these things. All this self examination – this fastidious probing – this hovering on the brink – its all wrong. I don't believe a writer can ever do anything *worth* doing until he has – in the profoundest sense of the word – ACCEPTED Life. Then he can face the problem & begin to question, but not before. But these people wont accept Life, they'll only accept a point of view or something like that. I wish one could let them go, but they go on writing novels and Life goes on being expensive – so poor little KM goes on lifting up her voice & weeping, but she doesn't want to!

Ive left Italy (Italy is a thoroughly bad place at present) and as you see Im in France. Its lovely weather – warm – mild – the air smells of faint far off tangerines with just a touch of nutmeg. On my table there are cornflowers & jonquils with rosemary sprigs. Here they are for you. The flowers are wonderful. How lovely the earth is. Do you know I had fifteen cinerarias in Italy & they grew against the sea? I hope one will be able to call these things up on one's deathbed.

This is not a letter. Its only to say I have yours which arrived TODAY. Its only to greet you – and to send my love & to beg you to get better quickly. All those things.

Good Night

K.M.

MS ATL. *LKM* II. 9–10.

[1] Sylvia Lynd (1888–1952), formerly Sylvia Dryhurst, was married to the Irish essayist Robert W. Lynd. Her novel *The Chorus* was published in 1916, and *Goldfinches*, a collection of poetry, including verses which Murry accepted for the *Athenaeum*, in 1920. KM did not see her after a visit to Portland Villas in Sept. 1919.

[2] King Edward VII died in early May 1910, while KM was staying at Rottingdean with Ida Baker, recuperating after an operation.

[3] The offices of the *Athanaeum* at 1 Adelphi Terrace.

To Charlotte Beauchamp Perkins, 31 January 1920

Hermitage | Menton
31.1.1920

My precious Marie,

At last I have time to sit down for a chat. I don't know whether you have received my last letters from Italy or not. Before I arrived here I had received NO news of any kind for a fortnight, neither was it possible to send a letter or a telegram! There was a complete postal strike with the office guarded by the military and a complete railway strike – which meant no supplies arriving of any kind. Plus that, my child we were attacked by bad men in the middle of the night – plus that your little sisters heart nearly gave out. Well, everything happened. Just before the strike began I wrote to Jinnie & explained my position. My dear, words cant describe what that woman has done for me. She found me rooms, arranged everything here – all *on the spot*, don't you know – got rooms for Ida – and sent a car from Menton to fetch me. Getting here was like the war all over again. The day the car came through an order was published forbidding all motor traffic between Italy and France. Our man managed to get there & then we made a run for it – among the mountain roads at the back of the towns to avoid the police. It was pretty horrid & cost £6 and 25 francs for the driver! Just as a last straw my nice thick overcoat was stolen from the

Casetta the day I left! Stolen out of the hall by a beggar while I was getting him some bread. Viva Italia. However we got here at last & Con & Jinnie were here. They had filled my rooms with flowers, bought cigarettes – an ash tray, all those small things which mean so much – and there was Jinnie. She opened her arms and said 'Well darling you're safe, thank God!' My child, I never was so near turning R.C. on the spot! 'Here' is a very large exquisitely clean and most sumptuous *maison de cure climatique*. Its not a nursing home. One is absolutely free and ones own mistress but at the same time there is a very nice Swiss masseuse on the premises, the food is particularly good & nourishing – one has heaps of butter & milk & so on and the bed-rooms are most comfortable with large windows, chaises longues, good beds, and central heating. Theres a gorgeous garden and view. A doctor lives on the premises & keeps an eye on one if one wants an eye kept – don't you know? But at the same time no *serious* cases are taken – people are just here to rest and so on. Its really ideal. I sometimes feel I died in Italy & have gone to Heaven! Its fearfully expensive but drat the expense as Mummy would say. I can do twice the work in this comfort & Oh Marie Im getting *better* – coming back to Life! Connie & Jinnie come in nearly every day with their baby Peke which is to be mine if we can get it back to England. They are going to try through some friends who have a car. Heaven knows why they should be so sweet and dear & friendly. I simply bask in their family affection. "Well, Con, how do you think the child is looking?" "Very sweet *my dear*". Cant you hear them? Ida is very happy. She comes every day – does my little odd jobs & so on. I am to walk next week & the baby Peke whose name is Chin-chin is to give me a lunch party. Well, thats enough about this child.

And you are? Marie – love – how are your feet? Are they massaged away? Do sparks come out of your toes? Do tell me just how you are. Jeanne, my child, where is your John Brown?[1] How is he. Will you lui serre la main from me? Kay says hes very doubtful about you both & wouldn't break a bottle of fizz on it either way. Did you see my book advertised in the Times? I can't ask you to buy it because it costs 10/6 but there it is out and on the market. Grant Richards is coming here next week & we are going to fix up a new one then. We are still looking for a house. The Lacket was too small. What a bother it is. Jack writes of nothing *but* houses. But in May I am coming to stay with you amnt I? I shall bring you both a mug with *Souvenir de Menton* on it, of course. Oh, you darlings – how I shall love to pop eyes on you again. Pa wrote to me from Freemantle. He sounded very chirpy and full of BEES. Dearest the gong has sounded. I must go to dinner. Heaven bless us all. Do write soon to your devoted

Katie

This is a crimson rambler of a letter. Its written on an empty stomach & I feel slightly drunk – do you know?

MS Newberry. Unpublished.

[1] A joking reference to Captain Charles Renshaw, Persian Rifles, who was engaged to KM's 18-year-old sister Jeanne.

To J. M. Murry, 31 January 1920

[L'Hermitage, Menton]
Saturday: January 31st 1920.
PLEASE READ THIS ALL THROUGH.
My dear Bogey

I wrote to you on Thursday last when I had heard from you of the arrival of my letters from here, but I did not post the letter. I held it over, hoping, with each courier, that the need to send it would be over. But now (Saturday) I can wait no longer.

I have received your letters about the house hunting & your Italian letters are coming in, in any order. I fully appreciate the fact that you are working extremely hard & that all your 'superfluous' energy is directed towards finding a house. At the same time, my dear Bogey, you have hurt me *dreadfully*. If you reflect for one moment you will perhaps realise how your 'hows money?' struck me.[1] Did I not tell you the expenses I had coming here – the bills to settle, the hire of the motor, the theft of my overcoat, the more expensive room, the 'extras' such as 'gouters' & frictions and Lesley to board & keep? Yes I have told you all these things. Now let me tell you what I 'imagined' you would do on receipt of my first letter from Menton. I imagined you would immediately wire me £10.[2] I 'imagined' you would have written 'its so gorgeous to know you are there & getting better. Dont worry. Of course I shall contribute £10 a month towards your expenses.' In addition I *counted* upon your loving sympathy and understanding, and the fact that you failed me in this is hardest of all to bear. I don't think you read my letters. I *cannot* think you simply dismissed them like that. This week I have been simply waiting for the letter that has not come & that wont come now. Its made it impossible to work. Now I must just readjust things & go on and I shall try and send you more for your paper. I have changed my room here for a smaller one but on Wednesday last, for instance, my lungs were radiographed. It cost me *200* francs & the cocher charged me 15 francs pour aller et retour. This morning the doctor lectured me about working (I put it down to 'mon travail') and ordered me an hours drive by the sea every day pour calmer les nerves. I cant afford it.

Therefore I ask you to contribute £10 a month towards my expenses here. If you cannot do so please *wire me at once* for I must make immediate other arrangements. *I cannot wait a day longer.*

It is so bitter to have to ask you this – terribly bitter. Nevertheless I am determined to get well. I will *not* be overcome by anything – not even by the letter you sent me in Italy telling me to remember AS I grew more lonely so you were loving me more.[3] If you had read that in a book what would you have thought? Well, I thank God I read it here and not at the Casetta.

I've nothing to say to you Bogey: I am too hurt. I shall not write again.

Your
Wife.

You will not put me off with just a sentence or two? Consider, Bogey, what you do!

MS ATL. *LJMM*, 463–4.

[1] Murry's letter on 26 Jan. had ended, 'How's money – let me know, please.' (Murry, 258.)
[2] Murry's response on 3 Feb. went to some pains to explain his financial position, his income tax, and why he hadn't sent money earlier. He also observed, 'But God above haven't we known each other long enough for you to *wire* "send £20".' (Murry, 263.)
[3] KM rather distorts what Murry wrote to her on 13 Jan.: 'I only love you; and when you're finding things terribly hard just think that I'm loving you more then, more intensely and warmly, more nearly, than at any other time.' (Murry, 249.)

To J. M. Murry, [2 February 1920]

[L'Hermitage, Menton]
Monday Morning.

My dear Bogey

I have just received your Thursday & Friday evening letters. Thank you from my heart for doing that for Gertie. It was a beautiful little act on your part and I am so proud that you should have done it.[1]

About the Grant Richards book (did I tell you he is coming South this month?) I think the Black Cap had better not be included.[2] But I will send you another story 'A Second Helping'[3] it is called, to go in its place. I shall try and get it typed here. My copy of *Je ne parle pas* or your copy – isn't it? – arrived yesterday. It *looks* lovely but I am not at all satisfied with the story.

About the house. Dear Bogey, why do you TORMENT yourself as you say?[4] Or is that only your way of saying it? I am sure it is the wrong attitude and it will only tire and exhaust you so that you will be "sick of the whole subject" very soon.

Its no good my writing every day. I cant. I simply feel you dont read the letters. I try and do my own work instead. Theres a much better chance that you'll read that one day – though why you should I dont know.

Yes, this is a very suitable place to be in – it is safe and very healthy.

Goodbye dearest

Wig.

Is there really a tearing hurry about the house? I fully appreciate the fact that you do not want to stay at Portland Villas. At the same time it would not matter if we were there until the middle of the summer. And when I come home L.M. can help with the house hunting. I mean she could always go for a preliminary inspection in the middle of the week & so save you useless journeys. This is well worth considering. She knows just what we want.

By the way – about that story Rutter has. I am awfully sorry to bother you – but I must see the proofs myself before it is printed.[5] If its typed 10 to 1 there will be mistakes and at any rate I cant expect anyone to go through it as I must go through. Every word matters. This is *not* conceit – but it must be so. Will you promise to send the proofs to me if he prints the story? Ill send them back express the same day. If you did not live at such racing speed I would beg you to go through the typed copy with the MSS and see that the *spaces* were correct – that where I intend a space there is a space. Its sure to be wrong. But I cant afford mistakes. Another word wont do. I chose every single word.

Will you please answer this when you write.

MS ATL. *LJMM*, 465–6.

---

[1] The housekeeper at Portland Villas had been told she should have an eye operation, but doubted her doctor's opinion. Murry sent her to Sorapure, KM's doctor in Hampstead, and assured her he would pay the fee.

[2] 'The Black Cap', published in the *New Age*, 17 May 1917, was omitted by KM from both the collections she put together, but was included by Murry in *Something Childish But Very Natural*, 1924.

[3] This story, which according to the *Journal* 1954, 198, she was still working out on 6 Feb., survives only as a manuscript fragment.

[4] Murry's recent letters had described the trials of walking about the country at the weekends in search of a suitable house.

[5] 'The Man Without a Temperament.'

To J. M. Murry, [4 February 1920]

[L'Hermitage, Menton]
This is written before your II card & telegram. I have opened this &
replied on pages III and IV.
Wednesday
Dear Bogey
A slip was enclosed in a letter card but I have received no letter which
explains itself. However I will just tell you the situation between
myself & G.R. [Grant Richards]
I wrote him asking if he would consider an MSS.
He replied delighted.
I replied saying I would send him one.
He replied the sooner the better.

Money has not been mentioned, but I think he ought most certainly
to have the first look. If he wants it I must ask for an advance & if he
refuses the advance – the affair is off. Please send me the note you refer
to – will you? As regards the advance money I would rather wait &
receive it for my book than that you should lend it to me. I MUST have
it for my overcoat, fare home, etc, & I certainly do not want to borrow
it from you. Perhaps I did not make clear that I ASKED you for the £10
a month. I mean NOT as a loan. I am afraid from this note you may
advance it for me & then take the book money. But I am afraid that
will not do.

Will you please tell me *why* money is tight?[1] I cannot understand. If
it is necessary to say [these] things why do you buy a mirror? I feel as
I felt when you referred before to your heavy debts that you are
keeping something from me all the time. You have expenses, you *must*
have that I dont know of. Oh, if only you would be frank about this: it
would make things so different. Can't you confide in me? Are you
helping somebody? I know you are saving up for the house but you . . .
dont put the house FIRST do you Bogey? Yet you find it necessary to
again write *money is tight*. I don't want – God forbid – to know your
private affairs but if you can tell me a little it would be a great relief.

Wig.

Bogey dear
Your telegram came this afternoon & your second card enclosing
the cheque but STILL not enclosing the letter came this evening.
First about the £20. You will doubtless adhere to your intention in the
letter card that it shall be an advance on my book – but you will see
why I do not want that. If you can agree to allowing me £10 a month
for my expenses while I am here I shall look upon this cheque as the
first 2 months instalment. I could perfectly understand your *money is
tight* had I NOT consumption, a weak heart, & chronic neuritis in my

lower limbs. About the overcoat you will doubtless explain how you want it paid for. For I cant write about these things. Neither will I touch the cheque till I hear from you.

My darling, I cant write every day. I love you but something has gone dead in me – rather – no I cant explain it. Explanations are so futile – you NEVER listen to them – you know. I shrink from trying any more. Give me *time* – will you? Ill get over this. I get over everything but it takes time. But darling darling that doesn't make me love you less. I LOVE you – thats the whole infernal trouble!

Bogey I cannot have the German Pension republished under any circumstances.[2] It is far too *immature* & I don't even acknowledge it today. I mean I don't 'hold' by it. I cant go foisting that kind of stuff on the public – *its not good enough*. But if youll send me the note that refers to it I will reply & offer a new book by May 1st. But I would not for a moment entertain republishing the pension. Its positively *juvenile* and besides that its not what I mean: its a lie. Oh no, never. But please give me the chance of replying to whoever wants to do so & offering another book.

                                                                                 Wig.

MS ATL. *LKM* II. 14; *LJMM*, 466–7.

[1] Murry replied with a detailed financial statement on 9 Feb., taking up and answering several of the points KM raises in this letter. See Murry, 271–4.

[2] The editor Michael Sadleir wrote to Murry on 30 Jan. 1920 that the publishing firm Constable would like to publish a volume of KM's stories, and that 'We should like at the same time to consider bringing out another edition of "In a German Pension" if that were possible.' (Murry, 261.)

On the same day KM wrote in her notebook: 'Horrible day. I lay all day & *half* slept in this new way – hearing voices – drifting off . . .

. . . Wrote to Jack about the *G. Pension*. No good.' (*Journal* 1954, 198.)

To J. M. Murry, [5 February 1920]

                                                          [L'Hermitage, Menton]

Forgive me for saying this.

Will you remember when you write that I dont go out or walk or see anybody to *talk* to, that you are my ALL. I lie in a chair all day. I am not strong enough yet to walk at all – & so when you say things like – that about insuring your life & breaking your neck you have me at your complete mercy. Can you understand? Try to imagine it!! It is terrific torture – terrific. Dont you care about me at all? If I must bear it I *must* but Im nearly at the end of my tether when you say such things.

Thursday. In bed.

Bogey darling

I have just received your Monday letter written on the back of the Constable note and hasten to reply. In the first place *your throat*. How is it? I cannot know. I must just wait then. And that remark flung at me about insuring your life. I beg of you not to say these things.[1] They are just like the most terrible frightful earthquake – much worse. My day breaks up into terrified pieces. You *know* that you know it *quite well*. Oh how CAN you. I dont understand. But one must be very careful and say nothing one would regret. I have no right to reproach you and I dont want to appeal to your pity – but my Bogey you make it very hard when you say such things thats all. (Everything I thought at the Casetta[2] got 'a long way from reality'.)

Now about Constable. If they will give £40 in advance & Richards wont it must be Constable of course.[3] I have explained my relations with Richards. A book including Prelude, Je ne Parle pas, and so on would be interesting. But I must make very sure of what they collect from Rhythm.[4] The story 'The Wind Blows'[5] from the Signature is in the collection. Its the only one worth reprinting. The book had certainly better include Prelude: it makes a longer book. I am afraid this is adding to your great press of work. Sadler says even if an arrangement is come to nothing can be published for several months. In that case the final decision as to *which* stories could perhaps be left for my return in the first week of May.

But this is all rubbish beside your sore throat and your remark about breaking your neck house-hunting. I must wire you and somehow *stamp down* my anxiety until I have your reply.

Yours
Wig.

MS ATL. *LJMM*, 467–8.

[1] Murry's letter on 2 Feb. followed up his mentioning a sore throat with 'I've also insured my life for £1000 in case I break my neck house-hunting.' (Murry, 263.)

[2] In the same letter Murry said he had just received her own letter of 13 Jan., written from the Casetta Deerholm, Ospedaletti.

[3] Murry explained on 1 Feb. that unless KM had pledged her new collection to Grant Richards, he would proceed with Constable. The next day he wrote of telling Sadleir 'that the whole question was one of the advance on royalties, and suggested £40. He seemed quite prepared to do that. . . . Accordingly, I have written to Richards telling him that everything depends upon how much advance he will give, & telling him frankly some-one else is after it. He may go more than £40, but I doubt it. He's rather a sharper on terms.' (Murry, 261, 262.)

[4] In fact none of her stories from *Rhythm* were included in her collection *Bliss*, which Constable would publish in 1921.

[5] 'The Wind Blows' appeared as 'Autumns: II', under the name of Matilda Berry, in the 4 Oct. 1915 issue of the short-lived magazine *The Signature*, edited by Murry and D. H. Lawrence.

To J. M. Murry, [6 February 1920]

[Menton]

HOW IS YOUR CHILL ANXIOUS TAKE GREATEST CARE REPLY TIG

Telegram ATL. Murry, 268.

To J. M. Murry, [7 February 1920]

[L'Hermitage, Menton]

In reply to your Tuesday letter.

My dear Bogey

I have your Tuesday evening letter. That you took my letter as being primarily concerned with money is horrible. However Ill answer that first. I send you back the cheque for £20. As you have paid £20 into my bank I shall use that at the rate of £10 a month and by the time it is finished that is at the end of March I hope that my book will be paid for and I shant have to ask you for any more money. You ask me if we havent known each other long enough for me to wire for £20. But Bogey haven't we known each other long enough for you to have said to me: *I realise* you must need money. But Im cleaned out this month. Ill send some next? If only you'd thought for me – or imagined for me: it was *that* that hurt.

You say I ought to have guessed you misunderstood. Curse money! Its not really a question of money. It was the question of sympathy, of understanding, of being in the least *interested* of asking JUST ONCE how I was – what I thought about & felt – what I did – if I was 'alright'? I cant get over the fact that it never occurred to you and it makes me feel you don't want my Love – not my living love – you only want an 'idea'. When that strike was on – fool that I was – my first thoughts always were 'what *I* feel doesn't matter so much. Jack must be in such agony. When he doesn't hear he'll try & wire and the P.O. will tell him no wires are delivered & he knows Im ill . . .' But your letter came 'drunk with the magnificence of the downs', a day's 'sheer joy', the 'note of hysteria would go out of my work', 'very fit'.[1] And when you *did* hear – good – your anxiety was over & you never referred to me again. So I *must* face the fact that you have put *me* away for the time. You are withdrawn – self-contained and you don't want in the deepest widest sense of the word to be disturbed. As long as Im on a suitable shelf – and ∴ YOU'RE not worried – ça va! Of course I still love you. I love you as much as ever. But to know this is torture until I get it in hand.

'A love that might break through *if she would let it*, the ghastly terror of her loneliness.'[2] Does not that show it up? Who could write such unspeakably cruel words if he loved? (at the moment). You suggest that my suffering was self-imposed, in so far as it was really a failure to love enough. If I had loved you enough I need not have suffered as I did. Bogey, you must believe me that is a *deadly* false view. A living, loving warm being could not believe that or say it. Its a vile intellectual idea – and it simply appals me. I can't wire the word Love because of it. (Of course I can of course I will. You do *love* me: its only you dont love me just now.) To make out my agony was my failure to love – oh that is really too much. ⟨You have stabbed me to the heart with these words.⟩

I want to mention something else. Lawrence sent me a letter today: he spat in my face & threw filth at me and said 'I loathe you. You revolt me stewing in your consumption. The Italians were quite right to have nothing to do with you' and a great deal more.[3] Now I do beseech you if you are my man to stop defending him after that & never to crack him up in the paper. *Be proud.* In the same letter he said his final opinion of you was that you were a 'dirty little worm'. Well, *be proud.* Dont forgive him for that, please.

Goodbye. I am bitterly disappointed with the answer to my letter but I *must* bear it. You say you are not ashamed: I dont want you to be ashamed. And then you say you sent the £20 the moment you had it. February 1 came too late. *Damn* the £20. I suppose from that you look upon yourself as a man who is being bled – *you* did all in your power but FATE and your wife would not wait. Its UTTERLY false. I wanted love & sympathy and understanding – were you cleaned out of those until February 1st? It is nightmare that you wont understand.

Your own
Wig.

[*Across top of letter*]
Of course you love me of course you do. Its only since Ive been away you have withdrawn yourself from me & ever since I broke down at the Casetta and appealed to you things have never been the same. Its only that you don't love me NOW. Oh, darling – do do break through. DO care. Its so hard – wait till Im strong before you run away for a bit. Its so awful. Bogey you must love me. Fancy writing so coolly to me & asking me to wire if I think you do. Would I be *here* if I thought you didn't – somewhere – deep down love me?

MS ATL. *LJMM*, 469–70.

[1] KM is taking up phrases from a letter Murry sent on 26 Jan. after a day looking for a house in the Sussex countryside.

² A subtly distorted version of Murry's letter to her on 3 Feb., as he tried to explain his reaction to her own letter of 31 Jan.: 'There are things in your letter that I just don't understand. One is what you say about the letter I sent you in Italy telling you "to remember as you grew more lonely so I was loving you more". I realize that is awkwardly put. But *if* I read it in a novel, I should know what the man meant, I'm sure. I would know that what he meant was that when his lover felt lonely, then she must think of him loving her more deeply than ever – loving her with a love that tried to break through, that might break through *if the world let it*, the ghastly teror of her loneliness. I feel that you must suspect me somehow, otherwise you could not have so failed to feel the intention behind the clumsy words. I'm not ashamed of them, even now.' (Murry, 264.)

³ Lawrence's letter does not survive. His friendship with KM had been marked by great warmth as well as by malice and anger. But his feelings towards her were complicated by those towards Murry, which ranged from the erotic during their time in Cornwall in 1916, to the contemptuous now that his writings on several occasions were rejected by the *Athenaeum*. It was this assumed editorial condescension that fuelled his present rage against KM, although Lawrence had been dismissive enough of *her* gifts, and any admiration they attracted.

To J. M. Murry, [7 February 1920]

[Menton]

OF COURSE YOU LOVE ME TIG

Telegram ATL. Murry, 271.

To J. M. Murry, [8 February 1920]

L'HERMITAGE | MAISON DE RÉGIMES DU Dᴿ P. GALLOT |
RUE PAUL-MORILLOT | MENTON (A.M.)

Dear Darling

I received a letter from you yesterday *saying* (1) you had bought me an overcoat. I wish you hadn't. It is obvious that you *raced* to buy it & that you bought it with your little brains & nerves . . . You are the man in the Daudet story you know the man with the golden brain.¹ But there. When it comes Ill see. Ill cherish it.

(2) You have paid £10 into my Bank. Now I am going to ask you if you can put another £10 in March. After that I shall need no more of your money.

(3) You've sold my book.² With the £40 I shall spend £10 for living expenses in the mois d'Avril & the £30 for fares and travelling home. Do you mind asking them to send the cheque to me. Pure childisness – but I want to see it with my own eyes & send it with my own hand to Kay – I feel the Bank will *close*. It is fearfully good of you to have done this for me & I feel it has been *no* end of a nuisance. Re the matter of the book – I suppose I have final say? I couldn't have The Woman at the Store reprinted par exemple.³ If its left to Sadler or if Sadler has a

say it would be bad. Anne's drawings don't matter.⁴ I do want the story called Second Helping that Im at now to be included. Enough. Richards is coming here you know to see me. That will be orkid.

Another change in the near future. I have not mentioned it, but this place is *intolerably* noisy. I am so sensitive to noise – oh – so sensitive. It *hurts* me really. They bang my door other doors shout shriek crash – I cant endure it & really cant work *or* sleep. The doctor suggested une forte dose de Veronal for sleep. Merci. But really its *bad*. I just mentioned this to Jinnie. She came one day when I was feeling it a bit badly. Today she arrived with a carriage & fur rugs & silk cushions. Took me to their Villa⁵ – it is really superb – *exquisite* outside & in. They had a chaise longue in the garden – a tiny tray with black coffee out of a silver pot – grand marnier – cigarettes – little bunch of violets – all ready. Then we went in to tea. Their villa is really – Boge – its a dream. I mean even the furnishing is *perfect*. Spanish silk bed coverlets. Italian china – the tea appointments perfect – stillness – maids in tiny muslin aprons flitting over *carpets* – and so on. Then they showed me into a room grey & silver facing South with a balcony – the only touch of colour a little rose brocade couch with gilt legs & Jinnie said "Now my dear we want you to come here – & live here. Its *dead* quiet – you can be alone all day if you like. There is the garden. We are here. First I must arrange that you see Doctor Rendall for him to sign that you are no longer infectious. If he does this – we want you here until May. Youre going to get well. Can't afford to fight or see ugly people or have ugly trays." And then she laughed & said "the Lord has delivered you into our hands & please God we'll cure you."

What do you think of that? They want me to stay there till May & then travel home together. Bogey this is really very important; its one of the most important things that ever happened to me. These women are *right*: they are what we mean to be in our life – they are wise & at rest & deeply happy – & they are very very exquisite. It all depends on Rendall.⁶ Subject to Rendalls signing I shall go but I don't know when. Not for a week at least: I will let you know. And I shall pay what I pay here – but of course no extras. I go *as* a patient – & Jinnie couldn't afford to leave the room empty. Also its right I should do that. But no money on earth could ever repay what I shall get there. You see Ill have that *Life* to share too, the meals & the room with great wood fires & the darling baby peke and the garden & the gardener – the orange trees the lemons – their maid to look after my clothes. You know what I mean? And my WORK always arranged for & thought of. A table in the garden & a bath chair with rug & cushions that I can lie in & write. WHY should they do that? WHY should Jinnie say: "then Ill be at rest about you, darling, I shall know youre safe". Its as though my *Mother* were here again. I miss her so. I often long to lean against Mother & know she understands things . . . that can't be told – that would fade at a breath – *delicate needs* – a feeling of great fineness & gentleness – but what Mother hadn't is an *understanding* of WORK.

The Villa is in style like Garsington – I mean that is the tone. It is very large – a huge hall lighted from above – a great double salon. It has delicate balconies – and a tower. I want you to see it. I cant make you see it. I want you to see the garden & the potting shed where I can walk & look at the little plants. Huge springing palms – great branches of orange against the sky – no I can't draw them. As soon as

Ive seen Rendall I shall know when I go. Have you read so far? Thats all, dearest. And that explains why I cant work here as I thought I could: the infernal noise – especially in the morning. You remember when I managed to ask you not to go on scraping your porridge saucer? It was so hard to say & I tried to say it nicely but I see now how you pushed the plate away & rumpled your hair & wouldn't eat or look at me – just *went blind*. It wasn't fair – you know, Bogey – really it wasnt. You knew how hard it was for me to say. Why did you take offence? You know I think & think of those things sometimes and I *cant* account for them! Its hereditary but I wish you didn't – *pay me out* for having to say: "I say old boy Im *so* sorry – but my nerves are so awful in the morning – DO you mind – I hate having to say it?" And oh, he shows her how he does mind! Do you "understand that in a novel"?[7] I suppose you do: I wish I did. No darling, at times you are very dark to me.

Your devoted Wife.

MS ATL. *LKM* II. 12–13; *LJMM*, 470–3.

[1] 'Le Legende de l'Homme à la Cervelle d'Or', in Alphonse Daudet's *Lettres de mon moulin* (1869), in which a man whose brain is made of gold gradually sells it off for a capricious wife.

[2] Murry wrote on 4 Feb. that Constable would publish KM's new collection on a 15% royalty, and pay £40 in advance on delivery of manuscript. (Murry, 265.)

[3] 'The Woman at the Store', which drew on KM's camping trip in the central North Island of New Zealand in 1908, and was written to Murry's editorial prescription for blood and colour, was published in *Rhythm*, Spring 1912.

[4] Michael Sadleir 'had asked whether you would like the book to appear with some little drawings by Anne Rice [Drey]' (Murry, 165.)

[5] The Villa Flora, to which KM would move the next week.

[6] Yet another doctor KM consulted in Menton, this time in order to obtain a letter assuring Jinnie Fullerton that her tuberculosis was not contagious.

[7] KM is scoring off Murry's phrase '*if* I read that in a novel', as he tried to defend himself against her charges of not caring for her sufficiently. See previous letter, n. 2.

To J. M. Murry, 9 February 1920

[L'Hermitage, Menton]
February 9th

Urgent.

My Bogey

I cannot stand it any longer. You must tell me the truth. Here is your Thursday letter: "Well Wig dont give me up entirely."[1] If you really contemplate the possibility of it then you no longer love me or believe in our marriage. You are simply killing me again and again with every letter. Your last, ASKING me to wire i̲f̲ I loved you! Now tell me at once, BY WIRE whether all is over or not. God! To have been driven by you to write such words. You cruel cruel – oh I am crying. Of course when I said I would not write again I only meant until I had your answer.

No you are *too* cruel. To throw away SUCH Love throw it away. Oh, how you must have lied to me! I thought we could not live without each other. But now put me out of my pain. I *cant* bear it. I am in utter despair. I must know.

Your Wife.

[*Across top of letter*]
This your Thursday letter makes mine about the Villa Flora just a silly dream. Again I *am* not. I just steel myself somehow not to weep before people – thats all.

MS ATL. *LJMM*, 473.

[1] The phrase that ended Murry's letter of 5 Feb. (Murry, 266–7.)

To J. M. Murry, [9 February 1920]

[Menton]

THURSDAY LETTER COME TELL WING WIRE IMMEDIATELY[1] YOUR COLDNESS KILLING ME TIG

Telegram ATL. Murry, 276.

¹ Murry replied to this telegraph the next day: 'Wire received all well he loves you desperately he can't do more. Wing.' And in a letter the next morning, he wrote: 'Wing has replied for me, because I don't know how to reply. How can I say in a telegram that I am not cold, that I love you passionately, that you are my all. How can I convince you, when I don't even know what it is in my letters that makes you think I am cold. I feel as though I were lost in a mist.' (Murry, 276–7.)

To J. M. Murry, [10 February 1920]

Anemones on my table.

[L'Hermitage, Menton]

Love

Note this coincidence. I wrote to Lawrence "I detest you for having dragged this disgusting reptile across all that has been."¹ When I got his letter I *saw* a reptile, *felt* a reptile – and the desire to hit him was so dreadful that I knew if ever I met him I must go away *at once*. I could not be in the same room or house. He is somehow filthy – I never had such a feeling about a human being. Oh, when I read your reply do you know I *kissed* it. I was lying on my face, dressed in nothing but a lace cap – Mlle Burger had gone off in the middle of doing my back – & I was alone for a minute. *As* I read it *as* I kissed it I had the queer, the *queer* feeling as though somehow one was caught in some wave of tradition that passes round & round the earth – as though hundreds & hundreds of years ago – a woman lying like I was – being massaged by someone had been handed a letter from her lover who swore to smite his enemy and she kissed it & laid it against her cheek. Thats NOT nonsense. But you must hit him when you see him – there's nothing else to do.²

My Life,

This letter of yours – its Friday evening's letter is almost like one of the old ones. I had a nuit blanche – fever – I couldn't help it. Yesterday nearly finished me and it was so strange. I was thinking at night as I smoked to stop crying I love you *more*. Even though you denied me and everything and refused to understand what I was getting at – even though that which *could* not happen, happened – you questioned OUR love – broke the chain that couldn't be broken, still I love you more. You know I never dreamed of doubting your love – must I dream of it? I simply felt you'd gone away, had enough for the

time being, and *that* was unendurable. The other – your idea – oh, you
dont love as I do – you cant have the capacity. God! At a breath of
such a possibility I am in anguish. But we are evidently very very
different. I havent 'illusions' really not though you think I have, but *I
love*. And loving I simply cannot face desolation – the desert *persists* in
blossoming – the flower *persists* in turning to the light. When you said
at the Casetta you not only believed differently but you did not want
to change – you remember – when we talked – or rather when I said
you seemed somehow to deny *fertility* – the living unborn child – when
you said that so deliberately I felt there was an essential difference.
And STILL I don't believe it. I STILL think it is not you. You see the
war – the tragedy of the war was that ever since I knew you you had
been trembling towards it. (This is a secret.) The war was no surprise
to you: it was a supreme justification of all you had trembled towards
(like a compass) all your life. Thats what nobody else can ever know.
It wasn't the war that broke a bright, radiant, ardent, loving, rich
spirit as all your friends and admirers think. You *never* wrote in
pictures or other than in that austere fashion, and you were talking to
Gordon[3] about weariness of the spirit, ultimate obscenity, vultures,
'our wounds' years & years before. But I always felt that behind all
that talk – "I am very tired" a quoi bonisme there hid – what I cant
help calling a bright burning angel – loving, turned to the light. Oh
my child! But like some daisy – innocent as others are not – *wise* as
others are not – dreaming, fulfilled, serene, a poet, the father of my
children. Oh, my pride to think that!

But the war came – your dark self pulled over, and finally at the
Casetta you said you did not even *want* the angel to triumph – and I
knew we would never have children – wed never be Adam and Eve
lying under a tree looking up through the branches with our own little
flowery branch lying between us. My own, you are always so terrified
that I want to intrude, to have you other than you are. You are always
thinking theres a need of escaping from MY idea of you. You are
wrong. I adore you as you are – your deepest self, but yes it is the
'angel' I adore and believe in for ever.

Wig.

[*Across top of letter*]
Ill send you a wire about the overcoat my darling the minute it walks
into this room. I am longing for it; my cape is no good for warmth.
Jinnie muffles me up in rugs when she takes me out but then I have to
be a mummy, just a head coming out and one does or I do like to wave

my arms and legs sometimes, unlike a boy I used to know.

MS ATL. *LJMM*, 473–5.

¹ KM's letter replying to Lawrence's does not survive.

² Murry also received a letter from Lawrence, in response to the *Athenaeum's* rejecting articles he had submitted, and calling Murry 'a dirty little worm.' (*The Letters of D. H. Lawrence*, Vol. III, ed. James T. Boulton and Andrew Robinson, 1984, pp. 467–8.) 'If ever I see him, no matter when or where, the first thing I shall do is hit him as hard as I can across the mouth. He seems to have become so degraded that I feel he is something of a reptile, and that he has slavered over me in his letter.' (Murry, 266.)

³ Murry had been close to Gordon Campbell, particularly in 1913–14. See *CLKM* I. 126 n. 1.

To J. M. Murry, [11 February 1920]

[L'Hermitage, Menton]
Wednesday. No. Yes.

My Precious,

Your Saturday evening letter has come with the 'explanation'.¹ Dont say another word about it. Lets after this put it quite away. Yes, I felt in Ospedaletti that you refused to understand and I have felt since I have been abroad this time that you have turned away from me – withdrawn yourself utterly from me. I have felt like a person in an open boat, tossing about on frightful waves calling and crying to be saved & you have seen me from your ship & refused to see me or rescue me because you were not made of whipcord or steel. Yes, Boge, it has been a suffering such as I don't feel you ever could know. But its over and its taught me a lesson and I don't regret it. I could turn to it now and kiss it. I can't enter into what it has taught me but the difference is there. It had to be. If Im *dead* sincere I must say that I believe in the mystery: *out of evil good shall come*.² But now – put it all away, my own. And you really must give up the word *desperate* with regard to our relations. Dont let it exist. Dont make an effort to love me – my silly darling – or to fly after enamel spoons.³ Just remember: *That From Now I Am not ill.* Because that is the truth. So lean on me, give me your things to hold, confide in me, worry me, treat me as your wife. Just *rest* on the thought of me. You are absurd when you say you are no good as a lover. That is just nonsense and its not fair to me. I dont want a slave and an admirer, my love. You would be a perfectly rotten slave & admirer. As a lover, you are – well simply you – just all my life and my joy and my *pride*. Call me your 'worm' – that is enough for me. But lets get over all this – what has been – has been. But remember *no desperate* efforts are allowed. Not being an intellectual I always seem to have to learn things at the risk of my life – but I do learn. Lets be wise, true *real lovers* from now on. Lets enter the Heron from today, from this very minute & I shall rejoice in you and if its not too great an effort – dear love – try and rejoice in me. Thats all.

I go to the Villa Flora on Sunday. All is arranged.

Heard from Mary Cannan this morning: she is at Capri & had heard from L. that I was a 'very sick woman' and you a 'great swell'. I thereupon wrote her an intimate letter & just put her right about US and just told her what you really were like & what your loyalty to L. had been and so on. I just felt I must do this. Heard from Grant Richards who is at Cap Martin – ½ an hour away – *very sniffy* but still wants to see me. He suggests bringing over a car & motoring me there. Well, Id better see him. No he doesn't suggest a car just that I shall go – so I don't know.

Its lunchtime. Im in bed I must fly up. My nib will not write. It must write that I love you & you only world without end amen. But you know it.

> *Yours*
> Wigchik

[*Across top of letter*]

Tell Wing to keep both eyes on you & when you disappear again he and Athy must just hunt you out and beat you – but not hard.

Are the snowdrops out?

The cuckoo has been heard at Hurstmonceux, Sussex.[4]

Chaddie has a wide 'border of yellow crocuses'. It sounds like an Alice Prosser[5] doesn't it?

C. & J. have given me the most exquisite fine woollen stuff for a dress & a dressmaker to go with it.

Your mother wrote me such a nice letter today & I replied.

(1) *Tell* Arthur about my change of Address after Saturday. Please *be sure to do this* and give the old boy a loving hug from me.

(2) Mark the linen.

(3) Whistle on the stairs.

(4) Walk out of the steps & down the front on your hands please just to show all's well.

(5) Ask Violet when she's going to be married & tell her its worth it. But do none of these things desperately.

MS ATL. *LJMM*, 475–7.

---

[1] Murry's letter of 7 Feb. confessed to 'a certain amount of real insensibility in me', and took responsibility for the recent spate of KM's recriminations. (Murry, 269–70.)

[2] A quite non-biblical sentiment, perhaps based on a memory of Rom. 3: 8: 'And not rather, (as we be slanderously reported, and as some affirm that we say,) Let us do evil, that good may come?'

[3] The same letter from Murry recalled 'our old quarrel of years ago about the enamel spoon', which Murry glossed in a note as a reference to a story by Anatole France.

[4] A fact presumably gleaned from her browsing of English papers.

[5] Murry's note, *LJMM*, 476, reads, 'I seem to remember that Charles and Alice Prosser were characters of Katherine's New Zealand days – a somewhat excessively refined clergyman and his wife who had come out from England.'

To J. M. Murry, [12 February 1920]

[L'Hermitage, Menton]
Thursday.

Monday evening letters (1) and (2) received.

(1) Very well, Isabel[1] about the Pension.[2] But I must write an introduction saying it is early early work – or just that it was written between certain years, because you know, Betsy[3] love, its nothing to be proud of. If you didn't advise me Id drop it overboard. But of course Ill do the other thing, & certainly it airs ones name. But why isn't it better! It makes me simply hang my head. Ill have to forge ahead & get another decent one written thats all.

(2) Ill repay you for the overcoat when Constables pay me. Thank you enormously for the figgers. They frighten me. You never mentioned your new suit. I don't know what colour it is or shape or anything – or whether there is any fringe on the trousers. I always rejoice when you buy clothes. When I am rich you will have such lovely clothes all real lace and silk velvet. You will have crimson satin sleeves slashed with indian green silk and embroidered gloves with sachets sewn in them – just wait.

(3) I had your wire last night about my story. Oh dear I hope you do find a moment just to say a little more against OR for. I burned for you to like it.

(4) You are a perfect darling to have bothered to say all this about the money. No, theres not much to play with indeed. We're both rather short of pocket money. If God would only give us a sheer 1d a week dropped from Heaven every Saturday morning just for us to go off & *spend*.

Ive told the people here Im leaving. It was *awful*. How I hate having to do this especially as they have been so immoderately kind. They make such a dreadful fuss of me – everybody – down to the servants. Even the masseuse says: it was so wonderful just to come into the room & then we all say we know Mrs Murrys room by the good smell outside the door – cigarettes & flowers. As to Armand – oh, its been *dreadful*. These people are so queer. Just because the room is arranged as we arrange a room and gay & I wear my little coats & caps in bed it seems to them *amazing*. Its not in the least.

Jinnie drives me round to the Villa Flora on Sunday. It will be a very famous day. Darling theres an american woman living with them – shes a bit of a millionairess & I *cant* stop her presents. If only I could post them on. I don't *want* them. Four boxes of marquise chocolate at one time – bouquets of violets & lilacs – cigarettes by the hundred. I think its the first time I have come across unlimited money. She is terribly unhappy & I know she feels I can help her. I can. Shes tremendous food for me – I mean literary. But I wish I could send you the gifts. Ill try & post the marquise chocolat today at any rate some of it. I don't care for such things.

Its such a delicate day – little birds are flying through it. I – love – you. I am very very well. Tell me about that house – have you any idears? I must jump up. The overcoat isn't here yet. But Ill send what I think the Constable book ought to contain & will you discuss it with me?

Yours for ever
Wig.

MS ATL. *LKM* II. 14; *LJMM*, 477–8.

[1] An affectionate term also used with Ida Baker, taken from a popular song which Murry had used when writing to her on 12 Mar. 1918.

> Come along Isabella
> Under my umbrella
> Don't be afraid
> There's a good maid
> Come along Isabella.   (ATL.)

[2] Murry insisted in his letter of 9 Feb. that *In a German Pension* was 'a splendid piece of work for 1911–1912', and that she must allow a new edition. To his other arguments he added, 'Finally you don't seem to understand the *kudos* that an entirely new edition of a book published nine years ago gives you. Why, I don't believe there's a single author under 35 who has had such a thing.' (Murry, 276.) For all that, the new edition did not appear.

[3] Another nickname she used with Murry.

To J. M. Murry, [13 February 1920]

[L'Hermitage, Menton]

Pray read this from the fayr Alice: its *comic* somehow! I bet I ask her to spend the day with us at the Country & bring little Hugh.[1] I FEEL myself asking her.

Friday.

My own

Your 2 Tuesday letters are here but they ARE too late – aren't they.

I mean – happily too late — [*an arrow leads from the drawing to a note at the top of the page*: Please show it to Wingchik.] We do understand everything & all is over – but really beautifully over – isn't it? Im out of the open boat & you have stopped sailing away and away —— ·

Precious love – you know the Italian china? The 2nd kind we liked even better than the first? Its shop is here – *packed*. Plates, cups, letter racks, china trays. I am going to buy a whole pile of it with my Art &

Letters money – if you agree? Do you? And have it packed in a crate. Its such a *perfectly thrilling shop* – one of our own shops you know. Its cold – deadly cold today. I am writing my review of Peter Jackson & the Dark River.[2] But I feel a rag: Ive got fever. Temperature 100. I shant stir a step. Its the chauffage qui ne marche pas. But it wont matter after Sunday. Jinnie came yesterday to see me, it was her birthday: she is 64: I thought she was about 47. We are the same age when we're together – thats whats so queer. But she is a saint – a real saint – a *holy woman.* Its a great privilege to have known her.

Boge I see Gaby Deslys is dead of pleurisy. I am so sorry. She had just given up the stage because of her lungs – she couldn't sing any more & she was going to be married to *the man* & now poor little soul she and all her hats are dead. God rest her soul![3]

Grant Richards is coming to the Villa Flora on Tuesday with a closed car, taking me to Cap Martin & seeing me home – guaranteed *no steps.* But he says may I hope to persuade you to let me have the first refusal of your next novel? Well, I suppose there is no harm done: Ill ask for £60 in advance & then he'll be sorry. Woman next door to me – inferior Belgian in bed – with fever – being sick all day & then sighing in between & making SUCH noises – 2nd class Ladies Cabin noises like Harwich & Antwerp. Its very fierce not to have this place properly heated, though. Addio my own darling precious ONE.

Your Wig.

MS ATL. *LJMM*, 478–9.

[1] Murry's secretary and her young son.
[2] KM's review of Gilbert Frankau's *Peter Jackson*, and Sarah Gertrude Millin's *The Dark River*, appeared under 'Orchestra and Solo' in the *Athenaeum*, 20 Feb. 1920.
[3] The French actress and *danseuse* Gaby Deslys (1884–1920), a music-hall celebrity at the Gaiety Theatre, London, as well as in Paris, died at Marseilles on 11 Feb. 1920, providing in her will for a hospital for the needy – 'I have danced all my life for the poor.' (*The Times*, 14 Feb. 1920.)

To Alice Jones, [14 February 1920]

Villa Flora | Menton.

Dear Mrs Jones

This is my permanent address until May for the papers. I hope the little one has got over his bronchitis . . . I shall love to see him one day.

Mr Murry once promised me Country Life. Will you ask him if he wants to break his promise?

K.M.

Postcard Texas. Unpublished.

To Dorothy Brett, [16 February 1920]

Villa Flora | Menton

Brett darling

This is my new & permanent address. You see what a nice easy one it is . . . *Please* take the hint. I long for a letter from you. I shall write a big answer. Im *fearfully* busy – but DO let me hear your news. Take care of yourself. It will be such joy to see you again – you darling! Ever your woolly lamb

K.M.

Postcard Newberry. Unpublished.

To Anne Drey, [c.16 February 1920]

Villa Flora | Menton

This is my address until May. DO send me a word!

My darling darling Anne

Ive just heard from Murry that Constable has accepted my book & that you may perhaps do some drawings for it. This last fact simply FILLS me with joy. Will you do them? It excites me so – the thought of them.[1] You know how I admire & love your work – you blessed woman – and how proud I am to have your name & mine walking bras dessus bras dessous. You know my BAG. It is my chez moi. It goes with me like Mary's lamb wherever I go. Whenever I get into another Strange Room – out comes the Bag & the Interior Decoration is complete. How many times I have greeted you as I put it on the sofa end or on the wardrobe handle. I don't believe a day passes but I think of you. It will always be so. There you just *are*. Whenever I fill the jar with anemones or peel a tangerine or see a tree covered with fruit or pick flowers or throw a stone into the sea or *laugh on the quiet* OR try on a hat or see a particularly ravishing bébé I think '*ANNE*'.

Ive been (dont laugh) ill since December 5th with a cursed heart – and I cant walk even yet. But the corner is turned and I shall be a well girl again very soon. You know Anne the 'art business' for me is the only Thing that Matters – I cant find a substitute which is 'both nourishing & satisfying'. I wish you were here – the weather is glorious. Italy is a cursed spot but France – is the old old story.

Salutations. Love – a great deal of Love to you & to le petit. Heaven bless *your* loves. I suppose you won't be in Paris in May by any chance? We might meet and fleet a golden hour together.²

I am always your
Katherine.

MS Lawlor. Unpublished.

¹ As KM's letter to Murry on 8 Feb. makes clear, she was indifferent to his suggestion that Anne Drey provide illustrations for her new collection, and the proposal came to nothing.
² A part memory of 'Fleet the time carelessly, as they did in the golden world', *As You Like It*, I. i. 124, which she had quoted to Murry from Bandol two years before. (See *CLKM* II. 33.)

To J. M. Murry, [c.17 February 1920]

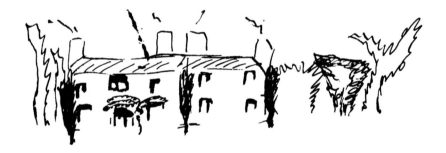

No its not like that

[Villa Flora, Menton]

Love

Will you put this letter from A. [Arthur Murry] & the drawing in the file? Both are so characteristic of him & so delightful they ought to be kept. And would you please post this letter to Anne? *No* post for me today – not a letter or a paper: I am so disappointed. I had none yesterday either. I am sure they have not gone to the Hermitage; they must be en route. And my overcoat. Bogey was it registered. When can I expect it? Can you know? I am worried about it. Its not that I want it so much just at the moment (though I do) but Im so afraid it may have gone astray & yet this is surely very unlikely with a parcel in the sac diplomatique. But was it insured? It is a vile day – a real Mistral. One is protected from it here – though. But Rendall says I can go for walks & that makes one impatient. I want to go for gallops to the china shop. Bogey if ever you have neuralgia or rheumatism or any pains of that kind take *irénine*. It is in the form of cachets & its absolutely ɪɴfallible. Dont forget darling. Any french chemist would sell it to you I expect. This isnt a letter today. J'attends –

Your own Wigchik.

MS ATL. *LJMM*, 479–80.

To J. M. Murry, [22 February 1920][1]

[Villa Flora, Menton]
Sunday.

My Very own Bogey

It is raining but such lovely rain; the drops hang in the rose bushes & on every tip of the palm fronds. Little birds sing; the sea sounds solemn & full & silver gulls fly over. I can smell the earth & I can feel how the violets are growing & all the small things down there under my window. It is exquisite. Talking about flowers you know gentlemens buttonholes? (A double daisy small). Child, they grow here in every conceivable colour – & massed together they are really a superb sight. I am sure Sutton[2] would have them. We *must* remember to grow them so in our garden a round bed. Country Life, of course makes it almost impossible to wait for a garden. When one reads the collection of flowery shrubs, par example – mock orange (you remember that: it was at Mylor[3]) four kinds of flowering quinces, mexican fuchsia . . . oh *dear* me! And then the annuals that sewn in January & February are flowering in Avrilo – there are at least 24 kinds & if you are clever you can grow them so that one kind marches up with banners after the other until the chrysanthemum is there. I think I shall become a very violent gardener. I shall have shelves of tomes & walk about the house whispering the names of flowers. We must have a tiny potting shed, too, just big enough for you & me. I see as I write little small forked sticks with labels on them – *daphne* grows in England: Eden Phillpotts has a great bush.[4] I shall write for a cutting. I read in Country Life of a most excellent apple called *Tom Putts*. Silly name,[5] but it seems to be a very fine fruit & the trees bear in their second year. Country Life intoxicates me – the advertisements and the pictures & the way they *harp* on hardy annuals. We must have a boy for heavy work but I want to do a fearful lot myself – large gloves, again (mine this time) & very short corduroy velveteen skirt – buff orpington colour.

Now I must lay down my trowel. Ive just remembered your bankruptcy discharge.[6] If it could be done it would be a very excellent thing but I *detest* the idea that Smith or any of your creditors should

get another sou. You cant borrow on me for Im not a good enough
Life – but could the house be bought in my name? Could any use be
made of me? Its very confusing. Boge, what is the amount? And what
would you be called upon to pay? I do wish you had never gone
bankrupt, but it seemed the only thing to do at the time. I think it was
not, though; I think you had evil advisers. The whole affair never
ought to have come about. Will you tell me more as much as you can
& just what you think best to do? God! what a comfort we are married
and no one can possibly start a divorce. We are *sound* as far as that is
concerned.

I have given L.M. her £10. Thank you again my darling for
arranging all that affair.

Bogey I find this italian inlaid work is really dirt cheap. I wonder if
you know what it is I mean. For instance J. has a tray here for coffee
cups. Its a kind of sea green inlaid with very delicate ivory coloured
trees & kids & little lovers playing among them & blowing on
trumpets. It cost *35* francs!!! There is, in fact, a whole shop of it & a
man who does the work here. Oh, I wish you were in Menton with me
for a little. We should have the most ravishing prowls, but perhaps
better not. I told you about the finger bowls – clear glass with faint
gold & green or gold & pink stripes – the green is prettiest. Ill never
rest happy now until we have a house fit to be visited by – by ——
ourselves. And I want very much these two french servants. They long
to come: & they love cats & chickens & country. I think it would be a
kind of final cachet – don't you? The one is Marie Louise and the
other Joséphine – and they both dress alike . . . Post has just come Ill
start another page.
  I have your Thursday afternoon letter & the A. & the T.L.S. First
the letter. I am afraid the house was not what it sounded because you
would have wired. Your childhood horrifies me.[7] You came upon
things so late & then they were so few, but how nice Way House
Minster *sounds* doesn't it!8
  Now darling – this is final about the coat. We must give it a bit
longer. (It really cant have been lost if it did go in the diplomatic bag.)
It must have been stolen in London, I fancy. But if it is hopeless, just
wire *no go*. I mean if I may definitely NOT expect it. For then Ill get one
made on the spot at a shop here called New England. They have
excellent materials – wool of the purest & thickest & will make one for
me in five days. L.M. has got *her* eye on a grey burberry – very chic.
She fancies herself in it. Burberry has a shop here. So just let me know
& Ill go ahead & with my £10 windfall get a coat.
  I note about stamps re reviews. And may I have more BOOKS. Poor

Mrs Leonard Merricks Mary-Girl cant stand more than a short notice.[9] Its just dreadfully bad & she's dead. Rest her! I cant say anything against her. Ill just send a synopsis. The books are rather difficult to do they are so BAD!

Grant Richards said at his hotel at Cap Martin a man saw him reading the Athenaeum and said thats the paper K.M. writes in. Shes very brilliant I know her well have known her for years . . . & so on. It was Belfort Bax[10] whom I *hardly* know really & havent seen since the old original New Age days. What great cheek. He thought himself such a gun then & now he boasts about poor little K.M. But don't imagine that *I* think myself brilliant will you, my precious. Very very far from it.

May has brought me a big branch of orange blossom all wet with rain. I must get up. If it clears after lunch we're going to take a car & go up into the mountains to see if we can find wild tulips for tea. Did I tell you Im having a lovely dress made – materials & dressmaker chosen by Connie. Its very fine supple black cloth with a puritan ivory crepe collar & cuffs. Do you like that? I like you to know about my clothes. I do feel one must have very distinguished clothes – Middleton Murry clothes. The little American millionaire[11] who is still here has a set of green and gold enamel dressingtable pots & trays. But I am going to bring you back a pile of presents. Unpacking will be a real adventure. No-one must be forgotten. There's your mother & Arthur, too. But the house – the house!!

There is a piece of orange blossom for you buds & leaves – but oh! I cant draw the scent. Goodbye my precious. Ever for ever your

Wig.

MS ATL. *LKM* II. 15–16; *LJMM*, 480–2.

[1] It is likely that letters to Murry from the preceding week have been lost.

[2] Sutton and Sons, a mail-order seed supplier in Reading, who advertised in *Country Life*, the weekly magazine which KM was then receiving. She would have read in their advertisement of 14 Feb. of 'Twenty of the Best Hardy Annuals', which she refers to below.

[3] After their unhappy attempt to live with the Lawrences in Zennor, KM and Murry moved in mid-June 1916 to a cottage at Mylor, on the Truro River, Cornwall, where they spent three weeks.

[4] There is nothing in *Country Life* that connects the poet and novelist Eden Philpotts with daphne, although his poem 'Wassailing the Apple Tree' appeared in the issue of 10 Jan. 1920.

[5] A letter to the Editor headed 'Tom Putt' on 14 Feb. 1920 pointed out that the apple was named after a late-eighteenth-century clergyman in the parish of Trent, Somerset.

[6] Murry had been declared a bankrupt in 1914, as a result of the publisher Charles Granville ('Stephen Swift'), who took over the financing of *Rhythm* from June 1912, himself going bankrupt, fleeing the country, and leaving Murry with the £150 debt to the printers. (See *CLKM* I. 110, 136, n. 1, 137, n. 1.) His concern now was that unless he went to the Bankruptcy Court

and paid the 30s. discharge fee, he would not be able to raise money for the house in the country they were hoping to buy. (Murry, 285.) He wrote, however, on 26 Feb. that he had decided to let the matter lie for a time – 'I don't want them prying.' (ATL.)

⁷ Murry's letter of 16 Feb. recalled the drab walks he was obliged to take with his father on a childhood holiday at Margate, and their coming on a field of corn with red poppies. 'That was the first time that beauty sent an arrow bang into my heart . . . I had never dreamed on anything like it.' (Murry, 288.)

⁸ The house he looked at in Minster, a few miles from Margate, was not suitable. See next letter.

⁹ No notice of Hope Merrick's recent novel, *Mary Girl*, appeared.

¹⁰ Ernest Belfort Bax (1854–1929), a barrister and journalist who trained first in music, and helped to establish the Socialist League with William Morris. He published volumes on history and philosophy, and was an authority on German thought.

¹¹ Mrs Bunnie Dunn, a friend of her cousin Connie's.

To J. M. Murry, [c.22 February 1920]

[Villa Flora, Menton]

Would you give enclosed letter card to my manager J.M.M. & ask him to get his menials to post the necessary books to the gent.[1] I think he ought to have a copy of Je ne parle pas & be told about the Constable book but thats as my manager pleases. As to Biographical Note:

Née 14 Octobre à Nouvelle Zélande.

Premier voyage age de six mois.

Premier histoire publié age de neuf ans.

La reste de ma vie est passé en voyagant et en écrivant les 'short stories'.

Written for Australian & English papers & reviews.

Wife of the brilliant poete et critique J.M.M. who is the famous editor of the newly brought to life and prominence Athenaeum –

Two cats.

K.M.

I am so sorry about Aldous. Do publish another review by another hand if you've a mind to. Ill understand absolutely – only I *could* not say more. Boge they were such BILGE.[2]

Wig-chik.

MS ATL. *LJMM*, 516.

¹ This information was obviously to be sent in response to an unidentified request – possibly from a French paper.

² Brownlee Kirkpatrick's *A Bibliography of Katherine Mansfield* (1989), 159, records among 'Rejected and Untraced' material: '27 February 1920: handwritten note attached to the *Athenaeum* issue for this date in the marked files of the journal: "Mrs Murry's review of *Limbo* [by Aldous Huxley] (1 column) to be paid for, by Editor's instruction £1/7/6." KM's review was not published; the only notice *Limbo* received was an unsigned note of three lines by JMM in the issue for 19 March.'

To J. M. Murry, [23 February 1920]

[Villa Flora, Menton]
Monday.

Darling

I have just read your Canterbury letter about Minster. I felt that Minster was not going to be much good. You didn't see Heaven when you were a little boy. Alas! they put you off with market gardens. I have a feeling that you wont find anything till I get back (which is in about 9 weeks as I suppose you realise: Wing knows.) I shall be able to tell what is possible & what is not: People lead you a dance love. For instance I was positive Battle was no go: the man seemed so – almost reluctant.[1] But dear love these last few days I keep on wondering whether the New Forest is any good? Ive a passion for it 'as an idea' & you could keep a horse & we might even run to a pony for me as well. You see Woodhay[2] which isn't our affair – but still *is* a highly desirable residence with garden, orchard, all improvements p.w.c.h. & c. and all kinds of pretty little kickshaws like awnings & summer blinds & so on only cost £2000 . . . And I am sure the forest is *superb*. And Father found it in one go. He just walked out & happened on it . . . What do you think? I feel a forest is a wonderful place to live near – & it certainly cant be enervating. What do you think, darling? By the way about my coming home. Dont come to Paris. Meet me in London with a car. There's no point in coming to Paris & as it is we shall be such a party. You wouldnt like it at all. Youd try & be a man & May would laugh at you. These two have 14 trunks of their own I have 3 L.M. 2. No, my child, don't come near Paris. Meet me in London at the station. Sit on a bench with a poetry book & clap it to when the steam comes waving under the roof & then find me very quickly. That will be far better.

Yesterday – it being midsummer – Mrs Dunn drove me in a kerridge & pair to Monte Carlo. I take back my words about the Riviera being *not* what it is made out to be. It *is* and more. It was the most marvellous afternoon. We drove towards the sun up hill down dale mountain roads, through lemon & orange groves – little children throwing bouquets of violets & hyacinths into the carriage – past the sea, under huge mountains – and the FLOWERS. Of course it is all quite artificial: theres no imagination in it anywhere. *Monte* is REAL HELL. To begin with its the cleanest most polished place Ive ever seen. The villas are huge and they have strange malignant towers. Immense poppies sprout out of the walls & roses & geraniums hang down like carpets. All the shops are magasin de luxe, lingerie, perfumes, fat unguents, & pawnbrokers & patisserie. The rooms are the devils headquarters – the blinds are down theres a whitish glare from the electric light inside – carpet on the outside steps – up & down which pass a continual procession of *whores* pimps, governesses in thread gloves – Jews – old old hags, ancient men stiff & greyish panting as they climb, rich great fat capitalists, little girls tricked out to look like babies – and below the room a huge outside café – the famous Café de Paris with *real* devils with tails under their aprons cursing each other as they hand the drinks. There at those tables, sit the damned. The gardens, darling. If you could see them – the gardens in Hell. Light bright delicate grass grown in half a night, trembling little pansies grown in tiny beds that are nourished on the flesh of babies – little fountains that spray up into the air all diamonds. Oh – I could write about it *for ever*. We came back through pine forests, past Cap Martin & then at the edge of the brimming sea. Ive never heard of Monte before – never dreamed there was such a place. Now I want to go to the rooms & see it all. Its *dreadful* but its *fascinating* to me.[3] We stopped the carriage outside the café & waited for about five minutes. I thought of the Heron & OUR life – & I thought how strange it was that at the Heron I should no doubt write a story about that woman over there that ancient long nosed whore with a bag made of ostrich feathers —— I wonder if youd like to see such a thing. Would you? I dont in the least know. Cruelty is there – & vultures hover – & the devil waiters wear queer peaked caps to hide their horns. Its another dead calm gorgeous summer – June – day – as I write – perfect weather! I wish you shared *that* at any rate. Take care of yourself my own – and dont forget for a moment how perfect our house is going to be. It will be far better than we imagined in the past because all is different now. No, I can never forget anything of what has happened because it has changed everything but I dont regret it. It *had* to be.

Your own
Wig.

I can get a lovely coat here I find, so don't forget to wire me if I must not expect the other, but parcils do take 3 weeks from Paris.

[*Across top of letter*]

Re the New Forest I was talking about it to Cousin Connie last night & she says its so difficult to get anything on gravel – and that *gravel* is the *most* important thing. One might as well dig a grave as live on clay.

MS ATL. *LKM* II. 19–20; *LJMM*, 483–4.

---

[1] Another incident in Murry's house-hunting, near Battle in Sussex.
[2] The house in the New Forest Harold Beauchamp provided for KM's sisters.
[3] Some of these feelings of Monte Carlo KM included in her story 'The Young Girl', written in Oct. 1920.

To J. M. Murry, [24 February 1920]

[Villa Flora, Menton]

We had baby lamb with infantile potatoes and nouveau né green peas today.

Tuesday.

There is a book which we must positively not be another week without. It is Forster's Life of Dickens. How is it people refer to this & have many a time & oft talked of it to me & yet – as though it was of course a very good Life a very good Life indeed – about as good as you could get & immensely well worth reading. But so dispassionately – so as a matter of course. Merciful Heavens! Its one of the most absolutely fascinating books I have ever set eyes on. I found today vol III in the bookshelves. Whether the other two are here or not I dont know but I do most solemnly assure you it is so great that it were worth while building a house in the country & putting in a fireplace, chairs & a table curtains, hot wine & you and I & Arthur & whoever else we 'fancy' exprès for reading this. Bogey its *ravishing*. What will you do when you come to the description of how his little boy aged 4 plays the part of hero in a helmet & sword at their theatricals & having previously made the dragon drunk on sherry stabs him dead which he does in such a manner that Thackeray falls off his chair laughing & rolls on the floor. No, thats nothing. Read of his landlord M. *Beaufort*, read of his house in Boulogne.[1]

Now I am exaggerating. Since I wrote all that I finished the book. Its not GREAT of course its not; its fascinating & its a bit terrible as a lesson. I never knew before what killed Dickens. It was money. He couldn't as he grew older resist money: he became a miser & disguised it under a laughing exterior. Money and applause – he died for both. How fearful that is! But still my own precious we must have the books. We must have his complete works . . .

I had your Saturday (home again) letter today. Fancy winter back again & here we go from sun to sun. Ill tell L.M. to write to Harlow Downs and Ill write to Belle[2] in case she hears from any of her friends of anything. Dont get agitated or desperate for a minute. When we're back we'll get what we want. I have no possible doubt. You *do* realise darling theres a chance I may have to return here next winter – a big big chance? Its for the *sun*, and I cant risk taking 10 years getting well when I might take 2. If I do come here of course it will be with Connie & Jinnie & Ill leave L.M. in charge of the house & you. Id come from November till May. Rendall saw me yesterday. He says my lung is better even in a week but my old rheumatism which has located itself at present quite definitely in the right hip joint is 'very troublesome'. It could be cured by baths but then my lungs wont stand baths – so Ill have to get them going before I can cure it. It doesn't prevent me from living my life however. Yesterday I had a wonderful afternoon. Mrs Dunn took a carriage & we (she) shopped. I bought for the house oh! dear! the most ravishing perfect —— surprises you ever did see. Youll *never* recover from them. She bought some too and a dress for me a girls dress blue chiffon with a pinky fringe – summer dress. No I cant draw it. But I really think what I bought for the house will boulverse you. I paid 77 francs of the £10 gave me & mean as I say to get more. This is a *frightful* town for shopping – glass, china, inlaid work, bits of brocade, trays —— We had champagne for dinner & Jinnie, seeing my softened mood gave me her missal to read. But *thats* no good darling. Who made God?

Wig. (I don't mean I did).

MS ATL. *LKM* II. 21–2; *LJMM*, 485–6.

---

[1] John Forster's *Life of Charles Dickens* (1872–4), vol. iii, Ch. 2 (Book Seventh, Ch. 4, in the more familiar one- or two-volume editions), describes Dickens's son Henry taking the leading role in Fielding's *Tom Thumb*, 'the small helmeted hero', and in another play adulterating the Dragon's drink with sherry. It was on a quite different occasion that W. M. Thackeray 'rolled off his seat in a burst of laughter', when 'Lord Grizzle performed his ballad of Miss Villikins'. Vol. iii, Ch. 4 is entitled 'Three Summers at Boulogne', where Forster describes the 'odd French place with the strangest little rooms and halls, but standing in the midst of a large garden' which Dickens rented in 1852, 1853, and 1854. He quotes from a letter of Dickens describing the remarkably generous landlord M. Beaucourt, 'a portly jolly fellow with a fine open face'.

[2] Her maternal aunt Belle Trinder, who lived in Tadworth, Surrey.

To Richard Murry, [24 February 1920]

Villa Flora | Menton.
Tuesday.

My dear old Boy

Yes I *did* get your letter written to a place called Hermitage *very much* called Hermitage, where Russian children stamped overhead & Rumanians roared below & French infants rushed at you in the lift. After Italy it seemed alright at first but then they began feeding us on haricot beans & I hate haricot beans. They have no imagination. What with that + the noise I turned against it & my cousin who has taken this villa for le saison asked me here. *Here* is about as perfect as it could be. A great garden, lemon & orange groves, palms, violets in blue carpets, mimosa trees – and inside a very beautiful 'exquisite' house in the style of Garsington but more sumptuous but unlike Garsington with a spirit in it which makes you feel that nothing evil or ugly could ever come near. Its *full* of life and gaierty – but the people are at peace. You know what I mean? They've got a real background to their lives – and they realise that other people have, too. I am basking here until I come back – sometime in May.

Menton is a lovely little town – small and unreal like all these places are but even here there are real spots. The colour and movement everywhere make you continually happy. Its all ruled by the sun. The sun is King and Queen and Prime Minister and people wear hats like this: [Drawing of small male figure, head and face invisible under equilateral conical hat.] I mustn't bring one back for Jack *or* you but they are very tempting!

Im not ill any more. Really Im not. Please think of me, dear old boy, as a comfortable cross between a lion and a lamb.

I wish you had a quiet spot where you could draw in peace. But your room at the Heron will be your *studio*. Its such a waste of Life to bark and bite like people do: I think we ought just to ignore them and go our way. Its no good getting mixed up in 'sets' or cliques or quarrels. That is not our job. *By their works ye shall know them*[1] is our motto. And Life is so short and there is such a tremendous lot to do and see – we shall never have time for all. Arthur, I wish we could find the house – don't you? I don't think Jack will find it before Im back (thats in 9 weeks time) but there will be a lot to do when it is found. Its just going to [be] the perfect place for us all – our *real* home. You must be down in all your spare time and when youre in London you must always have the feeling its *there* with the smoke coming out of its chimneys & the hens laying eggs & the bees burrowing in the flowers. I feel we must keep bees, a cow, fowls, 2 turkeys, some indian runner ducks, a *goat*, and perhaps one thoroughly striking beast like a unicorn or a dragon. I am always learning odd things such as how to light a scientific bonfire – but now you're laughing at me. However just come and see my bonfire one of these days, my lad, & you will turn up your eyes in admiration.

Sir, re small sum owing to R. Cobden-Sanderson, the author of tome said he would pay it for me as soon as he got back to England after Xmas.[2] Please ask him to settle it – will you?

In the Hermitage letter you asked me what were my views about Adam in this great swinging garden. Now thats awfully difficult to answer. For this reason. I cant help seeing all the evil and pain in the world: it must be faced and recognised – and I cant bear your sentimentalist or silly optimist. I know it all: I feel it all. And there is *cruelty* for instance – cruelty to children – how are you going to explain that, and as you say the beauty – yes the beauty that lurks in ugliness that is even outside the pub in the gesture of the drinking woman. I cant explain it. I wish I could believe in a God. I cant. Science seems to make it *im*possible – and if you are to believe in a God it must be a good God & no good God could allow his children to suffer so. No,

Life is a mystery to me. It is made up of Love and pains. One loves and one suffers – one suffers and one has to love. I feel (for myself individually) that I want to live by the spirit of Love – love *all* things. See into things so deeply and truly that one loves. That does not rule out hate – far from it. I mean it doesn't rule out anger. But I confess I only feel that I am doing right when I am living by love. I don't mean a personal love, you know, but —— the big thing. Why should one love? No reason; its just a mystery. But it is like light. I can only truly see things in its rays. That is vague enough isn't it? I do think one must (we must) have some big thing to live by, and one reason for the great poverty of Art today is that artists have got no religion and they are in the words of the Bible, sheep without a shepherd.[3] Now what lifts Jack high above them is his faith – which he calls *spiritual honesty* – that separates him from all the rest of them just as though he were a priest. We are priests after all. I fail and waver and faint by the way but my faith is this queer *Love*. One cant drift and everybody nearly is drifting nowadays – don't you feel that?

Its your fault I have written this. Theres a picture of me in a previous existence thinking it out. You say you didn't know what to talk about in the Hampstead days. It doesn't matter, old boy – and don't bother to write long letters (tho' I love your letters). I just feel we are true friends & that we understand each other "and thats the humour of it" as Corporal Nym says.[4]

When I come back

What Larks!

Always your loving
Katherine

MS R. Murry. *LKM* II. 16–18.

[1] KM's adaptation of Matt. 16: 20, 'by their fruits ye shall know them'.

[2] Payment for a copy of Murry's *The Evolution of an Intellectual*.

[3] A frequent image in the Bible. See for example Num. 27: 17, 2 Chr. 18: 16, Matt. 9: 36.

[4] Nym, one of Falstaff's low-life companions, plays incessantly on the word 'humour', including 'and that's the humour of it', *Henry V*, ii. i. 64.

To J. M. Murry, [25 February 1920]

[Menton]

REPLY URGENT.
Marie Louise – domestique de 30 ans, venant de Nord – peut faire la cuisine – travaille admirablement – desire venir avec nous comme cuisinière – femme de menage. Mais elle a avec elle sa nièce, jeune fille de 17 ans, *admirable* comme parlour maid et serving maid qui vent

venir aussi. Si je m'attache tous les deux? Please reply! Ce sont deux femmes superbes!!! Mais pas un mot d'Anglais. Je suis *très* anxious to bring them.[1]

Wig.

Postcard ATL. *LJMM*, 486.

---

[1] Although Murry thought the proposal an excellent one, it was not pursued, in view of the following letter.

To J. M. Murry, [26 February 1920]

[Villa Flora, Menton]

THE IMPORTANT LETTER.

Darling Precious little Husband

I want you to read this slowly and to remember that I am loving you with my whole heart and putting you first in my thoughts always. I know how terribly anxious you are to leave P.V. but what are you going to do if I go abroad for the winter. Rendall said today: it would be madness for me to spend the next 2 winters in England because whatever the luxury I live in the air is almost perpetually damp and there is very little sun. It is not as though I were a simple consumptive who can walk, lie about and so on: I am handicapped very severely by my rheumatism which cannot be cured until my lungs are cured. It is that which prevents me from leading the normal life in a cold climate which another consumptive can do. He says that for the next two years I ought to be here from November till May. I must take this opinion into account; it is shared by these 2 women and I dare not face a prolongation of my illness. Now if I do come abroad L.M. must be with me. She would not let me come alone & she says she dare not. I think she is right. You remember I once was cruel enough to suggest that we put off establishing our house: *I still suggest it.* Yes, I still think it would be 1000 times better to wait for 2 years. Please don't get angry. Please read on. You could surely get a weekend place for yourself every weekend. I would spend May till October in P.V. I suggest offering Violet & Roger the basement floor & her bedroom – with a door at the top of the kitchen stairs for them so that they live there. I would get the whole house & the feeding arrangements and so on into *perfect order* before I left and arrange that you were never left without a servant even when she was out. In the meantime you take your time, you look & if you do see the perfect thing & its cheap you make it your weekend cottage – and for us when Im there until I am well enough to live there. Youll say you cant stand P.V. any longer.

Not as it is now, of course, you cant. The house wants attention, care, organisation, the life of it wants changing; you must live like a gentleman and be served like one. But all that can be done when L.M. & I get back. Ill make it my job to see you are really comfortable and exquisitely housed. There's no reason why Sydney should not stay either. I KNOW you hate London but darling Heart you MUST be in London anyway for a time and you certainly could get every weekend off & *when* the house is found perhaps you could spend every weekend there. P.V. when Ive seen to it wont be in the least what it is now. And Bogey, you must realise that I want to give you your heart's desire *this moment* but I must consider well what is easiest and best for us. Life in the country without your wife would not do. It would make immense demands on your energy. It cant be done with[out] L.M. and me there all the time – and I really think I *dare* not face this rheumatism for two years. You see what it amounts to is: I come back thoroughly set you up – get all *really* exquisite – you find a country place or a pied à terre & go slow just for the present. Light a cigarette. Think it well, well over. I wish you were here so that I could talk it out with you. I do so feel its the right thing to do. Let Sydney know & ask him. Tell him how snug I mean to make P.V. & well kept in every way. And if you do agree please read this letter to Violet & give it to her immediately & darling please please wire me either *agree* or *dont agree*. I shall wait for that wire. Ill go into all the details once I'm home – & I promise you great comfort – no domestic worries and L.M. shall establish your country comfort.

Thats all.

Your devoted
Wife Wig.

MS ATL. *LJMM*, 486–8.

To J. M. Murry, [26 February 1920][1]

[Menton]

SENT IMPORTANT LETTER TRY NOT GO COUNTRY BEFORE READ LOVE TIG

Telegram ATL. Unpublished.

---

[1] KM must also have sent another wire the next day, as Murry wrote on 28 Feb. that he had replied 'to your telegram asking whether the reviews had been received' (ATL).

To J. M. Murry, [2 March 1920]

[Villa Flora, Menton]
Tuesday.

Fin de la greve(?)

My own Bogey,

A perfect pile of letters came today – one telling me about Dollie Radford.[1] Also there came the paper. I think it is vastly improved with the contents across p. 1. It looks a very good number. I have not had time to read any but your most *admirable* article[2] yet. Therell be no me this week I am afraid.[3] Letters have simply not been going to England. I suppose you don't realise là bas how serious this strike[4] has been here. I have seen the D.N. [*Daily News*] (Jinnie takes it) & it seems to be just dismissed but the french papers are *full* of it and *full* of its esprit revolutionaire. Were it not for the post Id snap my fingers at it. What does it matter here – when Jinnie takes up a piece of omelette & says "come on *hedge-sparrow*, peck away." Thats her name for me!

I want to write about a million things but I am held up because I do not know what you are feeling about my letter about the house. I feel your keen disappointment & Id give my eyes to able to retract it. But I *cant*. Its no good imagining that I can live in an English winter yet. I just dare not: it might cripple me for life. And we cant have a half life. You are the very last man on this earth to have to do with an 'invalid wife' – I know that so well. I know that the springs of our life together will be poisoned if I am not well – Italy taught me that & now this rheumatism which Rendall assures me is most obstinate & which I know for agony convinces me that nothing but sun from November till May will do. But *do* remember that I *realise* what that is to you when I say put it off . . .

L.M.'s letter came – & she was here so she let me read it. Bogey she cant sell her shares – not even for us and not even when it is such a sound proposition. She cant: she's *bound* not to, first by her solemn promise to her sister and I feel as well she *cannot* for another reason which is too obscure and difficult for me to write about. Its a *compound* feeling. If you'd like me to analyse it for you – I will.

Have my letters arrived? I've written every day & I have sent a review of *Pilgrims of Circumstance* & *Jewish Children*.[5] This week Im awfully badly off for books. Couldn't I have Rebecca Wests novel *The Judge* & *The Woman Called Smith* by Vember Heinemann & —— some others?[6] Its fearfully difficult to review things which ought not to have long reviews.

About the Constable excisions in je ne p.p. it depends what they ask – doesn't it?[7] I want to cut a small bit out of Prelude but that I can do in proof.[8] Bogey are you going to review my Story in the Athenaeum?[9]

Every week – I look – and dont see it. Your book was reviewed so I suppose its not a question of the staff at any rate it wouldn't be for I dont sign. But if youd rather let it alone – alright darling.

Your Blunden man —— oh what a curse. He doesn't really thrill me yet. I cant 'get away with it' – it seems to me the first poem [is] overweighted – overheavy.[10] But I KNOW I am not fair & I understand what he must be to you & all success to him! If anyone sent a poem from N.Z. from my school that had even *one* happy line —— But that is not your first interest in him, of course. Boge, do remember to be sober in your praise – temperate. You remember how little fired us when we were young & to be over generous is dangerous. You of course would shower love on anyone whom you thought was walking the right path – and I love you for it and yet – I know one *must* hold back a bit. If Im dead down sincere Ill confess that the fact he wrote you approached you through *Clare* influenced me for I have a perfect *horror* of Clare – the fact that he fell down in the mud at Byron's funeral & ruined his only clothes fills me with woe.[11] So theres a female for you!

I am so glad you love Brett so much. I used to feel in Italy that if I died you'd marry Brett very soon after – I nearly wrote to you about it. Shes wonderfully suited to you in a thousand ways.

Oh Love my pen moves stiffly till I hear from you. It wont run or leap and I want the strike to be over. Its *torture* not to be in the paper. E.M.F.[12] fills me with jealousy even tho he is such a Kleine Seele.

Bogey I don't think you ought to talk or bother about silly people. Be quiet if you want to. Just be yourself. Its all that matters. Dont even try & be anything else. I feel it is of the highest importance that you should not make an effort which you feel in your soul to be a wrong effort: Ive exposed you to that sometimes – but *never never* again. The weather day after day here is hot brilliant summer. We lie out, drive, bask – its hot enough for cold lamb salad champagne & fruit & cream – *really* hot. Menton is an exquisite little town. Every time I drive into it I think it more lovely. My lungs & heart are a million times better but my rheumatism is not. Its very bad – bad as bad can be just now. I love these women more every day I think. But I long to be HOME & making HOME for you – as perfect as I have learned how. Goodbye for now my own – my darling precious Bogey

Ever your devoted
Wigchik.

MS ATL. *LJMM*, 488–90; cited Meyers, 207.

[1] Murry told her of the recent death of Dollie Radford (1864–1920), a minor playwright and former Queen's College student, married to the Fabian poet and critic Ernest Radford (1857–1919). KM and Murry knew her through her close friendship with D. H. Lawrence.

² 'The Cry in the Wilderness', Murry's review article of *Rousseau and Romanticism*, by Irving Babbitt, in the *Athenaeum*, 27 Feb. 1920.

³ KM must have telegraphed that she could not provide her usual weekly review, for Murry wrote to her the same day, 'I've just got your wire about the review. I hope it was more the badness of the novels than actual brainfag.' (ATL.)

⁴ The rail strike which so disrupted mails.

⁵ KM's review of G. B. Bergin's fifty-ninth novel, *Pilgrims of Circumstance*, the *Athenaeum*, 19 Mar. 1920; her review of *Jewish Children*, by Hannah Berman, did not appear.

⁶ She did not review either Rebecca West's *The Judge*, or Marie Conway Demler's *A Woman Named Smith*, which she wrongly attributed to Vember Heinemann.

⁷ See p. 273 n. 3, for the textual changes to *Je ne parle pas français*.

⁸ Only very minor changes and spelling corrections were made from the Hogarth Press edition of *Prelude*, before its appearance in *Bliss and Other Stories*.

⁹ *Je ne parle pas français* was reviewed in the *Athenaeum*, 2 Apr. 1920, by J. W. N. Sullivan. The review rather laboured the point that KM owed more to Dostoevsky than to Chekhov.

¹⁰ On 25 Feb. Murry copied out for KM two poems sent to him by the young poet and scholar Edmund Blunden (1896–1974), who had attended Murry's own school, Christ's Hospital. Both poems were published in the *Athenaeum*, 'Wilderness' on 12 Mar. 1920 and 'Chinese Pond' on 7 May 1920.

¹¹ Blunden contributed the leading article, 'John Clare', on 5 Mar. 1920. It is not apparent where KM picked up the inaccurate story of Clare's behaviour at Byron's funeral.

¹² That week E. M. Forster wrote an incisively damning review of *The Strongest*, a novel by the French politician Georges Clemenceau.

To J. M. Murry, [c.3 March 1920] *

I cant draw our little girl till Ive got a fine pen, but he's not bad is he?

[Villa Flora, Menton]

Darling Bogey

I do wish I could draw. Im always wanting to put little small drawings on the tops of your letters & I had such a thrill when I made that little boy. We'll have to take our sketch books away this year. You know *re* the South of France I have grown to like it far more than ever I did. The mechanical *appearance* goes & theres something about

* This letter was re-dated to *c.* 30 March 1920, too late for inclusion in its proper place (p. 267 below).

the rocks & stones which reminds me of New Zealand – volcanic – & the sea is really a wonderful colour. Yes, Ive grown to *love* it. The air in the mountains is wonderful & then the trees – the pepper trees & the lemons. If only you shared my winters, & we had a minute Broomchen here where we grew jonquils, early peas & lettuces & anemones . . . You would be happy I know. I would not go to Bandol again because its not far enough South. Between here & Nice there are lovely little unspoilt corners in the mountains. But we can wait & come in 30 years' time. That will do.

MS C. Murry. *LJMM*, 509–10, 517.

To J. M. Murry, [4 March 1920]

[Villa Flora, Menton]
Thursday.

Dearest of all,

Your telegram saying you absolutely agreed[1] seemed to me the most wonderful gesture you had ever made. I felt your arms opened and I ran in and was folded up and *we* absolutely agreed. But all the same, dearest & most precious, I know what it meant to you – I know the cost. I deeply, deeply know it and feel it. Whatever we do it will be the Best – whatever we decide you know that my whole heart is in it *for you*. For I am yours, body and soul – my beloved – your own wife and every single day that passes here I feel as though I am dedicate anew to OUR FUTURE. This Spring is going to be our Spring – its going to be the crowning of our love. I wish I could explain that: I cant. But I feel Ive never before been really ready for Life – able to cope with it – strong enough to give and to rejoice. Now I am. And you are my all – my very one. Your letter about the house has come with the *quaint quaint* 1750 Bogey-eyed drawings. It sounds exquisite & I want to know what you decide. My only brick about it – is – not the size – but the cheapness. After a very big scrutiny of Land & Water I cant see why its not £3500.[2] What is the reason? There must be one. It cant be *distance* for a house that size would mean the people would keep a car . . . Otherwise it sounds marvellous. If only we could take it & play with it for the 2 years until its ours for ever & we are *really planted* there! But you will tell me in your next letter.

Queer you should feel that about Tchekov. I feel it simply profoundly, a kind of 'there you are' towards him with a smile which really means 'but no one understands him *truly* and delicately as Bogey and I do . . .'[3]

Please tell Wingley how very very much better his grandma is –

how *everybody* remarks on it & says she looks a different creature. If only her rheumatism would go I think she'd be almost well but it does not go at present . . . All the same – really my lungs are marvellously better & I hardly *ever* cough!

Its the most divine spring-summer weather – *very* hot. This is the kind of thing that happens at 1.30. A big car arrives. We go in from our coffee & liqueurs on the balcony. May is waiting to dress me – I wear 'somebodys' coat – 'anybodys' – we get in – there are rugs cushions – hassocks – & yesterday the tea basket and away we go. Yesterday we went to La Turbie (I cant spell it and am ashamed to ask.) Its up up high high on the tops of the mountains. Its a tiny ancient roman town, incredibly ancient, with old bits with pillars & capitals.[4] Oh – dear – it is so lovely. The road winds & winds to get there round & round the mountains. I could hardly bear it yesterday – I was so much in love with you. I kept seeing it all – for you – wishing for you – longing for you. The rosemary is in flower (our plant it is) the almond trees, pink & white, there are wild cherry trees & the prickly pear white among the olives. Apple trees are just in their first rose & white – wild hyacinths & violets are tumbled out of flora's wicker ark and are *everywhere*. And over everything, like a light are the lemon & orange trees glowing. If I saw one house which was *ours* I saw twenty. I know we never shall live in such houses but still they are ours – little houses with terraces & a verandah – with bean fields in bloom with a bright scatter of anemones all over the gardens. When we reached the mountain tops we got out and lay on the grass, looking down down, into the valleys and over Monaco which is, if anything in this world is Cinnamon's capital. The palace seen from so high – with its tufts of plumy trees, the harbour basin with his yacht & a sail boat and a minute pinnace. Angelica's chemises were hanging out to dry in a royal courtyard.[5] I saw them through the glasses. The hedge-sparrow had cushions & rugs for her. The american whose name is Bunny lay flat on her back smoking – Jinnie, never still for a moment roamed about & one heard her singing. She couldn't keep still & Connie (of course) unpacked the tea basket & fed us all & poured cream down us and then gave away the cakes to two funny little mountain children who watched us from behind a rock. We stayed there about 2 hours & then dropped down by another road to Monte. The light & the shadow were divided in the hills but the sun was still in the air all the time – the sea very rosy with a pale big moon over by Bordighera. We got home at 6.30 & there was my fire, the bed turned down – hot milk – May waiting to take off all my things. '*Did* you enjoy it Madam?' Can you imagine such a coming back to Life? Its simply incredible! But I was simply filled with thoughts of *you* all the time – every moment. I lay back in the car & talked to you . . .

How can one repay them for all this? Its not *money* its not because they are *rich* it is the spirit of it all the way they do it, their voices and looks and tones. It is living by love. How I do scorn all that horrible old twisted existence I mean really the weekends at Garsington – the *paralysis* of everybody the vanity and ugliness of so much. No wonder you cant speak. Its not for us such a life – but *this* is *plus* of course our work and our youth & deep deep love. Its *living* Bogey. I feel even the sun is part of it in some way – and shines differently.

MS ATL. *LKM* II. 18–19; *LJMM*, 490–2.

---

¹ That is, to her letter of 26 Feb.

² KM enjoyed reading *Land and Water*, the country life-style magazine where properties were advertised. The house Murry had been so taken with in Waltham, Kent, was selling for £1,500.

³ Murry contributed a long review of *Letters of Anton Tchehov to his Family and Friends*, translated by Constance Garnett, in the *Athenaeum*, 5 Mar. 1920. He told KM on 28 Feb. of his reading of Chekhov's 'extasies over his house. I felt, as I read it coming back in the train, that there was a kind of testing involved.' (ATL.)

⁴ La Turbie, a village on the Grand Corniche above Monaco, famous particularly for 'Le Trophée des Alpes', a monument to the victories of the emperor Augustus.

⁵ A reference to the feyly diminutive imagery in Murry's verse play *Cinnamon and Angelica*.

To Ida Baker, [4 March 1920]

[Villa Flora, Menton]

My dear Jones¹

I want to tell you a secret but I cannot when we are face to face. I feel you know what it is. But the fact is all I can tell you now. Later on, Ill laugh about it and talk about it and you can make fun of me but just at present Jones Im so sensitive that I couldn't even bear to hear you say you had got this letter. I tremble with shyness – that is *dead true*, my dear. Later on, I promise it won't be so, but for the present will you forgive me if I ask you not to even breathe a word of it to me.

This afternoon when we were lying on the hills (Ill tell you all about it one day) I knew there was a God. There you are.

One day (before I go back to England I hope) I mean to be received into the Church. I am going to become a Catholic. Once I believe in a god, the rest is so easy.² I can accept it all MY OWN WAY – not 'literally' but symbolically: its all quite easy and beautiful. But unless one really believed in a god even thought it is tempting to have that great inward gate opened – it is no good.

I mean to make Life wonderful if I can. Queer, Jones, Ive always a longing to *heal* people and *make them whole*, enrich them: thats what writing means to me – to enrich – to give. I want to do it in Life too.

I shall tell Jack this – sometime. Perhaps not for a long time. Perhaps I shall just leave him to find out. But you cant live near me & not know it & yet I could not bear you even to refer to a *book* I read. Do you understand this? I am so sorry to be so dreadfully secret & sensitive.

But I tell you for another reason too – and thats because youre my 'sworn friend' as they say. Jones – I am not at all well yet – terribly nervous and exacting and always in pain – but Ill get over it. But I need you and I rely on you – I lean hard on you – yet I can't thank you or give you anything in return – except my love. You have that always.

Katie.

MS BL. *MLM*, 149.

[1] Ida Baker noted on the manuscript, 'a letter left for me in her room, where I went each day'.
[2] KM was obviously impressed by the lives of her cousin Connie Beauchamp and her friend Jinnie Fullerton. Already on 8 Feb. she had made the notebook entry: 'I for the first time think I should like to join the Roman Catholic Church. I must have something!' (*Journal* 1954, 198.)

To J. M. Murry, [6 March 1920]

[Villa Flora, Menton]

I heard from Violet today & will reply via you tomorrow.

Dear Bogey

Your Monday note has just come (written at 200 miles an hour, I should think.) I haven't received the A. yet. My proof came last night: a thousand thanks for correcting it so minutely.[1] What a printer they have! Im posting it back today together with a review. Dearest please do not accept any invitations for me – will you. I am coming HOME because *I want to be with you* and in my room & not to spend part of the summer in Mrs Locke Ellis' house, tho' its very kind of her.[2] Id rather stay where I am than do that. And please dont ask anybody to dinner the day I come home or for the week following – not Brett – or anybody except of course my dear little 'brudder' whom Im going to ask to meet me at the station. I have not the remotest desire to see anybody but you and Arthur and my cats & the house and Sorapure and the willows and the shepherdess[3] and Violet & Gertie. I am afraid you don't know how homeloving I am & how it thrills me to think – oh bliss untold! of opening the grey door & being in the hall! My 'perfect times' here are only *pastimes*. So dont bother to cry 'hurrah' – funny one.

At the moment (and yesterday) Im in bed with rather a severe chill & fever but everybody is looking after me so 'hurrah' I suppose again ——

Yours for ever

Wig.

MS ATL. *LJMM*, 492–3.

[1] The proofs from *Art and Letters* of 'The Man Without a Temperament', which she had particularly asked to see before it was published.
[2] The wife of Murry's recent acquaintance, the occasional poet Vivian Locke-Ellis, had invited the Murrys to stay in their seventeenth-century home near East Grinstead.
[3] A favourite clock.

To J. M. Murry, [7 March 1920]

[Villa Flora, Menton]

My darling Bogey

After two days and nights of misery trying to make bricks out of straw I was forced to give up. I cant write on novels unless I can have some novels to write on. You see I have no intellectual stimulus here & my nerves are still so overstrained that they just fail me.

I am also exceedingly worried about you. Except for that hurried note in reply to my important letter you have not referred to it: you have not talked it out at all. I tried my very best darling to make you realise how deeply I felt it for you but I am afraid I did not succeed at all. But try not to forget that we are *all in all* to each other and that you when you 'confess you are selfish' and talk of the no compensations in London you are saying things which I not only know just as deeply just as finely as you – we have talked of them all in the deepest intimacy – but you hurt my love in speaking as though I were a stranger. Must you? Try not to! It is like your other letter saying: 'My days are very laborious & I am none too pleased with Life.' Can't you feel how these words strike another? Oh so strangely and sadly, dearest.

As soon as I get back (in 7 weeks) I shall arrange everything for you. I think the Cottage idea is the right one & we shall have a whole month there in the summer. L.M. & I will make it perfect. I do not ask you to spend one penny on P.V. I never have. All that we buy will be for the Heron & P.V. is our storehouse. Remember this, Bogey dear. I have already spent 200 francs on most lovely things for us here – cups, saucers, trays, boxes, exquisite oddments. I bought them with such deep joy but your letter makes me feel perhaps my joy was a little premature & you will not care so greatly. Its a great effort to love just now – isn't it? Ah, Bogey –

Darling – do not drink more wine than you need.¹ It does you great harm. Won't you get Sorapure to give you some injections as you are over tired? May I write & ask him to come & see you?

And will you tell me in your very next letter whether you want Waterlow to stay on. As regards his money – I will pay the £13 a month. If you want him we must fit him in somehow. It is for you to say but please tell me won't you?

I feel your fatigue is dreadful. Take care of yourself my precious boy & remember that in seven weeks please God you will be able to hand over many of your worries to your own devoted for ever –

Your very own
Wig.

Do confide in me if you possibly can – won't you?

MS ATL. *LJMM*, 493–4.

---

¹ KM also sent a telegram which does not survive asking Murry not to drink any more wine. He answered on 11 Mar., 'Now that Ottoline's parties are over there's no need.' (Murry, 292.)

To J. M. Murry, 10 March [1920]

[Villa Flora, Menton]
March 10th.

My dearest Bogey

Please reply to all of this in detail for I shall be home now in six weeks and I must know certain things.

(A) I have just received a letter from you about your country expedition with Brett. I am in complete agreement about the cottage. As long as you can find one L.M. and I will do the rest. But I am certainly not well enough to spend the 6 months (and not 4 as you ever so airily suggest darling!) in a cottage. As I have already told you I return to England on the 30th of April & do not leave before November. I must ∴ have Portland Villas and I beseech you to realise that QUITE DEFINITELY. I long to spend a country holiday with you but I intend when I return to see Doctor Sorapure, to go very slow and certainly it were impossible for me to pass those 6 months in the country. We shall have to make a financial scheme by which this will be 'easy'; I am sure we can. (Does 2 months make so little difference to you? Darling, what a queer lover I have!)

(B) P.V. is too small to contain Waterlow during the months that I am there, in my opinion, and I would very very much prefer to have our own home for those months. I long to be alone and at home with you more than ever I did. And I am afraid I do not like Waterlow at all – or his wife. I distrust him. But the question of space and our own intimacy makes it I think impossible. If you agree will you please tell him immediately to leave P.V. in the last week in April so that there will be time to rearrange the rooms & so that Violet can clean them. If I do not hear from you in regard to this I shall be quite at sea.

(C) About Violet. You 'ignored' my plan. Did you give her my letter?[1] How shall I write to her if I dont know? And I must write at once and make arrangements for my coming home. Did you discuss my plan with her? I know you received it for it was in the letter you in part answered.

I cannot tell you, my darling Bogey, how distracting it is not to know these things. You write to me as though I had been away 8 years.

(D) We shall do all that is necessary to the house & don't buy anything till I return – will you dearest?

(E) Please ask Sullivan to review my story if it is not too late.

Well, darling, I am sorry to worry you but I am so very very anxious to know these things. I felt when you talked of my 8 months away as though you hardly cared if I ever came home again. It *did* hurt!

Yours for ever
Wig.

MS ATL. *LJMM*, 494–5.

[1] This letter to the maid at Portland Villas does not survive.

To Richard Murry, [c.13 March 1920)

[Villa Flora, Menton]

Of course I don't now how to light a fire with damp wood, damp paper and 1 match BUT please reply telling me how to as who knows how soon I may have to do it (do you see the hint conveyed in these words?)

Villa Flora | Menton.

Giant Heron

Ill get you a corduroy coat if I can & send it packing. Im very very happy to have your letter. Please note: Seats is booked in the train *if* the train goes for April 27th and I do hope, time and tide permitting, you will meet me at the station – will you? Isn't it gorgeous to think we have 6 months in front of us and whats to prevent you and me from flitting over the heath & while *he* draws & paints enchanted landscapes *she* lies on the grass & tells him about the lions & tigers & crocodiles & boa constrictors that she used to feed under the palm trees at Mentone. Do you know the heron has got beautiful blue legs? I read that the other day.

You speak of the sadness of peoples minds being as they are. Yes, it is dreadful. I read Jack's article on John[1] it was very good & its tragic to think a painter can sin against Art. But lets remember the 'credit side' − and work for that. I have a real horror of the 'John crew' in London and of all those traitors to Life − for thats what they really are.[2]

Your little drawings are most awfully nice. Ill draw you some palms, there are so many different kinds. My favourite tree I really think, tho', is the lemon tree. Its far more beautiful than the orange. And then the prickly pear has a lot of drawing: its a *very* queer affair & then there's the pepper tree hung of course with pepper pots − but I wish you were here to sneeze at it with me.

Jack seems so very busy that he never has time to write me a real letter. I miss them so! For the Tig you know is an animal which removed from its native soil, however golden the cage & however kind & charming the people who hand it things through the bars or even pat it, LONGS for fat envelopes to eat and when left without them she finds it an awful effort not to just creep into a corner and pine. But it can't be helped. I have asked Jack for them so often that Im sure he'd send them if he had them − he just hasn't − that's all.

Will you be quite changed when I come back. Please carry something that I can recognise you by such as − an emerald green handkerchief printed with a design of pink shrimps *or* a walking stick [Drawing of crooked stick with large bow on top.] tied with a large bow of pale blue ribbon. No, Heaven bless you I shall know you anywhere and you'll know me. Here's one kind of palm. [Drawing of four different palm trees, one with fruit under which she has written '*dates* in the middle'.] No I cant draw them I must wait until I go out & do them from nature. [Drawing of female figure with parasol standing looking at two palm trees, sun above, cat running behind.]

Yours ever
Katherine.

MS R. Murry. *LKM* II. 30−1.

---

[1] Murry had written 'The Modernity of Mr. John', in the *Nation*, 6 Mar. 1920.

[2] KM painted an acerbic picture of the artist Augustus John and his women friends in a letter to Ottoline Morrell in July 1917. See *CLKM* I. 316.

To J. M. Murry, [14 March 1920]

[Villa Flora, Menton]

Just got your telegram about Sydney.[1] God bless you my darling – I don't know what to say. It was FEARFULLY IMPORTANT.

'House' letter.

My Precious dear,

I hasten to answer your letter (Thursday night) about the house. Look here, we can decide practically nothing while I am away but the main lines Bogey must be arranged ———

I dont see how you *can* have Waterlow. Where is he to sleep? I must have the south bedroom, Ida the small room & you *must* have your dressing room with a little bed in it in case I have to sleep alone. But quite apart from that, oh Bogey the idea is *detestable* to me. Surely he'd understand that he can't be there in the summer. It seems to me so sensible. The house is *much* too small & the bathroom, lavatory & so on aren't a bit suitable. But the chief question is I cannot put to you too strongly my desire to be HOME and he is NOT part of my home. I want to dine "en famille" – to be alone with you – to have all the rooms. Ill leave the winter scheme & Violet & Roger en l'air until I return. I can see you would rather I did. Its a poor look out to let the house furnished I must say as I want it to be so lovely but that must be as you wish. At any rate I cannot consider for one moment a furnished house in the country for the summer! Oh, you dont understand me a tiny bit. Im in furnished houses all winter. P.V. is HOME. I want to be there with our things – our cats – our own little bits. I CANT GO ANYWHERE ELSE. Lets go to your cottage and well make that cottage perfect & have a month in it but I must have my own home. I cant be without it. You must decide what you like in the winter. If you would prefer rather dingy rooms & your cats (who will look after *them*?) and who will look after you? No, we really had better not discuss all this till I return.

Ill write to Violet leaving all plans 'pending'. I rely on you to get rid of Waterlow – and to let us be alone for those six months. ⟨Heavens! What a request. I would have thought you could not have borne to share our life with him in the little while we are together.⟩ If you would rather not – let me. Ill write at once. But it must be done at once. *Please wire me* if you would rather I wrote or not – will you? But let me at least have our life together unspoilt by strangers for the little time we have together. Does that sound too "queer" to you? Please at any rate try & leave it all till April 30th and DONT unsettle Violet. I don't think you know how we depend on her. No, dearest love – the only thing is to wait but to get Waterlow out if you can or if not let me explain to him AT ONCE.

Your own
Wife.

——————→ A *heart* flying to greet you & panting after the water brooks.[2] Ill have to add to this. Marie has just brought your telegram about Waterlow. Im so happy I have turned a Katherine wheel & feel inclined to cheer. *Just wait till I get home* thats all the best. And we shall be alone & all the house ours and a perfect table & the new cups & saucers with their flowers & fluting. And the windows shall be open – youll be in old clothes, Ill be in fair ones – Wing & Athy there – fruit in our italian dish – HAPPINESS happiness. We'll be really truly alone. Ill be able to pick up your hand, look at it – kiss it – give it back to you. Ill say Boge my own, youll say yes Wiggiechik? We'll look at each other and laugh. Wing will wink at Athy and pretend to play the fiddle –

Oh I love you

Je t'aime

Wig.

MS ATL. *LJMM*, 495–6.

[1] Murry acceded to KM's demand that the Waterlows leave Portland Villas.
[2] 'As the hart panteth after the water brooks, so panteth my soul after thee, O God.' Ps. 42: 1.

To J. M. Murry, [17 March 1920]

[Villa Flora, Menton]

I am glad that Waterlow has been so decent Boge & I fully accept all you say. At the same time . . .

Dearest Bogey

I have just received your Sunday letter answering my questions. Thank you darling. Now we'll cry PAX till I do come home – its so soon now. At the same time I had a letter from Brett. I hesitated before opening. I felt it was not going to be pleasant . . . & it wasn't. She told me all about the 'orgies' and the 'drink' & the parties etc. I had known more or less before, but I do wish she had left me with my 'less'. I could never never be part of such a world, dear Bogey, however desperate I felt. A great gulf separates me from it for ever. And then that precious Arthur writes that HE thinks the sun has risen over the Heron and will never set. Well, I hope it wont, for him. I shall do my very best to make him feel it is there and bright and warm when I come home. Don't ever let him see the 'orgies' or wine parties, will you Boge?

Poor Brett. She asks me to forgive her. Of course I forgive her – but she ought to take herself in hand. She cant afford to drift. And one cant fall drunk "into a Lav" & then talk of the beauty of Cinnamon & Angelica. I do feel so very deeply the need for dignity in this present Life. Its the only protest one can make – to be dignified and sincere and to – somehow keep *love* of human beings in ones heart. Really, its no wonder that people are so unhappy. Well, I cannot afford to judge any man. And after all I have lived another remote and different Life. My eight months are like eight years. The "girl you left behind you"[1] really did die after all in that Casetta and is buried there for ever.

My dearest little mate – we shall have a month together in the summer all alone – and peaceful beyond words. We shall lie in the grass & look up at the clouds and play soldiers & you shall wear a daisy in your buttonhle & we'll blow some o'clocks[2] & tell lady birds to fly away home.[3] That is MY kind of gaierty, Bogey darling.

Take care of yourself and don't forget that I love you 'absolutely', and that I am

Your own
Wig.

You see that combines a kiss ordinary and a heart with an arrow. It is ∴ a very powerful magick . . .

MS ATL. *LJMM*, 496–7.

[1] An Irish melody with the title 'The Girl I Left Behind Me' was printed in 1810; the present words by Samuel Lover in 1855.

[2] To 'play soldiers' is the children's game of attempting to knock off the plaintain heads of one's opponents; to 'blow o'clocks' is puffing the seeds off dandelions.

[3] The children's rhyme which contains the old adjuration for ridding oneself of troublesome spirits: 'Ladybird, ladybird, fly away home, | Your house is on fire, your children are gone.'

To Dorothy Brett, [18 March 1920]

Villa Flora | Menton

Dearest Brett

There is no question of 'forgiving'. If there were it is I who should ask it of you for having written to you so unpardonably 'frankly'. Of course you couldn't reply! I shouldn't have shown my wounds: I should have shown you only bandages but at that moment there seemed to be no bandages to show. But you must forget the letter: I am so deeply ashamed of it. If it does still exist, tucked in your desk somewhere – *will you please burn it.*[1]

I am going back to England at the end of next month & staying until the end of October when I return *here*. Here is a villa owned by relatives of mine: its an exquisite house with an enchanted garden and we are very very happy. We bask in the sun, picnic on mountain tops, go for long long drives. And the country is in its full beauty – flashing white cherry trees among the silver olives, the orange & lemon groves in perfection – the pink & white almond & blue rosemary still in flower and all the little flowers and plants – myriads of hosts. Sometimes we drive to Monte Carlo and shop and eat ices and look at the poor gay world at the Casino, or we buy *hats* – spring hats – this villa seems to have a hat complex at the moment. All this is so far away from London. I confess, Brett, that I *hate* the 'orgies' and gossip. But then I have been away for at least 8 YEARS and in that time I have seen and felt so much else.

This is the place for working. My lovely room, full of sunshine looks over the broad gardens ablaze with cinerarias today – over to the sea. It is so wonderful to think I shall come back here next Autumn. Why don't you try for a winter in the South? If I were a painter I should never spend those dark days in London. One needs to be *renewed*: thats one of the secrets of life, I think.

Well, dearest we shall meet this Spring at 2 Portland Villas. I long to make the house really nice. I am afraid poor M. has had an uncomfortable winter but perhaps his gaierty has not made him realise it too much.

Be happy. Be well.

Yours ever
Tig

MS Newberry. Unpublished.

<hr>

[1] Brett destroyed the embarrassing letter to which KM refers.

To Anne Drey, [c.18 March 1920]

Villa Flora | Menton.

Anne

I must reply paid but don't you bother to. Ive got eight golden pages from you and I have just eaten the perfect infant. Chère chère!!!

What a being to have produced. My three new spring hats are off to the darling. There he sits – absolutely confident that the ancient incredible old world is spinning round because he is sitting there and just laughing at the joke of it all. Let me love him when I come home. Bless his fingers and toes. Tell him he has an Aunt Katherine who cant look at him without turning into a kind of rainbow smile. Darling – to use our private, old time language I think you have absolutely boxed it as far as the baby business is concerned. Tell him Ill turn catherine wheels if hell laugh at me and tell him that his mother has really been whiffling[1] to some purpose!

Im leaving here April 27th and coming to England until the fin d'Octobre when I return here. Ill be in Hampstead for the summer. We must meet soon. Im *ever* so much better & can walk and talk but part of my left lung is gone and that means my heart is not a boxers heart & Ill never be able to climb trees or run or swim again. Isn't that a bit steep of Almighty God. Im always praising him too, but there you are – Im terribly happy all the same and I don't *think* the world has lost an athlete darling – do you?

The weather here is simply supreme. Its summer – hot enough for cold chicken un peu de salad, champagne & ice cream all of which are very much here! The flowers are marvellous Anne. We go for picnics up among the mountains and long day excursions by motor. We fly into Monte & buy hats for some reason "c'est l'heure des chapeaux" at present & hats seem to be flying in the air – a whiff of the Rooms gives one civilization encore & the bands the gay frocks the children pelting the car with tiny bouquets – all seem part of the spring picture. All the flowers I share with you & the lemon groves & orange trees. I see little houses perched up on the wild hills & dream we are there sur la terrasse. I shall always love you like that. When the light is lovely I think 'Anne' would see it & when a funny old man stands in the middle of the road cursing at his goats its a drawing by Anne – Tell le cheri he is going to have a lapin niçois brought home for him that waggles its ears *so* beautifully that you have to shriek or die at the sight.

I am lying here with 'relations' the dearest people *only* they are not artists. You know what that means? I love them and theyve just been too good & dear to me but they are not in the same world that we are & I pine for *my own people* my own 'wandering tribe'.

I am so glad you liked my old story. A&L are publishing another.[2] I hope you'll like that. I have done a heap of work here – the sun makes one work & it just shines & shines.

Murry seems terribly busy and occupé always. I think he has nearly forgotten me by now.

My best love, dearest of women & a big big warm hug. Please serre Drey bien le main for me & kiss the Joy Baby under his left ear

for

Your

Ever devoted

Katherine.

[Drawing]
me among the Pallums . . .
X

MS ATL. *LKM* II. 23–4.

¹ A joke that went back to the time KM and Anne Drey spent together in Cornwall in May 1918, where KM was taken with the local expression 'whiffing for pollocks', for fishing with a handline. See *CLKM* II. 199 n. 3.
² 'The Man Without a Temperament', *Art and Letters*, Spring 1920.

To J. M. Murry, [19 March 1920]

[Villa Flora, Menton]

Darling Bogey,

I have just received your Monday letter. I am so sorry a faint chill sounded from mine about Mrs Locke Ellis.¹ I did not mean it to be there. And my feeling for P.V. isn't really as unnatural as you think. I *fully* enter into yours; but you see it is OUR home to me until we have another – and ∴ the centre of my affections. I am sure when you have your cottage & when L.M., Miss James, Singer & Co and Wig have spring clung P.V. youll feel it is rather nice and bearable until we have our permanent home. But you see until we do it is my home and I have lived my months away from it – away from the cats and the – no, Ill spare you. How thrilling about the table. But I see what you mean about chairs. I *said* dont buy any because I was sure you didnt want to. If you *see* any of course theyd be a joy. Those red ones are too hard for anybody to sit on. What are Heals like?² Do they 'go' with the table? Ill write to Violet about the spring cleaning. If only luggage were not such a great bore here. We are not allowed more than 100 lbs each. More than that is rejected or one has to take an extra full ticket for it. Isn't that *maddening*. Im having the china sent by rail post: its the only way. It will be a long time coming but that cant be helped. The cups are really very very lovely – big, fluted and covered with little small flowers. But I want to buy other things here and just cant because of getting them away. I shall have to wait and bring them back next year.

I have been rather lucky about clothes here and I have some very nice hats. Perhaps you may think me a rather pretty girl when I put them on but you needn't say so. They are all presents, of course.

About our holiday. What about the New Forest? And picnics in it? I hear it really is a perfect place. Would you like it? I could ask Marie to find us rooms. I cant go to awfully poky little cottages Boge – you know what I mean is – oh Blow! You know what I mean. I thought we might go to an inn – what do you think? Of course BEST of all would be a cottage but how does one find them? And we cant do for ourselves, my darling. Its no fun. We want to be free and not to have to worry about anything. What is your idea? Perhaps the Locke Ellis' know a good place. From here I feel rather helpless, you see. Its high time I did without a personal maid for a month. Yesterday I was going out driving with Bunny & I really could not dress myself. Couldn't find my hat or veil or anything. I had to ask her to lend me her nigger servant as May was out. But we must find a very simple place where we can come in with leaves in our hair . . . And what month will it be? A hot one so that we can brown nicely. I am very brown now: the sun burns today again and after the rain there is a special sparkle on everything. I wrote a review last night of 4 books of short stories – 2 columns. Its the only way to treat them – I mean to do them by the bunch.[3] How you have had to work! Bogey – you *must* have your holiday. Would it be too expensive & unpractical to go to Ireland? Get Beatty[4] to find us a place? I feel it would be such a thorough change for you but on the other hand it is a waste as far as cottage getting is concerned & – youre english & I want to see the English summer country. But you must have a *complete* rest & Id like you to have bathing or boating –

I am very anxious for you to send me a copy of Prelude if you can. Will you? And darling if you can send back B.C.'s [Beatrice Campbell's] Christmas card I can get a *perfect* frame for it here – in any colour. I wish you would. Is that possible? Just slip it into the pages of Prelude: that would be all the best. Mrs Dunn's millionaire husband arrives today. His name is James Dunn[5] & he has just floated the British Cellulose Company with 2 millions of treasury money to help him. L-G bought and old Squiff bought as well.[6] A powerful fellow – a very bad man, I imagine. We (J. C. & I) smell a cloven hoof already. But that doesn't interest Bogey. Are the tulips above ground. How is our raskal?[7] Do you love him as much as ever? And Athy? The Chaucer is exquisite: I know the poem. I remember it.[8] I read Alexander Smiths essay on Chaucer yesterday: its very good.[9] Hes a very pleasant fellow. Goodbye for now my blessed one.

Your very own little

Wig.

MS ATL. *LJMM*, 497–9.

[1] In his letter of 15 Mar. Murry remarked on 'a faint chill in your note' of 6 Mar., responding to the Locke-Ellises' offer of hospitality.

[2] The same letter from Murry reported his buying a new table which meant they would also need new dining-room chairs. He had been to look at some at Heal's in Tottenham Court Road.

[3] Her review of three volumes of short stories, *The Clintons and Others* by Archibald Marshall, *The Surrender and Other Happenings* by Mary Gaunt, and *A Bit at a Time* by Dion Clayton Calthrop, appeared in the *Athenaeum*, 2 Apr. 1920.

[4] Her old friend Beatrice Campbell (see *CLKM* I. 262 n. 1), who lived just out of Dublin. Murry had mentioned on 26 Feb. meeting her husband Gordon Campbell, Lord Glenavy, after some years.

[5] James Dunn (1875–1956), a Canadian trained in the law, who became Chairman and President of the Algonia Steel Corporation, Ontario. He had substantial British investments, and was made a baronet in 1921.

[6] David Lloyd George (1863–1945), Welsh Liberal MP who, after a career as Chancellor of the Exchequer, Minister of Munitions, and Secretary of State for War, took over from Herbert Asquith (1852–1928) as Prime Minister in Dec. 1926. Asquith's generous drinking habits explain his soubriquet of 'Squiffy'.

[7] Their cat, Wingley.

[8] On 19 Mar. Murry quoted Chaucer's *Troilus and Criseyde*, iii. 1205–11.

[9] Alexander Smith (1830–67), Scottish poet and essayist. His essay 'Geoffrey Chaucer' was included in *Dreamthorp*, first published in 1863, and reissued as an Oxford World's Classic, with an introduction by Hugh Walker, in 1914.

To J. M. Murry, [20 March 1920]

[Villa Flora, Menton]

Darling,

Sullivans a wicked liar. I never said more than two years.[1] Kill him & pay no attention to his dead groans. Oh you are working too hard much too hard far too hard & its still five weeks before I am home. I am so impatient now. I want to be *there* with you. Its High Time you were looked after and not by substitutes but by your own Heronia. Can you keep going till April 29th. Then you must just throw everything at me. Once you get your cottage it will be better.

> Come up here o dusty feet
> Here is faery bread to eat
> Here in this enchanted room
> Children you may dine
> On the - ˘ - of broom
> And the smell of pine.[2]

I forget it & its not good but it rings in my ears – faëry bread – I feel you ought to be nourished on it – and you ought to push under your plate all the horrid old city winter crusts. Precious love, at a wave a week my slow boat has five waves to get over.

Im waiting for Ida to come for my reviews and a telegram for you. Im furious about Marie D.[3] For Heaven's sake tell her you are too busy. Shes attached fast to the horrid Trinders.[4] Shell never be allowed to sink. Why should you have to worry about her. I am so angry with Chaddie that I feel inclined to throw my inkpot from here to Wooden Hay.

Ida has been and gone with the reviews and telegram. The cannons are being fired for the royal wedding at Monaco.[5] Monaco is very romantic! Last night it & Monte were illuminated & there were Bengal lights & a torchlight procession & serenades under the palace windows & a great ball in the gardens. I always wish in a way we were Prince Bogey of Heronia and the Princess Wig. You would have made a good Prince . . . but I wouldn't have been up to much.

Bunny Dunn is revealed as a Beatrice Hastings of the worst kind. She is frightfully jealous of me & has been telling disgusting lies behind my back & altogether behaving so odiously that I cant even *look* at her. Happily she returns to the Ritz & Claridges[6] in a day or two and she don't signify. But Society women when they do turn and are not well bred take a good deal of beating, Boge. Ive got her presents for good and all & I dont really care.

Oh, its such a day – the sea purrs. Its so hot & fine and golden. You would bathe & brown & youd eat oranges with me in a green shade.[7] I love and love & love you for ever. Goodbye for now my own *precious* darling. Dont forget Im coming and that I am for ever your very own little mate

Wig.

MS ATL. *LJMM*, 499–500.

---

[1] Murry wrote on 16 Mar. that 'Sullivan told me he had had a letter from you in which you said that you had to go away in the winter for years, i.e. more than two years more.' (ATL.)

[2] From Robert Louis Stevenson's *A Child's Garden of Verses* (1885), which had been a favourite book of KM's as a teenager. The stanza KM misquotes from 'Fairy Bread' reads:

> Come up here, O dusty feet!
> Here is fairy bread to eat.
> Here in my retiring room,
> Children, you may dine
> On the golden smell of broom
> And the shade of pine . . .

[3] Marie Dahlerup had recently asked Murry's advice in looking for a job.

[4] Her maternal aunt Belle, married to the shipping magnate, Harry Trinder.

[5] Celebrations for the wedding on 19 Mar. of Princess Charlotte-Louise of Monaco, Duchess of Valentinois, to Pierre, Count of Polignac.

[6] Two opulent London hotels, the Ritz in Piccadilly, and Claridges in Brooke Street, Mayfair.

[7] A conflation of two memories from Andrew Marvell, 'He hangs in shades the Orange bright' ('Bermudas', 1. 17), and 'Annihilating all that's made | To a green Thought in a green Shade' ('The Garden', 11. 47–8).

To J. M. Murry, [c.23 March 1920]

[Villa Flora, Menton]

My darling Broomy[1]

Is the cottage to be ours? I do long for a telegram saying that you have secured it. It sounds a perfect little GEM & so cheap. If the worst comes to the worst we can always live there on nothing and 1d a year darling & eat the 2 acre fields. But I long to know more. Can we make a bathroom? What is the water supply? How is it heated? Can the Dairy be made an extra room? I feel we ought to attach to it a government hut for six rooms wont go far with 3 people and a maid. We cant live there *without* a maid. It sounds just what you are looking for & the position is ideal. Is there a shelter for a trap? But as we shall only be there weekends & our summer holiday we won't want a trap. A bicycle for you will do. I loved your letters today darling. I am longing to be home. It is a great strain to live away from ones own tribe – with people who, however dear they are – are not ARTISTS. These peoples minds are about 1894 – not a day later. They still talk of such-a-pretty-book & whether one can or whether one cant (OH YE GODS) have a platonic friendship with a man & (oh ye gods!) agree that you cant while the male is male & the female female!!!!!! I 'shock' them but if they knew how they shock me. Bunny talks as Ive never heard a prostitute talk – or a woman in a brothel. Her mind is a *sink*: shes sex mad. They make me feel inclined to roll up my sleeves, pin back my hair, lock the door & take myself & my knife off to the dissecting room – where all such idlers are shut out for ever.

Oh, how PURE artists are – how clean and faithful. Think of Tchekov & even Johnny's talk and Anne's laughing, generous way – so remote from all this corruption. Dearest love, let us remain chaste & youthful with our work & our life & our poetry. Even Chaddie and Jeanne wont do, you know. One can't afford to MIX with people. One must keep clear of all the worldly world. And we can do it. I feel our happiness will be simply without end when we are together again. But now that I am turned towards home I am impatient to be there. I want to make 2 P.V. perfect in its way & Ill ship out of it what we want for Broomies. But Broomies will be exquisite, too. No doubt about that.

Im deaf today – with booming noises in my head. Almost idiotic with it. It must be a slight chill. So please forgive a silly letter in answer to your two darling ones. Won't Wing love the new house. He shall go down in a bastick.

Goodbye for now dearest own. Ill try & bring the trays. I want us to have them. One thing I have got here is a present of a dressing table set of pots and so on which is the loveliest thing of its kind I have ever seen. Do you like your pen tray? I have bought 2 more for writing tables. PLEASE SAY.

Du reste je t'aime de tout mon coeur – je suis pour toujours – toujours – mon bien-aimé.

Your
Broomy I.

Broomy regina.

MS ATL. *LKM* II. 24–5; *LJMM*, 503–4.

---

[1] Murry wrote on 20 Mar. that he had found a cottage called 'Broomies' on North Common, Chailey, Sussex, half-way between Hayward's Heath and Lewes, which he thought ideal for their life in the country.

To J. M. Murry, [24 March 1920]

[Villa Flora, Menton]

[*Across top of letter*]
Booked Tickets for April 27th. There happened to be 2 first class returned for that date (wagon lits). After that there are no seats until the end of May. Rendall says I must not stay here for the month of May: its too enervating. So we shall be home about *May 29th Victoria 9 p.m.* So will you see that Waterlow knows in time for the rooms to be put right again? The more I think of it Boge the more I realise he mustnt be there. The house is much too small and besides I cant help it, I feel he is my enemy and I greatly dislike him.[1] The luggage complication is awful. We can only take 100 lbs each & Ive bought all these things which *must* come. I wanted to buy 2 trays – large – one blue inlaid with cream and one silver grey with black & white inlay – VERY exquisite – 40 francs each – but perfectly *exquisite*.
My precious Bogey
    I had 2 such lovely letters from you yesterday – one written on Wednesday and the other on Thursday. They were quite *old-fashioned* letters, telling me things and they brought us so near together. I read & re-read them. Thank you, my very own. About the novels. Id rather do them until I come home. Then we can talk it over.[2] But youve sent me enough now to go on with & I *do* hope to work more this week. Its all I can say. I feel very refreshed today and my chill has quite gone. Rendall (the doctor man) had a talk with me on Friday evening. He says I do absolutely right to go back to England now & to return here in November & this time next year I *ought* to be as well as I ever shall be i.e. as well as Mother was. She & I seem to be *exactly* the same: my

heart trouble I mean is just like hers. I don't mean my temporary Casetta heart trouble for thats gone but my permanent kind, love which will never go. You see part of my *left* lung n'existe plus – so my heart has to do a two man's job to pump the blood through quickly enough to oxygenate the system. It can do it of course but it wont bear strain. I mean it wont bear violent exercise ever, so if a bear runs after me you *must* run after the bear & not climb your juniper tree. But I can walk and could even ride when my arthritis is better and can do all normal things *at my own pace*, thats all. I have written to Father about this because I must have my £300 a year for life certain. And I must work no end but I am very very happy – and if all is well between us, my own, we shall have our wonderful life: it will be far more wonderful than we imagined. Oh, how I long for it! Here, I could not be more exquisitely cared for and loved and spoilt. They are more than sweetness & goodness to me in every way and the maids are the same – & the Doctor is a treasure of kindness BUT I want to [be] alone with you – quite alone with my own Bogey for ever so long – away from *everybody*. Id like a tiny baby house where just a little boy brought the milk an butter & an old man came selling cream & raspbugs & we sat at the door in the evening & read poetry[3] . . . Thats *my* heaven: to have you to myself. Nothing less would do. Lets have a month of it – oh *do* let us. Nobody else, though. I felt in these 2 letters that perhaps you hadnt forgotten after all what we used to be to each other darling and that made me long to have you near . . . Goodbye for now. Tickets are taken for April 27th. After that there are no more seats till the end of May. Ill be back by the 29th 9 p.m. Victoria.

Your own
Wig.

MS ATL. *LJMM*, 501–3.

[1] Although this is a point KM reiterates, there is no evidence that Sydney Waterlow was in any way her 'enemy' or acted against her interests.

[2] That is, whether she would continue with her weekly reviewing for the *Athenaeum*.

[3] A half memory, perhaps, of her depiction of such an 'ideal' setting-up house, and its ambiguous conclusion, in 'Something Childish But Very Natural', a story she wrote in Paris in 1914, but which was published first in the posthumous volume whose title Murry took from that story.

To J. M. Murry, [25 March 1920]

[Villa Flora, Menton]

My dearest Bogey

I was reading your letter so happily this morning until suddenly I came across your remarks about Beatrice Hastings.[1] Darling, your

memory is very short lived. Yes, it is true, I *did* love B.H. but have you
utterly forgotten what I told you of her behaviour in Paris – of the last
time I saw her and how because I refused to stay the night with her
she bawled at me and called me a femme publique in front of those
filthy frenchmen? She is loathesome & corrupt & I remember very
very well telling you I had done with her, explaining why &
recounting to you how she had insulted and abused me. I should have
thought you could not have forgotten those things. Indeed I shall
never forget your enemies – never forgive them – never forget if you
tell me you have been insulted. London is a veritable sink of
corruption if such mists gather & mislead your fine & pure
understanding.

But darling, even though as you say you cannot cope with the world
– don't for god's sake for that reason go to meet the world in any way.
Withdraw. Be morose. Be silent. But oh Bogey Do be proud. What is
our love worth if it hasn't taught us *pride* if we don't defend each other
and keep the shield bright for each other. Your honour is my honour;
Ill not betray you. Ill defend you: Ill keep very very straight & good
because I am a Heron. I will NOT be caught on their lime twigs even
for one moment. Love, you are too lenient. Is it much to ask you to be
yourself & to condemn what you don't approve of? Those horrible
parties of Ottoline when you were gloomy with wine.[2] Oh how hot &
ashamed I am to think those sniggering fools could so egg you on!
Wouldn't you rather it were said of us 'Try as Lady A. did she could
not persuade Middleton Murry to attend her parties or if he did his
despair was manifest' than 'he came & was perhaps a trifle more
gloomy than was natural'. Oh I am so deeply truly anxious that we
shall be an example & in our small way hand on a torch. I could *never*
– or I swear I never will – attend such functions unless I am my most
sincere self. Ill keep away & make enemies by silence rather than by
the words I wish I hadn't said. It is really a fault in your nature that
you are not proud enough. Will you one day forget & forgive
Lawrence – smile – give him your hand? Oh that I should dare to
write that.[3] Forgive me. But my own, do I beseech you keep clear of
bad people until I return. Be fastidious. HURT bad people – rather
than be hurt by them. Remember that B.H. is bad, has insulted us –
insults us worse by thinking she has only to write to you for you to wag
your tail.

I think I am too changed. Perhaps you will think Im too exacting
altogether & that it cant be done. Well, if it can't, if we cant remain
pure – let us not try & be artists. Thats all. I have such a profound
respect and reverence for our work & for *the universe* – for all that is
being discovered, for all who really seek the truth that I want to
belong to them *alone*. And if you muddle up Ottolines parties – no, no

more of them. Brett should be ashamed of herself to tell me she 'fell into a Lav'. What does she expect me to say to that? Must I admire – pity – grin? I turn away in disgust. But will you, my gentle Knight please defend me against my enemies – and I shall defend you and keep our name unspotted.

Let us be GREAT – FAMOUS Broomies[4] through & through.

I solemnly warn you that if you stir B.H. you will discover such a nest of serpents that you will repent it. Dont forget *Our Pride.* Not that shes so important in herself; its what she stands for. Dont you see?

Broomy II.

MS ATL. *LJMM*, 504–6.

[1] Murry wrote on 22 Mar. that he had received a card from KM's old friend and now bitter enemy, Beatrice Hastings (see *CLKM* I. 97, 109, n. 1), asking for work on the *Athenaeum*. 'She's no friend of mine, it's true; but you, I know, have memories of & feelings towards her. She must, I suppose, be hard up to apply to me even in the most formal way. I'd be willing to give her something; but, you see, I never thought anything of her work . . . I wait for your suggestion.' (Murry, 298.)

[2] Murry's letter had recalled 'the impossible people' at Lady Ottoline Morrell's parties, and that his drinking at them 'was the best way out of the difficulty' (Murry, 297).

[3] KM's suspicion was correct. Murry was to write *D. H. Lawrence: Two Essays* in 1930, and *Reminiscences of D. H. Lawrence* in 1933, finding much good to say about Lawrence, who 'had been my greatest friend'. (F. A. Lea, *The Life of John Middleton Murry* (1959), 118.)

[4] 'Broomies' joined the 'Heron' in their private language to suggest an enduring happiness together, a private life of insulated freedom.

To J. M. Murry, [26 March 1920]

[Menton]

FORGIVE MY EXTRAVAGANT WIRE YESTERDAY![1]

Text Murry, 301.

[1] The earlier telegram, which KM apologizes for in her next letter, does not survive.

To J. M. Murry, [26 March 1920]

[Villa Flora, Menton]

My little King of Broomy Castle,

Ever since I sent that long wire Ive been ashamed of it: it wasn't the wire to send *you*. Forgive me, please. This afternoon a wave of rage against myself seized me so I put on my ta-ta & went off to the poste & sent another. I couldn't *bear* to think you had that odious one for the weekend. It was so wicked of me not to have considered that your intentions were perfect and that you are too busy, my precious dear, to remember everything. Forgive me again & please kiss and be friends. Im a wicked Wig who flies off at tangents. Ill try not to . . . Being out, & full of love, desperately in love in fact I went & bought a tray – about the length of this page, about ¾ the breadth, a divine shade of blue with little ivory birds in ivory boughs singing all over it – A tray for letters to be handed in & cards – to be kept on the hall table – Perfeck. This made me feel slightly better. I ordered a large one for tea & then bought another, small & square, just for handing a cup or a glass of milk – *very* lovely – silver grey with a centre design – <u>7.50</u>!! I then went & bought Connie a bouquet for her birthday tomorrow, stocks & bluets. They tied it with gold string which was very kind of them for it only came to 2.75. Then I bought a large packet of lined envelopes for 1 franc (about 5d) hailed a very spanking little voiture & came home by the sea. Came in. Had tea, cherry jam & cream cake – threw my hat up several times & caught it – remembered we start for home tomorrow a month – looked at your photo said *Boge* to it & . . . .

well, here I am. Can't get calm. Have fallen in love with a dark haired young man with beautiful hazel eyes.

I had a letter from Brett today & answered same. She was terribly sad & kept asking me to put her into the dustbin. (Like a Dickens character). Poor dear. I do hope I have cheered her up a little bit. Its the tag end or fag end of that ghastly winter, I expect.

Oh child we'll have such a July – a holiday complet as you say. What about phonetically speaking "Bewley" in the New Forest.

There's an inn there & water. One can sail in a walnut shell with a match end for a mast and an ivy leaf for a sail. I must wait & see what Marie says. We shall certainly find something & I want you to hire a horse & go for a ride every day – leaving me under a tree. Thats my idea. We shall take a camera & photograph each other, too & well go off in the morning with our lunch and our poetry book & picnic & make a fire (on est permit to make fires in the forest) and drink tea out of a muslin bag.

Do you know Bogey I love you. Yes, you know very well, Isabel. In the New Forest I expect they will think we are Newly married and give us the best of everything. Wont it be perfect? Think of summer evenings – when weve put on our slippers & had supper & Im lying down & youre sitting up & we read & then go over to the window & look at the stars. I love you much more than I used to – because Im different. But that doesn't matter. I don't expect you will notice.

I hope Wing & Athy are practising their Chorus of Welcome – I long to pick up little Wing & see his dear eyes again –

Well I must finish my review for tomorrow morning's post. Goodbye, my true love. Do please try & rest a little & DONT make any preparations for me except a car to be at the station. If Violet wants to know things just say "look here Violet Im awfully tired. Be a brick & just manage best way you can." And she will. Tell Arthur its time he wrote to me. How is he?

My own little mate I am yours for ever with all my heart & soul

Your
Wig-wife.

MS ATL. *LJMM*, 506–7.

To Dorothy Brett, 26 March 1920

Villa Flora | Menton | France
26 iii 1920

My darling Brettushka,

If I write letters which convey my feelings so ill I ought to be stopped. God in his infinite wisdom ought to touch my pen with wings & make it to fly hence from me for Ever. He ought with his Awful Breath to breathe upon the ink so that it catcheth on fire and is consumèd utterly[1] . . . Will you let me put my arms round you and give you a quick, small hug? Thats what I want you to feel I am doing *this moment* – and after that – lets sit down and talk for five minutes – I've a review to write. We shall keep our big talk until the end of Avrilo when you must come (will you?) and spend the day & bring your slippers in a satin bag as one used to when an infant and "invited out" . . .

But why can't I give you – send you for a present – this day like a pearl. There's no sun; the sky is folded, the sea moves and that is all. It is so still, the air is so gentle that every tiny flower seems to be a world unto itself. I am sitting at the window and below a silent, silver coloured cat is moving through a jungle of freesias. "There, by the Grace of God, goes K.M." – you know.

Don't feel bitter! We must not. Do let us ignore the people who aren't real and live deeply, the little time we have here. It really does seem that the world has reached a pitch of *degradation* that never could have been imagined – but we know it – we are not deceived. And the fact of our knowing it and having suffered, each in our own way *cannot* make Life – the Life of the Universe – what we mean when we stand looking up at the stars or lie watching the ladybird in the grass – or feel – talking to one we love – less marvellous. I think that we – our generation – ought to live in the consciousness of this huge, solemn, exciting, mysterious background. Its our religion – our *faith*. Little creatures that we are we have our gesture to make which has its place in the scheme of things. We must find what it is and make it – offer up ourselves as a sacrifice. You as a painter and me as a writer. What is it that urges us? Why do you feel that you *must* make *your* discovery and that I *must* make *mine*? That just because we are artists and the only free people we are obedient to some law? There's the mystery! And we shall never solve it – we shall only know a little more about it by the time we die and thats all – and its enough.

But, Brett, just because we DO feel this – I know you do, too – we cant afford to be bitter and oh, we musn't let the wrong people into our Holy of Holies. Dont think, darling, I am become an elderly fogey. I believe like anything in happiness and being gay and laughing but I am sure one can't afford to be less than ones *deepest self* always. Thats all I mean by renewing oneself – renewing ones vows in the contemplation of all this burning beauty. We belong to the Order of Artists and its a strict order but if we keep together and live together in love and harmony we'll help each other. Oh, Brett, I worship Life. I fall on my knees before Love and Beauty. If I can only make myself worthy . . .

There! I had to say these things for I cannot bear that you should feel there is a door closed between us.

I send you my love *always*

Tig.

MS Newberry. *LKM* II. 22–3

[1] 'How are they brought into desolation, as in a moment! they are utterly consumed with terrors.' Ps. 73: 19.

To J. M. Murry, [28 March 1920]

You and Arthur & me on a mule expediting.

[Villa Flora, Menton]

Old Sir John to Hell has gone
Burn, devils! Burn him!
When one side well is fried
Turn Devils! Turn him

I thought you might quote that one day. Its quite genuine & in a churchyard in the Isle of W.

My Blessed One

Its winter again – pouring rain, ghashly cold, pipes burst, oranges burst, big fires, bottils, marsala, frenzied palms. I d̲o̲ love Bogey so. Why?

Just because he is Bogey and he is mine & I am his. I dreamed last night I got home, arranged all my presents on a tray brought them to you & the ONLY one you picked out was *the Russian spoon*. "Tig what a charming spoon. Why didn't you buy ½ a dozen." And there was the tray with all the lovely things & I had to say – Dont you remember you sent it to me for my birthday? Wasn't that fearful. It really was. Country Life has come. It has some flower pictures in it. Do you know Bogey (this is literally true) flower pictures affect me so much that I feel an instant tremendous excitement and delight. I mean as strong as if a great band played suddenly. I read a description of a certain pink magnolia which grows in Asia 150 feet high – the blooms are shell pink on silver stems & there are no leaves so that it has the appearance of a great flock of flamingos. This was illustrated. Boge I REALLY nearly fainted. I had to lie down – But when I come home & show you what Ive bought you you must nearly faint too. We'd better have Arthur there with buckets of water. I love Arthur Bogey. He writes me such darling letters with small pictures in them & I love to think of him so honest and true and good – and a Boy. I think he wants the kind of spoiling he could get chez nous – not a mother's spoiling but a sisters (quite a different fing). When I have money he shall be my heir. We must also bring him here with us one year – & you & he must go climbing up in the mountains – I can go on a mule. [Drawing of a figure on a mule and two walkers with walking-sticks.] See us? the mule looks rather a silly. Knock at my door. Jinnie. "Is our little girl comfy". "Yes, very". "Are you warm enough, darling?" Now she has gone & the baby peke has dashed off with my pink mule. Its so wonderful to think I come back here *with* them in November to this same room even – Bogey you would love these women & there is *no* effort – no need to talk or to be other than your own self – absolutely. They make old age a joke – Connie is nearly 70 and shes a *girl*! Bless them but above all bless my little mate.

MS C. Murry. *LJMM*, 500–1.

To Richard Murry, [c.29 March 1920]

Villa Flora [Menton]

To Arthur of Heronia
    Greeting!
I got your letter today. It was a very special one with lovely printing on top, a darling little drawing & How to Light a Bonfire. Ill lend my hair if you like but I bet I couldn't make one. I'll keep the wind off & watch you and Wing will prowl and ᴘʀʀʀowl around. Doesn't the little small Heron sound fascinating. Yes we must have a pig sitting under the pig-tree. Talking about English flowers

> Bring hither the pink and purple columbines
> And gilly flowers
> Bring coronations and sops-in-wine
> Beloved of paramours
> Strew me the ground with daffa down dilly
> With cowslips and kingscups & lovèd lilie
> The pretty paunce and the chevisaunce
> Shall match with the faire flower delice.[1]

I quote from memory, but thats hard to beat don't you think? But I am all for feathery topped carrots – don't you love pulling up carrots, shaking them clean and tossing them on to a heap? And feeling the cauliflowers to see which one is ready to cut. Then OUT comes your knife. When I was about the height of a garden spade I spent weeks –

months – watching a man do all these things and wandering through caves of yellow butter beans and smelling the spotted speckled broad bean flowers and helping to plant Giant Edwards and White Elephants. Oh, dear, I do love gardens! Think of little lettuces and washing radishes under the garden tap. Id better stop. I just saw you climb in to a cherry tree and leaning against the trunk of the tree I saw and smelt the sweet sticky gum. But we'll have all these things.

I bought you one of the most exquisite little boxes yesterday Ive ever seen. You know how some things *belong* to people. It stood on a shelf in the shop and said A.M. so I carried it off and Ill bring it home.

Ivor B's novel has just come.[2] I say – I don't think *much* of the look of it, do you? The print is alright but the jacket & lettering . . . what is your eggspert opinion?

Its not *May*. Its *April* 29th. Victoria 9 p.m. Thats all the difference. If you knew how she longs to see her brothers!

'Broomy' – of Broomies.

MS R. Murry. *LKM* II. 29–30.

[1] KM imposes her own line arrangement on the fifth stanza of Edmund Spenser's 'A Ditty, In Praise of Eliza, Queen of the Shepherds', as Sir Arthur Quiller-Couch entitled his selection from the April Eclogue of *The Shepherds' Calendar* in her favourite source of quotations, *The Oxford Book of English Verse*. Murry wrote to KM on 4 Apr. that 'Arthur . . . says that in your letter to him you quoted a long piece of poetry about flowers. I guessed it was your favourite Spenser piece – sops-in-wine & the purple columbine. Was I right?' (ATL.)

[2] KM reviewed unfavourably Ivor Brown's *Lighting-up Time* in the *Athenaeum*, 30 Apr. 1920. The novel was published by Cobden-Sanderson, for whom Richard Murry then worked.

To J. M. Murry, [30 March 1920]

[Villa Flora, Menton]

primula & leaf

My precious little mate

Ive had three letters from you today – one before the pen tray, one after, & one about Broomies. I want you to tell me C.Y.H.S.D.[1] if you thought the pen tray at all 'special'. Because then I shall know what to buy. I think its simply exquis but perhaps I have gone a trifle mad-dog, after so long "on my own". I shant refer to Beatrice Hastings again. Its explained, isn't it, love. And now shake off Marie D. [Dahlerup] Thank Heaven she'll never be with us. Oh, please tell Tommy to take his 'sprightly stone axe' for me & bang Miss Willcocks on the head with it. Really her Balzac!!!![2] It is the last word in utter drivel. Your Miss Cavell is *superb*.[3] You're doing just what I hoped you would do in the Nation; putting big things into the scales. Its VERY good. Now dont forget to tell Whos Who all about yourself.[4] And your recreations are – what? Oh, I wish I looked over your shoulder! But be sure to do it. I shall always be *idly* turning over the pages and rereading what you say. *Dont forget to do it in time. Could you send me a copy of Prelude please?* And thank you for my bouquet in the A. for March 26th. It was a very nice one.[5] Love, I am all for Broomies. I, too, have this idea we may retire there and live on love when we are old. I love the little place. Its the right size and its remote and very simple. William & Dorothy [Wordsworth] might have lived there or any of our *own kind*. If we do have money we can always make it better and better but I am greatly desirous of our owning it (bad English). I think its *us*. We can leave it to Arthur. It seems to me nicer than anything else. I see it under the stars – so quiet – its thorn hedges spangled with moonlight – our pony cropping – my dear love at the window telling me how fine the night is. Please let us decide on it if you agree. I want it with all my heart.

I have (practically) taken a flat here. Connie & Jinnie have also taken one. They don't want to risk this huge place next year. Were in the same building on the same landing – just our 2 doors next to each other. The house is exquisite really most beautiful in very fine style.[6] It faces due south – so do all the rooms except the kitchen ones & the bonne's which is west. It looks towards the frontier – There are balconies at all the big windows. Lovely rooms – a superb bathroom & geyser & the kitchen part is shut off from the salons & chambres a couchers by big doors. There is a gas stove, 3 best bedrooms, salon, salle a manger, bonne's room, kitchen w.c. bathroom & housemaid's pantry. Theirs is identical across the way. So I am in hopes you may come out for a month next year or at least for a very peaceful and lovely Xmas. What do you think?

To revert to Broomies for a minute. If the A. gives up at the end of its two years you drop £1000 a year. Well, we want to be in a position where this doesn't matter two shakes of Wing's tail & we should be if we had a cottage like Broomy. You'd just turn into a poet & vegetable grower if you wanted to. At any rate there'd be nothing BIG to keep up or to be a drag – & you being what you are, my dearest, its always best to remember we *can* live on the cheap.

Heres supper. Its a roaring night so we are drinking champagne to put it out of mind. Connie bought me *another* hat today – that makes *six*. She must stop. She "dresses" me just as though she were my grandma and I have more clothes than ever before. "Now that would suit you, darling. Youre such a little slight thing youll only need 2½ metres & Ill have it made with just a touch of . . ." & she holds it up against my cheek. Oh, it *does* remind me of Grandma so! Its awfully sweet.

Goodnight dearest dear. I love you for ever and ever amen.

In fack I ADORE you.

 Your own Wife.

. . . Tell me how you love me in your next letter . . . You see I love you so terrifically & Thursday is the 1st and then its only 27 days – 27 bregchiks, three 'laundries'. *3* Sundays – Think of it – three Sundays and I shall be HOME. I feel quite *shy* with bliss. Youll whistle when you come in – won't you & Ill look over the stair. Then you must gallop up or Ill let down a little ladder – Well have very good dinners (all new food) & coffee & liqueurs. Oh oh oh I could go on for ever. What will you wear at the station. What hat? When I see your precious darling face & hand lifted & feet running I may fly into a 1000 pieces. Well walk arm in arm – forgetting our luggage. Will you be as happy as I will? Oh Boge!!

MS ATL. *LKM* II. 25; *LJMM*, 507–9.

[1] 'Cross your heart straight dinkum', a favourite KM expression from childhood to ensure a directly honest reply.

[2] In his regular *Nation* column, 'The World of Books', on 27 Mar. 1920, H. M. Tomlinson disclaimed any critical expertise other than a 'gimlet to test for dry rot' and 'a stone axe'. His piece concluded, 'the only essentials in literary criticism are to avoid solemnity, and to use even the stone axe with spritely joy'. Mrs P. Willcocks, an occasional writer for the paper, concluded that same week her long two-part article, 'Balzac'.

[3] Under 'Memorial or Incubus', Murry wrote in the *Nation*, 27 Mar. 1920, a strong attack on the monument erected in London to Edith Cavell, the English nurse executed by the Germans in 1917. Its taste, Murry argued, both 'traduces' the English public and is 'monstrous as a testimony to such a spirit as Miss Cavell's'.

[4] Murry had been asked to provide a biographical entry for *Who's Who*.

[5] Sullivan's review of *Je ne parle pas français*, under 'The Story-Writing Genius'.

[6] The villa Isola Bella, where KM would live when she returned to Menton in Sept. 1920. She sublet from her cousin and Jinnie Fullerton, who rented the Villa Louise next door.

To Sydney Schiff,[1] 1 April [1920]

I
IV
1920

                                    Villa Flora | Menton

Dear Mr Schiff

Last night I had a letter from Mr Grant Richards telling me that you were at Roquebrune. May I drive over and call on your wife or would you both come & take tea with me here in my room? It would be very pleasant to talk over Art & Letters.

                          With kind regards
                          Yours sincerely
                          Katherine Mansfield Murry.

MS BL. *Adam* 300, 96.

---

[1] Sydney Schiff (1868–1944), a wealthy and eclectic patron of the arts, who published largely autobiographical fiction under the pseudonym of Stephen Hudson. KM reviewed Hudson's *Richard Kurt* with muted praise in the *Athenaeum*, 7 Nov. 1919, unaware of this connection. He was also the financial backer of the periodical *Art and Letters*, and he and KM had apparently experienced some kind of editorial *contretemps* the preceding year. See p. 89, n. 2.

Schiff replied to KM's letter the next day, inviting her to visit him and his wife at the Villa Violet in Roquebrune. He delivered his reply by hand, and KM wrote across the bottom of his letter: 'Marie told me un m'sieu très grand was waiting for an answer & I went into the salon to discover the most soigné creature in the world – in the false grey flannels – waiting for me. I'm going tomorrow in a car. He seemed *horrified* by me & I don't know what he had expected. He kept saying "sit down I *implore* you. Pray forgive me imagining you could take a tram." I wish people didn't always expect me to be on the point of death. It's horrid.' (ATL.)

To J. M. Murry, [1 April 1920]

                                    [Villa Flora, Menton]

My precious little mate

April Fool's Day and only 27 days before I start for home – I think you & Wing might begin taking one bead off the counting frame each day now. Did you learn to count on a frame? and so on? I did. I remember how blue the blue beads were now. Your Monday letter came last night. It will not be at all difficult to supplement the well supply with a good colonial tank and a great tub for rain water – barrel I mean. The more I think of it the more I am in favour of a small place that we can live EASILY in – with our own eggs & chicks & fruit & veg & nothing to worry us about money. We oughtn't to take a place like the Canterbury one because I cant help feeling its a burden for people like us. Its all right *for a time* but we are in harness. And Id rather live exquisitely – dress for supper have every possession fine as fine at Broomies. We are not really & truly earth children. I want to be very comfortable (have to be) and never to do house work or horrid cooking or anything like that. Im sure I couldn't light a fire even if I tried – but I don't want us to find out were spending heaven knows what a week & have to *pull together* & manage somehow. No – lets live at Broomies when we can enlarge it a bit – keep it for our faery house until then & keep on good old poor old despised by you loved by me P.V. for the present.

My flat idea is all in the air again. For Jinnie now wants to buy this small chateau & to give me rooms in it to be my very exclusive own for next year & the year after. I am torn in two for its true the exquisite *protection* of being here no money could buy & if I had my own den it would be different. Well, Ill manage all this as I think best. Dont give it a thought. It is after all my own look out and nothing to do with you. (I mean that 'nicely & kindly' love). Jinnie wants me so much I expect I shall be here and not at Garavan. She said "one of my aims in life is [to] make you well and you mustn't deny me that." – Ive nothing to say when she puts it like that.

An awful thing happened here yesterday. Just a week ago a young woman was seen wandering about under the trees at Cap Martin & crying – all day. *Nobody spoke to her.* At dusk a little boy heard her crying for help. She was in the sea about 15 ft. from land. By the time he told somebody it was dark & she had disappeared. Her purse & jacket were on the beach. She had a *return* ticket to Nice – five francs & a handkerchief in it – that was all. Yesterday morning the sea washed her up just opposite the Villa. She came rolling rolling in with each wave & they waited till she was tumbled on the beach. All her clothes were gone except her corset. Her arms & feet were gone and her hair was bound round & round her head & face – dark brown hair. She doesn't belong to a soul. No one claims her. I expect theyll shovel her under today. Poor soul.

Wig.

MS ATL. *LKM* II. 25–6; *LJMM*, 510–11.

To J. M. Murry, [2 April 1920]

[Villa Flora, Menton]

Vendredi Saint.
My darling Boge,

Your letter on the gnu typewriter came yesterday. What a pearl it must be. Ive never seen one I liked better. It is so distinguished that its quite possible to write personal letters on it without feeling you've shouted them into the common ear – as you do with the old-fashioned kind. Two compliments flew from your letter: I am very thankful you liked the reviews. The Beresford book was *awful*[1] Bogey – dead as a tack. These people have no life at all. They never seem to renew themselves or to GROW. The species is now adult and undergoes no other change until its head feathers turn white & fall out . . . Awful!! Even if one does not acquire any "fresh meat" – one's vision of what one possesses is constantly changing into something rich and strange – isn't it? I feel mine is; 47 Fitzherbert Terrace,[2] p.e. is colouring beautifully with the years & I polish it and examine it and only now is it ready to come out of the storeroom and into the uncommon light of day.

Oh my stars! How I love to think of you and me as *workers*, writers – two creatures given over to Art. Not that I place Art higher than Love or Life – I cannot see them as things separate – they minister unto each other. And how I long for us to be *established* in our home with just a few precious friends with whom we can talk and be gay and rejoice . . . Ecce quam bonum et quam jucundum habitare fratres in unum! Sicut unguentum in capite, quod descendit in barbam, barbam Aaron.[3] (Now that surprised you – didn't it?) Im a cultivated little thing, really.

Its a cold and windy day and makes me cough. I still cough, still walk with a stick, still have to rest nearly all the time. They still talk about me as tho' I were the size of a thimble. So you mustn't expect a very large fierce girl and you mustn't be disappointed if I have to go slow. Ignore it. Take it all as part of the present me. Its nothing to worry about – and Im going to be 1000 times better as soon as Ive seen Sorapure. Now goodbye for now, my own blessed *darling* little mate. You must be very sure not to make *any* preparations for me or to add one single worry to all your worries.

Ever your own devoted
Wig-wife.

[*Across top of letter*]
I see the D.N. [*Daily News*] quotes your Nation article.[4] I feel theres a *smile* in the remarkable "It doesn't even make *him* laugh". You seem very famous nowadays. I bought a lovely early morning T tray shaped ⬭

MS ATL. *LKM* II. 26–7; *LJMM*, 511–12.

---

[1] KM's review of J. D. Beresford's *An Imperfect Mother* and R. H. Bretherton's *Two Sisters* appeared under 'Two Modern Novels' in the *Athenaeum*, 9 Apr. 1920. Her remarks on Beresford's 'pale book' concluded with, 'it's essential emptiness. The house is not furnished at all; nobody lives there. We should not be surprised if Mr. Beresford had written "To Let" on the last page.'

² Where KM lived in Wellington after her return from Queen's College in Oct. 1906, until she again sailed for London in July 1908.

³ The Vulgate version of Ps. 133: 1–2: Behold, how good and how pleasant it is for brethren to dwell together in unity! It is like the precious ointment upon the head, that ran down upon the beard, even Aaron's beard.' KM would have read it in her cousin's Missal, where the verses appear as the Gradual of the Mass for 10 Mar., the feast of the Forty Martyrs.

⁴ His piece on the Edith Cavell monument in the *Nation* on 27 Mar.

To J. M. Murry, [4 April 1920]

[Villa Flora, Menton]

Dearest Own

Easter Sunday – pouring rain 'parky' beyond words – pools in the garden, rows of galoshes in the bathroom umbrellas in the marbil basins.

I got lovely presents. A silk egg full of chocs, a silk jersey trimmed with silver, a cigarette holder, two boxes for my dressing table, a pot of white cyclamen. The eggs were in the table napkins which were cunningly contrived birds nests. The Athenaeum came at lunch, but was seized & taken by Jinnie. I haven't seen it yet. I long to. Course I couldn't go & see old Schiff in this weather. I was *very* glad I couldn't. Your Thursday letter came today, darling. I think it would be a famous idea to have sketches & stories.¹ I wrote one on the spot, called 'Daphne'² – about a plant. Ill try & bring a whole lot home – & you could stick them in under noms de plume – if you wanted to.

Yes, its true about Catholics:³ their world is not our world – my *duty* is to *mankind* – theirs is to a personal deity – a really-living KING with a flashing face who gives you rewards. I read a panegyric by a Jesuit t'other day which did astonish me – "God shall be our most passionate love. He shall kiss us with the kisses of his mouth" and so on. It disgusted me. They horribly confuse sexuality & the state of beatification – I know really a good deal about Catholics now – Of course there's no doubt Jinnie is a saint. But she has given herself up to the whole thing. She works like mad for the glory of God – lives for his glory – refers everything to God & his saints & in fact it is to her what Art is to us. But it has *warped* her – even her. I try to pretend she can see our point of view but then she says in Je ne parle pas 'how *could* you say her big belly. I feel our Lady would have disliked it so much.'⁴ *Well* – what are you to say to that?

Oh – *most* exciting. Cousin Mac (the surgeon Laurie Macgavin) lives a few miles from Broomies. Knows it. Has been over to see it wanted it for Cousin Lou & Len (the deaf & dumb one Connie's sister & brother great uncle Horatio Beauchamp's children.⁵) Mac says it was too isolated for them but its a great bargain, excellently built, could be made up-to-date at a very small expense and is just the very climate for me – He wrote "Katherine couldn't have a better spot." He has a place called Dewbridge where he lives there: I believe its lovely, and we are not far from the Leslies encampment – old Kate Leslie and her crew.[6] They know Broomies too. But don't be frightened, dearest love. I wont let them disturb you. Laurie Macgavin is a fearfully nice chap tho' – a Scottish surgeon. You'd like him & I value his opinion. We *must* have that house. If we did want to sell it any time we could always do so to one of their ramifications. But I *don't* want to sell it.

Boge could you buy an ordinary folding canvas chair for me – small – one that L.M. could carry on to the Heath for me & put under a tree – so that I can work there? Ive got the out of doors habit now & like all people with lungs I feel *stifled* indoors for long. I mean to be the Mysterious Lady of Hampstead Heath this year. Wing can be trained to carry me visitors cards cant he. Addio – precious darling love.

Ever your very own
Wig.

MS ATL. *LKM* II. 27; *LJMM*, 512–13.

---

[1] Murry wrote on 1 Apr. that he was eager to start publishing stories and sketches each week in the *Athenaeum*, and that as the only 'first-rater' KM would need to provide a lot of them.

[2] This seems not to have survived. 'Daphne', one of the unfinished stories Murry included in the posthumous *The Dove's Nest*, is another story written in 1921 – the first-person narrative of an English portrait painter visiting Wellington.

[3] Murry's letter of 1 Apr. discussed the question of KM's living with her cousin the following year, remarking, 'It *is* in the long run always impossible to live with people who are not artists; and it's absolutely impossible I'm sure in the case of Catholics who, however generous & kind they may be, are definitely anti-artistic . . . they really live in a strange world to which you have not & don't want to have access.' (Murry, 303.)

[4] KM recorded this episode more fully in a notebook entry, *Journal* 1954, 202.

[5] Horatio was the brother of KM's grandfather, Arthur Beauchamp.

[6] Distant relatives, from a connection the Beauchamps were proud of: Harold Beauchamp's paternal grandmother was the sister-in-law of the painter Charles Robert Leslie, RA (1794–1859), author of *Memoirs of the Life of John Constable* (1843).

To J. M. Murry, 6 April 1920

[Villa Flora, Menton]
6.iv.1920.

My own precious Bogey

We are motoring to Nice this afternoon – Early lunch in hats & then down come the maids with cushions & rugs for the car – the baby dog is captured "coming for nice tatas with missie" – and he growls with joy. "Has little Murry got her fur?" "Where's Connie?" – You know that kind of *upheaval*. It reminds me of my early days. May is going to look after me – The others want to shop & I cant rush even if I would so May carrying the baby dog trips along. "Oh *Ma*dam! Isn't the little pot ever so sweet – and on a *blue* tray Madam with just a *little* cloth not too big and a Mappin & Webb[1] tea service!" I can hear her already. Shes such a little gem, carries the parcels and looks after one beautifully, and the peke sits on her arm. "Now Chinnie, be a good girl, my ducksie-pet!" Does that all sound very strange to you? I love it. I *bathe* in it – and its all gay & there are flowers and music and sparkling sea and we go & have tea in a queer place and eat ice cream – and little Murry has no choice but must drink chocolate. "L'auto est là Madame."

Later. I'm in bed and have just had supper with brandy for a drink. The drive to Nice is really wonderful Boge, through Roquebrune, Monte, Eze, Villefranche, Beaulieu – but Nice is *vile*. At least the shops are. I do hate great glaring glittering glass & gold shops where one walks miles to the ascenseur & where the employées look as tho' they lived on 10 francs a month. Mountains of jumpers, haystacks of crepe de chine chemises – ugh! I retired & sat in the car & read the paper. On the way back we were stopped by the Deschanel cortège.[2] Very gay – the streets marvellously decorated – a bataille de fleurs for the gentleman. It was rather fun. We cut in after the presidential car & before La Presse & L'Eclaireur flying their flag & were part of the procession – received the salutes & flowers & Vive Madame Deschanel. We bowed very nicely. At Roquebrune we stopped for a presentation & the people crowded round gaping. Connie (the Beauchamp in her) enjoyed it very much. I wish you could have seen Monaco with the minute soldiers guarding the palace & the little pepper-tree fringed roads that lead up to it. Monaco is certainly *your* town. But oh! I do hate the middle class. Nice is the paradis des bourgeois.

All the same Boge the Riviera isn't over rated. Its superb. More than that one gets fearfully fond of it. It does in bits remind me so much of home – of N.Z. the rocks and sea and the flowers. I am afraid I do want a Broomies here as well – two tiny houses – one in Sussex one not far from Menton. Would you hate that my darling?

My darling Boge

Ive just got your note about Je ne parle pas. No, I certainly won't agree to those excisions if there were 500000000 copies in existence. They can keep their old £40 & be hanged to them. Shall I pick the eyes out of a story for £40.[3] Im *furious* with Sadler. No, Ill never agree. Ill supply another story but that is all. The *outline* would be all blurred. It must have those sharp lines. The Times didn't object.[4] As to The Wind Blows I put it in because so many people had admired it.

(Yes its Autumn II[5] but a little different.) Virginia, Lytton – and queer people like Mary Hamilton & Bertie all spoke so strongly about it I felt I must put it in. But this had better be held over till I get back. Ill never consent. Ill take the book away first. Dont worry about it. Just tell Sadler hes a fool. As to The German Governess it was *on* my list & I asked you to include it!![6] (Caught out!) But dont you worry love. It will have to wait. Of course I wont consent!

Wig.

MS ATL. *LKM* II. 28; *LJMM*, 513–15.

[1] Mappin and Webb, the china shop in Regent Street.

[2] Paul Deschanel (1855–1922), after serving as President de la Chambre for the past eight years, became President of France in Jan. 1920. He retired because of ill health the following Sept.

[3] Murry wrote on 31 Mar. reporting on a letter from Michael Sadleir at Constable asking for considerable changes in the text of *Je ne parle pas français*. See Murry, 308–9, where the letter is erroneously dated 7 Apr. See also Alpers' notes, *Stories*, 559–61.

[4] An unsigned review by Harold H. Child, *The Times Literary Supplement*, 29 Jan. 1920.

[5] Murry's letter urged KM to include in the collection 'Autumn II', which first appeared in the *Signature*, 4 Oct. 1914, and which she revised as 'The Wind Blows' in the *Athenaeum*, 27 Aug. 1920, before its inclusion in *Bliss*.

[6] 'The Little Governess' had appeared over two issues in the *Signature*, 18 Oct. and 1 Nov. 1915, and was on the list of stories for the new book sent to Murry.

To J. M. Murry, 7 April 1920

[Villa Flora, Menton]
7.iv.1920

My darling again

Its Wednesday. Im off to lunch at Roquebrune with the Sydney Schiffs[1] and to see their Gauguins and their Picassos. Your Sunday letter has come. Would you rather Arthur didn't come to the station. Tell me and tell him. Bogey, I feel I was too undisciplined about my story & Constable. I leave it to you. Youre my Cricket. If you agree to what they say – why then, alls well. (And I *DO* want the money.) Je t'aime.

Our queer correspondences again. I have steeped in Shakespeare these last days with a note book[2] – looking up every word finding what are inkles and caddises – & I have felt that we *must* read more – you & I – read together. I nearly know the sheep shearing scene from A Winters Tale by heart. Its the most *bewitching* scene – but thats one of my favourite plays. If I am strictly truthful I know nearly all of it *almost* by heart. And I began reading the songs in Twelfth Night in bed this morning early.

Mark it Cesario, it is old and plain;
The spinsters and the knitters in the sun
And the free maids that weave their thread with bones
Do use to chant it – it is silly sooth
And dallies with the innocence of love
Like the old age.
Clo: Are you ready Sir.
Duke: Ay, prithee sing. Music.
Clo: Come away, come away, death etc.[3]

Oh how that does all ravish me. I think I could listen to that for a small eternity. My dear love we must read together, read aloud to each other. Do you know, by the way, Alexander Smiths Essay on Chaucer?[4]

Goodbye for now dearest dear – What a miracle that we should love each other and love the same other loves.

Your own
Wig-wife.

MS ATL. *LKM* II. 28–9; *LJMM*, 515–16.

[1] This was the lunch postponed, because of weather, from the previous Sunday.
[2] Murry's letter on 4 Apr. had spoken of how he wanted 'gradually to work through English Literature notebook in hand' (ATL).
[3] *Twelfth Night*, ii. iv. 44–51.
[4] Already referred to in her letter on 19 Mar.

To Sydney and Violet Schiff,[1] *7 April 1920*

Villa Flora | Menton
7.iv.1920

Dear Mr and Mrs Schiff

I feel that I deceived you today about my health and I succumbed to the awfully great temptation of deceiving myself. Really and truly, thinking it over, I am afraid I am not well enough to live in that darling little flat.[2] You see, there are days when Im completely hors de combat; I can't walk a step further than I walked today and I have to take horrid and extravagant care of myself always. Sometimes I get a week when I can't move and Im always under a doctor's care & if I do go out Im supposed not to breathe the dust. This sounds ridiculous; I wish I didn't have to say it. I feel there is *plenty* of room to be well in une petite appartement but there is not enough room to be ill and I have to provide for it. When I said I had to write for pennies I didn't mean for the essential pennies but for all the luxuries which are alas! my necessities. Yes, forgive me, I was carried away today & I forgot I must behave like an invalid. But when I came in and lay down and rested I thought: "You know these things aren't for you, and you were deceiving those two dear people. You must let them know at once."

Will you forgive me? And thank you for a lovely day. Im lying here living it over and seeing in my mind's eye your garden and house & hearing the torrent – and – much more important than those things – delighting in the fact of having met you.

Yours ever sincerely
K.M.

MS BL. *LKM* II. 29.

¹ Violet Schiff (1876–1962), the sister of Ada Leverson, novelist and close friend of Oscar Wilde.
² The Schiffs had offered her the use of a flat in Roquebrune.

To J. M. Murry, [9 April 1920]

[Villa Flora, Menton]
Friday. Winter. Wind &
raging sea. Cold. Big Fire.

My very very own,

Do not overpraise me. When I read what you had written about the drawings I flew two pink flags.¹ But if you like them a little I'll do you some more – better – and put them in a frame for you when they're good enough. I entirely agree with your suggestions re je ne p.p. Please invest yourself with Full Powers, darling and forgive me for giving you so much trouble. This month will end it. This letter (Tuesday) is the most astonishingly sweet letter. Its one of those letters which make me feel quite faint for joy. I feel I *must* see you – *must* hold you, *be held*, must say "you know . . . Bogey . . . my darling" – "My darling" – thats what you are – Darling – darling – and my heart is full of love. I feel deeply your obligation to make the A. a success. It must be done. You can do it – its your duty towards your neighbour. Yes, you're a poet, but you are too true a poet not to be a poet of your time. When I heard old Schiff the other day praising the paper (praising it so rightly) and saying what you were doing for English literature I felt you *could* not let all these people down – you *must* carry the torch. They do look to you. Mrs S said "he was pointed out to us at Tom Eliot's lecture. Everybody was talking about him."

You know, even from the superficial point of view Squire isnt taken seriously: he's looked upon as a newsmonger – and you (I don't exaggerate) people feel you've got the fate of English literature in your hands, I believe. When Schiff said the other day: "I feel confident that in a few years it will make or mar a man – the criticism passed on him by the Athenaeum." Its pretty terrific – or rather – *you* are. L.M. is blowing off to the poste this afternoon with a wire re Constable.[2] Act on it darling, won't you – and if you *can* so fix things that they send me the money *as soon as possible* you will greatly oblige me. You see I am practically determined to take either a flat or small villa for next year. I want to – pay for it while the exchange is high. Not pay all – that I couldn't do but pay part of my Constable money immediately. *This is very important* to me, old boy. As it works out I think the advantages are greater in being my own mistress. Of course you can't advise me, Mr Absurdity. You're my *literary* adviser thats all. I want it to be in Menton if possible because I simply love this little place – LOVE IT. If it weren't for you England wouldn't see me again for a very long day. Id live at La Turbie in the summer & here in the Winter. But YOU are in London and so my whole heart is there until we are free enough to live between Broomies & the S. of France. Even then I don't want to live far from Menton – because I can't live all the year round away from *music* & opera especially. One can get both here and at Monte. You need never go. But Ill often take a slave and descend to either town to hear a symphony.

But above all I long for the time when we shall be together 'all the year round'. Its not yet but it will come & now we know how to receive it. Life – strange Life – teaches – or no – one *learns*. I wouldn't be without these months for anything in the world. Do you feel that? Without them we were going all wrong – getting into an entirely false position. This separation has been and will be for ever the great fact of my life – my secret when you know "something happened". No one knew what – but after that "all was changed" – I had a lovely letter from the old boy today & one from Brett – pathetic.

L.M. arrived take letter.

Goodbye darling

Own Wig.

MS ATL. *LJMM*, 518–19.

---

[1] Murry wrote on 6 Apr., after receiving her letter of *c*.30 Mar.: 'I had a letter from you this morning which contained 2 of the most adorable drawings of children I have ever seen. Seriously I consider them little masterpieces of this kind. I think the little girl is beyond words exquisite, & a marvellous piece of drawing.' (Murry, 305.)

[2] The telegram presumably anticipated the advice of Murry's letter she received the next day. 'If you think you can accept these omissions will you just wire to me "Omissions accepted," when Constables will send you a cheque immediately.' (Murry, 309.)

To J. M. Murry, 11 April 1920

[Villa Flora, Menton]

Would you LEND me your copy of Prelude[1] if you have one?

Sunday. April 11th 1920.

To Bogey of Broomies.[2]

My very own,

All yesterday, off and on, I had waves of delight at the thought of Broomies. I could not have imagined that the fact of us being real little landowners could make such an extraordinary difference. The feeling of *security* – have you got it, too? The enormous pleasure of putting up a wall if we choose or putting in a fireplace. Ill never be able to say what Broomies means and you found it – my own explorer. Its our *island*. I feel the anxiety about money in the future is lessened, too, don't you? All our geese will lay golden eggs before they become swans —— But more than anything I keep writing short prefaces & putting in the left hand bottom of page corner 'Broomies 1922'. Also "we shall be at Broomies until the fin d'Octobre when we leave for Genêt Fleuri[3] – our small villa in the South . . ." Oh, Destiny, be kind.[4] Let this be. Let these two children live happy ever after. By the way – what with these two names we shall be calling our small son Richard Plantagenet Murry if he doesn't hurry up. I see SUCH books. Golden bees fly out of them – young dandelions sprout between the pages – the critic discovers the first small aconite on page 54 and by the end of the book he is even slightly freckled. Im very silly. Forgive me.

L.M. spends all next week hunting for a villa or flat for next year. I am decided not to be with these people: and the flat I saw – perfect tho' it was – had a trifle more stairs than I like to remember. She'll find something & Ill take it, however. The weather was awful yesterday, il pleure averse today. But a bird sings & its very warm. I do hope May will be warm. Yes, my precious, well divide our time between Sussex which is you and the South of France which is me – mystically speaking. We shall never saddle ourselves with any big responsibility or large house – but well live beautifully. It makes another great joy in my coming back here this winter to know Ill have the Schiffs at Roquebrune. Do I take violent fancies? Boge? I must say at present, I love Violet Schiff. I think you would too. [You] would certainly find her very beautiful, as I do. I want you to see her and to talk to her. Shes extremely sympathetic.

Jinnie has just come in with your Thursday letter. What a shower of pearls and diamonds tumbles out of your letters! Heavens, how I do love you! Yes, you are perfectly right about the book.[5] Let it be as you wish. I am only too willing to abide by your decision. I am sorry to have given you so much trouble, dearest love.

Hardy thrills me. Its an anniversary I expect – but whose?[6] Oh, its *very* thrilling. And that he should have chosen you. I confess Id dearly love to go down & see him with you one weekend – very quietly. I wouldn't talk but Id like to see him and see you together. Its very good about the American publisher;[7] Arthur, of course rushed to tell me.

How sweet you are. You are so wonderful. I wonder people don't see the gold ring round your hair. I think you're perfeck.

I fearfully want to see your review of James letters.[8] Boge, the paper wants a touch of Lytton or Forster – it looks a trifle depressing, too. Theres so much small type. But thats just en passant. Goodbye for now my blessed one –

Wig of Broomies.

MS ATL. *LJMM*, 519–20.

To J. M. Murry, [11 April 1920]

Your proposed amendments of Je ne parle pas are read, admired and heartily approved by
Your affectionate Client
Katherine Mansfield Murry
(Prize Scholar,
English Composition,*   *Subject: 'A Sea Voyage'.
Public School
Karori)

Text. *LJMM*, 516.

[1] Murry informed her on 3 Apr. that the Woolfs had no more bound copies of *Prelude*, which their Hogarth Press had published in July 1918.

[2] Murry had wired KM on 9 Apr.: 'BROOMIES YOURS BOGE' (ATL), and wrote to her on the same day that he had bought the cottage for £480. Because of his bankruptcy, the purchase was in her name, although she was never to see the cottage.

[3] KM gives their imaginary villa the name of her favourite perfume.

[4] Murry had written on 6 Apr. of Broomies, and 'two little daisy children' when they settled in their new home. 'I don't think it's asking too much of Destiny, who has been so fond of banging me on the head in the past.' (Murry, 306–7.)

[5] On 8 Apr. Murry encouraged KM to accept Sadleir's changes to *Je ne parle pas français*, as 'people like my mother' who otherwise would admire her stories 'will be shocked by the few things the omission of which is . . . suggested' (Murry, 309.)

[6] Thomas Hardy sent his poem 'The Maid of Keinton Mandeville' to the *Athenaeum*, with the stipulation that it appear on 30 Apr. as a tribute on the sixty-fifth anniversary of the death of Sir Henry Bishop.

[7] There were negotiations, which came to nothing, for an American edition of *The Evolution of an Intellectual*.

[8] Murry cried off his review for the *Nation* of the two-volume edition of *The Letters of Henry James*, ed. Percy Lubbock, possibly because, as he told KM on 9 Apr., 'I am bored, unutterably bored with them.' (Murry, 310–11.)

To Violet Schiff, [c.11 April 1920]

[Villa Flora, Menton]

My dear Mrs Schiff

I should love to come on Thursday if I may. The weather looks so unpromising in the morning but Ill come unless the wind is fierce on Thursday – with great pleasure. No I havent changed my tickets. Silly events of no importance – but disagreeable events make me want to leave the Villa Flora as soon as I can.

With love from
K.M.

Is your cold better? Im sorry to hear of it.

MS BL. *Adam* 300, 96.

To J. M. Murry, [12 April 1920]

[Villa Flora, Menton]
Monday.

Dearest of All

Time seems to be flying this month and I have only 2 more Mondays here after this one. If only the wedder is fine and fayre in May! I don't think it would be possible to have fogs now – do you? This gorgeous air and almost certain sunshine gives me quite a horror of such things. Today for instance its 9 a.m. its *hot*. The sun is pure gold and a great swag of crimson roses outside my window fills the room with a sweet smell. Oh, how I have come to *love* this S. of France and to dislike the French. The french here don't count; they are just cultivateurs au bord de la mer but its the voice of la France *officielle* which I loathe so. You should have read L'Eclaireur on this last crise;[1] it was a very pretty little eye-opener. But Bogey I do so long for you to know this country in the spring. Its like the Middle Ages, somehow. I feel its Elizabethan spring – earlier – far – oh, I don't know *when*. But driving up those valleys & seeing the great shower of flowers & seeing the dark silver olives & the people working in the bean fields – one feels as though one were part of the *tradition* of spring

– Outside my window there live two lizards. Sometimes they come in & look at me & their throats pant in a funny way. I wish I could bring them home.

Oh my dearest I love the sun. I made a fuss about it at San Remo but that was because I was ill – but I love it. To WORK and to play in our garden – in woods & fields and on mountains and pebbly shores – with You. And to sometimes draw on thin suede gloves & go into cities & look at pictures and hear music and sit at a café with a long drink watching the passing show (you with a large parcel of books on the chair by you.) Thats the life for me – To live like artists, always free and *warmhearted* – and always *learning*. I can say great long pieces of poetry for you now – heavenly bits . . . & you must tell me things.

Yours yours for ever
Wig of Broomies.

MS ATL. *LJMM*, 520–1.

¹ The Paris newspaper's views on the recent strike.

To J. M. Murry, [14 April 1920]

[Villa Flora, Menton]

Precious Bogey *darling*

The Schiffs have just been. They are giving a luncheon party for me tomorrow and they came in to beg me not to bother to talk. "Let *them* do the running." Also Schiff wanted to tell me he'll send a car for me & send me back in it. He has had my disease so he rather exaggerates the care one ought to take. But its all in *more* than kindness. Well, if I do take fancies to people, love its nothing to the fancies they take to your Wig-wife. It makes me feel so horribly unworthy & it excites me so. I long to be worthy of these sweet things they tell me. Im not: its all nonsense, but they find something strange in me like people do in you. Were *Broomies* & they know it. But Mrs Schiff says suddenly: "youre such a lovely little thing I want to cry." (I only tell you that in dead privacy.) She feels like Anne feels. Its not *false*. There are certain people who make me feel *loving* warmhearted – tender – and – like children feel. Anne is one. Violet Schiff is another. Did I tell you that (its confidential) Schiff wrote Richard Kurt?

Oh, to be among people with whom one can discuss *prose* – and its possibilities. Not very seriously or well but at any rate to discuss it and be understood. But you must meet Violet Schiff. Shes one of the most attractive *women* that we have known – physically *and* mentally. You'd admire her – You'd like her and her mind. I am frightfully fatigued with talking to people who care for *the CHURCH* or (Bunny & Co) dress – envy hate and all uncharitableness.

God mend all![1] I've had no letters today, my darling. As the time passes I get awfully impatient for letters. Today fortnight we shall be in Paris. Oh, my plans for the future! Oh Bogey will you really want to be *alone* with me as I shall with you? Will you really say: darling I must have you to myself and mean it beyond words. To be in a room with you – hear you – *close*, seeing you, hearing you, watching you – my heart. To look after you again and see that you [have] lovely food & that all is in exquisite order. Oh, will it matter to you – having a wife? Will you ask people to dine with us & will you ask me sometimes to lunch or come to tea with me? Oh – to love as I love you!!

Know that Jaegar wooly you bought me. I got a skirt of the same stuff today – all wooly and furry. It looks the *spit* of Broomies with a very funny hat which might have been made of chopped bracken. Its the best country ensemble Ive ever seen because its very amusing but at the same time it is distinguished.

                                                    Wig of Broomies.

MS ATL. *LJMM*, 521–2.

---

[1] 'God mend all.' An expression of Queen Katherine in Shakespeare's *Henry VIII*, I. ii. 201.

To J. M. Murry, [15 April 1920]

                                                    Thursday
My darling,

I envy you 'madly' going to see Cymbeline.[1] If you knew how full my mind is of Shakespeare! Its a perfect world – his pastoral world. I roam through the Forest of Arden & sit on the spiced Indian sands laughing with Titania.[2] When we *do* get a small quiet moment – *what* talks! But you are going to Stratford on Avon. Lucky, lucky boy! And you won't remember for a moment that was the first English country your wife saw & she used to walk about there with her hair down her back wearing a pinky grey hat & even in those days carrying one of those small green Shakespeares – but of course it was Amleto, then. Talk about excitement – inward excitement. I wish I could keep it down. The fire – the beacon you know – the Bon Feu of bonfires is blazing away already with a kind of soft silent roaring most difficult to bear. We meet – heaven defend us – this day fortnight at 9 of the clock.

Yesterday afternoon Ida & I went driving up to Castellar. Its more lovely than Gorbio even. You *must* come here one spring. L.M. is hunting hard for a flat or villa. Ill have to pay about £60 for the season – i.e. £10 a month. It can't be done for less in comfort – and it must be in Garavan – thats the other bay – the one towards Italy with the superb old town and old ancient port built to one side of it. L.M. has gone over there today bathing.

I love your comment on The Fair Maid of the West.[3] *My* day book contains a regular gallimaufry of things – from "curtains for studio windows & landing windows must be lined" to hints for lunches and dinners taken from Annette here to notes & drawings of flowers & their leaves buds and seed pods minutely described to observations on a peke burying a nonexistent bone to – Shakespeare again. Thus the whirligig . . . Its grey; its rather cold. Its going to rain. I shant be able to go to my party. Oh weh oh weh!

×× ×   ×× ×

Fair young ×King of Broomies× thy dear Love & Queen salutes thee.

×× ×   ×× ×

Wig Regina.

MS ATL. *LJMM*, 523–4.

[1] The following week Murry would attend the Shakespeare festival at Stratford-upon-Avon as drama reviewer for the *Athenaeum*.

[2] KM is running together the lines from *A Midsummer Night's Dream*, ii. i. 124–6:

And in the spiced Indian air, by night,
Full often hath she gossiped by my side,
And sat with me on Neptune's yellow sands . . .

[3] Murry's letter is missing that told KM of his attending the Phoenix Society's production of Thomas Heywood's *The Fair Maid of the West; Or, A Girl Worth Gold*, at the Lyric Theatre, Hammersmith, the previous weekend.

To J. M. Murry, [16 April 1920]

[Villa Flora, Menton]

My own Bogey

Your Saturday afternoon letter is here about King John. Its such a dull old play, too. How horrid that you must do it.[1] I simply long to read your article on James. What I saw in The Times horrified me – arrogant, monstrous pomposity – even from early youth. I thought the article was a bit of fearful pretentiousness too and not worth a brass farden.[2] James makes me ashamed for *real* artists. He's a pompazoon. I am thankful we never received any favours. They can keep him – & then holding up his shocked hands at Thomas Hardy. How *great* Hardy is beside the other.[3] Oh, I do hope you will speak your mind & put all right for those who are frightened to say.

Yesterday I went to the Oceanographical Museum & Aquarium at Monaco. It was one of those experiences which make you stamp with fury because you are not sharing it. I wanted to telegraph you to promise that one day we'd spend a whole week in Monaco together & live in this place. My dearest – one is richer for life by such a museum. The AQUARIUM finished me & I had to lean over a tank of slumbering tortoises & weep because of the fishes I had seen & the worm high worm built forests. Ive got the guide for you. Ill show it you one Sunday afternoon. The little town of Monaco is the cleanest on earth I should think. You must see the palace courtyard with its cannons & cannonballs (all toy) pepper trees, limes & plantanes ancients in green with red facings, gold lace shoulders & hats

like that. Tis a sweet place. There are benches where one can sit & look at it all in tumpany with nurses in black velvet bodices white chemisettes & lace caps tossing up month old patriots. But all these things *without you* – thats the rub, Bogey. There was a little cream house with powder blue persiennes & a carpet of rose geraniums hung over its pink wall. I wanted to live there with you – another life. You know I love you beyond repair – and Ill be home a fortnight today. Oh dear – *And* we are proprietaires!!!!! My love –

Wig of Broomies.

MS ATL. *LJMM*, 522–3.

[1] Murry reviewed *A New Variorum Edition of Shakespeare: The Life and Death of King John* ed. H. H. Furness, in the *Athenaeum*, 30 Apr. 1920.

[2] 'The Letters of Henry James', an unsigned review by Virginia Woolf in *The Times Literary Supplement*, 8 Apr. 1920.

[3] KM is echoing Murry's letter on 9 Apr., where he was irritated by Henry James's condescension to Thomas Hardy, 'sneering at *Tess of the D'Urbervilles* – a book worth the whole of HJ's work lumped together . . . He needs to have a critical skewer poked into his swollen carcase.' (Murry, 311.)

To J. M. Murry, [18 April 1920]

My own

This letter was never posted and here's Sunday, déja.[1] I did go to my lunch after all. It was very enjoyable. A man called Tinayre[2] sang, and the Schiffs house is made for singing.

Yesterday Saturday horrible things happened. I had my review all ready to send and Ida never came. It was not a day to go out in – I was dead tired. I finally did go out, feeling certain to meet her carriage & didn't meet it & had to rush – & couldn't get a carriage & reached the poste 5 minutes late & got a carriage & tore up to the station where nobody would help me or tell me anything. I posted it in a box there then wired you,[3] then got back into the carriage – & you see me don't you darling – weeping away *furiously* in face of all Menton. I got out at Rumpelmeyers & drank boiling black coffee & ice water, came home a very pore girl & lay down with a brandy for tumpany. Schiff came in later & sat with me. His rage against the world because I had had such a bad time didn't make it better – and even now I can't get over it or quite forgive Ida until I know it has arrived. If you only knew what agony it is to fail you – what an effort to work (8 interruptions yesterday) in strangers houses! I don't want to make a moan tho'.

I have taken my flat – paid the deposit and asked Mrs Harrison to find me a cook for next season. The flat is *ideal*.[4] Three bedrooms, maids room, salon, salle a manger, bath with geyser, kitchen with gas housemaids pantry, cabinet de toilette for your dressing room. Its exquisite – furnished by an italian contessa – all dark wood & in my bedroom grey velvet curtains & hangings lined with blue brocade & a blue silk edredon. Quite *lovely*. Big soft carpets everywhere – fine glass, with plenty of small silver teapots and so on – and at least 1 dozen copper saucepans in the tiled kitchen. I shall be able to give little parties next year to my friends here – for the Schiffs will be here. The Tinayres, Lytton's married sister,[5] and so on. Ive paid the deposit & shall leave part of the rent to be paid at the present exchange. Then I want you to come for Xmas if you can – & I thought Brett might come for a month here (12 guineas, Id ask her – couldn't do it for less). It has the most superb view & a concierge on the premises. It looks very like Sir John & Lady Middleton Murry – which pleases me.

Darling, I love the thought of North Devon.[6] You'd better write *soon* to that hotel. Of course I don't mind it being far from the railway – why ever should I? But do you mind very much if I take a maid with me? Its such a bore dressing & undressing & packing & getting things & shed be a comfort travelling. Its such a waste of time & energy for you to do all these things & I can't do them & we want a *holiday*. I don't see very well how we can do without a maid for a month. All our buttons will come off & well have no clean hankies. I thought perhaps Violets or Gerties sister might come or Ill get someone from an agency for the month.

Well my own precious Boge. Of course I understand about the £10. But Id like to help you but I can't.[7] You see Ive had to pay for 2 wagon lits & 1st floor rooms in Paris – & then there is all the tipping etc here. Ill be très hard up by the time I get back. Be sure to order a Hampstead car wont you that will take the luggage & make certain of it, darling. Oh dear I can't believe it not even now. I just *go on.*

                                                                Your own wife.

MS ATL. *LJMM*, 524–5.

[1] Murry identifies this, *LJMM*, 524, as the second of the letters he dates 15 Apr., here dated 16 Apr.
[2] A musical friend of the Schiffs.
[3] The telegram does not survive.
[4] In the Villa Isola Bella.
[5] Dorothy Strachey (1866–1959), married to the French painter Simon Bussy.
[6] Where Murry suggested they holiday after KM's return to England.
[7] Murry wrote on 14 Apr. that he could not that month pay into her bank the £10 according to their arrangement, and wondered if she might pay back from her Constable money the 9 guineas for the overcoat he had recently sent on to her. (Murry, 312.)

To J. M. Murry, [20 April]

                                                    [Villa Flora, Menton]

My precious darling,

All being well I shall be at the *Palais Lyon*[1] on Wednesday until Thursday. Do you think L'Hote would come and see me on Wednesday afternoon – or Valery.[2] If they'd leave a 'bleu' letting me know when to expect them Id be delighted. I want to see them for the firm – to have a chat, don't you know & hear what is happening. Its the most divine day. Im staying in bed until lunch as I had a heavy day yesterday buying small presents to bring back and so on. Exhausting work because one gets so frightfully excited as well. Connie went with me in the morning & bought *me* an antique brooch, very lovely; three stones set in silver. Then she bought me a pastel blue muslin frock with frills like panniers at the side. Ida who was by said she thought Connie had a very bad influence on me because she spoiled me so. And the poor old dear got pink just like Gran ma used to & said "well, the child has had no fun, no life, no chance to wear pretty things for two years. I'm *sure* Jack would want to do what Im doing . . ." You remember in Italy how I longed to return to Life with all kinds of lovely possessions. Funny it should have all come true. I also bought the most exquisite fruit plates with small white grapes & gold leaves on them pour la famille Murry & a dish, high, to match, to take the breath. Ive no money. I think I must be a little bit mad. Oh, could I bring the flowers, the *air* the whole heavenly climate as well: this darling little town, these mountains – It is simply a small jewel – Menton – and its *band* in the jardins publiques with the ruffled pansy beds – the white donkeys standing meek – tied to a pole, the donkey women in black pleated dresses with flat funny hats. All, all is so terribly attractive. I'd live years here with you. Im immensely attached to it all & in the summer we'd go up to the Alpes Maritimes & live in the small spotless inns with milk hot from the cow & egg-wegs from the hen. Wed live in those steep villages of pink & white houses with the pine forests round them – where your host serves your dinner wearing a clean white blouse & sabots. Yes, dearest darling, Im in love with the Alpes Maritimes. I don't want to go any further. I'd like to live my life between Broomies & them.

Your Sunday & Saturday letter has come. You are a darling to have made the garden so fair & had the grass cut. Ive been thinking about that grass. You are having a worrying time about Arthur,[3] dear love. Couldn't the discussion be left till I talk it over with you. But after all there is nothing to talk over with me that you havent mentioned. If Arthur is going to be a *real artist* he must have his chance & if I have the good fortune to make money you know Ill always help. As matters stand I spend every penny I have because you see I *can't* live except in a rather luxurious way & I can only get better by resting – taking carriages – living as though I had £800 a year of my own instead of £400. This journey home for L.M. & me, for instance has cost – I really cant say what – telegraphing to Paris, to the boat, to the other side – with wagon lits and so on – but I can't do it except like that. Ive written Rutter *3* times for the money for my story[4] & Ive not had a penny, nor have I had a cheque from the paper this month. But all the same we shall be alright I know & we shall take Arthur & when he is here with me he'll not cost you a sou.

I read your article on Negro Sculpture last night.[5] It was *excellent*. I thought Fry most feeble in the Athenaeum.[6] As usual he was afraid to say what he felt. He wanted – a small fry – to be in the cultured swim. Will you take me to see some pictures when I come home?

Im lunching with the Schiffs tomorrow. It will be our last meeting until they come back to London. Schiff – well, you'll see what he's like. I was at a big lunch the other day (about 10 people) at their house & you should have heard the talk against The Nation – and FOR the A. [*Athenaeum*] Massingham, according to some really rather intelligent men there, gets his facts hopelessly wrong about French affairs,[7] but I learnt a great deal of interesting facts about the French – *not* to their credit. Ill tell you in about 3 years time when the other things have been told. Darling *dont* make my homecoming an effort – don't curse the upset of it all. I will try not to show how glad I am & so frighten my darling little mate. Dont feel you *have* to meet me even. It is very dreadful to know that even Love is an effort to you at times & I don't want you to make that effort. Feel – oh well, she'll make things easy and L.M. will be on the spot and I shant have to think of puddings. Years ago I wanted to change things in you – I wanted you less 'vague', less silent, more – almost – practical. But you must always remember that was years ago. Now I don't want you to be *anybody* but your natural self – free to wander away or to keep quiet just as it pleases you. I want you to feel that with me you can be absolutely *free* in spirit. If I find your hats too awful I shall buy you other hats, or if your hair is too dreadful I shall seize the moment and brush it straight – but you must not *exert* yourself or pretend that you have to look after me. I'm very independent please altho' I am your

Own little Wig.

MS ATL. *LKM* II. 31–2; *LJMM*, 526–8.

[1] The hotel near the Gare de Lyon where KM stayed.
[2] André Lhote, the French critic and artist (see *CLKM* II. 347), and the poet Paul Valéry were friends of Murry particularly, and both wrote for the *Athenaeum*.
[3] There were discussions about Richard Murry attending the Slade School of Art, and Murry's needing to supplement his brother's scholarship with an additional £30 a year.
[4] 'The Man Without a Temperament', published in *Art and Letters*, Autumn 1919.
[5] Murry's 'Negro Sculpture', reviewing an exhibition at the Chelsea Book Club, the *Nation*, 17 Apr. 1920.
[6] Roger Fry discussed the same exhibition under 'Negro Sculpture at the Chelsea Book Club', the *Athenaeum*, 16 Apr. 1920.
[7] H. W. Massingham, Murry's friend and the editor of the *Nation*, regularly wrote on European affairs.

To J. M. Murry, [c.20 April 1920]

[Villa Flora, Menton]

Please tell the old boy.

Dearest Bogey

This is about Arthur. Of course I am entirely in favour of the scheme.[1] It is splendid to think we shall have a painter in the family and I rejoice greatly –

As regards money – he can, as you say, always have Broomies at his back – a sure haven. And then Id like him to know that I am certain to have money one of these days – certain – I mean money that will be left me. This, as long as our children are provided for, Arthur can always count on. At any rate, however big our family (no fear of that) I shall always leave (give) Arthur enough to live on without working. I am determined within the next few years to have a house in the South here. He can always come and paint and be free of all money worries.

I love and admire Arthur and its simply the greatest good fortune to have a chance of making him happy. Here we are. He can take from us without ever dreaming of paying back: he can just be our brother – in art as well as in life – and all success to him and a proud sister's blessing –

We *must* see him through.

Goodbye for now my darling

For ever and amen your
Wig.

MS ATL. *LJMM*, 528.

[1] Murry had written on 16 Apr. telling KM that Dorothy Brett was advising his brother on which of his drawings to enter for a scholarship at the Slade Art School. Murry was willing to contribute an additional £30 a year, should Arthur (Richard) be successful, and there was Broomies also as security.

To J. M. Murry, [22 April 1920]

[Villa Flora, Menton]
Thursday.

My dearest,

Your letter with the piece about Raquel Meller has just come.[1] I hope you have good weather at Stratford. Kay writes its awful and that Ill never stay over there. I *wish* it would be finer. Its quite frightening to think of the English climate, or of Paris even. As to *London* with its sights and sounds – I was only saying to L.M. last night it needs a very great gasp to swallow it. But you and home and the kittens – all are in Hampstead so Hampstead is the tall rock rearing its awful form with the sunshine nestling on its head. But pray pour le beau temps!

About your Cinnamon and Angelica Im frightfully anxious to see reviews. Arthur & C.S. have done it beautifully[2] – Yesterday Connie began reading part of it aloud – Angelica & Mrs Carraway (oughtn't she to have been Mistress?) I wish to God it will be a success. Its only a question of time but I know what it means to be recognised *immediately*. There is nothing so wonderful or that has so renewing an effect upon an author. My love, I wish it for you with all my heart.

Just let me look at your list of friends again.[3] No, we cant really include Virginia. I don't know Tomlinson at all personally – I cant call him or T.Eliot or Group (3) my friends except in so far as they are people whom I feel certain *are* right people – Tommy & Eliot because of their books the other (3) because you know and like them. Brett is a dear creature but again – yes – she's s friend – but much more a friend of yours than mine. Violet Schiff Id include and Schiff without the smallest hesitation or doubt. I like him as much as I do his wife but in of course an entirely different way. He attracts me *tremendously* and his great kindness, sensitiveness, almost childishness endear him to me. In fact Id head my list with those 2 but thats because I look at people from a different angle to what you do. Then Id include Anne Rice – *definitely*. I love her as a 'being' as Kot would say. What a silly I am. Now I see you only call your list 'nice people'. Then I subscribe to it of course. Im sure they are nice – but thats not enough, is it?

I am glad the singer is wonderful. I shall go to hear her as soon as I can. Let me be frank. Your article on her bears the impress of great fatigue. It saddens me that you should be so painfully overworked – painfully unable to respond "without an effort". "We shall learn it chiefly from the assiduous frequentation of our own great heritage."[4] There – thats what I mean. You must not feel too strongly your duty to bear the age we live in upon your back. At any rate, faced with a fellow artist, Id greet her *as* an artist & let them understand what they may. Thats our privilege. We can explain later – obliquely. Do I talk nonsense?

Wig.

MS ATL. *LJMM*, 528–9.

[1] 'The Art of the actress Raquel Meller', Murry's review of the Spanish actress and singer at the Hippodrome, appeared in the *Athenaeum*, 23 Apr. 1920.

[2] *Cinnamon and Angelica*, designed by Richard Murry, had just been published by Cobden-Sanderson.

[3] In his letter of 19 Apr. Murry wrote:

'What you say about Violet Schiff interests me very much. She seems to me to be the real thing. A real addition to the nice people would be splendid; at present they are, in my opinion,

(1) Tomlinson ⎫
    Brett   ⎭

(2) Tom Eliot
    Sullivan
    Sydney Waterlow

(3) Dunning
    Locke Ellis
    Delamare

You see there's only one woman: another wd. be very helpful. I don't think I can really include Virginia. Anyway I'm not sure. I don't mean (3) is inferior to (2) but merely that I don't see very much of them & therefore they belong to a different class.

I think we agree about all of them except Sydney.' (Murry, 315–16.)

Bill Dunning was a yogi master Murry later stayed with in 1922 when KM went to
Fontainebleau.
⁴ A sentence from Murry's Meller review.

To J. M. Murry, [24–25 April 1920]

[Villa Flora, Menton]
Will you ask Eliot¹ to supper on Sunday? I want to see him very much
& have messages for him. But if youre not inclined its no matter,
dearest.

My own dearest
A dinner party here 18. Im wearing my purpil dress. I thought I
shouldn't be able to get into it – but pas de chance. Im also wearing
real small pearl ear rings – a farewell present. They are very lovely –
being real they have such a different feeling. I rather dread the dinner.
Oh Id so much rather go to my Schiffs. Mr Schiff is a kind of literary
fairy godfather to me. He looks after me so perfectly and so gently &
Violet Schiff seemed to me the last time far more beautiful and more
fascinating than before. She will *fascinate* you – the movement of her
lips, her eyes, her colour, all her beauty. And their house is always for
me the house where *lovers* dwell. He loves her perfectly. And her quick
'darling' and hand outstretched . . . I mustn't talk of these people for I
could talk too much. They are so real and dear & beautiful to me &
they understand ones work. Our farewell has been postponed until
tomorrow. We are going to Eze by car. Its a tiny Saracen village
on the Grand Corniche Road. Stratford sounds *awful* my darling –
hopelessly awful² – & no pyjamas to crown all! If we'd been there
together we should have fought for good dry beds but even then we
couldn't fight for good dry skies. I think Ill learn plays by heart and
give representations like Mrs Hannibal Williams³ used to.

I sent you today four assiettes tres anciennes and a fruit dish. They
are *perfect*. There were no more to be had. And they cost me – *oh dear*.
Now I am quite broke really broke – its awful!

About Devonshire – is it too remote? Are the sanitary arrangements
perfect? Can one drive. Your wife cant be planted on a cliff yet – alas –
& Im a little bit frightened of your hotel. I feel I ought to be nearer
civilisation. But lets decide that when I return. I have an *idear*.

Sunday. Brilliant fine. Oranges for breakfast & a *huge* bouquet of
sweet peas – AND a letter from you. That Festa, my own boy must
have been a most disgusting affair. Oh, how I agree about Shylock! I
think The Taming of the Shrew is so *deadly* too.⁴ I am certain Bill
never wrote it; he bolstered up certain speeches but that is all. Its a

hateful silly play – so badly constructed and arranged. Id never go to see it. I think we shall have a Shakespeare festival one year at Broomies – get actors there to study their parts – act out of doors – a small Festa – a real one. Ill be stage director. *I am dead serious about this.* Your Stratford makes me feel it.

Really its grilling hot today! I feel inclined to make a noise like a cicada. Just now Miss Helen Fullerton shouted from the garden "Little Murry, come on to the balcony & be took." She had her camera. She'd just returned from early Communion. Jinnie has just come in from Mass.

Oh this climate this weather this place. Ill *never* leave here another year before the end of May. Its too perfect. Even June is exquisite Im sure. Adorable South of France. How I have loved it. Well I wont write again. Goodbye my precious little mate. Go slow and be a good boy – not a tired one. Be sure you have a car *engaged* – won't you. Now begins a new chapter – much newer – quite different, so I imagine, to what you think –

Your own wife
Wig.

MS ATL. *LKM* II. 32–3; *LJMM*, 530–1.

[1] Although T. S. Eliot wrote to Murry 25? Apr. 1920 that 'We are looking forward to seeing Katherine', his private opinion of her was expressed to Ezra Pound on 3 July 1920: 'I must say that [Murry] is much more difficult to deal with when K.M. is about, and I have an impression that she terrorises him. . . . I believe her to be a dangerous WOMAN; and of course two sentimentalists together are more than two times as noxious as one.' *The Letters of T. S. Eliot*, ed. Valerie Eliot, vol. i (1988), 382, 389.

[2] Murry wrote from the Stratford Hotel, Stratford-upon-Avon, on 21 Apr., saying that he found the hotel 'simply unspeakable', the people 'abominable', and 'the plays a mixed bag' (ATL). His reviews in the *Athenaeum*, 30 Apr. and 7 May 1920, were unenthusiastic about the Bridges Adams company in *The Merchant of Venice, Richard II, Much Ado About Nothing, The Taming of the Shrew*, and *Cymbeline.*

[3] Mr and Mrs Hannibal Williams, New York elocutionists, performed in Wellington in the winter of 1900, the couple taking all the parts in recitations of Shakespeare plays.

[4] Murry's letter on 22 Apr. reported that *The Taming of the Shrew* was 'well done and in the right spirit', but said of Murray Carrington's Shylock that 'of all ludicrous conventions this one as the realistic Ghetto Jew . . . is the worst. As if Shakespeare couldn't have written Tank God, if he meant Shylock to say it.' (ATL)

To J. M. Murry, [? April 1920]

[Villa Flora, Menton]

My precious dear

Will you please guarder these snaps for me in a book? Don't forget mignonette, because Ill weep over the steps & the arum lilies – in memory.

Do you think they are good of your girl? Please tell.

Wig.

MS ATL. Unpublished.

To J. M. Murry, [early 1920][1]

[Villa Flora, Menton][2]

My darling

I add a tiny note. It is raining & the wet rose bush blows about full of great drops. I suddenly for no reason remembered you at Clovelly[3] with 3d of ice for the butter – and you and I in our boat – a *queer* place or getting ready to go out to dinner. Weren't we happy! You were *such* a darling: I loved you so and you were grave and rather silent even then. Do you remember the white shoes with blue laces we bought in Paris? Oh, Bogey don't get older! Let us always be in our heart of hearts very very young.

MS ATL. Unpublished.

---

[1] From internal evidence, this undated note perhaps belongs with the letter on p. 223.

[2] Murry pencilled on the top of this page '1920. Villa Flora.'

[3] KM was living at 69 Clovelly Mansions, Gray's Inn Road, when she first met Murry in December 1911. He moved in with her in April 1912, and they remained there until September.

INDEX OF RECIPIENTS

GENERAL INDEX

Lightning Source UK Ltd.
Milton Keynes UK

177157UK00005B/2/A